ILLINOIS JUSTICE

ILLINOIS

*The Scandal of 1969 and the
Rise of John Paul Stevens*

Kenneth A. Manaster

With a Foreword by Justice Stevens

JUSTICE

The University of Chicago Press
Chicago and London

The University of Chicago Press, Chicago 60637
The University of Chicago Press, Ltd., London
© 2001 by The University of Chicago
All rights reserved. Published 2001.
Paperback edition 2015
Printed in the United States of America

24 23 22 21 20 19 18 17 16 15   2 3 4 5 6

ISBN-13: 978-0-226-50243-4 (cloth)
ISBN-13: 978-0-226-35010-3 (paper)
ISBN-13: 978-0-226-35024-0 (e-book)
DOI: 10.7208/chicago/9780226350240.001.0001

Frontispiece: John Paul Stevens (*left*) and Sherman Skolnick. Reprinted with special permission of Chicago Sun-Times, Inc. © 2001.

Library of Congress Cataloging-in-Publication Data

Manaster, Kenneth A.
   Illinois justice : the scandal of 1969 and the rise of John Paul
Stevens / Kenneth A. Manaster ; with a foreword by Justice Stevens.
      p.   cm.
   Includes bibliographical references and index.
   ISBN 0-226-50243-0 (cloth)
   1. Judicial corruption—Illinois—History—20th century. 2. Stevens,
John Paul, 1920– I. Title.
   KFI1725.5.D5 M36 2001
   345.773'0234—dc21
                                                          2001000378

♾ This paper meets the requirements of ANSI/NISO Z39.48-1992
(Permanence of Paper).

To Cole

Contents

Photographs follow page 100

Foreword

In his Gettysburg Address, Abraham Lincoln made the famously in-
accurate prediction that the "world will little note, nor long remember" what he had to say. That statement is powerful evidence that even
the most talented professionals may be poor judges of the significance
of their own work. The danger that one might *over*estimate its value is
particularly strong when members of a joint venture share a mutual
respect developed during the course of a stressful assignment. Readers may therefore be well advised to discount both my reaction to Ken
Manaster's meticulous recounting of the tale of the Special Commission and his overly generous observations about the part that I played
in that story. I do believe, however, that many readers will not only
find his account interesting, but will also discover in it some important
insights into the legal profession. For my part, I shall comment briefly
on how that assignment has affected my perception of the work of special prosecutors and my own work as an appellate judge.

Thurgood Marshall had an effective method of emphasizing the difference between unconstitutionality and unwisdom. He would often
remind us that there is nothing in the Constitution that prevents Congress from enacting stupid laws. I have never doubted the constitutionality of legislation authorizing the appointment of independent
counsel to investigate allegations of wrongdoing by high government
officials. Some of the cases those lawyers have argued in our Court
have, however, raised questions in my mind about the wisdom of their
assignments. My perspective in such cases was undoubtedly influenced by the contrast between the duration and scope of those
lawyers' authority and the narrow assignment given to the Special
Commission.

    Two limitations in the order creating the Special Commission were
of critical importance: the deadline and the scope of our inquiry. The
commission was created in the middle of June and ordered to deliver
its report by the end of July. Its only task was to investigate the "integrity of the judgment" in one specific Illinois Supreme Court case,

People v. Isaacs. Because we began our work with little more than newspaper accounts of allegations made by an uncooperative informant, we were unable to assess either the difficulty or the significance of our assignment. If we were to find that there was no substance to the allegations, there was ample time in which to prepare a report explaining why that was so. But we obviously had to recognize that a different possibility existed, and therefore had to budget the time to organize an effective investigative team, conduct sufficient discovery to determine whether public hearings were warranted (for it would have been highly improper to make public disclosures of the inner workings of the supreme court if there was no probative evidence of misconduct), conduct those public hearings, assess the evidence, and write a report summarizing our findings. It would be an understatement to say that time was of the essence.

Although it then seemed to present a serious problem, the deadline actually produced two important benefits. First, it required us to assess the relative importance of various possible lines of inquiry and to concentrate on the most promising. We did go down a few blind alleys and engage in some skirmishes that, as Ken correctly notes, seem almost comical today. On the whole, however, our constant awareness of the deadline forced us to focus on what was most relevant to our assignment and to forego collateral inquiries. Second, it forced us to be prompt in reaching our conclusions and in sharing them with the public. The decision to conduct public hearings was not made precipitously, but it was made as soon as our investigation demonstrated that such hearings were appropriate. And it was the deadline—not any extraneous motivation—that controlled the timing of the formulation and public disclosure of the conclusions set forth in the Special Commission's final report.

The specificity of our assignment produced similar benefits. During the course of our inquiry, we received a good many suggestions for lines of investigation that were not even tangentially related to the decision in the *Isaacs* case. If we had had the sort of open-ended assignment that characterized the work of some independent counsel appointed under the now-expired federal statute, we could have kept a much larger team busy for a much longer period of time. I am also convinced that such an open-ended charter would have made it much less likely that we would have completed our assigned task as effectively as we did. If and when Congress should enact a new provision for the appointment of independent counsel, I am convinced that it would be wise to place strict limits on both the duration and the scope of any authorized investigation.

*   *   *

Knowledge that I acquired during the investigation has influenced my work as an appellate judge in at least three respects, as Ken mentions. Each involves a departure from practices followed by many other judges. One is a product of reflection about the Illinois Supreme Court's method of assigning responsibility for the preparation of court opinions. Cases were assigned to a particular judge through a rotation system in advance of argument. Because we were in search of possible skulduggery in the assignment of the *Isaacs* opinion, it immediately occurred to us that anyone who wanted to exert improper influence in a particular case might first seek to discover the identity of the probable author of the opinion. Although the presumed integrity of all appellate judges makes the risk of this kind of influence minimal, the possibility should never be ignored. More likely—and therefore of more concern—is the risk that a preassignment procedure will cause members of the court other than the designated author to be less diligent in their preargument preparation, particularly in the less interesting cases on the docket. Any procedure that elevates the role of a single judge above that of his or her colleagues before the court addresses the merits of a case tends to undermine the central purpose of a multijudge tribunal. In my judgment, it is even less appropriate to delegate the task of preparing a preargument bench memo for the entire court to a member of the staff—no matter how gifted and impartial that staff person may be. My abstention from my current colleagues' process of assessing petitions for review on the basis of a single memorandum prepared for a "pool" of justices is, in part, a product of my work for the Special Commission.

Second, my reaction to so-called pro se petitions—those filed by lay litigants without the assistance of counsel—is also markedly different from that of my colleagues. Rarely does such a petition raise an issue that merits full review by the Court. For that reason, and in the interests of efficiency, my colleagues have, through the years, entered numerous orders restricting the ability of such litigants to file repetitious claims or to proceed without the payment of costs. I have always thought it more efficient to deny the frivolous petitions on their merits rather than to place them in a disfavored category. My memory of the unexpected merit that we found in the allegations made by Sherman Skolnick has remained a powerful reminder that categorical prohibitions against repetitive filings can create a real risk of injustice. Although I seldom clutter up the U.S. Reports with formal notations, at virtually every Court conference I find myself dissenting from three or four orders imposing special burdens on this disfavored class of litigants.

Third, I do clutter up the U.S. Reports with more separate writing than most lawyers have either time or inclination to read. For many years before the *Isaacs* case was decided, most appellate judges refrained from expressing their disagreement with the views of the majority except in exceptional circumstances. Some of our greatest jurists wrote dissenting opinions that they never published. Dissents were often viewed as a threat to the collegiality of the appellate court. Moreover, they tended to undermine the illusion that the law is a seamless web of certain, definite, and harmonious rules. Even today in most European tribunals, dissenting opinions are gauche, if not verboten. I am sure it was that prevailing view that explains why Justice Schaefer—one of the finest judges who ever served on the Illinois Supreme Court or, indeed, any court in the country—decided not to publish his dissent in the *Isaacs* case. When I learned in the course of our investigation that he had in fact dissented from the majority's decision, my immediate and strong reaction was that the public should have been informed of that fact when the decision was announced. If there is disagreement within an appellate court about how a case should be resolved, I firmly believe that the law will be best served by an open disclosure of that fact, not only to the litigants and their lawyers, but to the public as well.

There have been significant changes in the practice of law during the years since we investigated the integrity of the judgment in the *Isaacs* case. Law firms seem to get larger and larger, and presumably they generate larger and larger profits. I remain convinced, however, that the principal rewards available to the best lawyers have nothing to do with money. The profit motive had no impact whatsoever on the work of the five leaders of the Illinois bar who served as members of the Special Commission, or of the six junior lawyers and the accountant who staffed the investigation. Even though all twelve of us served without compensation, I am confident that we shared the conviction that our time had been well spent. So it is, I believe, with Ken's account of the investigation. I think he can—and will—be justly proud of the story he has told. I will not venture a prediction about the extent to which the world will "long remember" what he has to say, but I am confident he will be amply rewarded by readers' assessment of his work.

JUSTICE JOHN PAUL STEVENS
UNITED STATES SUPREME COURT

Preface

On a hot summer night in a crowded courtroom in Chicago, all eyes are fixed on one man, the chief justice of the Supreme Court of Illinois. He is, as always, a formidable presence—distinguished, handsome, and amiable. He enjoys the respect of the legal profession in his state and elsewhere in the country. He is considered a contender for the current vacancy on the United States Supreme Court, the vacancy created just two months ago when Justice Abe Fortas resigned in disgrace.

The chief justice is speaking, but he is not speaking as a judge in this case. Tonight he is a witness. He is seated in a chair in the witness box, and he is, in effect, a witness in his own defense. He is answering questions about his financial dealings and their connection to a case his court decided two years earlier.

At the moment, he is having trouble with some of the questions, and his throat is getting dry. He turns to the raised bench to his right, looks up and back, and then prepares to pour himself a glass of water from the pitcher at the front of the witness box. The audience is struck again by how extraordinary this trial is, for presiding over this case is not a judge, but a lawyer. He and four other lawyers are hearing the evidence; the lawyers are judging the judge.

The chief justice begins to pour the water, but his nerves betray him. He knocks over the pitcher, drenching the papers in front of him and sending a slow cascade dribbling down the dark marble front of the witness box. Suddenly he looks helpless, for he doesn't know what to do about the water. And the despair on his face says something more: that he also doesn't know what to do about the questions he is being asked. The water has gotten away from him, and so has this case—and so, ultimately, has his career.

At this defining moment, everyone still watches the chief justice, now a diminished and almost pathetic sight. No one is watching the lawyer who has been questioning him. This unimposing man with the bow tie is not well known to people in the courtroom or elsewhere.

No one knows that in just a few years—in part because of his work tonight—this lawyer will become a justice of the Supreme Court of the United States, where he will serve the law and the nation for many years.

A Scandal's Lasting Impact

In June 1969 two justices of the Illinois Supreme Court were accused of misconduct, and that court "was suddenly shaken to its foundations."[1] In response to the accusations, an unprecedented investigation was begun. The immediate result of the investigation was that Chief Justice Roy J. Solfisburg Jr. and Associate Justice Ray I. Klingbiel were forced to leave the court in the wake of findings of serious improprieties in their conduct.

There are people who believe, and with good reason, that without this scandal, Roy Solfisburg might very well have become a member of the United States Supreme Court. There also are many people who believe that without this investigation, John Paul Stevens would not have become a justice on that Court. Stevens himself is one of those people.

When Stevens was nominated to the high court in 1975, he described the investigation as "one of the principal, important professional achievements of my life." He also linked it more informally to his ascent to the Supreme Court, referring to it as "the proceeding that got this whole business started." He spoke of it again in a 1992 speech before the American Bar Association: "All I can say is had I not participated in that matter, I'm sure I would not be occupying the position I occupy today."[2]

The story of this scandal bears telling for many reasons, starting with its role as a catalyst for Stevens's judicial career. The case also tells us some other things about Stevens, for his professional values and legal talents are illuminated by his work on this scandal. Even in a few specific and surprising respects, Justice Stevens's work on the bench can be better understood as having been distinctly shaped by this experience.

The scandal also stands as a dramatic and instructive example of the subtlety of some forms of judicial corruption as well as of the complexity of ferreting them out. The case had great impact on the drafting and adoption of the Illinois Constitution of 1970, which created a new system for investigating and punishing judicial misconduct. Even beyond that impact, other lessons for future investigations and reforms can be learned from the unique process by which the accusations against the justices were brought to light, investigated, and resolved.

The investigation of the two justices was part of a larger saga of corruption in Illinois government in that era. Within a few years after this case, revelations of similar and virtually simultaneous wrongdoing by some of the same people involved in the 1969 scandal led to the criminal conviction of Otto Kerner, the former governor of Illinois. At the time of his conviction, he was a judge on the U.S. Court of Appeals for the Seventh Circuit. The 1969 scandal was the prelude and parallel to this other drama.

Finally, this story warrants telling for the diverse reasons most everyone enjoys recounting an exciting tale, especially one we have lived through and learned from. I served as a young lawyer on the legal staff that conducted the investigation in the summer of 1969. In recollecting these events now, I am heeding advice given to the staff many years ago by one of the most prominent figures in this story. He said, "I hope that each of you will remember this experience for a very long time and will draw some inspiration from it in other days."[3]

ACCUSATION

The First Half of June

Chapter 1

A Citizen's Suspicions

The first accusations of wrongdoing were made by the vocal and eccentric leader of a group called the Citizens' Committee to Clean Up the Courts. It was the creation and alter ego of Sherman H. Skolnick, a "self-taught Chicago legal researcher"[1] already well known in Illinois courtrooms. Estimates of the size of his group varied from thirty to much larger numbers. On one occasion in 1969, Skolnick testified under oath that the committee had about nine hundred members "scattered over a geographical area of the Midwest."[2]

In previous years Skolnick had brought many lawsuits in his own name, or in the name of his committee, against a variety of government officials and agencies, although he seldom met with success. Prior to 1969, Skolnick's greatest litigation victory had come in a class action suit he filed claiming that the constitutional "one man–one vote" requirement was violated by the ward boundaries drawn by the Chicago City Council.[3]

Skolnick was thirty-eight years old in mid-1969. He had been paralyzed since suffering polio at age six and was always in a wheelchair when seen in public. He worked out of his family's house in a neighborhood on the southeast side of the city. A later newspaper profile reminisced somewhat affectionately about Skolnick's appearance in 1969: "He wore thick glasses, had buck teeth, dressed forgettably and showed absolutely no respect for authority."[4]

In 1958 Skolnick and his parents sued a brokerage firm they accused of mishandling a stock fund his parents had established with $14,000 in life savings to help meet their son's future needs. That suit was unsuccessful, and Skolnick was bitter about the loss. He initiated a series of lawsuits against various attorneys who allegedly had some role in the stock litigation or its aftermath.[5] In a 1964 ruling by the Illinois Supreme Court, a lower court's dismissal of one of those suits was upheld. Among the members of the court who participated in that decision were Ray Klingbiel and Roy Solfisburg.[6] Skolnick never forgot the court's ruling against him. He also never forgot, and did not forgive, Solfisburg and Klingbiel in particular.

Skolnick became obsessed with rooting out the corruption he perceived to be rampant in Illinois government, especially in the judiciary. As Skolnick later observed, "We sued to get our money back. We went all the way to the state Supreme Court—Solfisburg and Klingbiel were on it then—and lost. I vowed to my parents that I would devote my life to helping others in the courts."[7]

As early as 1966 Skolnick began hearing rumors of conflicts of interest involving the Illinois Supreme Court. In February 1969, according to a subsequent account by Skolnick, an anonymous source suggested to him that he should investigate the stockholders of the Civic Center Bank & Trust Company (CCB) in Chicago.[8] The bank was only a couple of years old and was located on the northeast corner of La Salle and Randolph Streets in immediate proximity to the principal state and local government offices in Chicago's downtown political, legal, and financial district. Skolnick and his associates began to search public records relating to the bank for any hint of judicial misconduct. They discovered, in a list of CCB stockholders in the Cook County Recorder's Office, that two grandchildren of Associate Justice Ray I. Klingbiel of the Illinois Supreme Court owned a hundred shares of CCB stock.

Klingbiel was a Republican who had joined the court in July 1953. He received his law degree from the University of Illinois in 1924, and then practiced in East Moline, with twelve years as city attorney before serving six years as mayor. During those years he was considered something of "a kingpin in the Rock Island County and Downstate political power structure."[9] He then spent eight years as a circuit judge before being elected to the supreme court. He served as chief justice for one year beginning in 1956 and then again from the fall of 1964 to January 1967. In 1969 he was sixty-eight years old.

The Newspapers Start Digging

In the spring of 1969, Skolnick communicated his interest in Klingbiel to two very different newspapers—the *New York Times* and the *Daily Calumet.* On a Sunday in early May, a reporter from the *Times* came to Skolnick's house to discuss an unrelated matter. Skolnick told the reporter his suspicions about Klingbiel and the Civic Center Bank stock, and on the spot the reporter telephoned Klingbiel at home in Moline. Klingbiel told the reporter that he had purchased the CCB stock. After that conversation, the *New York Times* did not pursue Skolnick's concern about Klingbiel any further.

Skolnick found more sustained interest at the *Daily Calumet,* a small community newspaper serving an area that included Skolnick's neighborhood. The *Daily Calumet* was controlled by two young men, James A. Linen IV and Jameson Campaigne, with Linen the principal owner. Skolnick brought his information to Robert Seltzner, the paper's managing editor and an experienced newsman to whom Skolnick often talked. Over the course of a few months, prompted by Skolnick's nagging, Seltzner and a novice reporter prepared a series of articles setting forth Skolnick's research and suspicions. These articles relied heavily on what Skolnick told them and on a variety of documents he showed them. Seltzner also made some telephone calls, including one to Klingbiel later in May, while the court was in session in Springfield. The *Daily Calumet* became the first newspaper ready to publicize Skolnick's interest in Klingbiel and the Civic Center Bank stock.

The *Daily Calumet,* however, did not break the story. Linen and Campaigne earlier had retained as corporate counsel the large Chicago firm of Kirkland, Ellis, Hodson, Chaffetz & Masters. Don H. Reuben, a Kirkland partner then forty years old, was the leading libel expert in the state. He represented both the *Chicago Tribune* and its sister paper, *Chicago Today.* He also represented the *Tribune*'s radio and television stations, numerous other broadcasting clients, and other major publishers, including Time, Inc. Many people at that time viewed Reuben as the single most influential attorney in Illinois, though consumer activist Ralph Nader described Reuben more critically: "No lawyer in any other city is as powerful or feared as Don Reuben is in Chicago."[10] Reuben was friendly with all the members of the Illinois Supreme Court, having argued before them many times.

In late May, Linen submitted Seltzner's articles to Reuben's firm. After reviewing what the *Daily Calumet* was planning to publish, Reuben emphatically advised Linen not to do so. Reuben's view was that the paper would create "very big exposure" to liability for defamation if it printed Skolnick's suspicions about Klingbiel. Reuben pointed out that charges coming from Skolnick at this stage lacked the legal protection that attaches to statements made in connection with judicial proceedings.

Furthermore, even under the relatively recent *New York Times v. Sullivan*[11] constitutional requirement—that a public official must prove actual malice in order to win a libel case—Reuben believed the newspaper would be in great jeopardy. He told Linen to imagine Skolnick, the source for this story, on the witness stand for two hours, and then to try to imagine a successful defense argument that the newspaper had not acted with reckless disregard for the truth. Reuben bolstered his legal opinion with dire warnings about the probable loss of the *Daily Calumet*'s liability insurance, and of the Kirkland firm's representation, if the articles were published. Linen's partner, Jameson Campaigne, found Reuben's advice "brutal and threatening" and tried hard to persuade Linen to disregard it, but Linen refused and the *Daily Calumet* did not publish the accusation against Klingbiel—at least not first.

Although it may seem odd that newspapers as dissimilar as the *New York Times* and the *Daily Calumet* were the first to consider Skolnick's suspicions, there is an explanation. During the previous years of his litigious crusade against Illinois courts, Skolnick's credibility with the major Chicago newspapers had declined considerably. There was thus a better chance he would be listened to by a reporter from out-of-town, where he was not well known. Paradoxically, he probably also felt comfortable approaching the small South Side newspaper where he *was* well known, well enough for the editor to realize that sometimes he might actually be on to something. As Seltzner of the *Daily Calumet* later recalled, "Nobody else would talk to him."

Skolnick Lights the Fire

Undaunted by the initial lack of publication, Skolnick did not give up. He was in Springfield on Wednesday, June 4, to testify before a state legislative committee investigating organized crime. During his testimony, he included his customary broad array of allegations about corruption in government. He also distributed a diverse batch of written materials, including a "fact sheet" that listed some of the stockholders of the Civic Center Bank. One stockholder entry on the fact sheet mentioned Klingbiel:

> Illinois Supreme Court Justice Ray I. Klingbiel (while he was stockholder he exonerated Theodore J. Isaacs, Secretary and General Counsel of Civic Center Bank, who was being prosecuted for state contract fraud—see, *People vs. Isaacs,* Illinois Supreme Court decision written by Justice Klingbiel).

With this parenthetical notation on the list of stockholders, Skolnick lit a match to the dry kindling of Klingbiel's stock ownership: he suggested that Klingbiel owned the stock at the same time that the Illinois Supreme Court, in an opinion authored by Klingbiel, upheld the dismissal of criminal charges against Theodore J. Isaacs.

Isaacs and Kerner

In 1964 Isaacs, an influential Chicago lawyer and a key political ally of Otto Kerner, was indicted in Springfield for conflict-of-interest violations allegedly committed while he served as Director of the Illinois Department of Revenue as an appointee of Governor Kerner. Beginning in 1965, Isaacs became actively involved in the organization of the Civic Center Bank.

Isaacs was Kerner's "right-hand man."[12] One Chicago newspaper summarized the many links between Isaacs and Kerner:

> A native Chicagoan, Isaacs opened his law practice in 1934. When World War II erupted, he joined the army and spent five years in the European and Pacific theaters. Afterward, he joined the 33d Illinois National Guard. Kerner was a major general attached to that unit; Isaacs held the rank of lieutenant colonel. Isaacs managed Kerner's successful 1954 campaign for county judge. In return, Kerner named Isaacs attorney for the Chicago Election Commission—an agency under his jurisdiction.
>
> Two more political campaigns followed: Kerner's reelection as county judge in 1958 and his election to governor in 1960. Isaacs was in there pitching all the way. On December 29, 1960, Kerner announced he was naming campaign manager Isaacs to head the revenue department. News articles noted that Isaacs had "a closer association with Kerner than any other appointee" though he was an unknown quantity as a public administrator.[13]

While Kerner was governor, Isaacs was "the dominant behind-the-scenes personality in the administration," and the relationship between the two men was "deep and trusting."[14] Isaacs later was described as "a man who lives in shadows," and certainly for much of his life he operated in the large shadow of Otto Kerner, then one of the most distinguished public figures in Illinois.[15]

A graduate of Brown University, Kerner obtained his law degree from Northwestern University in 1934. His father, Otto Kerner Sr., was a political ally of Democratic Mayor Anton J. Cermak, whose support led to the elder Kerner's appointment to the federal court of appeals in Chicago. Cermak's daughter became the wife of Otto Kerner Jr.

Following Kerner's World War II duty, he served from 1947 to 1954 as U.S. Attorney in Chicago and then for six years as a Cook County judge. In 1960 he was slated for the governorship by the Democratic Party. He later was described as "a central-casting candidate," "the state's first ready-made television candidate," with "bright eyes, well-chiseled features and resonant voice suited perfectly" for that medium.[16]

With Isaacs as his campaign manager, Kerner defeated the incumbent by over half a million votes. In 1964 Governor Kerner was re-elected, defeating Charles H. Percy. Once again Kerner called on Ted Isaacs to manage his campaign.

On July 27, 1967, Kerner was appointed by President Lyndon Johnson as the chairman of the National Advisory Commission on Civil Disorders. At that time Kerner was not a nationally renowned figure. In March 1968 the commission produced its landmark report, warning of continued racial polarization in American society. By this time, both the "Kerner Commission" and its chairman had become much better known and widely respected.

A few weeks before the report was released, Kerner announced that he would not run for a third term as governor. Speculation arose that President Johnson would name Kerner to another important position, perhaps the U.S. Supreme Court.[17] In May Kerner resigned as governor to become a judge on the Court of Appeals for the Seventh Circuit in Chicago, the same federal court on which his father had sat. Kerner joined the court of appeals on May 20, 1968. As of that date, there was every reason to believe that his already distinguished career of public service—as soldier, state judge, governor, and namesake of the Kerner Report—would now be extended as a federal judge at the court of appeals level, or even higher.

Chapter 2

Alarm Bells in the Newsrooms

Among the members of the press receiving Skolnick's fact sheet on June 4—suggesting the damning link between Klingbiel's stock and Isaacs's criminal case—were two who became very interested. Ed Pound was a twenty-five-year-old investigative reporter from the *Evening Telegraph* in Alton, a town of about thirty-nine thousand people located across the Mississippi River from St. Louis. The other reporter, Charles Nicodemus, at thirty-seven, was the political editor and an investigative reporter for the *Chicago Daily News,* one of the four major daily newspapers in the city then. Nicodemus already knew Skolnick and had a cautiously favorable impression of him.

Nicodemus had not attended the hearing where Skolnick testified that day. Later in the afternoon, however, Skolnick went to the Press Room in the Capitol and told Nicodemus he had a story the reporter ought to be interested in, especially since the *New York Times* had failed to follow through on it. Skolnick summarized the prosecution of Isaacs and Klingbiel's authorship of the supreme court decision dismissing the case. Skolnick showed Nicodemus the fact sheet and claimed he had examined the CCB stock lists on his own initiative, knowing that Isaacs was a key organizer of the Civic Center Bank and that Kerner also was a stockholder. Nicodemus agreed to follow up on Skolnick's information.

Ed Pound of the Alton paper had listened to Skolnick's testimony, and Pound's "interest was drawn by the brashness and scatter-gun charges made by the self-styled reformer who told the state senators, without batting an eye, that some Chicago judges were crooked." Pound felt that Skolnick was the type of person a reporter never should write off: "an aggravating gadfly who, in his persistent digging, sometimes hits paydirt." While Skolnick and Nicodemus were talking, Pound was leisurely reading Skolnick's written materials, including the fact sheet. When Pound saw the notation about Klingbiel, "newsroom alarm bells were sounding inside him" and he went into action:

> Pound popped out of his chair and went in search of Skolnick. He found him talking to a newsman. Pound pried the Chicagoan free and asked him to enlarge on the Klingbiel bank stock affair. Skolnick told the *Telegraph* reporter that records in the Cook County Recorder of Deeds in Chicago would show that on September 5, 1968, some 100 shares of Civic Center Bank stock were transferred to two of Justice Klingbiel's grandchildren in care of the justice.
>
> "But," Pound told Skolnick, "this does not prove, as you state in your fact sheet, that Klingbiel was a stockholder when he wrote the *Isaacs* opinion in 1967." "We believe," Skolnick told Pound, "that Klingbiel got the stock at the time of the *Isaacs* decision. We think by checking, it can be proved."[1]

Before doing anything more, Pound asked Nicodemus about Skolnick. Nicodemus advised Pound that although Skolnick was controversial, he did know how to do factual research and to dig up information others might overlook. Both reporters were beginning to see what Skolnick was seeing, a possible link between a supreme court justice's financial interests and a decision of the court in an important criminal case.

Each of the reporters quickly, but separately, got to work on the story. Pound used the next few days to learn more about the prosecution of Isaacs and to get approval from his Alton publisher to pursue Skolnick's hunch. On Sunday, June 8, along with his fellow reporter Ande Yakstis, Pound drove the three hundred miles from Alton to Chicago. The next day they checked the public stockholder records in Chicago, talked further with Skolnick at his home, and began a series of telephone interviews with Klingbiel and Isaacs. They also called some other justices, plus Robert M. Perbohner, a friend of Isaacs and a member of the Illinois Commerce Commission who was coming to light as having had an intermediary role of some sort in Klingbiel's acquisition of the CCB stock.[2] These calls produced seriously conflicting versions of how Klingbiel got the stock.

At the same time as Pound's search, Nicodemus was also on the trail. He and other *Daily News* colleagues questioned Isaacs, Klingbiel, Perbohner, and others through telephone calls. These calls produced glaring inconsistencies and later on would become important incriminating evidence.

The Editor and the Justice

By the beginning of the next week, Nicodemus had roughed out a story disclosing that Klingbiel had been given stock by Perbohner, a close friend of Isaacs, and that Isaacs's fate had been determined in a supreme court decision written by Klingbiel. On Monday, June 9, this rough draft reached Roy M. Fisher, the editor of the *Daily News*. Fisher then called Isaacs on both Monday and Tuesday, to give him "an opportunity to talk about the implications of our findings."[3] He also spoke with Perbohner.

But Fisher moved more slowly on the story than Nicodemus wished. He proceeded cautiously in part because he was concerned about the views of two important people. One was Justice Walter V. Schaefer, the senior member of the Illinois Supreme Court. Schaefer and Fisher were acquainted with each other and had many mutual friends. Fisher had great respect for Schaefer and occasionally would call him for background guidance on stories. Fisher called Justice Schaefer on Monday and asked him about the possibility that Klingbiel had assigned the *Isaacs* decision to himself. Schaefer explained why that was not a possibility, but declined Fisher's offer to explain why the question was being raised.[4]

Another justice, Robert C. Underwood, was also being pursued by the press. On Monday a *Daily News* reporter called him to relay some of what Justice Klingbiel already had said to the *Daily News*. Underwood "was pretty upset about the situation" and immediately tried to call Klingbiel to "find out what the situation actually was—whether they had talked to him or whether this was simply a means of attempting to get me to make a statement."[5]

Klingbiel was on vacation overseas, and Underwood was unable to speak with him until Tuesday night, reaching him in Spain.[6] Immediately after that call, Underwood called Schaefer, relayed what he had just learned from Klingbiel, and asked him to talk to the other justices in Chicago. Underwood also made another request, as Schaefer later described:

> Mr. Justice Underwood was calling to ask me to call Mr. Fisher of the *Daily News*—I don't know whether he mentioned him by name, I think he did—to ask him to hold off publication of any story until Justice Klingbiel returned to this country, which was to be the following Saturday evening. Mr. Justice Underwood said that he had talked to some other members of the court, and that he wanted to get my judgment as to whether that should be done, and he wanted to know whether or not I would be willing to do it.

Schaefer agreed, and promptly called Fisher at home, waking him up
at about 11 P.M.

Schaefer later recounted the unusual conversation between the justice and the editor:

> I made my request. I told him that Mr. Justice Underwood had
> called, and he told me in considerable detail of the newspaper's in-
> vestigation of the situation. I asked him to withhold publication un-
> til Justice Klingbiel came back.
>
> He told me at that time that the paper planned to write nothing in
> their first edition the following day, but to run—and I remember his
> exact words—to run a truncated story in their second edition. He
> said that he would consider my request, which I had put to him as a
> request of the court in fairness to Mr. Justice Klingbiel.

The Editor and His Boss

Fisher's plan to publish a "truncated story" in the second edition apparently had been firmed up Tuesday afternoon, after a discussion
with the other person Fisher was concerned about: Bailey K. Howard,
president of the newspaper division of Field Enterprises, which owned
both the *Daily News* and the *Sun-Times*. Coincidentally, Howard was
a friend of Isaacs and, making the situation even stickier for the newspaper, was also one of the five original organizers and stockholders of
the Civic Center Bank. He had been a member of its board of directors
from the outset and served as its first chairman.

Howard was known as an energetic, shrewd, and extremely well-
connected businessman. Fisher and Howard had known each other
for a long time. Fisher joined the *Daily News* after World War II, but
left in 1958 to join the World Book Encyclopedia division of Field Enterprises as editorial director and vice president, with Howard as his
boss. When Howard assumed control of the Field newspapers in 1965,
he brought Fisher back to the *Daily News* as editor.

The *Daily News* was widely considered the best written of the
Chicago newspapers, with more journalism awards to its credit than
all the others. Nonetheless, it was fighting for survival against the pressures of evening television newscasts and urban lifestyle changes that
were hitting afternoon newspapers especially hard.[7] By 1969 it was
losing money for Field Enterprises, and Fisher found himself repeatedly trying to fend off top management's inclination to close down the
paper or take it in directions that Fisher and other journalists found

repugnant to its traditions. Fisher frequently found himself at odds with Howard during these trying times.

When Fisher went to see Howard on Tuesday afternoon, he was accompanied by a small delegation. It was clear that Howard would have to make the final decision on this story, since it had real potential to hurt, or at least embarrass, him and his business associates. Fisher went to see Howard along with the newspaper's lawyer, Daniel Feldman, and Emmett Dedmon, the parent company's editorial director for both of its newspapers. According to Fisher's subsequent account, as well as Feldman's recollections, Howard "was prepared to go with the story" but also "expressed a desire that we check out everything thoroughly." Fisher later claimed that Howard's interests were not a factor in the paper's coverage of this subject, and that the paper "handled it exactly right."[8]

Charles Nicodemus, the *Daily News* reporter in Springfield, was not aware of the meeting with Howard or of the plan to publish the truncated version in Wednesday's second edition. By Tuesday evening, Nicodemus had refined his story and was urging Fisher to publish it in the first edition the next morning. He felt this urgency because he had been told by Skolnick that Pound was in Chicago working on the same story, and because Skolnick was telling Nicodemus that he was going to take some action himself since the newspapers were taking too long.

The Story Breaks

While the *Daily News* went through its deliberations, the *Alton Evening Telegraph* got ready to publish. The story was written by Ed Pound and Ande Yakstis and appeared in the Alton paper's regular edition on Wednesday afternoon.[9] The Alton reporters wrote that Klingbiel had received the stock as a gift from Isaacs while the court had *People v. Isaacs* before it. Their headline read "High Court Judge Linked to Bank Deal," and their lead sentence declared: "Illinois Supreme Court Justice Ray I. Klingbiel in 1967 upheld the dismissal of criminal charges against an officer of the Chicago bank in which the judge had received a gift of stock worth about $2,000, a *Telegraph* investigation revealed today." The *Telegraph* story also reported that Governor Kerner and Joseph E. Knight, former state Director of Financial Institutions, had received stock in CCB as well.

The Alton story stated that Skolnick had asked, "in a motion mailed to the court," for an investigation of the *Isaacs* decision. The reporters were careful in the phrasing of that statement, for the motion indeed was Skolnick's, but it actually had been mailed to the court by Pound on Tuesday as a favor to Skolnick. Pound now recalls that—as a naive downstate reporter—when he mailed the motion, he made a tactical mistake that aided the *Daily News* in its competing coverage. Had he not complied with Skolnick's request quite so quickly, thus putting the citizen's allegations on the public record, the Alton paper could have published its findings much sooner than the *Daily News*—probably one full day sooner.

About 9 A.M. on Wednesday, as the Alton story was being sent to the Associated Press, Justice Schaefer arrived at his chambers in downtown Chicago. He found a message that Roy Fisher had already telephoned, and Schaefer quickly returned the call. Fisher first asked the justice an additional question about what Klingbiel had said to Justice Underwood. Schaefer later recalled what transpired next:

> He said they were going to have a conference shortly about whether to withhold publication or to publish. Either at that time or the evening before, I told him that I had had a call from the *Alton Telegraph*—my recollection is that he knew that the *Alton Telegraph* was also interested in the case. After my conversation with him, he said, they would have a conference and he would tell me the result of that conference.
>
> And I then started to open my mail, and the second document, the second envelope that I opened, was a copy of Mr. Skolnick's motion, and I immediately called Mr. Fisher back and told him that that document had been mailed to the clerk, so I didn't want them to be courteous to the court and to be scooped. As long as it was public knowledge, I felt that I was obligated to call him at once and tell him that it was public knowledge.[10]

Schaefer was giving Fisher a green light. Furthermore, on Tuesday Fisher had called Paul S. Cousley, the publisher of the *Alton Telegraph,* to find out when the *Telegraph* was going to publish. Cousley refused to discuss his paper's plans with Fisher, but the Chicago editor surmised that the downstate paper was close to finishing its story.[11] Also, on Wednesday morning Isaacs failed to return another phone call from the *Daily News,* following up on Isaacs's commitment to produce records showing that the stock transfer to Klingbiel was a normal business transaction. With Isaacs's telling silence, the Alton paper's competitive pressure, Schaefer's and Howard's acquiescence, Nicodemus's urging, and Skolnick's petition on file with the court, it clearly was time for the *Daily News* to go to print.

The *Daily News* published its story in its second edition at about eleven o'clock.[12] It ran, without a byline, at the top of the front page under the headline "Gift to Klingbiel Bared." Nicodemus was dismayed that the story had not run in the first edition as he had expected. He was even more distressed because what appeared was "very obviously in a form that was different from the way I had proposed the story."

The opening paragraph, the lead, was astonishingly bland: "One hundred shares of bank stock given to Illinois Supreme Court Justice Ray I. Klingbiel as a campaign contribution in 1966 ended up two years later with the justice's grandchildren." The next few paragraphs simply quoted Robert Perbohner—the Illinois Commerce commissioner—as having given the stock to Klingbiel, and the justice as having acknowledged receipt of it, as a campaign contribution. Not until more than halfway through the story did any references to the Civic Center Bank and Isaacs appear:

> Perbohner said the stock was part of the original issue of the Civic Center Bank & Trust Co. He said he bought it for $2,000 from Theodore Isaacs, an officer of the bank.
>
> At the time of Perbohner's gift to Klingbiel, a case involving Isaacs, former state director of revenue, was pending before the court.
>
> Klingbiel was assigned to write the Supreme Court opinion, which was favorable to Isaacs.

Although the *Daily News* later claimed that its story "created an immediate sensation in Springfield," it is difficult to believe this story would have stirred much public concern anywhere. It simply reported that the justice had received the stock as a campaign contribution but later gave it to his grandchildren. Only in a veiled manner was the stock linked to "a case involving Isaacs," a case not identified as a criminal case in which he was personally charged as a defendant.

Nicodemus concluded that out of deference to Justice Schaefer, a desire to avoid tarring the supreme court, and concern for Bailey Howard, Fisher had decided to print only the bare minimum. Fisher, as an experienced newsman, habitually proceeded with caution when preparing to print a story that could damage people's reputations. In this instance, however, the beleaguered editor found himself in an additional acute bind—caught between his investigative reporters' zeal, his boss's potential involvement in the budding scandal, and the expressed concern of Schaefer and other justices for careful treatment of the supreme court. The attempt to reconcile these conflicting pressures was reflected in the truncated article.

The Alton paper's story evidenced no similar constraints, and the two downstate reporters were proud of it. Charles Nicodemus found his own paper's burial of the Isaacs link "disgraceful."

Chapter 3

Uproar in Springfield

The written motion Skolnick filed with the court on Wednesday, June 11, was entitled "Motion for Leave to File Appearances as Amici Curiae and Request for Court Investigation." It was submitted by Skolnick along with Harriet Sherman, staff member and investigator of the Citizens' Committee to Clean Up the Courts. The motion recited various findings of the Citizens' Committee in its "research and investigation project involving the Civic Center Bank & Trust Company." Among the findings were charges that in the fall of 1966, while the *Isaacs* matter was pending before the court, and with Klingbiel then serving as chief justice, Robert Perbohner received a hundred shares of CCB stock in a transfer from Isaacs, his "very close friend." Skolnick next alleged that Perbohner "gave as a gift the said 100 shares" to Klingbiel. Skolnick claimed that his inquiry

> points to the involvement, by undue influence and appearance of impropriety, of both Justice Klingbiel as well as Justice Roy J. Solfisburg, Jr., and statements by Robert Perbohner tend to show that Perbohner was a conduit, or courier, for the said 100 shares from Isaacs to the opinion-writer and decision maker, Ray I. Klingbiel.

Skolnick accused Solfisburg, who now was chief justice, of secretly being an attorney for the bank. Other findings named about twenty other CCB stockholders, including Otto Kerner, but without any assertions linking them to *People v. Isaacs*.

The motion concluded that "there has been a fraud upon this court," that the court "has inherent power to investigate the integrity of its judgments, orders, and decrees," and that the "decision in the instant case is tainted and is invalidated by fraud upon the court." Skolnick asked that the court undertake an investigation of the *People v. Isaacs* decision "and that upon investigation, that the records of this court be purged of the decision in this case."

The court had no immediate public response to the motion, but newspapers in Chicago—and in Aurora, where Solfisburg lived—quickly reported that the chief justice had stated that the matter would come before the court at a previously scheduled session in Springfield the following week. Solfisburg also said it "would be improper for me to comment on a pending case." Nonetheless, he indirectly denied the allegation that he had been a lawyer for the bank. Since becoming a judge in 1956, he said, he had not practiced law, had any clients, or received any fees.

Similarly, when Skolnick's assertions about Kerner's CCB stock ownership were mentioned to him by a reporter as the judge walked to his chambers in the Federal Building, he said, "Up here, we don't comment, so there'll be no response." Isaacs's immediate response was far less judicious, although oddly phrased for a native Chicagoan. He described Skolnick's accusations as "complete falsehood and a lot of tommyrot."

The Legislature Weighs In

The next morning, Thursday, June 12, the Executive Committee of the Illinois House of Representatives convened to consider a resolution offered by Democratic Representative Anthony J. Scariano of Park Forest. The resolution called for an investigation of Klingbiel's CCB stock ownership. Scariano was one of a number of progressive Democratic members of the legislature.[1] These legislators had frequent informal contacts with members of the press in Springfield. One such discussion took place in the Capitol Press Room between Scariano and Charles Nicodemus of the *Daily News* on Wednesday afternoon. They talked about Skolnick's accusations and agreed that the legislature should undertake some investigation of the matter.

At Scariano's request, Nicodemus prepared a draft resolution, calling for the creation of a special committee of the House. Nicodemus later reflected that in drafting the resolution, he was playing "a much greater insider role than journalism these days would consider acceptable." Such involvement was acceptable then, he recalls, "as long as you could maintain your integrity, and still turn around and throw stones."

The meeting of the House's Executive Committee on the draft resolution was stormy, with legislators loudly disagreeing over whether the House had authority to undertake an investigation of this sort. The Executive Committee also sparred over whether to hear from Skolnick. The committee chairman finally allowed him to testify on the spot, and Skolnick repeated his allegations and urged the Executive Committee to have various justices explain themselves to the legislature.

Following this meeting, a modified resolution was offered before the full House. The new version was described as written in "plain, unexplosive language as a substitute for [the] more controversially worded resolution" offered by Scariano. Some House leaders had viewed Scariano's draft as accepting "at face value" the charges made by Skolnick. The substitute resolution was sponsored jointly by House Speaker Ralph T. Smith of Alton, a Republican, and Minority Leader John P. Touhy, a Democrat from Chicago. Their resolution, unanimously adopted without debate, succinctly recited that "there have been allegations of judicial impropriety by a member or members of the Illinois Supreme Court." It then directed the appointment of a special committee to investigate the allegations and report to the House by September 15.

The speed with which this action was taken stemmed in part from displeasure the legislature already was harboring toward the court. Some members of the supreme court had been pressuring the legislature to enact pay raises for the judiciary, and many legislators were feeling badgered. A bill to raise judicial salaries was before the legislature and included a provision raising the supreme court justices' annual salaries from $37,500 to $40,000.[2] Additionally, some legislators saw political benefits to be gained in the eyes of the public if they appeared responsive to the charges against Klingbiel. It was, of course, less than a month since the highly publicized resignation of U.S. Supreme Court Justice Fortas under a cloud of alleged ethical infractions. In this climate, and with a mixture of motivations, the House members adopted the resolution and created the House Committee with unusual haste.

Speaker Ralph Smith tapped Republican Representative George W. Lindberg, a lawyer, to chair the House Committee. Another Republican member was Henry J. Hyde, a forty-five-year-old Chicago lawyer who had begun his service in the Illinois House in 1967. Four other members of the committee were also lawyers, and another was an accountant. The *Chicago Sun-Times* reported that "observers considered the committee a high-powered group, indicating the depth of concern in the General Assembly over the allegations against the two justices."[3]

Hyde was given the responsibility of finding an out-of-state attorney to serve as counsel to the House Committee since, as Lindberg explained, the committee wanted "to avoid any conflict of interest which might result by employing an Illinois lawyer." Lindberg noted that many qualified Illinois lawyers had appeared before one or more of the present supreme court justices at one time or another. Lindberg also expressed the committee's desire to have the House authorize an expanded investigation, going beyond the charges against Klingbiel and Solfisburg to investigate improprieties at all levels of the Illinois judiciary. Additionally, the committee sought to extend the time period for its work into 1970. Both of these changes were unanimously adopted by the House.[4]

Skolnick continued to make himself heard in Springfield at the time of Lindberg's statements. The *Chicago Tribune* reported that Skolnick "haunted the House corridors" that day. Skolnick asserted that the six lawyers on the House Committee should disqualify themselves from serving on it if they had cases pending before the supreme court. He also urged the committee to ask the supreme court to allow all litigants with cases pending before the court to obtain continuances "until this cloud is lifted." Lindberg simply replied that the committee would take up Skolnick's suggestions at its next meeting. When Henry Hyde was asked by reporters whether the committee would be overly cautious in investigating Skolnick's allegations against the supreme court because most of the committee members were lawyers, he replied, "Like hell we will."

To guide Hyde's search for an attorney for the committee, members suggested that he contact law schools in the East, bar associations in New York, and members of Congress such as Abner Mikva, a former member of the progressive Democratic group in the Illinois House. Hyde first contacted Louis Nizer, a nationally known New York lawyer and author, to see if he would take the job. When Nizer proved to be unavailable, Hyde invited Edward Bennett Williams, a prominent Washington lawyer and college friend, to become counsel to the House Committee. Williams declined, recommending instead another Washington lawyer, William G. Hundley.

Hundley was the former chief of the Organized Crime Section of the Criminal Division of the Department of Justice under Robert F. Kennedy. A Republican holdover from the Eisenhower administration, Hundley earned Kennedy's respect through impressive handling of high-profile criminal cases for the department. He accepted the position, but even with its own counsel on board, the House Committee was in a difficult position. The legislature was to adjourn for the summer on June 30, so there was little time available to proceed with the investigation. Nonetheless, the House Committee was widely regarded as a forum with potential long-term impact. George Lindberg recalls that soon after the committee's formation, Justice Schaefer asked to meet with him to discuss how to protect the supreme court's reputation. Although Lindberg shared the widespread perception of Schaefer as "a very beloved figure" and "probably the greatest judge in Illinois history," the legislators refused to meet with him. Ralph Smith, the speaker, considered an informal meeting of that sort inappropriate in the midst of this confrontation between the legislature and the court.[5]

A Crisis Emerges

At this point the stage was set for dramatic action: Skolnick's charges were before the court and the public in a formal, albeit somewhat unusual, legal document. Newspapers around the state were devoting more ink and larger typeface to his allegations and to their own investigative results. The legislature had established a new investigative body, hired a lawyer, and threatened to insist that the justices appear before the legislators to explain themselves. Investigations were being initiated in other quarters, too. The Chicago Bar Association appointed a committee to "determine the facts," and the Sangamon County State's Attorney, Richard A. Hollis, announced that he was looking into possible criminal activity involved in the transfer of CCB stock to Klingbiel.

Finally, in addition to Klingbiel and Solfisburg, the names of many other figures in Illinois government and business were being indirectly besmirched for their association with the bank either as shareholders, directors, or friends of the bank organizers. The most extensive disclosure of prominent people associated with the Civic Center Bank appeared in the *Los Angeles Times*.[6] The article listed not only the two targeted justices, but also Kerner, many Chicago trial court judges, various Chicago aldermen, Chicago Congressman Daniel Rostenkowski, U.S. Senator Joseph Montoya of New Mexico, a variety of state and local officials, and some associates of organized crime leaders. The paper seemed to relish giving particular attention to "leading figures in the communications industry in Chicago" who were investors in the bank, including not just Bailey Howard, but also other executives and editors associated with all four of the major Chicago newspapers.[7] Skolnick, the perennial citizen gadfly darting around the Illinois courts, this time had started something big.

Chapter 4

A Special Commission

As the crisis grew, the supreme court realized that somehow it had to respond. The two accused justices wanted to find a forum in which to clear their names, and other justices wanted to remove the court from the public spotlight and the taint of the accusations. The challenge was to find a credible process leading toward these objectives.

Searching for a Process

Since the mid–nineteenth century, judges in Illinois have been selected predominantly by political party nomination and partisan election, even at the supreme court level. The political nature of elections for the supreme court has been further accentuated by the state's division into separate judicial districts. After the 1962 amendments to the Judicial Article of the 1870 Constitution, the seven supreme court justices were elected from five judicial districts: three from the district covering Cook County, and one each from four districts around the state.

Under this system, as a practical matter a judge could most effectively be removed by a party's decision not to renominate the judge for reelection.[1] The 1962 changes, however, added a new nonpolitical procedure. An incumbent judge would go before the voters unopposed and without party designation, and the voters would be asked to decide simply the question of retention of the judge in office.

The new Judicial Article, which took effect in 1964, also granted the Illinois Supreme Court the authority to create a commission with power to remove any judge for cause, as well as to retire a judge for disability or to suspend a judge without pay.[2] In May 1964, acting under this constitutional mandate, the supreme court established the Illinois Courts Commission and promulgated a rule to govern the Courts Commission's organization and proceedings. The rule, however, had a crucial procedural deficiency, for under its terms the Courts Commission could do nothing unless it was convened by the supreme court to hear each individual complaint.[3]

The Courts Commission had been convened on only two occasions, in May and June 1967.[4] Seeing this paucity of activity, many Illinois lawyers felt that the system was ineffective, and a joint committee of the Illinois State Bar Association and the Chicago Bar Association was formed to recommend changes. Among the proposed changes to the rule was a provision directing that the Courts Commission be convened permanently. These recommendations were presented to the supreme court in May 1969, but the court did not adopt them until the end of June.

When Skolnick's motion was filed on June 11, the Courts Commission still could only be convened on the specific order of the supreme court. The obvious awkwardness of this procedure, particularly in the charged atmosphere at that time, forced the court to seek an alternative. If anyone had doubts about the need for an alternative in this instance, one look at the commission's membership erased them: the chairman of the Courts Commission was Klingbiel.

The Order and the Commissioners

On Monday, June 16, the court met in Springfield. Justice Klingbiel had returned on Saturday from his trip abroad. En route Solfisburg urged him by phone to come to Springfield on Sunday, rather than following his usual practice of arriving at the court on the Monday morning of the new term. Klingbiel heeded the advice, giving the justices additional time to talk about the situation.

At their meeting on Monday, the seven justices discussed Skolnick's motion further and agreed on a course of action. The next day the court issued an order creating the Special Commission. Although a variety of rumors circulated as to the source of the Special Commission idea, the dominant view was that it came from Justices Schaefer and Underwood because of their strong interest in protecting the court as an institution.[5]

As the court groped for a solution in the days leading up to the order, there was what one justice described as "a vast amount of conversation" among them.[6] Some of them, particularly Klingbiel, also sought advice from outside the court. Klingbiel spoke to Don Reuben, the influential Chicago libel lawyer who earlier had advised the *Daily Calumet* not to print its story about Skolnick's suspicions.

Reuben believed the court should summarily dismiss Skolnick's motion, because obviously Skolnick had no proper role—no "standing"—in the criminal case against Isaacs. Reuben even questioned whether Isaacs's due process rights would be undermined by any action the court ultimately might take in response to an interloper's motion. Reuben's advice not to create any sort of investigative mechanism was disregarded, however, especially because, as he later recalled, "Wally Schaefer and Bob Underwood wanted to do it," and Solfisburg and Klingbiel thought the Special Commission would help them out of their plight.[7]

The court's order was entered on June 17 within the framework of the *People v. Isaacs* case. It denied the portion of Skolnick's motion seeking approval for him and Harriet Sherman to appear as amici curiae, friends of the court. The order then referred to Skolnick's request for the court to investigate its decision in the case, but the court took no direct action on the request, neither granting nor denying it. Instead the court declared:

> On the Court's own motion a Special Commission is appointed to investigate the charges contained in the motion insofar as they relate to the integrity of the judgment entered by this Court in this case.

This declaration effectively granted Skolnick's motion, but for unstated reasons—probably to save face and try to move Skolnick to the periphery—the court disingenuously described its action as being on the court's "own motion." Under prevailing legal doctrines, the court undoubtedly did have inherent power to investigate allegations that fraud or corruption had affected a specific decision it had rendered. Indeed Skolnick had done his homework well, for his motion correctly referred to the leading U.S. Supreme Court precedent on this point.[8]

The court's order next indicated the composition of the commission. The court had decided on Monday to name the presidents of the Illinois State Bar Association and the Chicago Bar Association to head the Special Commission. That afternoon, Justice Schaefer had asked Alfred Y. Kirkland of Elgin, president of the State Bar Association, if he would be willing to serve. Kirkland was reluctant. He had practiced law for many years in Kane County, where Solfisburg also had practiced, and he questioned whether the court should appoint a lawyer from the same county as the chief justice. Furthermore, Kirkland pointed out, he knew Solfisburg well, not just professionally but

socially, too. He asked Schaefer whether his appointment might appear to raise a conflict of interest, and he also mentioned that his term
as bar president expired in a few days.

In the wake of Kirkland's cautious response, and the realization
that the terms of the incumbent presidents of both bar associations
were almost over, Schaefer did not extend the second invitation the
court had asked him to convey. John Joseph Sullivan, outgoing president of the Chicago Bar Association, was not approached as planned.

At this point, members of the court were surprised and disappointed. Some of them specifically wanted Kirkland and Sullivan to
handle this task. These justices undoubtedly believed that the two bar
leaders' treatment of the court, and of the two targeted justices in particular, would be gentle. Kirkland himself later shared the opinion,
widely held at the time, that Sullivan would have been strongly inclined to reach a conclusion favorable to the accused justices. Sullivan
was friendly with many of the justices, and in fact those friendships
would be spotlighted within a few weeks in startling ways.

Having determined to rely upon the bar presidents, but swayed by
Kirkland's reluctance and the news of the term expirations, the court
instead invited the incoming bar leaders to head the Special Commission. Later on Monday, Justice Schaefer contacted Henry L. Pitts, the
new president of the Illinois State Bar Association, and Frank Greenberg, who was due to head the Chicago Bar Association. After brief
reflection, they agreed. Pitts later described these events:

> [The Special Commission] broke at the time of the ISBA annual
> meeting at Pheasant Run [resort] when the outgoing president, Al
> Kirkland, got called off the golf course by a phone call from Wally
> Schaefer, who said the court was requesting him and Joe Sullivan,
> the outgoing president of the CBA, to organize a special commis-
> sion to review the *Isaacs* decision. Al, who knew Roy Solfisburg
> well, socially and professionally, got off the hook by calling this to
> Wally's attention, pointing out that the media would play this up. Al
> immediately alerted me to expect a call from Wally, which came
> within a few hours. He said the court had decided to ask the incom-
> ing presidents of the ISBA and the CBA to take on the assignments.
>
> I was no more eager than Al and quizzed Wally about why this
> rather questionable action was being taken and what the legal basis
> was for bypassing the prescribed constitutional procedure. Wally as-
> sured me it was a part of the inherent power of the court and assured
> me they had thoroughly researched the question and had no con-
> cerns about it. He pressed me to accept the job and asked me who

was the incoming president of the CBA, because he intended to call
him immediately if I would agree to accept.[9]

The court's order thus named Pitts and Greenberg to the Special Commission, directed each of them to select an additional member, and directed them jointly to select a fifth member. Both men were corporate
lawyers in downtown Chicago firms.

Pitts promptly chose Mason Bull of Morrison, former president of
the State Bar Association, as an additional commission member.
Greenberg selected Edwin C. Austin, a name partner in the Chicago
firm of Sidley & Austin. For the fifth slot, Greenberg and Pitts jointly
chose Daniel M. Schuyler, a professor at Northwestern University
Law School and a partner in the Chicago firm of Schuyler, Stough &
Morris.

Frank Greenberg was promptly designated by the other commissioners as chairman of the Special Commission, which thereafter was
frequently referred to as the Greenberg Commission. Greenberg and
Pitts had not been personally acquainted with each other previously,
and at their first meeting, Greenberg asked Pitts his feelings about
which of the two should be chairman. Sensing that Greenberg wanted
the position, Pitts acceded, so Greenberg took the lead role and Pitts
became the vice chairman.

Additional language in the court's order gave the Special Commission power to subpoena witnesses, order production of documents,
and conduct public or private hearings. Witnesses were to have the
right to be represented by counsel, and hearings were to follow the
rules of evidence. The order's final directive to the commission was
perhaps its most remarkable provision: "The Commission is directed
to proceed expeditiously and to file its report on or before August 1,
1969." By that date, the report was to be filed with the clerk of the Illinois Supreme Court, the House Committee, and the Illinois Courts
Commission. A handful of busy practicing lawyers and bar leaders was
to undertake a thorough investigation into a court decision and financial transactions of great complexity stretching back over a period of
at least five years, and it was to do all of this in six weeks.

Presumably the court wanted the work done rapidly in order to get
the controversy behind it fast, especially since it was facing two cases
of tremendous legal and political significance. Perhaps the court was
also being considerate of the newly named members of the Special
Commission, not wanting to prolong the burden on their law practices, their new duties as leaders of the organized bar, and their summer. Perhaps also the court—or at least some members—did not want

the investigation to go too long because they did not want it to go too deep. As Pitts said many years later, "I was always confident that Walter Schaefer and others then on the court fully expected that the Special Commission would pull their chestnuts out of the fire with a perfunctory and bland report."[10]

The penultimate portion of the order also was quite unusual. In it the court explained some traditionally confidential aspects of the justices' deliberations, draft opinions, and votes in the *Isaacs* appeal. The full significance of this explanation, and the controversy surrounding it, would later become much clearer.

The Fight for Financial Disclosure

The last portion of the court's order noted that all of the justices had filed the statutorily required annual financial statements with the Administrative Office of the Illinois Courts. The court directed that those statements and the "relevant income tax returns of the members of this Court and their wives will be made available for inspection by the members of this Commission only." Under the court's implementation of the 1967 statute that required the filing of these financial statements by judges, only an order of the court itself, or an action of the Illinois Courts Commission, could open the sealed envelopes.[11]

The court's allowance of access only to the Special Commission angered members of the House Committee. George Lindberg proclaimed that "those sealed envelopes and their contents are public property and the legislature should have access to them." House Speaker Smith also strongly favored legislative access to the statements.

In the next few days, a major confrontation began brewing between the legislature and the court over the House Committee's power to obtain the financial statements of Klingbiel and Solfisburg. The committee had already discussed the possibility of subpoenaing the two justices and their financial records, but decided instead to invite them to provide the financial information without the issuance of subpoenas. The legislature's subpoena power might be used if the justices refused, however. Proposals and counterproposals went back and forth between the legislature and the court, but as of Thursday the impasse remained.

On Friday more troublesome information came to light. That morning the *Chicago Sun-Times* carried an Associated Press report turning the spotlight on other financial dealings by Solfisburg. The article summarized a lengthy story that had appeared on Thursday in the

Cleveland Plain Dealer, raising questions about financial interests
Solfisburg had held in nine different banks and other businesses since
joining the Illinois Supreme Court in 1960. It was obviously strange
that this information about the Illinois chief justice should first appear
in a newspaper article in Ohio. As will be seen, this oddity reflects the
extremely dubious handling of this same information earlier by a major Chicago paper.[12]

Another *Sun-Times* story around this time alleged that eight hundred shares of CCB stock had been transferred, while the *Isaacs* case
was before the supreme court, to a "secret Aurora land trust" involving associates of Solfisburg. Furthermore, Skolnick had amended his
original motion to magnify the charges against Klingbiel. He alleged
that a total of 4,110 shares of CCB stock, gifts from Isaacs, were held
for the benefit of Justice Klingbiel by the justice's daughter and five
other persons with whom she allegedly was associated. These five
people all immediately denied knowing Klingbiel or his daughter, although most of them acknowledged owning CCB stock. The amendment also asserted that Isaacs gave a hundred CCB shares to Joseph
E. Knight, who was the state's Director of Financial Institutions when
the bank received its charter.

The newspapers were giving prominent attention to all of these new
accusations. With this explosion of adverse publicity, and with the legislature adamant about getting the justices' financial statements, the
two justices finally relented. Later on Friday, they sent a letter to the
House Committee in which they agreed to provide their statements to
the legislators "at a convenient date next week." A Pandora's box was
soon to be opened.

Chapter 5

The Case Against Isaacs

The Illinois Supreme Court mandated that the Special Commission investigate the charges in Skolnick's motion "insofar as they relate to the integrity of the judgment entered by the Court" in *People v. Isaacs*.[1] The case grew out of Isaacs's business activities while he was Director of the Illinois Department of Revenue from 1961 to 1963.

On September 30, 1964, Jack Mabley, a columnist and reporter for the *Chicago's American* newspaper, blasted Isaacs in a set of articles headlined "Kerner Aide Admits Link to Major State Supplier!"[2]— the result of an investigation Mabley conducted with the Better Government Association, an Illinois watchdog group. Mabley also contacted Raymond L. Terrell, the State's Attorney of Sangamon County.

Mabley met with Terrell to present evidence that Isaacs owned a substantial amount of stock in a Chicago printing company, Cook Envelope & Lithographing, Inc., which had received over a million dollars' worth of state printing contracts while Isaacs headed the Department of Revenue. Although the contracts were awarded through sealed bidding and although Cook Envelope was a very new company, it enjoyed remarkable success in landing them. Terrell looked into Mabley's information and began to believe that state officials might have provided the printing company with secret strategic information on how to structure its bids. In view of Isaacs's prominence, the political dynamite was tremendous, especially since Isaacs then was managing Kerner's reelection campaign against Charles Percy. *Chicago's American* even included with Mabley's articles a statement issued by Governor Kerner declaring his "highest confidence in the integrity and ability of Mr. Isaacs."[3]

As Terrell later recalled, "extraordinary pressure" was applied to him, through a variety of Democratic and Republican sources, to let the matter die. Instead, over a two-and-a-half-month period, Terrell presented the evidence to a grand jury in Springfield. During this time, Isaacs left his position as campaign manager for Kerner.[4] Although critics of Terrell, a Republican, charged that he was trying to indict Isaacs so as to damage Kerner's reelection chances, Terrell had not finished his presentations to the grand jury by election day in November and had not aimed to do so.

The Indictment Rises and Falls

On December 16, 1964, the Sangamon County Grand Jury returned a thirty-five-count indictment against Isaacs, Cook Envelope, and John J. Lang, later described as Isaacs's "hand-picked state superintendent of printing" in the state Department of Finance.[5] The indictment alleged that from 1961 to 1963, Cook Envelope entered into contracts to supply the state with envelopes, paper, and printing services. The indictment also asserted that the contracts could have been consummated with other bidders that would have supplied the state with the materials for much less money, and charged that Isaacs, Lang, and Cook Envelope had violated a variety of statutory provisions relating to state contracts, criminal conspiracies, state taxes, and official misconduct.

The circuit court in Springfield held a hearing on July 27, 1965, on motions filed by Isaacs and Lang to quash the indictment. On November 12, thirty-four of the thirty-five counts were quashed and dismissed by Judge Creel Douglas; the remaining count was not ruled on because it named only Cook, which had not yet made a formal appearance in the case.

The Appeal

Because the judge's ruling raised constitutional issues, the state was able to appeal directly to the supreme court. Terrell filed the appeal in December, and it officially went on the supreme court's docket in February 1966. Briefs were filed over the next few months, and the case was argued before the supreme court on September 15. The state conceded the invalidity of one of the thirty-four counts quashed by Judge Douglas, so thirty-three counts remained in dispute.

One of the pivotal charges was that Isaacs had violated the first paragraph of section 12 of the Illinois law on state contracts by holding a "direct pecuniary interest" in a state contract while employed by the state. The indictment also charged that Lang had aided and abetted

Isaacs in this offense. Isaacs was additionally charged with violating the second paragraph of section 12 by having a direct pecuniary interest in the state's contract with Cook by owning more than 25 percent of Cook's common stock and being entitled to more than 7.5 percent of the corporation's total distributable income. With the addition of other counts broadening these allegations into charges of aiding and abetting and conspiracy, these violations were the basis for ten of the counts reviewed by the supreme court.

The defendants were also charged under nine more counts with additional conspiracies. Eleven additional counts either charged Lang with collusion in violation of the law governing state contracts, or charged Isaacs and Cook with conspiring with Lang to defraud the state. Two additional counts asserted conspiracies to violate the Retailers' Occupation Tax Act. Finally, Lang alone was charged with official misconduct in acting beyond his lawful authority. Lang specifically was alleged to have caused the state to enter into the contracts with Cook Envelope while knowing that Isaacs was a state employee and one of the owners of Cook.

The Rulings

The supreme court faced a variety of constitutional and statutory objections to this array of charges. In resolving these objections, the court rendered an opinion that was highly technical, convoluted, and dry in its dissection of the statutory language and relevant precedents. Later commentators described the decision as "mind-bending,"[6] although "mind-numbing" is probably more apt.

The court's opinion, written by Justice Klingbiel and issued on March 29, 1967, affirmed the dismissal and quashing of all counts against Isaacs and all but eight counts against Lang. Those eight counts charged Lang, as an employee of the Department of Finance, with corruptly colluding to defraud the state. The trial court order dismissing these counts was reversed, and the case was remanded for further proceedings against Lang. No dissenting votes or opinions of any of the other justices accompanied Klingbiel's opinion.

Rehearing and Mandate

Terrell was disappointed, of course, with the decision. He thought the result "flew in the face of reason and common sense." Nonetheless, he had no basis to suspect that anything nefarious had contributed to the outcome. Terrell's assistant, Laurin Wollan, who had helped to research and write the state's brief, was surprised by the decision, but it did not seem terribly odd to him given the complex and technical nature of the issues. It did strike him that Lang seemed to have become the "fall guy" in the whole affair.[7]

On April 12, 1967, Terrell filed a petition for rehearing of the court's ruling on count 10, which Terrell considered the heart of the case against Isaacs. That count had charged both Isaacs and Lang with a conspiracy to violate the second paragraph of section 12, and the court had concluded that this paragraph could impose liability only on corporations and not on their individual stockholders. The court also had found that this count, like some others, was not stated with constitutionally adequate specificity.

The court denied Terrell's petition on May 16 without further explanation. The court's official order sending the case back down to the circuit court for further proceedings was issued on May 25. This date, as well as the dates of some of the other events during the *Isaacs* appeal, later would take on great importance during the Special Commission's investigation.

"Finally Disposed Of"

In the wake of the supreme court's decision, Lang appeared before circuit court Judge Paul C. Verticchio and pleaded guilty "to the crime of official misconduct in the manner and form as charged in the indictment." Lang, then a forty-nine-year-old department store employee, was fined $1,000 and half the costs of the proceedings.

The third of the original defendants, Cook Envelope & Lithographing, had made its appearance in the case early in 1966. A few months later it followed the other defendants' example by moving to dismiss the charges against it. Shortly after the supreme court's decision in the *Isaacs* case, Judge Verticchio ruled on Cook's motion, quashing all but one count against it and declaring, albeit without much explanation, that the count based on the second paragraph of section 12 stated "a good and sufficient charge."[8]

On the same day Lang pleaded guilty, Cook Envelope entered a guilty plea to the section 12 charge. Fined $2,500 and half the costs of suit, Cook subsequently went out of business, even though the state still owed it $67,000.[9]

After the sentences were imposed on Lang and Cook Envelope, Terrell said: "I'm very happy it's finally disposed of after 2½ years of going through the courts. I feel the pleas justify the time spent by the Sangamon County grand jury, which sat for 2½ months on this case, the courts of the county, and our office on this matter." Looking back at the broad scope of the original charges and at the furor they aroused, and comparing those charges to these modest plea bargains, it is hard to believe that Terrell's heart was in this statement. What he could not then know, of course, was that *People v. Isaacs* was not finally disposed of. As one commentator later observed, "One might have thought that this affair was over and the facts buried in the archives. This was not to be."[10]

[John Lang died in 1995. His years following the guilty plea and fine were difficult, exacerbated by the taint that the conviction attached to his name. In 2003, his daughter submitted a petition to the state seeking posthumous executive clemency for Lang. After nearly 12 years of silence by the state, on January 9, 2015, his name was cleared. Governor Pat Quinn granted Lang a pardon and expungement order.]

INVESTIGATION

Mid-June to Mid-July

Chapter 6

Stevens and His Team

After the Special Commission was created, it fell to Chairman Greenberg and Vice Chairman Pitts to quickly assemble a legal and investigative staff. On Friday, June 20, the Special Commission announced that it had chosen its counsel: John Paul Stevens, a forty-nine-year-old partner in the Chicago law firm of Rothschild, Stevens, Barry & Myers, which then had about ten attorneys. He was not widely known among Chicago lawyers, but a segment of the Chicago bar knew him as a skilled litigator and antitrust expert whose name was not associated with any highly publicized cases. A registered Republican with no significant involvement in politics, he had been active for many years in various committees of the Chicago Bar Association.

Stevens was a native Chicagoan, with deep roots in the city. His paternal grandfather had come to Chicago in the 1890s from southern Illinois. Successful in business, he formed an insurance company and acquired real estate holdings. Stevens's great-uncle was a prominent merchant, owning the Chas. A. Stevens department store in downtown Chicago. Stevens's mother, Elizabeth Street Stevens, came from nearby Michigan City, Indiana, and was a high school English teacher. His father, Ernest J. Stevens, was a lawyer, but followed his own father's footsteps into the business world and did quite well, at least until 1929. By that time he had built two hotels, the La Salle and the Stevens, but lost ownership of them after the Crash. The Stevens Hotel, a massive landmark on South Michigan Avenue, still bore that name, however, for many more years until it became the Conrad Hilton.

The Stevens family lived in the Hyde Park neighborhood on the South Side, near the University of Chicago. Two of John's three older brothers, William K. and Richard James, became lawyers. John was educated at the University of Chicago's elementary school and high school. One of the most memorable moments of Stevens's early years as a Chicagoan occurred at a 1932 baseball game between the Chicago Cubs and the New York Yankees at Wrigley Field. The twelve-year-old Stevens was there and watching closely when, in the fifth inning of the third game of the World Series, Babe Ruth called his shot and hit his most famous home run.

Stevens stayed at the University of Chicago for college, majoring in English, editing the *Daily Maroon* newspaper, acting as student head marshal at convocations, achieving high academic honors, and graduating Phi Beta Kappa in 1941. That summer he began working on a master's degree in English at the university. The dean of students, who was doing confidential work for the U.S. Navy, persuaded him to sign up for a navy correspondence course in military encoding and decoding. A few months into the course, the navy invited him to apply for a commission, and he signed up on December 6, the day, of course, before the attack at Pearl Harbor. Eventually Stevens couldn't resist joking that his enlistment apparently had precipitated the war.

After initial service in Washington, Stevens was sent overseas to serve in the Pacific theater in communications intelligence, gathering information from intercepted Japanese radio transmissions. As the war's end finally approached, he planned to return to his studies in English, but a letter from his brother Richard James convinced him to go to law school instead. His brother practiced in a small firm in Chicago, and John recalls that the thoughtful letter emphasized the service a lawyer can provide to people and the satisfaction that comes from helping a client solve a problem. When he returned from the Pacific in 1945, John Stevens began his study of law at Northwestern University, the G.I. Bill mostly paying his way.

Stevens was a superlative student at Northwestern, serving as an editor in chief of the *Law Review* and graduating first in his class in 1947. He was also reputed to have achieved the highest grade point average ever reached at the law school. As he was finishing law school, prominent Northwestern faculty members invited him and another student to take two available clerkships at the U.S. Supreme Court. A flip of a coin decided which student would get which clerkship. Stevens went to Washington for a year as law clerk to Justice Wiley Rutledge.

After returning to Chicago, Stevens joined the law firm of Poppenhusen, Johnston, Thompson & Raymond, known in later years as Jenner & Block. Stevens there began his practice in antitrust law. In 1951 he returned to Washington to serve as associate counsel to a congressional subcommittee conducting a much publicized investigation of antitrust concerns in various industries, most notably major league baseball. As a result of his work with the subcommittee, some people in organized baseball took notice of him, which in the 1960s led to his representation of Charley Finley, the controversial owner of the Athletics. Stevens recalled with amusement many years later, "There were actually three different people who told me they were the one who recommended me to Charley."

In 1952 Stevens formed a new firm in Chicago with Edward I. Rothschild and Norman J. Barry, young lawyers who had shared an office with him at the Poppenhusen firm. There they had developed a strong friendship and a resolve eventually to leave and create their own firm. This resolve began to form right after they took a one-day trip to Springfield for the swearing-in ceremony that made them members of the bar. They returned to discover they had been docked a day's pay.

The firm they created was a little unusual among Chicago firms then, for it blended a West Side Catholic (Barry), a north suburban Jew (Rothschild), and a South Side Protestant (Stevens). A referral from another lawyer soon brought them their first major antitrust client, a large milk company owned by a wealthy and prominent Chicagoan. From that starting point, Stevens and the others developed a healthy practice, with Stevens concentrating on antitrust cases.

Soon he also began teaching antitrust law, first filling in at Northwestern for a regular faculty member, and then on a frequent basis both there and at the University of Chicago Law School. The invitation to teach the "Competition and Monopoly" course at the University of Chicago came from Edward Levi, who had taught the course before becoming the law school's dean. Many years later, Levi was to play an even more fateful role in Stevens's career.

As of mid-1969, Stevens envisioned an ongoing career in his firm. There had been no mention of the possibility he might become a judge. As a litigator, frequently involved in complex federal cases, he was accustomed to hard work and had gone through a number of two- or three-week-long trials. Nonetheless, very few of his prior cases were as grueling and all consuming as what he was about to get into.

In turning to Stevens, Pitts and Greenberg knew they would be getting a talented trial lawyer. Additionally, since most of Stevens's practice was in federal court, any potential backlash from the state justices involved in this matter would, they hoped, be less of a deterrent to Stevens than it might have been for some others.[1]

The invitation came from Henry Pitts on June 19, as Stevens later described:

> I remember being outside on a spring evening in front [of my home] playing with my kids, and I was called to the phone. It was Henry, and he asked me if I'd do it. I think I just agreed on the spot after thinking about it, thinking it's the kind of thing that I ought to do. I didn't at the time realize that it would be a full-time assignment for the next six or seven weeks.

Stevens had several fairly important cases in the works then, but as the scandal unfolded, he says, "I did virtually nothing on my practice while this thing went on."

Running into Torshen

Stevens recruited Chicago attorney Jerome H. Torshen as his assistant counsel. They had come to know each other on opposite sides of a case in federal court in northern Indiana a few years earlier. Torshen, a thirty-nine-year-old graduate of Harvard Law School and a sole practitioner, had a broad range of litigation experience and an engaging and unpretentious manner.

The big break for the development of Torshen's practice was a multimillion-dollar insurance fraud case in federal court. He was asked to assist another firm in its representation of John F. Bolton Jr., a Chicago lawyer appointed by the state as the rehabilitator of a large insurance company. Although Bolton was skeptical about having this young, relatively unknown lawyer represent him, Torshen's strong performance in court made a believer out of Bolton. A couple years later, Governor Kerner named Bolton Director of the state Department of Insurance, and Bolton asked Torshen to represent the department in the investigation of insurance company practices.

In this role, Torshen did a lot of high-profile litigation, and he also began to get cases from another important source: Bolton's law partner Thomas E. Keane, the most powerful member of the Chicago City Council and a close ally of Mayor Richard J. Daley.[2] Through the work Torshen did for Bolton, Keane got to know Torshen's abilities, and he too liked what he saw. As Bolton and Keane directed legal work to Torshen, he became widely known among Chicago lawyers, judges, and journalists. Although not directly involved in politics, his linkage to Keane also led others to see him as having clout.

When Stevens asked Torshen to work with him on the investigation, Stevens was not thinking about clout. He just needed help on this unusual project from a good lawyer, especially one that Stevens knew had "bounced around" in the state courts a lot more than Stevens had.[3] The day after his appointment as counsel was announced, Stevens ran into Torshen in downtown Chicago and, on the spur of the moment, invited Torshen to assist him. Torshen's recollections of that encounter reflect a skepticism about the investigation shared by many lawyers at the time:

> As I was going into my office building, John came walking down the street. I congratulated him upon his appointment. He asked if I could work with him by giving him a couple of days in June. I agreed to that commitment. Neither of us knew that "a couple of days in June" would become a sixteen-hour-a-day, seven-day-a-week job into August. On that Saturday morning, we both thought that Skolnick was off on some sort of mad frolic.[4]

The Other "Volunteers"

Four other attorneys from Chicago law firms signed on as associate counsel: Joseph E. Coughlin, William J. McNally, Nathaniel Sack, and myself, all in our mid-twenties and not long out of law school. With military service, judicial clerkships, and other detours on their various paths to La Salle Street, the four brought to this investigation precious little actual experience as practicing lawyers.

The recruiting of the four was done through senior attorneys in their firms who were active in the Chicago Bar Association. Frank Greenberg took the lead in making contact. Sack, like Torshen, had initial doubts that this was a major assignment. He surmised with self-deprecation that he was called in simply because, as a junior associate, he "was probably regarded as the most expendable lawyer in the office."[5]

My invitation to work on the investigation came in a conversation with A. Bruce Schimberg, who was on the managing board of the Chicago Bar Association and a partner in the firm I worked for, Leibman, Williams, Bennett, Baird & Minow. He told me he wanted a lawyer from our firm to help out with the investigation, thought I would be a good man for the job, and said the project probably would just involve a few meetings in the next few weeks.

Even as he assured me it would not require much time beyond my regular chores as a new lawyer at the firm, I feared that destruction was imminent for any chance of a relaxing summer. Pondering this unhappy prospect, I clumsily hemmed and hawed. Just then another young associate, Henry L. Mason III, happened to walk into Schimberg's office. Schimberg turned to him, and Mason, whose strategic instincts I already admired, heard the partner's sketchy description of the task. Mason somehow quickly seemed to sense—for reasons obscure to me—that this was an opportunity not to be passed up. Perhaps because I trusted Henry's instincts more than my own, but more likely out of a competitive impulse to get this possible plum for myself, I instantly accepted the assignment.

A couple of months later, Stevens wrote to me, "There are a good many young lawyers who would have been happy to accept an opportunity to participate in the Special Commission's investigation."[6] Knowing how close I came to passing it up, and how ignoble my motivation to sign on actually was, I privately found Stevens's statement ironic, and a bit embarrassing.

To complete the team, the commission obtained the services of James G. Nussbaum, a young accountant with Price Waterhouse & Company. He, as well as the commissioners, counsel, and legal staff, served without compensation. Only Ed Powers, a private investigator hired by Stevens to assist in the work, was paid.

The Court's Press Release

On June 18, the day after it created the Special Commission, the court explained its action more fully, indicating that it was responding "to inquiries as to the reasons why the Supreme Court did not convene the Illinois Courts Commission with respect to the charges attacking the integrity of the judgment in the case of *People v. Isaacs.*" The justices declared that although the court had the power to investigate the charges itself, in this instance "the most prompt, impartial and effective investigation could be conducted by a Special Commission." The court also stated that it had appointed the incoming bar presidents "to insure the absence of criticism which might result from this Court's selection of the members of the Special Commission." Besides being a bit illogical, since the court in fact had selected the two leaders of the commission, the last comment was also futile, since a wave of criticism had already been released.

The court noted, with some understatement, that because Justice Klingbiel was the current chairman of the Illinois Courts Commission, any investigation by the Courts Commission would "likely be viewed with some skepticism." "The problem at the moment," the justices said, "was to select a competent, responsible investigating agency independent of the existing connections between this Court and the personnel of the Illinois Courts Commission." In addition, the court declared, "Of paramount importance was the fact that the confidence of the bar and the public in the integrity of the Court not be further impaired."

A Skeptical Reaction

The court stated that it was "hopeful, in order that its work would not be unduly impeded, that creation of a Special Commission would eliminate the need for additional investigations which might prove largely duplicative." This statement plainly was aimed at derailing, or at least discouraging, the additional investigation just beginning through the House Committee. The legislators understood immediately what the court meant, and they viewed the creation of the Special Commission as an affront to the legislature and an attempt to undercut the House probe. One member of the House Committee was quoted as saying: "What you've got here is the agency that's under investigation setting up its own investigators. The agency is laying the ground rules for the conduct of that investigation and then, in effect, trying to freeze out all other investigations. The Legislature cannot tolerate that." This statement reflected the doubts many people had about the Special Commission approach. Certainly those doubts were understandable, as Henry Pitts observed many years later: "In more than forty years of practice I found that lawyers generally cannot be relied upon to take on high members of the judiciary. I suspect that the members of the court who created the Special Commission were relying on this belief."[7]

Skepticism at the time was widespread. The Chicago Council of Lawyers, a recently formed group of about 250 young attorneys, sent a letter to the court asking for reconsideration of the order. The council stated that an investigation conducted by "practicing lawyers who may argue cases before the judges whose conduct they are investigating cannot possibly serve to inspire public confidence in the impartiality of their commission's work," and urged the court to change the Special Commission's composition by appointing a majority of non-lawyers, with the only lawyers being those "who do not practice actively before Illinois courts."[8]

Predictably, the most strident expression of criticism came from Sherman Skolnick. He flatly pronounced the court's creation of the Special Commission a "whitewash." He also filed a petition asking the court to vacate its order creating the Special Commission. He asserted that the order was void because the two accused justices participated in it, thus ruling on their own controversy.

The court's press release had candidly anticipated the extensive skepticism, for one of the court's concluding comments sounded a defensive, almost fatalistic, note: "The court realized, of course, the inevitability of criticism of any course it chose, but the court felt the investigating method chosen was substantially less vulnerable in this respect than use of the Illinois Courts Commission at this stage."[9] As events would turn out, the court's realization was both wrong and ironic. In the end there was very little criticism of the court's method. Of the criticism expressed, however, the harshest came from members of the court themselves.

Chapter 7

Limiting the Questions

The questions facing the Special Commission and its staff were initially defined by the accusations in Skolnick's motion. Most of what Skolnick had charged, and the newspapers had been fleshing out, translated into four areas of inquiry: the commission had to examine the *People v. Isaacs* opinion itself, the decisional process by which the court had issued that opinion, Klingbiel's acquisition of the CCB stock, and Solfisburg's alleged role as attorney for the Civic Center Bank. Beyond these four areas, new allegations about the justices seemed to call for expansion of the questions at hand. But would the commission broaden its investigation in response?

The Decision and Its Process

The substance of the decision in *People v. Isaacs* had to be considered. It was obvious that if a close reading suggested it was legally shaky in its own terms, the integrity of that judgment would be far less assured. The court's deliberative process in the case also had to be explored. With Klingbiel as a Civic Center Bank stockholder at some time before, during, or after the *Isaacs* case, just what role had he played in the deliberations leading to his opinion for the unanimous court in that case? On June 12, the day after Skolnick's motion was filed, the *Chicago Daily News* revealed three alarming facts about how *People v. Isaacs* was actually decided.

The first revelation was that before Klingbiel wrote the opinion that ended the criminal case against Theodore Isaacs, Justice Robert Underwood drafted an opinion that would have upheld some of the counts against Isaacs and forced him to stand trial. The Underwood opinion, however, failed to win adoption by a majority of the court; only Underwood and Schaefer voted for it.

Second, it was only after the failure of Underwood's opinion that Justice Klingbiel was assigned to write his decision throwing out all counts against Isaacs. Third, when the Klingbiel opinion was finally adopted by the court, the vote was not unanimous. Underwood and Schaefer voted against it but had chosen not to record their dissent in the published report of the case. No one knew there had been any disagreement within the court about Isaacs's fate until the *Daily News* brought it to light.

To some observers these unexpected disclosures by the *Daily News* suggested odd behind-the-scenes dealings in the court's handling of the case. Recalling that Klingbiel had been chief justice when it was argued, some newspapers drew their own inferences from the new facts, going further in tarring Klingbiel than the *Daily News'* disclosures warranted. The *Los Angeles Times,* for example, wrote that before Underwood's opinion was known to the public, "Klingbiel withdrew the case from Underwood and assigned it to himself." The *Chicago Sun-Times* wrote that after Underwood prepared an opinion unfavorable to Isaacs, "Klingbiel took the case back." A week later, Charles Nicodemus of the *Daily News* wrote an opinion column in which he expressed the distress he and many others felt about the new information:

> What has not been noted is that when cases are assigned to a justice, members of the court first hold a conference on the case, and then take a vote on how they believe the court should rule. That vote then provides the justice handling the case with some guidance as to how his colleagues feel. What this would seem to indicate is that when Underwood went home from Springfield and wrote a proposed opinion recommending that Isaacs stand trial, he was reflecting what he believed had been the majority indication of the court, no matter how tentative. Yet, when he returned with the opinion, he was in the minority. Somebody, it seems, had changed their vote.[1]

Faced with the disclosures, when the court issued its order creating the Special Commission, it took the unusual step of expressly commenting on them:

> Normally the internal proceedings of this Court in conference are not disclosed. However, in view of the circumstances of this case we release the following information: It is not uncommon for the mem-

bers of this Court, or any other reviewing court, to disagree as to a decision. This case involved questions which were not easily resolved and the members of the court were not in agreement as to their proper solution. The trial court had dismissed all counts of the indictment under which defendant Isaacs was charged. An opinion of this Court was prepared which sustained the judgment of the trial court as to twenty-three of the counts, including Count 10, but reversed that court's dismissal as to ten counts and required Isaacs to stand trial. That opinion was not adopted by the Court. An opinion was subsequently adopted which sustained dismissal of all counts as to defendant Isaacs. That opinion was adopted by a 4–2 vote. No dissents were filed. The petition for rehearing, which was denied, requested a rehearing with respect to Count 10 of the indictment only. Mr. Justice Ward did not participate because as State's Attorney of Cook County, he had been involved in an investigation of matters concerned in the indictment.

In making this unprecedented statement, the court was trying to offer a candid, harmless explanation for the suspicious events. Nonetheless, the court's candor was selective: as a later, even more alarming revelation would show, there was another strange aspect of the decision-making process that the court knew of but didn't mention.

The *Daily News* also did not reveal everything it knew, for it never told the public exactly who had made these disclosures to the newspaper, thereby breaching the court's confidential processes. In fact, the breach must have been made by Justice Schaefer, during his first phone conversation on June 9 with the editor of the *Daily News,* Roy Fisher.[2] The next day, when Justice Underwood reached Klingbiel by phone in Spain, Klingbiel told him that the *Daily News* "had that information when they called me."[3] In a deposition two weeks after the *Daily News'* disclosures, Schaefer acknowledged telling Fisher both that the writing of the *Isaacs* opinion initially "had fallen to Justice Underwood" and probably also that Underwood's opinion had not been adopted.[4]

In retrospect, it is hard to believe that Schaefer's keen intelligence and political sensibilities were not triggered by Fisher's inquiry, and that he did not realize he was divulging highly confidential information. A newspaper editor calling up a justice to ask whether another justice had assigned himself to write the opinion in a politically charged case was not an everyday occurrence. Schaefer's answer was not given off the cuff, for he had to do a bit of research first, since the case had been decided over two years earlier.

Perhaps, sensing that something troublesome involving Klingbiel was brewing, Schaefer was trying to distance himself and Underwood from whatever chicanery might come to light. Edward Rothschild, one of Stevens's law partners, was close to Schaefer and recalls hearing rumors in earlier years about questionable activities of Klingbiel and Solfisburg. On a few occasions Rothschild mentioned the rumors to Schaefer and warned him to be cautious regarding the two. Schaefer told Rothschild to stop passing on these rumors to him, for he was tired of hearing them. Perhaps, however, Schaefer remembered Rothschild's warnings when Fisher called to ask about Klingbiel and the *Isaacs* case.

In contrast with Schaefer's openness with Fisher, Justice Underwood adamantly refused to discuss the court's confidential deliberations when asked about them by the *Daily News*.[5] Either Schaefer did not share Underwood's level of commitment to the court's confidentiality, or Schaefer acted out of a keener sensitivity to the potential for scandal that could engulf the court. Whatever Schaefer's motivation, he decided on his own to share this information with the newspaper. The testimony of other justices would soon show that some of them were none too pleased about this breach, but also that neither they, nor anyone else, realized that Schaefer, the court's most revered member, was the source. Justice Underwood soon would say under oath, when asked about the source of the *Daily News'* information, "I have no idea."[6] Justice Byron House was equally mystified but expressed much greater anger about the leak:

> I don't know how they ever found out. That is a mystery to me how anyone ever knew what the vote was in that conference room. That is a leak we are going to find out before this thing is over, and somebody is going to be in trouble, because no one has any business leaking something out of that conference room. I was literally astounded . . . but we don't know yet where that came from. It is a monumental thing to me.[7]

Evidently it was not a monumental thing to Schaefer.

Klingbiel's Stock

The third area of inquiry facing the Special Commission was Klingbiel's acquisition of the Civic Center Bank stock. As of June 4, when Skolnick distributed his fact sheet to the reporters in Springfield, all he knew was that in 1968 Klingbiel held CCB stock, registered in care of himself for two of his grandchildren. As Skolnick originally explained to Ed Pound, the Alton reporter, Skolnick believed that Klingbiel got the stock earlier, during the *Isaacs* case.

When Skolnick filed his motion with the Illinois Supreme Court, he filled in some of the blanks in his conjecture about Klingbiel: his motion claimed that Robert Perbohner, Isaacs's friend on the Commerce Commission, gave the hundred shares to Klingbiel as a gift in the fall of 1966, while the *Isaacs* case was pending. The Cook County records did indicate that Isaacs transferred a hundred shares of CCB stock to Perbohner on October 11, 1966, about a month after the *Isaacs* case was argued before the supreme court. The records showed that these same shares were registered by Klingbiel almost two years later.

Other allegations Skolnick put into his motion were not the fruits of his own research. They came instead from the *Alton Evening Telegraph* and the *Daily News,* which made available to him some of what they were learning on their own, most of which came from parallel sets of telephone conversations initiated by the two competing newspapers. These conversations produced an astonishing array of contradictory statements.

Klingbiel was first contacted by telephone by Nicodemus of the *Daily News,* who reached him in Morocco. Klingbiel stated that he bought the stock from Perbohner only long after the *Isaacs* case was decided. Perbohner, in contrast, told the *Daily News* that the stock was a gift to Klingbiel for which Perbohner himself had merely been a conduit, since the gift really came from an unnamed client of Perbohner's. When asked whether he paid Isaacs for the stock, Perbohner told Nicodemus he "didn't handle the finances," since he was just a "middleman." Perbohner told Ed Pound and Ande Yakstis of the *Alton Telegraph* a different story, saying he bought the stock from Isaacs and then sold it to Klingbiel at about par value.

Isaacs, in turn, gave the newspapers only a limited explanation of his role, but at least he told them both the same thing: that he sold the stock to Perbohner without any awareness that it later would go to Klingbiel, and that the stock was part of a large block of shares Isaacs had technically owned, but really had just held temporarily on behalf of the bank as part of the arrangements for its initial organization. Isaacs agreed to provide the *Daily News* with records confirming that Perbohner had purchased the stock.

When Nicodemus called Klingbiel a second time, reaching him in Torremolinos, Spain, the justice said he now remembered receiving the stock in the fall of 1966 from Perbohner and Robert Dolph, another Commerce Commission member. Dolph, who had since died, had been very closely allied with Solfisburg and had served as his cam-

paign manager when the judge first ran for the supreme court. Klingbiel, who had gone before the voters in November 1966 on a retention
ballot, told Nicodemus he considered the stock a campaign contribution from Perbohner and Dolph. He also explained that he did not register the stock for about two years, until in the fall of 1968 he finally did
so in the names of his daughter's children, but in care of himself. He
said this delay was the result of family considerations, a desire to avoid
playing favorites between his daughter's and his son's children. Klingbiel acknowledged his failure to use the "campaign contribution" for
campaign purposes and gave the same version of these events to the
Alton Telegraph.

When the Alton paper raised Klingbiel's campaign contribution explanation with Perbohner, he blithely said, "If he says I gave it to him,
I guess I did." When telling the *Daily News* essentially the same thing,
he justified the gift—with apparent and brazen candor—by reference
to his position on the Commerce Commission: "And you know in my
position with the Commerce Commission, I have to keep an 'in' with
the Court. You know how that is. So it was just something nice to do
for the judge." Perbohner also told both papers that he bought the
stock from Isaacs, paying $2,000 by a check made out to the bank.

As portions of these conversations were made public through the
newspapers, it became evident that none of the key participants was
giving a clear account of Klingbiel's receipt of the stock: Klingbiel offered two versions, first saying he bought it and then saying it was a
campaign contribution. Perbohner put forth three different stories,
variously claiming that a client of Perbohner's bought it from Isaacs
and then gave it to Klingbiel via Perbohner, that the justice simply
bought the stock, and that Perbohner himself bought the stock from
Isaacs and then joined with Dolph in giving it to the justice as a
friendly campaign contribution. Isaacs disclaimed any knowledge of
Klingbiel's link to the stock but asserted simply that Perbohner purchased it "as a normal business transaction." Isaacs, however, did not
make good on his promise to produce documentary proof of the sale.

The *Daily News'* first story on the scandal quoted Klingbiel and
Perbohner only as explaining the stock as a campaign contribution.[8]
The newspaper said nothing about the other contradictory explanations it had heard. In contrast, the *Alton Telegraph*'s initial report recounted the various, conflicting telephone conversations with Klingbiel and Perbohner. As Stevens and his staff began the investigation, it
was clear they had to delve into these suspicious inconsistencies.

Another questionable element in the mix was a trip Isaacs took the
day after the story broke. He flew to the town of Woodruff in northern

Wisconsin—over three hundred miles from Chicago—to visit Perbohner in the hospital, where he was recovering from hip surgery. Certainly the timing looked strange, for with the scandal heating up, Isaacs would seem to have had enough to keep him busy in Chicago and Springfield. At the very least, he was supposedly still trying to find documents confirming his claim that Perbohner bought and paid for the stock. Nonetheless, Isaacs hurried to Perbohner's postoperative bedside. The newspapers got wind of this trip, but were unable to find out why Isaacs decided to see Perbohner just then and what the two had discussed. Isaacs would only curtly acknowledge that he had indeed "passed through" Woodruff.

Solfisburg as Attorney for the Bank

The fourth issue facing the Special Commission was Skolnick's assertion that Chief Justice Solfisburg was secretly the bank's attorney. Skolnick had an odd reason for making this charge. When Ed Pound and Ande Yakstis went to Chicago in early June, they did some of their investigative telephoning from Skolnick's house. During one of Pound's calls to Perbohner, Pound asked whether Perbohner knew of any connection between Chief Justice Solfisburg and the Civic Center Bank. Perbohner replied, "Oh, yes, he's an attorney for the bank." When Pound jumped on this startling comment, Perbohner said, "I mean he's a friend of attorneys for the bank."[9] Perbohner's quick attempt at a correction cast doubt on the accuracy of his initial response, so Pound and Yakstis did not include this possible link between the chief justice and the bank in their breaking story. They did, however, tell Skolnick what Perbohner had said.

On that shaky basis, Skolnick added Solfisburg to his motion, thus making a simple, yet highly inflammatory accusation against the chief justice. Of course, Skolnick didn't know what Perbohner's statement really meant. Had Perbohner made an innocent slip of the tongue in speaking to Pound, or had Skolnick come upon yet another layer of scandalous connection between the justices and the bank?

The View from Cleveland

In addition to these four areas of inquiry, there were new press reports about even more alleged shenanigans of Klingbiel, Solfisburg, and others linked to them. For example, the *Chicago Sun-Times* summarized a lengthy two-part report on Solfisburg then appearing in the *Cleveland Plain Dealer*. The report linked Solfisburg to nine different banks and detailed his involvement with an insurance company, brush and machinery manufacturers, and a securities firm.[10]

Hardly anyone knew why this extensive information about the chief justice was coming to light in Cleveland, rather than in Illinois. The author of the Cleveland articles was Donald L. Barlett, a thirty-nine-year-old investigative reporter for the *Plain Dealer*. His report relied on an extensive examination of Solfisburg's business connections conducted in 1968, during his two-year stint at the *Chicago Daily News*.

Barlett gathered the information on Solfisburg in conjunction with the Better Government Association, the same watchdog group that four years earlier had helped to develop the evidence leading to Isaacs's indictment. Much of the investigative journalism undertaken by Chicago newspapers around that time was done in alliance with the BGA, so it was not unusual for a reporter and BGA investigators to combine forces. What was unusual, however, was to home in on possible misdeeds of a judge, especially one at as high a level as the state supreme court. As Barlett and others remember the journalistic customs of that era, "courts were off limits."[11]

Also unusual was that none of the information about Solfisburg was published in 1968 and ultimately did not even first come to light in Illinois. The investigation had begun in response to tips from various sources regarding Solfisburg's extensive political activities and business dealings, tips that Barlett and the BGA began pursuing in early 1968, with the support of Roy Fisher. Through detailed document searches and interviews with confidential informants and business associates of Solfisburg, they amassed a tremendous array of facts about the justice's activities off the bench.

In late April, they talked with a young woman in Springfield with whom Solfisburg reportedly had an extramarital relationship. The very next day, Barlett was shocked to receive word from Fisher that the *Daily News* and its reporters, including Barlett, were to have no further interest in Solfisburg and make no further inquiries about him. As Barlett later said, it was "one of the only investigations in my forty years in the business that was outright killed."

Barlett assumed that Bailey Howard was a party to this decision, and that Roy Fisher was just the messenger of a decision reached at a higher level. Some other Chicago journalists later learned of the killing of Barlett's story, and there was speculation about what the path to the *Daily News* leadership might have been and who might have gone to bat for Solfisburg.[12] In June 1969, after Barlett's report appeared in Cleveland and was summarized in the *Sun-Times*, the

Daily News acknowledged that it had developed extensive information about Solfisburg a year earlier. The paper justified its failure to publish the information on the basis that under the lax ethics laws in force in Illinois at the time, "such outside business interests are not in themselves illegal for Illinois judges." As the *Daily News* reminded its readers, only at a future date were Illinois judges required to divest themselves of positions as officers or directors of profit-making enterprises. Even then, the newspaper noted, stock ownership in banks and other businesses would still be legal for judges.

Not many people knew the circumstances of the killing of Barlett's investigation, so the newspaper's face-saving explanation had an air of plausible respectability. What the explanation overlooked, however, was the possibility that, even assuming Solfisburg's business and political activities were technically legal, some of them may have raised conflicts of interest or otherwise have been highly inappropriate for the state's chief justice to engage in.

Donald Barlett left the *Daily News* at the end of 1968 for a more supportive opportunity at the *Cleveland Plain Dealer.* When Solfisburg's name surfaced in the growing scandal in 1969, Barlett relished the opportunity provided by his new employer to finally bring out in Ohio the information he had developed in Illinois.

Resisting the Rumors

The *Sun-Times* had reported mysterious information about eight hundred CCB shares going to a "secret Aurora land trust." The newspaper asserted that the trust also held an Aurora building in which Solfisburg had his local office, with the rent paid by the state. The story noted that Robert Dolph, the late ICC commissioner and close friend of both Solfisburg and Perbohner, had held the beneficial ownership interest in the building and received the rent.[13] The *Sun-Times* soon added a new angle on the office space in a front-page story reporting that Solfisburg's former law clerk, David H. Armstrong, had conducted a private law practice while clerking for the justice; the problem was that the clerk had used the justice's Aurora office space for his private practice, even though the space was rented by the state for the justice's use. Adding greater interest to these revelations were the clerk's business associations and career path: he and Solfisburg had been active in the formation of Financial Security Life Insurance Company of Moline, and by 1969 Armstrong was the chairman of the Illinois Commerce Commission. The web of Solfisburg's involvements was tangled indeed.

Klingbiel, too, was now the object of additional suspicions. Publicity was being given to Klingbiel's longtime position as a director of a bank in his hometown, East Moline. Two days after the first newspaper stories about his CCB stock, a federal grand jury indicted two of the top officers of the bank for mail and securities fraud. Newspapers quickly confirmed that Klingbiel had no role in the allegedly fraudulent activities, but still his connection with the indicted bank officers further darkened the cloud over him.

Finally, in the midst of this journalistic feeding frenzy, George Lindberg announced that the House Committee was going to look into the conduct of Sangamon County Circuit Court Judge Creel Douglas, who had presided over *People v. Isaacs* at the trial level and issued the initial ruling quashing the indictment against Isaacs.

Some of these new charges and questions seemed serious, while others seemed tangential or contrived. Nonetheless, in the aftermath of the Fortas resignation in May—largely because of his extrajudicial activities, associations, and income—it might have been tempting to the commission and the staff to explore at least some of the more substantial accusations now coming to light. The press and much of the public would probably have been supportive of an expanded inquiry, for they were more sensitized than ever to the type of "ethical blind spot displayed by Abe Fortas" and seemingly by Solfisburg and Klingbiel as well.[14]

The commissioners and Stevens, however, resisted the temptation. They knew their legal mandate was limited to investigating Skolnick's charges "insofar as they relate to the integrity of the judgment" in *People v. Isaacs*.

Chapter 8

The Chief Justice's Stock

On Tuesday, June 24, the House Committee headed by George Lindberg went to the Administrative Office of the Illinois Courts in Springfield to see the financial reports Klingbiel and Solfisburg had reluctantly agreed to divulge.[1] Extracted from a sealed envelope in a safe, Solfisburg's 1968 statement made front-page headlines across the state. It revealed that Solfisburg had a $14,000 investment in Civic Center Bank stock, held in a trust at the Old Second National Bank of Aurora. The chief justice's 1969 statement, however, did not mention the shares.

In a separate letter to the committee, Solfisburg explained that he purchased seven hundred shares for $14,000 on May 27, 1966, using money borrowed from a bank in the town of St. Charles. He added that by 1969 he had sold all of the stock, and once again denied ever representing the bank "as an attorney, secret or otherwise."[2] With the revelation of this stock purchase, made while *People v. Isaacs* was pending in the supreme court, suddenly a fifth question was raised for the Special Commission: Did the chief justice's stock purchase and ownership have any bearing on the integrity of the judgment in the case?

Klingbiel's financial statements did not list his CCB stock, apparently because its value was under the $5,000 statutory minimum required for reporting. In a separate letter to the committee, he explained that he gave the stock to his daughter's children in 1968 in an attempt to balance other gifts of property he gave to his son's family in the previous year.

What the *Daily News* Knew

The press previously had not reported any link between the bank and Solfisburg, other than Skolnick's charge that he was secretly its attorney. Earlier in the month, however, two crucial statements were made about Solfisburg in one of the phone calls by Roy Fisher of the *Daily News* during the paper's initial investigation. On June 10, Perbohner told Fisher that Solfisburg bought CCB stock before Klingbiel got any shares. Perbohner also told Fisher that the idea of giving CCB stock to Klingbiel came from Solfisburg and that after buying the stock from Isaacs for Klingbiel, Perbohner passed it on to Solfisburg "because he had asked me to do it."

Strangely, Fisher told none of this to his principal reporter on the story, Charles Nicodemus. Neither Nicodemus nor the public heard anything about Perbohner's statements until late in July, when Fisher testified publicly about them. At that time, he acknowledged that he never tried to verify Perbohner's assertions about Solfisburg and that the *Daily News* had never printed them. He also said, "This is the first time I have told anybody about it," although he had given the information to Stevens in writing at the end of June.[3]

It is difficult to believe that the significance of Perbohner's double-barreled disclosure—linking the chief justice to the bank and to the stock Klingbiel received—could have been lost on an experienced newsman like Fisher. Of course, talk of a justice's "purchase" of stock did not sound the journalistic alarms set off by reports of a "gift" to a justice. Perhaps Solfisburg's visibility and prospects for higher office also heightened Fisher's habitual caution about impairing reputations. Fisher certainly remembered the top management edict that had killed Donald Barlett's earlier investigation of Solfisburg.

Fisher later explained his caution toward Perbohner's statements by saying, "According to practices of good journalism, you print what you are sure of. We were [only] sure about that one hundred shares going from Perbohner to Klingbiel." Unfortunately, Fisher's invocation of "good journalism" does not provide a complete explanation, for the paper's presentation of other things Perbohner said was also extremely selective. The initial article, for example, quoted Perbohner as saying that he gave the stock to Klingbiel "because I wanted to do something nice for him." Perbohner's actual words were significantly different.

In a later *Daily News* article, and more fully in the written statement Fisher gave to Stevens, Perbohner was quoted as clearly stating that the gift to Klingbiel was Solfisburg's idea. Fisher then asked, "Why would Roy Solfisburg ask you to do this when it was for Judge Klingbiel, Bob?" Perbohner's full reply was:

Well, he was close to Klingbiel. And we all thought it was a good idea to do something nice for him. He was completing his term as chief justice and Roy thought this was the nice thing to do. And you know in my position with the Commerce Commission I have to keep an "in" with the court. You know how that is. So it was just something nice to do for the judge.[4]

Obviously there is a major difference between the published statement—"I wanted to do something nice for him"—and the actual statements that "we all thought it was a good idea to do something nice for him" and "Roy thought this was the nice thing to do."

Fisher later implied that he had made a conscious decision to print less than he knew at the outset in the hope that by taking the lid off, the rest would come "crawling out."[5] Ordinarily this would be a remarkably tentative approach for a major newspaper editor to follow. Given the sensitivity of the subject and the broader pressures he was under from *Daily News* management, however, perhaps his strategy was the best he could do in a bad situation. Nonetheless, Fisher's failure to follow up on the information about Solfisburg, and to share it with his reporters, is not easy to explain.

Solfisburg's Rising Star

Solfisburg, a politically active Republican and a 1940 law graduate of the University of Illinois, spent about a year as a trial judge and three years as a member of the Second District Appellate Court before being elected to the Illinois Supreme Court in 1960. There he was chief justice in 1962–63 and began another, three-year term as chief justice in January 1967, succeeding Klingbiel. He was now fifty-two years old.

Rumors had circulated in previous years that Solfisburg hoped someday to run for governor.[6] More recently, reports appeared that Solfisburg was on a list of people being considered for nomination by President Nixon to fill the U.S. Supreme Court seat vacated by Justice Fortas in mid-May. A few days after Fortas's resignation, the *Chicago Tribune* reported on possible successors, including four prospects mentioned by a Republican leader in the U.S. Senate. The article then stated: "Another Illinoisan, State Supreme Court Justice Roy Solfisburg, of Aurora, met with Sen. Dirksen [R., Ill.] several weeks ago, it was learned today, in hopes of being considered for the nation's highest court. Dirksen said he would 'throw the name in the hopper at the appropriate time.'"[7]

The *Tribune* was not alone in viewing Solfisburg as a possible nominee to the high court. Stevens later recalled that Solfisburg had a strong reputation as a jurist at the time and was supported by people at the *Tribune* and elsewhere for the vacancy in Washington. Even Donald Barlett's highly critical report in the *Cleveland Plain Dealer* acknowledged that "Solfisburg has enjoyed a largely favorable press while holding public office in Illinois." Moreover, it mentioned that several Chicago lawyers had recommended Solfisburg to Senator Dirksen and Senator Charles Percy, and that Dirksen "reportedly already has passed on the endorsements to President Richard M. Nixon."[8]

Lobbying Dirksen

Solfisburg's U.S. Supreme Court prospects in part reflected his own lobbying efforts. He had met with Nixon in Miami the previous summer during the Republican National Convention. On May 1 he had met with Everett Dirksen in the senator's office. About a week later, Solfisburg followed up with a short letter thanking the senator "for the generous time that you gave to me for our discussion" and enclosing a one-page biography "pursuant to our conversation." The biography included ordinary personal and professional data about Solfisburg, as well as political background.

At the end of the biography—just under "Hobbies: Hunting and fishing"—Solfisburg added something strange:

> CONFIDENTIAL!
> *NOTE:* Since the Judicial Article of 1964 prevents judges from making political contributions I have not officially made any since 1964. However, my wife is a sponsoring member of the Illinois United Republican Fund and a member of the 500 Club.

Ordinarily it would not have been unusual for an aspirant for a political appointment in Illinois to make sure that his intended patron was aware of the office seeker's financial contributions to "the party." In this instance, however, Solfisburg's addendum was odd in two respects.

First, he acknowledged the constitutional restriction on a judge's political contributions, but he then qualified his observance of the restriction by saying he had not "officially" made any contributions. If he had fully complied with the restriction, no qualification was necessary, and in fact no comment at all on contributions would probably have been most appropriate. If he had circumvented the restriction, through his wife's activity or otherwise, what was to be gained by highlighting the subterfuge? Solfisburg's Republican credentials could not be doubted, and it is hard to believe a politician as sophisticated as Dirksen needed this type of confidential note in order to find motivation for Solfisburg's cause.

Second, given the position Solfisburg was pursuing, it is difficult to fathom his judgment that this added statement was worth making. When Solfisburg met with Dirksen and wrote his letter, he was not seeking appointment to Justice Fortas's seat on the Supreme Court, for that seat was not vacant and there was no reason yet to think it soon would be. The *Life* magazine article that crippled Fortas had not even been released when Solfisburg and Dirksen met, and Fortas did not resign until May 14.[9] Instead, what Solfisburg wanted was a nomination to be chief justice of the U.S. Supreme Court: the position that first President Johnson and then President Nixon had been working on filling for months, ever since Chief Justice Warren's announcement that he would step down in June. Could Solfisburg seriously believe that his candidacy for that monumental position would be advanced by a reminder that he had not "officially" been contributing to the Republican Party since 1964, but that his wife was a good party loyalist?

Solfisburg's entreaty prompted Dirksen to help him, but not much. There is no way to know what Dirksen's personal opinion of Solfisburg actually was, or what other candidates or political agendas the senator might have been interested in relative to the Supreme Court, but Dirksen clearly was not persuaded to be more than a perfunctory messenger for Solfisburg.

Dirksen wrote to Attorney General John Mitchell on May 13:

> Dear Mr. Attorney General:
>   The time is probably not too far in the future when a Chief Justice must be appointed and it may be that suggestions will be invited from many sources.
>   Let me bring your attention to the name of Roy J. Solfisburg, Jr., Chief Justice of the Supreme Court of the State of Illinois.

The biographical data (omitting the confidential note) was then presented, leading up to a final sentence that fell far short of making a recommendation: "I thought I would get this in your hands so that it would be brought to your attention." Everett Dirksen, a politician legendary for his choice of words, had chosen to say something circular that amounted to next to nothing.

Even so, given the considerable stature of his positions in the Senate and the Republican Party, a letter from Dirksen must have gotten Mitchell's attention, and Solfisburg's hopes must have been raised by Dirksen's intervention, whether or not Solfisburg ever actually saw the letter. On the same day Dirksen wrote to the Attorney General, he also wrote a brief note back to Solfisburg. The senator did not mislead Solfisburg and avoided saying anything very encouraging. The entire letter read: "Thanks for the biography. I will send it right along to the Attorney General without delay. Just what will come of this, I do not know but as I have often indicated, nothing ventured, nothing gained."[10]

Aspiring to Move Up

Solfisburg's efforts at self-promotion were not focused only on Senator Dirksen. In late May the National Conference of Metropolitan Courts sent a letter urging Solfisburg's nomination to President Nixon, with copies to both Illinois senators. Founded in 1961 by U.S. Supreme Court Justice Tom Clark and some trial court judges, the conference was intended to provide a forum for presiding judges and court administrators from the nation's largest metropolitan areas to share information about judicial administration and efficiency.

Solfisburg had been an active participant in the organization, serving as its chairman from 1962 to 1965. In 1969 he still served on the Executive Committee. His involvement was unusual because, unlike all the other Executive Committee members and virtually all of the conference members, he was not a trial judge. The Executive Committee met in Chicago on May 30 and authorized its president to write the letter of recommendation for Solfisburg, detailing Solfisburg's judicial experience and extolling him as a "sound, practical, able and experienced justice." The letter also touched the "law-and-order" nerve widely perceived to be critical in the president's thinking about filling vacancies on the Supreme Court.

In addition to this unusual letter, the conference had taken another unusual action. In late April a public statement had been issued by Solfisburg and nine other judges on the Executive Committee at an earlier meeting in Chicago. The statement recommended, as the *New York Times* described it, "that violators of the law in college campus disorders be prosecuted whether or not school officials wish prosecution."[11]

It is difficult to know for certain just why the leaders of this group, organized for limited purposes related to judicial administration, spoke out on campus disorders in April and then recommended Solfisburg in May. It does not appear that the conference has taken similar actions at any time before or since these events.[12] Nonetheless, since Solfisburg had both charm and ambition in good measure, had been present at one or both of the Chicago meetings, and probably even played some of the role of host at them, it is almost certain that Solfisburg exercised considerable influence on the Executive Committee's actions. Both actions could only help to boost his prospects as a potential nominee.

After learning of the conference's letter endorsing Solfisburg, the skeptical reporter Barlett made an inquiry with the conference president. The president's representative confirmed that the organization didn't usually make such recommendations but said that in this case "the recommendation was made by the Executive Committee." When the reporter asked who chaired that committee, the aide said, "Why, the present chairman is Judge Solfisburg." He then added, "I hope publicity won't harm anything."[13]

Sometime in the spring of 1969, Attorney General Mitchell presented President Nixon with a list of 150 names of people who merited consideration for the position of chief justice. The same list, plus a few additions, was used in the filling of the Fortas vacancy. By then the list "had grown to more than a hundred and seventy names, many of them federal judges, some state judges, some prominent attorneys." There is a good chance, with all that he had going for him, that Solfisburg was on the list.[14]

As June began, Solfisburg's star certainly seemed to be rising, and he undoubtedly thought so himself. Before the month was over, a drastic reversal of direction had begun. It started with the opening of a safe in Springfield and the discovery that he too owned stock, and quite a lot of it, in the Civic Center Bank.

Chapter 9

Starting the Search

Stevens had his team of investigators in place early in the week of June 23 and quickly got them to work. They knew that their results might be presented at public hearings, if the Special Commission chose to hold open sessions before the August 1 deadline. Although the press assumed there would be public hearings, Stevens was not so sure. He was concerned that "fairly serious invasions of privacy" might be inflicted on the justices and others whose confidential financial information was to be examined by the commission. To make this type of information public would be inappropriate, he believed, unless there was "a substantial basis for thinking something wrong had taken place." He couldn't decide if there was such a basis until he and the staff had dug into the facts.

This case was unlike any Stevens had worked on. He had never held a job "remotely like a prosecutor." Perhaps because of this, he didn't think of his role as counsel to the Special Commission as prosecutorial. Although he later realized that he was acting essentially as what came to be called an "independent" or "special" prosecutor, at the time he viewed his task as just "a fact-finding mission." With this orientation, he chose two obvious lawyerly tools to search for the facts.

The first method was depositions, the taking of testimony under oath before a court reporter outside of courtroom proceedings. He and Torshen, both experienced litigators, would have the responsibility for taking depositions from the persons most likely to have information about the allegations. The second method would be analysis of the paper trail. James Nussbaum, the staff accountant, would have the lead role in examining the records pertaining to the organization of the Civic Center Bank, distribution of its stock, and the two justices' holdings. These two techniques obviously intersected: depositions would identify documents to be pursued, and analysis of documents would illuminate more questions to be asked in depositions.

What was not so obvious was the public relations problem these conventional tools presented. Depositions would be taken in the normal manner, in closed sessions usually held in private law offices. Similarly, documents would be examined out of the public spotlight. The perceived "secrecy" of these initial investigative steps fueled the widespread doubt that the court-appointed Special Commission could be anything other than a "whitewash." Stevens concluded, however, that "we had to take that heat" in order to avoid unnecessary invasions of privacy and damage to reputations.

Stevens had no sure way of knowing whether his staff members would work together effectively. With the exception of Torshen, he had not selected any of them or even met most of them before. Fortunately, Stevens's optimistic habit when working with other lawyers was to assume their decency and competence until evidence to the contrary appeared. In any event, given the short deadline set by the court, he knew he had no choice but to do the best he could with the help he was given.

Meeting John Stevens

I earlier had met Stevens briefly on a couple of occasions in the fall of 1968. We were among numerous Chicago attorneys participating in strategy meetings on behalf of our clients, various library book distributors who were defendants in an antitrust case.[1] Having only been in private practice for a month or two, I was struck by the deference paid to Stevens's strategic views by other experienced lawyers, presumably because of his antitrust expertise.

It also caught my attention that the only ties he wore were bow ties, but I knew other lawyers with that fashion preference. Something else I noticed about him, however, continued to puzzle me: everyone included his middle name when referring to him. I learned only many years later how the custom had developed. When Stevens began to practice law, he decided to use his full name when signing pleadings, briefs, and other legal papers on the strength of advice given to him while he was still in law school. Homer Carey, a prominent Illinois property lawyer, told him that every lawyer needs some sort of distinguishing characteristic to help establish his professional identity. Stevens thought that perhaps the use of his middle name when signing legal papers would add that touch. Although he hadn't really intended it, the custom spread widely among his professional acquaintances to speak of him, and even sometimes directly to him, using his complete name.

The Commissioners Get Organized

While the staff was recruited and the initial staff assignments organized, the five members of the Special Commission were also busy. They held their first meeting on Saturday, June 21, when they completed their "Report on the Organization of the Special Commission," which they then filed with the Illinois Supreme Court.

Part of the report was the commission's Order Number 1 relating to procedures to be followed. The labeling of this document as "Order Number 1" was one of the first indications of Chairman Greenberg's fondness for the ceremonial trappings of the law. He undoubtedly felt that the use of legal formalities would underscore the seriousness with which the commissioners approached their responsibilities. While he was probably ultimately right about that effect, he was nonetheless wrong in his evident expectation that there were more "orders" to come, for there was never an Order Number 2.

Order Number 1 authorized Stevens to employ an investigator and a court reporter, and to utilize discovery procedures including the taking of depositions. The order also authorized the chairman and vice chairman to sign subpoenas and orders for document production. This authorization was a follow-up to the court's original declaration that the commission would have the power to subpoena witnesses; however, the court had said nothing at all about how this power actually might be enforced against uncooperative witnesses, and, unfortunately, the staff soon would have to find a way to fill that gap.

Coordinating with the Legislature

While the Special Commission was starting its work, the House Committee began its own investigative steps. Representative Lindberg and some of his colleagues were among the many people who viewed the Special Commission skeptically, doubting its backbone since it was the court's own creation. From that perspective, as Lindberg later put it, "We only trusted ourselves."

William Hundley, the Washington attorney hired by the House Committee, had begun to conduct investigative interviews, including a meeting with Skolnick. The committee met in early July to hear Hundley report on his work. It also was announced that Hundley would make another report at the next meeting, scheduled for August 5—after the Special Commission was to have reported its findings to the supreme court. It seemed obvious that the House Committee would not try to accomplish anything major until the Special Commission's work was completed.

In fact, the two groups had come to a mutual understanding. Even though Greenberg struck Lindberg as kind of a "cranky character," the House Committee agreed to hold its investigation in abeyance until the Special Commission was done. As Stevens recalls, the committee members backed off even though there were probably political benefits to gain by aggressively pursuing their own inquiry. Stevens especially recalls that Henry Hyde was among the firmest voices in favor of deferring to the Special Commission. Hyde remembers that the House Committee didn't want to get in the way of the commission and its staff.

Rules of Procedure

The commission also drafted its own Rules of Procedure, principally through the labors of Greenberg and Pitts.[2] The first portion of the rules was entitled "Function of Commission" and stated: "In keeping with the [court's] order, the Commission will conduct an investigation of the specified charges but will not adjudicate the rights or liabilities of any person."[3] With this statement, the commissioners sought to emphasize the limited role the court had entrusted to them. The principal reason for including this statement in the Rules of Procedure was to make clear that the commission did not have to conduct its proceedings in the manner of criminal trials, with the full array of procedural due process protections that apply to defendants in such cases.

A few weeks earlier, the U.S. Supreme Court had decided an important due process case that lawyers in Henry Pitts's office had analyzed closely for its bearing on the Special Commission's procedures.[4] With their advice in hand, the commission included its "Function of Commission" statement both to head off constitutional objections and to allow it to tailor its procedural rules to the peculiar task it faced and the very short time period it had been given for accomplishing it.

This statement also may have been intended to reassure critics who feared that the commission might attempt much more than the court had authorized. Some were afraid that the commission might make findings on the culpability of specific individuals, thus intruding into the domains of grand juries, criminal prosecutors, and the Courts

Commission. Most critics, of course, feared quite the opposite, that the commission would do much less than it was authorized to do—that it would be just a "whitewash."

The commission's Rules of Procedure went on to declare that hearings of the Special Commission could not be televised, broadcast, recorded, or photographed. Also, individuals could apply to the commission to be designated as "interested parties" if they believed their interests might be materially affected by any hearings held. If such an application was granted, the "interested party" had the right to cross-examine witnesses and present evidence.[5]

The Skolnick Chase Begins

As Stevens charted his course, it was obvious that he had to question Sherman Skolnick. It was, after all, Skolnick's motion that had started the whole investigation and defined the main issues. Stevens was still in the dark, however, as to just exactly how much Skolnick really knew; he hoped Skolnick might have some hard facts to offer and would be a cooperative source of assistance. His hopes were drastically, even farcically, misplaced.

From the outset, Skolnick's response to the Special Commission was hostile. Two days after the supreme court's order created the commission, he had asked the court to vacate the order, insisting that a "whitewash" was in the works. Not surprisingly, the court denied Skolnick's request.

At the outset of his work, Stevens had invited Skolnick to give testimony and furnish documentary support for his charges, but Skolnick repeatedly refused. On June 25 a subpoena signed by Greenberg was served on Skolnick, requiring him to appear for a deposition and produce relevant records two days later. Skolnick immediately told reporters he would ignore the subpoena because the commission was "illegally constituted" and "they plan to question me in secret." While Skolnick branded the deposition a "star chamber" tactic, Greenberg and Stevens asserted that the subpoena would be enforced.

Skolnick Sues Again

With a confrontation now developing, Skolnick did one of his favorite things: he sued. On June 26 he filed a complaint in federal district court in Chicago against the Special Commission.[6] Having done so, he did not show up the next day for the deposition. When Stevens telephoned him at the appointed hour to again request his cooperation, Skolnick again declined.

Skolnick's federal suit attacked the Special Commission's legality, on basically the same grounds he had urged in his motion a week earlier before the Illinois Supreme Court. This time he added general allegations of illegality under the U.S. Constitution as well. In a typically paradoxical move, Skolnick asked the district court to hear his case and simultaneously asked all the judges of that court to disqualify themselves. He stated that he did not believe he could obtain a fair and impartial hearing from any of them because among the courts his Citizens' Committee to Clean Up the Courts was investigating were the federal courts in Illinois. The court's Executive Committee nonetheless immediately directed that the case be assigned to a judge "according to the rules."[7]

The case went to the chief judge, William J. Campbell.[8] Judge Campbell was familiar with Skolnick, since the judge had presided over other cases brought by him and Skolnick had sued Campbell for his handling of some of them. Continuing to express his animosity toward Judge Campbell, Skolnick swiftly moved to disqualify him from the case and to bring in "another U.S. District Judge, not from this District, not from this Circuit, and not from any adjoining circuit, to hear and determine this matter." Skolnick also suggested an extra reason for wanting Judge Campbell out of his case, charging that "there appears to be a link between the Isaacs matter" and a company in which Judge Campbell's wife was "a substantial investor."

On July 1 Judge Campbell issued a written memorandum and order dismissing the case. He first denied, as "totally without merit," Skolnick's motion to disqualify the judge himself and various other judges. Campbell noted in passing that Skolnick's sweeping motion would have prevented any judge from the Sixth, Seventh, and Eighth Circuits—covering fourteen states—from hearing the case.

Judge Campbell next turned to the merits of Skolnick's complaint against the Special Commission. He emphasized "the limited power of this Court to review the decisions of, or in any other way interfere with, judicial proceedings pending before the supreme court of a state," and noted that Skolnick was not the subject of any investigation himself and had only been summoned to testify "as to information he claims to possess concerning the judiciary of the state's highest Court." Campbell found that the Special Commission "in no way violates, or even remotely threatens to violate, any of plaintiff's federally guaranteed rights."

Although Campbell's opinion could probably have ended there, it didn't. He went on at some length to present his view that the Special Commission's role was closely linked to the Courts Commission under the Illinois Constitution. Although the supreme court had acknowledged the possibility "that proceedings before the Illinois Courts Commission may eventually become necessary," the court repeatedly emphasized the need to create an "investigating agency independent of the existing connections between this Court and the personnel of the Illinois Courts Commission." In contrast, Judge Campbell viewed the investigation as "an integral part of the Courts Commission process."

In the final portion of his opinion, Campbell touched on Skolnick's charge that the supreme court's order was invalid because it was signed by the two justices specifically accused by him. Campbell construed the Special Commission's mandate as relating only to misconduct by these two justices, and he emphasized that the supreme court's order was "also signed by the remaining five Justices, whose conduct and integrity are not challenged." Therefore, he found "nothing whatsoever invalid" about the order.

In its immediate result, of course, Campbell's decision was just what the Special Commission wanted: a rejection of Skolnick's attempt to dismantle the commission and to prevent the staff from taking his deposition. As Judge Campbell explained his reasoning, however, the decision was more than that. It was a preview of further conflicts yet to come about just what type of legal entity the Special Commission was supposed to be, and just what authority it ultimately might have.

Chapter 10

Building the Answers

While the struggles with Skolnick were under way, staff work went forward on other, more productive fronts. Stevens began taking depositions, assisted at times by other staff attorneys. The staff accountant and one of the lawyers set up camp at the Civic Center Bank and began to examine documents there. In less than three weeks, the team took about twenty depositions, dissected hundreds of pages of financial records, and researched a variety of fairly obscure legal questions. At the same time, they scrambled to respond to continuing attacks on the Special Commission's authority, while preparing for possible public hearings. Each staff member reported frequently to Stevens, usually on a daily basis. Stevens later described this period as "totally absorbing."

Through this compressed process of collecting and sifting evidence, Stevens and his staff tried to ascertain whether any of the charges under investigation would undercut the *Isaacs* decision. None of what they learned was revealed publicly while they were learning it. There were, in short, no leaks.

On the Paper Trail

James Nussbaum joined Price Waterhouse & Company as an accountant in 1960. When asked by Frank Greenberg to provide accounting expertise to the Special Commission, a partner in that firm turned to Nussbaum. Although only thirty-three years old and not yet a partner, he was at a high staff level and had already worked on many financial audits. Among those were a few bank audits, although in those efforts

Nussbaum always had been part of large teams. Stevens sent Nussbaum to the Civic Center Bank as the only accountant on the assignment.

Stevens also wanted someone with legal training to be in on the scrutiny of the bank's records, so he assigned me to accompany Nussbaum at the bank. I, of course, had no experience particularly relevant to this task. In contrast, Nussbaum's auditing experience led him to consider this a very basic assignment, involving a plain and simple search for checks, stock registers, and other documents relating to the acquisition of the CCB stock by Solfisburg and Klingbiel.

We began on the morning of June 26. Accompanied at first by Stevens, we first had a short meeting with the bank president, Harold H. Stout. A large and affable middle-aged man, Stout received us correctly, if not warmly, giving us the use of a large conference room adjacent to his office. Just outside the door was the desk of his secretary, our contact when we needed to find additional materials or make photocopies.

Awaiting us in the conference room that day was a sloppy, disorganized collection of bank files and notebooks containing a variety of records and correspondence. Also included was a small advertising pamphlet for the Civic Center Bank, trumpeting its location at the "crossroads of Chicago's financial-business community." This description was a bit disingenuous. Even though the bank was just a few blocks from the heart of Chicago's financial world, clearly the crossroads at which the bank stood, and for which it was named, was more political than anything else: With the State of Illinois Building directly across La Salle Street, the combined City Hall and County Building edifice right across Randolph Street, the new Civic Center one block farther down Randolph, and politicians' watering holes and restaurants in the Sherman House and Bismarck Hotel just a few steps away, something more seemed to be implied in the pamphlet's proud declaration: "We can't think of a better place for a bank."

We worked at the bank for about two weeks. Toward the end of that time, Nussbaum created large charts comprehensively displaying the progress of the bank's organization and the flow of its stock into various hands. These charts would later become the centerpiece of his testimony before the commission. With Nussbaum's assistance, I prepared as a companion to his charts a lengthy memorandum for Stevens that attempted to tell as much of the story of the bank's organization and of the two justices' CCB stock as we could learn from the paper trail.

The Depositions

Stevens took his first deposition from Illinois Supreme Court Justice Walter V. Schaefer at Stevens's office on the morning of June 25. This first deposition illustrates just how fast the investigation was moving. Stevens had been asked to serve as counsel to the Special Commission on the evening of June 19 and began to delve into the charges against Klingbiel and Solfisburg on Friday, June 20. Five days later he was taking the deposition of the most senior and widely respected justice of the Illinois Supreme Court, a man often regarded as one of the two or three top state court judges in the nation.[1]

Actually Stevens already knew Schaefer fairly well. Schaefer had been one of his professors at Northwestern, and Stevens's law partner, Edward Rothschild, had managed Schaefer's 1951 campaign for election to the supreme court. Despite this prior acquaintance, or perhaps because of it, Stevens had to prepare to question the eminent justice not only with speed, but with thoroughness as well.

Stevens remained on a fast track for more depositions. Two days after the Schaefer deposition, he deposed Justice Robert C. Underwood. During these few days, of course, he also was monitoring the efforts of Nussbaum and me at the bank, guiding the work of William McNally on a quick trip to Springfield to review court records there, trying to get Skolnick to show up for a deposition, helping to resist Skolnick's federal court lawsuit against the commission, sending out deposition notices and negotiating for the scheduling of other depositions for the following weeks, studying documents as they came in, and somehow still trying to take care of some regular clients.

Stevens chose to begin the depositions process with Schaefer and Underwood for strong reasons, which he subsequently described:

> I started with Schaefer and Underwood because I felt that those were the two that were almost certainly going to be trustworthy and candid, and that if we started by getting them to be willing to disclose their internal files, drafts of opinions, and stuff like that, it would have been much harder for anyone else to claim privilege. I deliberately started with the witnesses I thought would be the most forthright.

Stevens's feeling proved sound: Schaefer disclosed information about the court's internal deliberations in the *Isaacs* case that other justices were not inclined to reveal, and both he and Underwood candidly revealed information that left Stevens amazed.

On Monday of the following week, June 30, Stevens took Justice Klingbiel's deposition, and the next day he deposed Chief Justice Solfisburg. Stevens later explained why these two were next: "Then we took Klingbiel and Solfisburg because they were under the most suspicion. My thinking was that, in fairness to them, we should give them the first opportunity to say whatever they did, once we had understood the basic way the court operated through Schaefer and Underwood." Earlier on the day of Solfisburg's deposition, Stevens also deposed Klingbiel's daughter, a Chicago attorney. When Skolnick had amended his original motion to the supreme court, he charged that she and others held over four thousand additional shares of CCB stock for Klingbiel.

After these first five depositions, the staff took others almost every day until the public hearings began, when they still took about a half dozen more. Stevens took most of the depositions, with some conducted by Torshen, McNally, Nathaniel Sack, or me. This division of labor also reflected the time pressure the staff faced, for although Stevens and Torshen were experienced litigators, neither McNally nor I had ever taken a deposition before. In fact, the first deposition McNally had ever even observed was the Schaefer deposition conducted by Stevens.

Deposing the Court

The most extraordinary aspect of the deposition process was that all seven justices of the Illinois Supreme Court came to Stevens's office and had their depositions taken there. Their testimony obviously had to be obtained. The court's order establishing the Special Commission had focused on the "integrity of the judgment" in *People v. Isaacs,* rather than just on possible misconduct of Klingbiel and Solfisburg. The order's language was broader than federal Judge Campbell's narrow interpretation limiting the investigation to Klingbiel and Solfisburg. Any one of the seven justices might be found to have acted in some way that impaired the integrity of the *Isaacs* decision. Also, any one of the justices might know or have observed something about another justice's activity that had bearing on the decision.

Even if any of them found it repugnant or undignified to go to a Chicago lawyer's office to be questioned under oath about one of their own decisions, they had committed themselves collectively and publicly to the process they had created. All the justices thus submitted to the depositions, which are unique in the history of the Illinois judiciary; indeed, nothing quite like them has probably ever occurred before or since anywhere else in the nation.[2]

Chapter 11

Blind Alleys and Roadblocks

On July 3 the Special Commission formally announced that it would begin "public en banc hearings for the taking of testimony and other evidence in its investigation, as mandated by the Supreme Court of Illinois, on July 14, 1969, at the hour of 9:30 A.M. in the forenoon in Courtroom 1501, the Chicago Civic Center, Chicago, Illinois." Letters to Isaacs, Perbohner, Solfisburg, and Klingbiel advised them that the commission intended to call them as witnesses.

Stevens had a lot of work to finish before July 14, including some key depositions. In contrast with the serious drama of the seven justices' depositions, two other important depositions he was about to take would prove to have considerable elements of comedy. They also demanded a lot of time from Stevens and his colleagues, but with little to show for their efforts in the end.

The Skolnick Chase Continues

Now that Judge Campbell had dismissed Skolnick's suit to dismantle the Special Commission, Stevens again was ready to take his deposition, but Skolnick still resisted. The subpoena to him had been issued under authority the Illinois Supreme Court had granted the Special Commission in its original order. There was a gap in that order, however, for it was silent on how to enforce a subpoena against an uncooperative witness like Skolnick. To try to fill the gap, Stevens and Torshen submitted a petition to the supreme court, asking for its approval of certain procedures "to aid and effectuate this subpoena power." On July 7 Justice Schaefer signed an order authorizing any circuit court to respond to disobedience to a commission subpoena by issuing an order to compel testimony. Schaefer added, "Any failure to obey such order of the circuit court may be punished by that court as a contempt upon itself."[1]

John S. Boyle, chief judge of the Cook County Circuit Court, agreed to assign Edward F. Healy, whom Torshen considered "a no-nonsense, streetwise judge," to enforce the commission's subpoenas. On Wednesday, July 9, Stevens and Torshen filed a petition asking Judge Healy to order Skolnick to submit to the deposition. Skolnick was ready with his customary salvo of written motions, challenging both the Special Commission's legitimacy and the ability of any Cook County judge to resolve this dispute fairly toward him. Thursday morning Healy rejected Skolnick's motions and granted the commission's petition, directing Skolnick to appear for the deposition at Stevens's office almost immediately. In response to Skolnick's expressions of distrust about being questioned "in secret," the judge allowed Skolnick to be accompanied by others at the deposition, including members of the press. When he showed up, he was accompanied by more than a dozen reporters, and everyone squeezed uncomfortably into a small conference room. For the next couple of hours, Stevens and Skolnick skirmished through a cycle of specific questions and vague answers. Only two things were clearly revealed: the depth of Skolnick's mistrust of the legal system, and the depth of Stevens's commitment to fulfilling his responsibility in the investigation. As this gulf between the two men's perspectives was revealed over and over, no useful evidence came to light.

Skolnick's replies were tantalizing in their implications, but they failed to provide anything concrete. When asked to explain and document specific accusations, Skolnick replied generally, while insisting that he had a mountain of supporting documents and "strategically placed informants" for his charges. He emphasized that he knew the Special Commission and its staff were "agents for the judges" and would "destroy everything we have spent months working on." Under no circumstances would he provide Stevens and the commission with any of his specific proof of wrongdoing.

Nonetheless, Stevens pressed on and posed the question that led to the deposition's most serious impasse:

STEVENS: Have you been told by someone whom you are unwilling to identify that Mr. Isaacs has been seen in the presence of Justice Solfisburg during the period of time that the *Isaacs* case was under advisement in the Supreme Court of Illinois?

SKOLNICK: What is the point? I am not going to tell you who our informant is, why he is strategically placed and all that. I don't trust you with that information.

Stevens posed this question because a few minutes earlier Skolnick claimed that Solfisburg "was often seen consulting on legal matters with Mr. Isaacs in various places." Stevens emphasized to Skolnick that "this would go to the very heart of our investigation, if the statement you make is true." The principal accusation such observations would link to, of course, was Skolnick's charge that Solfisburg secretly was an attorney for the Civic Center Bank. The remaining few minutes of the deposition were consumed by further jousting over Skolnick's refusal to identify his sources and Stevens's announced intention to get a court order from Judge Healy forcing Skolnick to divulge more information.

It was obvious that nothing resembling evidence had been obtained, although the newspapers nonetheless quickly reported some of Skolnick's most startling statements, including a wide array of unsupported charges of unlawful conduct by many prominent people. During one colloquy with Stevens, Skolnick asserted that there were actually four justices of the Illinois Supreme Court involved in "the fixing of the *Isaacs* case."

Skolnick indicated that one of these justices took office on December 13, 1966, voted in Isaacs's favor in the *Isaacs* case, and was financially involved with Isaacs and others through a different Chicago bank, the Archer National Bank. Taking his cat-and-mouse game to its most absurd level, Skolnick wouldn't use the name of the "third judge." Instead he said, "There is only one judge on the state supreme court who cast the retroactive vote. It is easy enough to figure that out." It was indeed easy to figure it out. The judge he was implicating had to be Justice Thomas E. Kluczynski, who had been elected to the court in November 1966. Of the two newly elected justices at that time— Justice Daniel Ward being the other—only Kluczynski voted in *People v. Isaacs*. Although Stevens also knew this, he purposely did not mention Kluczynski's name in the deposition. Nothing specific had been said to tie Kluczynski to misconduct in the *Isaacs* case, and lacking any evidence, Stevens would not put Kluczynski's reputation in jeopardy.

In the deposition's final moments, Skolnick fumed that Stevens, by planning to get a court order to compel him to identify his sources, now was accusing the righteous accuser, rather than the wrongful justices. Skolnick ended defiantly:

SKOLNICK: You could send me to prison, but you are not going to get the name of a sensitive witness.

STEVENS: I have no desire to send you to prison.

SKOLNICK: That is what it is going to take.

As he threw down the gauntlet, Skolnick wasn't kidding. He had succeeded, however, in making Stevens and the commission his adversaries. Stevens already had cautioned: "This is not a laughing matter, Mr. Skolnick." As Skolnick soon would find out, Stevens wasn't kidding either.

A Day in Wisconsin

While the depositions of the seven justices and various other witnesses were under way and the Skolnick chase continued, a struggle over another important witness had been brewing. Stevens was trying to take the deposition of the man whose name had surfaced at the beginning of the affair: Robert M. Perbohner. Although the potential rewards from getting Skolnick to talk were speculative, Perbohner definitely seemed worth pursuing.

Perbohner was a member of the Illinois Commerce Commission and a friend of Isaacs. Originally from Chicago and now sixty-eight years old, Perbohner had been involved with politicians for many years. His specialty was political lobbying, especially involving the legislature. Perbohner was a man who relished doing favors for influential people. As his son later described him, "My old man did everything for everybody. He never said no to anybody."

When Skolnick's accusations first piqued the interest of reporters Ed Pound and Charles Nicodemus in early June, they had each telephoned Perbohner. They asked him about the hundred shares of CCB stock originally registered in Isaacs's name, then in Perbohner's, and then in Klingbiel's, but the various explanations they heard from him and others were wildly contradictory.[2] Stevens wanted to hear from Perbohner in person and under oath. It seemed he could tell the investigators a lot, assuming he was willing and able to talk.

Unfortunately, it was far from clear that Perbohner was either willing or able to testify. He was still convalescing from hip surgery in a hospital in Wisconsin. Nonetheless, Stevens obtained an order from a Wisconsin court for the issuance of a subpoena directing Perbohner to submit to a deposition at the hospital.

Soon after the subpoena was served, Stevens was contacted by Perbohner's Chicago lawyer, Samuel Adam, and told that Perbohner was

not in suitable mental or physical condition to testify. After some consultation with Perbohner's doctors, Stevens and Adam agreed to postpone the deposition until Friday, July 11. On July 10 Adam called
Stevens again, asserting that Perbohner still was not competent to answer questions in a deposition.

Torshen telephoned Perbohner's principal doctor, Dr. Joseph Farrington, who assured him that Perbohner was capable of testifying in a
short deposition. With this assurance, Stevens and Torshen flew to
Wisconsin on July 11 to take Perbohner's deposition. They were accompanied by Michael J. Shapiro, the head of the team of Chicago
court reporters who covered the depositions and hearings.

The deposition began at 11:30 A.M. in Perbohner's hospital room,
with something of a crowd gathered around the patient-deponent in
his bed. In addition to Stevens, Torshen, and the court reporter, Perbohner's lawyer Adam was there, along with Chicago lawyer Patrick A. Tuite for Isaacs, and an Aurora lawyer representing Solfisburg
and Klingbiel. Perbohner's wife was present, plus Doris Steigberg, his
secretary.

The deposition began chaotically and never recovered. Before
Stevens could begin, Adam tried to offer Perbohner's wife and secretary to testify, "not necessarily under oath," about his condition.
Adam also claimed that another doctor at the hospital had just opined
that "the competency of Mr. Perbohner at this time to answer any
questions is somewhat in doubt"[3] and reiterated his intention to advise Perbohner not to answer any questions.

After telling Adam of the contrary medical opinion Dr. Farrington
had given the previous night, Stevens began his attempt to question
Perbohner, first assuring him that the questioning would be delayed or
interrupted if the witness "has moments where he would like to rest or
prefer that we not go forward." Perbohner's immediate responses—
"We've got nothing to hide. I am ready to go right ahead"—raised
Stevens's hopes.

Unfortunately, a moment later and out of the blue, Perbohner said,
"As far as insurance is concerned, Mr. Torshen knows the whole side."
Mrs. Perbohner and Adam both quickly reminded the witness that
"insurance doesn't have a thing to do with it." Adam again advised his
client "to answer no questions other than your name and address."

At this point, the intrepid Stevens had the court reporter administer the oath to the witness. Even this formality, however, failed to get
things on track. Perbohner's wife immediately began berating her husband, telling him, "You are not listening to your lawyer. Honey, you
are not capable of anything." After Perbohner asked his wife first to

"sit down" and then to "get out," she turned to the lawyers and said: "Please, he will befuddle everything. You men don't understand. I have to cover up for him so much." Perbohner retorted: "You don't have to cover for anything. I have got nothing to hide. I am not a crook. What the hell is the matter with you?" After Mrs. Perbohner's sad reply, "I know, I don't want you to be hurt, that is all," she and the secretary were ushered from the room, and Stevens tried again.

For about half an hour, Stevens tried to probe Perbohner's memory for a variety of things, including his relationship with Isaacs, his involvement with Civic Center Bank stock, his dealings with Solfisburg and Klingbiel, his own bank accounts, and his telephone conversations with the newspapermen. Stevens got nowhere. Occasionally Perbohner would acknowledge remembering a certain person or conversation, but most often he denied having any relevant recollections.

At times his answers had a baffling, contradictory content. For example, when asked whether he recalled telling Roy Fisher that Solfisburg had asked him to handle getting CCB stock to Klingbiel, Perbohner answered, "I didn't say it and I don't recall it." When asked about Nicodemus's initial call to him, Perbohner first said that the reporter had "misrepresented himself," then said "the guy is a liar," and then denied any memory at all of telephone conversations with him.

Throughout these frustrating exchanges, the lawyer Adam peppered the record with a steady stream of objections and with admonitions to Perbohner not to answer. Increasingly Perbohner heeded those admonitions. Soon Perbohner was declining to answer any of Stevens's questions. Stevens reluctantly ended the deposition.

The day's events were not over, for the entourage traipsed around the corner to the Woodruff Medical Clinic, so Stevens could take a short deposition of Dr. Farrington. The doctor reiterated his opinion that Perbohner was capable of testifying if it wasn't on a prolonged basis.[4] Five minutes later, Adam took the deposition of another doctor, Henry Ashe, who explained that Perbohner had been in great pain with a long-standing orthopedic problem when he came to the Woodruff hospital. Perbohner, he said, had been using "rather fantastic quantities of drugs and alcohol to relieve the discomfort." He also explained that although the doctors had been gradually getting Perbohner off the drugs and alcohol, "he is still in a depressed mental condition, he is still getting certain drugs . . . , and in my opinion there is reasonable question as to how competent this man is to make responsible decisions at this time."[5]

The final event, initiated by Adam, was a short deposition of Doris Steigberg, Perbohner's secretary. Adam questioned her to bring out information about Perbohner's bank accounts that Perbohner had been unable to explain that morning. Adam also asked the secretary about her opinion of Perbohner's mental capacity to be deposed, and her opinion was that he was "definitely not mentally alert."

Stevens asked whether Mrs. Steigberg recalled Perbohner's telling her that he wanted to help Isaacs at the time of Isaacs's indictment. Her answer was yes, and Stevens suddenly seemed on the verge of extracting key information. Adam objected vigorously to Stevens's expanded questioning, and he urged the witness to consult with an attorney before answering.[6] A flustered Steigberg quickly took Adam's hint and told Stevens that she didn't want to answer any questions until she had gotten herself a lawyer. Stevens's frustration at this point was evident. Amidst his anger, however, Stevens sensed Mrs. Steigberg's distress and quickly assured her that he didn't want to embarrass her.

Finally, Stevens asked Steigberg whether she was Perbohner's personal employee or an employee of the Illinois Commerce Commission. Her reply gave the proceedings a somewhat lighter tone: "I am Mr. Perbohner's personal employee. I would not work for the state of Illinois under any circumstances. I am an independent Swede." On this note, Stevens threw in the towel. He conceded that it was time to suspend, pending further proceedings, adding, "I don't know just what to say other than that."

Although the trip had been comical, the effort to get Perbohner to talk remained serious business. The time and energy invested in Perbohner by Stevens and his team, and the corresponding investment by Perbohner's own lawyer and the lawyers for Isaacs, Klingbiel, and Solfisburg, reflected the importance of what Perbohner could say. His elusiveness, the ambiguity of his mental condition, and the efforts to shield him from testifying all emphasized that he might hold the key to much of what the Special Commission needed to learn.

Text of the Decision

Since the text and substance of the *People v. Isaacs* decision might shed light on the integrity of that judgment, Stevens read it closely. He quickly concluded that on its face there was nothing suspect about the court's opinion. Stevens later said, "I thought the whole case was sufficiently opaque that it would be very, very difficult to use that opinion as a basis for questioning the integrity of any judge who wrote it."

This conclusion was bolstered by information emerging in the depositions of the seven justices, or at least of the six who had participated in the *Isaacs* decision. The staff's questioning of the justices about the process through which the case was decided—including the initial rejection of Justice Underwood's draft opinion and the final adoption of the opinion written by Klingbiel—further emphasized that there were many genuinely debatable points of law raised in the case. On most of those points, all six of the participating justices were in agreement, and there was nothing plainly irrational in the outcomes reached. Even on the points on which there was disagreement, there was nothing to suggest that legally insupportable or blatantly incorrect conclusions had been reached.

Isaacs's Roadblock

On Thursday, July 10, four days before the public hearings were to begin, Isaacs filed a motion with the supreme court, relying on a rule requiring some Illinois Courts Commission proceedings to be confidential. He asked the court to order the Greenberg Commission not to conduct public hearings. The commission's response noted that its members unanimously had determined to hold open hearings. The response also stressed "the conviction of the Special Commission that only in this way can the conduct of the investigation merit the confidence of the legal profession and the public in the integrity of the Commission which the Court has appointed." Clearly the Special Commission was prepared to reject, as emphatically as possible, Isaacs's argument that the Special Commission somehow was an offshoot of the Courts Commission. The Special Commission understood itself to be something different and unique.

The final portion of the commission's response conveyed a "hands-off" message to the court:

> And your Commissioners further respectfully represent to this Court that each of them accepted appointment to this Special Commission, and undertook the responsibility given to them by this Court, only in accordance with the terms of the order entered June 17, 1969, and with the understanding that their discretion in the holding of either public hearings or private hearings or a combination of both would not be interfered with.

With this statement, the commissioners conveyed an unmistakable threat that some or all of them would terminate their service if the court were to apply confidentiality constraints or otherwise interfere with the commissioners' decision to hold public hearings.

The commissioners had considerable leverage with the court at this point. The court surely would suffer further public embarrassment and criticism—and probably a revival of investigative zeal in the legislature and other forums—if the commissioners withdrew because of interference by the court. Any such embarrassment would be particularly damaging to the court at this juncture, because it was just then grappling with two of the hottest political issues Illinois had faced in years. The legislature recently had adopted the state's first income tax law, and a challenge to the constitutionality of the tax was to be argued before the supreme court one week later;[7] furthermore, the court was on the eve of deciding a major case on the legality of the law establishing a Constitutional Convention to draft a new state constitution. With cases of this historic magnitude before it, this was not a good time for the court to look bad.[8]

Having made the threat to quit, the commissioners soon learned there was no need to act on it. The court denied Isaacs's motion on Saturday, two days before the public hearings would start.

TRIAL

The Second Half of July

Chapter 12

The Trial Begins

On the hot and humid morning of Monday, July 14, the public hearings began in the Chicago Civic Center's Room 1501, a large, high-ceilinged, formal courtroom. Over the weekend, after the Illinois Supreme Court rejected Isaacs's attempt to prevent the hearings, there was growing anticipation that something significant and very unusual was about to start. On Sunday the *Chicago Today* newspaper capsulized perspectives on the imminent trial:

> The opening tomorrow of unprecedented hearings into charges of impropriety against two Illinois Supreme Court judges brings to a climax the first major probe involving the state's highest tribunal. At stake are the careers of Chief Justice Roy J. Solfisburg of Aurora, and Ray I. Klingbiel of East Moline. Those supporting the jurists believe the public's faith in the whole judicial system will also go on trial at the hearings and that exoneration of the pair will restore that shaken faith. Those aligned against the judges also believe faith in our system of "justice" is a primary issue. But they contend removal of the two would constitute the first local step toward "cleaning up the courts."

Charles Nicodemus, in an insightful commentary in the *Chicago Daily News,* focused on Stevens and the Special Commission's quandary:

> For an attorney, the only job in Illinois more thankless than membership on the Special Commission created to investigate the state Supreme Court is the job as counsel for that commission. On the Commission's chief counsel, John Paul Stevens, and his assistant counsel, Jerome Torshen, rests the burden of doing the groundwork

for next week's historic hearings on the integrity of Illinois' highest
court. It is a job no attorney relishes—a job from which, in fact, numerous lawyers literally ran away, pleading that they had to "go on
vacation" or elsewhere when they were queried about serving in the
all-important staff posts. The counsel's job is particularly taxing because, like the commission members, the staff gets it from both
sides—painfully.

Nicodemus went on to emphasize the bind that the commission and its
staff faced as they were "laboring hard enough to draw—privately—
the ire of some members of the Supreme Court, only to find themselves prejudged by a segment of the public as 'The Whitewash Commission.'"

Greenberg in Charge

The hearings began at 9:30, with the commissioners seated at the elevated courtroom bench, which had been expanded by carpenters over
the weekend to accommodate all five of them. Arrayed before them
were about ten lawyers at counsel tables. Skolnick was in his wheelchair in the middle aisle of the room. Although neither Klingbiel nor
Solfisburg was present, Isaacs was at the counsel table with his
lawyers. Reporters filled the jury box.

Greenberg began by summarizing the mandate of the Special Commission and introducing its members. He alluded generally to Skolnick's motion before the Illinois Supreme Court and emphasized that
the court's order directed the commission "to investigate the charges
contained in the motion insofar as they relate to the integrity of the
judgment entered by the supreme court in the case of People against
Isaacs." He added, "This is the only investigation which this commission is empowered to make."

The chairman then touched on procedural aspects of the hearings, including the allowance for certain individuals to be designated
as "interested parties," who could be represented by counsel, cross-
examine witnesses, and present evidence. Skolnick had submitted a
written request for this status, but Greenberg announced that the
commission had decided to deny it. This ruling was not a surprise to
anyone, except perhaps Skolnick. The skirmishing between him and
the commission staff had neither endeared him to the commissioners
nor convinced them that he had anything useful to add.

Greenberg invited the lawyers to identify themselves. First to speak
was the prominent Chicago lawyer Albert E. Jenner Jr., representing

both the Civic Center Bank and Theodore Isaacs. Jenner's first two statements were rather unfocused. He announced that Harry Busch, Isaacs's criminal defense attorney, wished to withdraw his appearance on behalf of Isaacs in this matter. Busch, however, had not actually entered an appearance yet. Second, Jenner moved "for leave to withdraw the motion filed last week that these proceedings be private, and on behalf of Mr. Isaacs we withdraw that motion and accept cheerfully that these proceedings be public."

The next lawyer to identify himself was Lambert M. Ochsenschlager of Aurora, representing both Justice Klingbiel and Chief Justice Solfisburg. He requested that they be designated as interested parties. At this point Jenner interrupted to request that interested party status also be granted to Isaacs.

Stevens Makes His Appearance

Stevens entered his appearance as counsel and introduced Torshen, McNally, and me at counsel table, and Sack and Joseph Coughlin, seated nearby. Stevens commented that Jenner's request to withdraw the motion for the hearings to be private was obviously out of order: "The motion was filed with the supreme court and not with this body, and it has already been ruled upon."

More importantly, he succinctly described his plan for the hearings:

> It will be our intention to present evidence generally in the order in which it has been developed during our investigation, and of course we will urge the members of the commission to withhold judgment on aspects of the evidence until all of the evidence is in, because there are various incidents about which witnesses will testify but, obviously, we cannot put all the evidence in at one time.
>
> Generally speaking the order will be, first, certain members of the supreme court will be asked about certain aspects of the *Isaacs* litigation, certain evidence will relate to the Civic Center Bank, and then we will call upon interested parties and certain other witnesses to comment on the matters that have been produced.

As Stevens made this undramatic statement, he also unknowingly stepped into the public spotlight on a path that would lead him far beyond this courtroom.

Greenberg announced that the commission was granting Solfisburg, Klingbiel, and Isaacs the status of interested parties. Harry Busch's appearance—if there ever was one—was allowed to be withdrawn. Jenner's attempt to withdraw Isaacs's motion for closed hearings was expressly not ruled on, since it "was filed with the court, and acted upon by the court." The hearings were off to a mostly smooth and businesslike start.

Inside the Court

The first witness was Justice Byron O. House, a member of the Illinois Supreme Court since 1957. House was from Nashville, Illinois, where he had practiced law for thirty years. The courtroom was packed for this unprecedented appearance of a supreme court justice as a witness before a group of lawyers investigating one of the court's decisions. Early in House's testimony, during attempts to adjust the witness's microphone, he and Greenberg each acknowledged with dry humor just how unusual their respective roles were:

> GREENBERG: Mr. Stevens, may I interrupt a moment? Will you see if that mike is working? We are having a little difficulty hearing Justice House. This not being our regular courtroom—
> HOUSE: Nor mine.

Stevens's questions confirmed that House had known of Theodore Isaacs from the time of Isaacs's position as director of revenue in the Kerner administration in the early 1960s, but House had met Isaacs only once, at a banquet of state officials in Springfield. House also acknowledged knowing Robert Dolph, whom he identified as a lawyer and a friend of Solfisburg's. Once or twice House had gone to Dolph's apartment in Springfield for dinner, because "Dolph was quite a chef, he liked to cook, and he invited all the members of our court several times."

House was asked whether he or any of his relatives or associates had ever owned Civic Center Bank stock. His answer was unequivocal: "None whatsoever. I didn't even know there was such a bank." Stevens then turned to the principal evidence to be presented through Justice House, focusing on the court's decision-making process in *People v. Isaacs* and whether there was anything out of the ordinary in the way that case was handled.

House explained that immediately after the *Isaacs* case was argued, the justices took an "impression vote." As he began to explain these events, however, House interjected his strong belief "that it is improper for anyone in the conference room to divulge anything that happens in the conference room." House nonetheless said he was glad to testify since the information already had been released publicly. He was plainly referring to the *Daily News'* disclosure a month earlier of information about Justice Underwood's draft decision to keep the prosecution of Isaacs alive, the failure of a majority to adopt that decision, and the four-to-two vote adopting Klingbiel's opinion throwing out the case. This was the information Justice Schaefer had divulged to the newspaper, although it still did not seem that other justices had identified Schaefer as the source. Greenberg quickly assured the justice that the commission shared his regret that these secret conversations had to be explored publicly.

House's agenda book notes on the impression vote showed that he, Solfisburg, and Klingbiel were inclined to affirm the lower court's dismissal of the indictment of Isaacs, while Schaefer voted to reverse. Justice Underwood was listed as voting a "question mark," indicating uncertainty as to how he would decide the case. At that time, there was a vacancy on the court because of a death, so the sixth and remaining justice who could have participated was Justice Harry B. Hershey. The dash House had written next to Hershey's name was uninformative, for House could not recall whether it signified that Hershey was absent on that day or simply expressed no vote. Hershey's health was failing then, and he occasionally missed oral arguments.

House explained that the *Isaacs* case was assigned in September to Justice Underwood for a written decision under the court's normal system of assigning opinion-writing duties on a rotational basis. Every two months, the court convened in Springfield for a new term of a couple of weeks of arguments, conferences, and decisions. The cases to be heard each term would be numbered starting with Number 1. Working from the most junior justice to the most senior, each term's case Number 1 would be given to the justice next in line after the assignments from the previous term, and the succeeding cases would similarly be assigned in order.

Although it might have seemed odd that Underwood was to write the court's opinion despite his "question mark" vote, House made clear that the rotation system was the sole basis for the assignment. It was simply Underwood's turn. Underwood's opinion was not voted on when the court reconvened at the November term, however, apparently because it was not yet finished.

Instead, the Underwood opinion came before the court in the January 1967 term. By that time there had been a few important changes in the court's composition. Klingbiel had been retained in office by the voters in early November. His position as chief justice ended in January, and Solfisburg assumed the post. Justice Hershey had resigned, and his position and the prior vacancy were filled by the November election of Justices Kluczynski and Ward.

Underwood's draft opinion would have kept some counts of the indictment against Isaacs alive. In the voting on this opinion in January, Justice Ward did not participate, just as he did not participate in many of the criminal cases then before the court. He had been the State's Attorney of Cook County at the time of the *Isaacs* prosecution in Springfield, and his office had given some assistance to the Sangamon County State's Attorney. Accordingly, he recused himself from the case, leaving six justices to decide. Five of them had heard the oral argument back in September. The sixth, Justice Kluczynski, apparently was to follow a new justice's normal practice of studying the briefs, listening to a tape recording of the oral argument, and then participating in the decision.

The Underwood opinion failed to get the four votes necessary for adoption. House testified that only Underwood and Schaefer voted for it, while he, Solfisburg, and Klingbiel voted against it. Justice Kluczynski "passed," which House described as meaning he probably wanted more time to look it over because he was not on the court at the time it was argued. The Underwood opinion then was considered rejected, for it had not garnered the necessary four votes and would not even if Kluczynski were to vote for it. House explained that when an opinion is rejected, the case "goes back into the hat and goes to the next justice after the one who took the previous case."

Up to this point, there was nothing startling about Justice House's testimony. Much of what he said had already been divulged in the *Daily News* and other newspapers. Now, however, he had reached a critical juncture: the reassignment of the *Isaacs* case from Underwood to another justice.

The Skipping of Justice House

The big question was why the case went to Klingbiel. Stevens had heard the answer during the depositions of the justices, and now House was to be the first to try to explain publicly one of the most suspicious aspects of the court's decision-making process in *People v. Isaacs*—an aspect that the court had failed to mention in its order establishing the Special Commission. The court had not revealed that when Klingbiel got the reassignment in January to author a new *Isaacs* opinion, it was not his turn. Furthermore, no one could explain why Justice House was skipped over in the rotation in favor of Klingbiel.

House testified that at the end of the January term, after Underwood's opinion was rejected, the next justice in normal rotation for the reassignment was Underwood himself. Reassignment to him obviously made no sense under the circumstances. Next in line after Underwood was Solfisburg, but House's records showed that Solfisburg already had an unusually large number of cases assigned to him, so he was skipped. Next in line after Solfisburg was House, but instead the assignment went to the next in order after him—Klingbiel. Stevens asked House if he could explain why this had happened. House replied, "I have no idea. I just don't know."

Stevens then explored House's attempt to reconstruct the reassignment through examination of records, paying particular attention to the justices' common practice of trading cases among themselves for any number of reasons. Stevens asked again whether he had been able to determine why he been skipped. House answered, "No, sir, I tried. I tried to work out every trade, but couldn't find out how it happened."

In an ordinary legal proceeding, this line of questioning would have ended, for the witness had no memory of how and why the reassignment went to Klingbiel and had been unable to reconstruct an answer through study of past records. As House's testimony made evident, and other justices' depositions and testimony would confirm, the court's record keeping on the assignment of cases was surprisingly unreliable and incomplete. Each justice kept his own agenda book of notes on assignments, and often the notes were fragmentary and inconsistent from one justice to the next.

All House could do now was speculate, and Stevens wanted him to do so. Stevens realized, of course, that under basic rules of evidence it would be improper to ask a witness to speculate, especially on such a key question. Stevens also knew that Isaacs's lawyer, Albert Jenner, would almost surely object to any question Stevens might pose to invite House's speculation. Jenner already had objected to a number of Stevens's less important questions. The two justices' lawyer, Lambert Ochsenschlager, also might object, although it was not yet clear whether he and Jenner were following a coordinated strategy.

Stevens made a delicate effort:

STEVENS: So the best you can do is to speculate on how it might have happened?

HOUSE: Yes.

STEVENS: Based on your handling of other matters over the years you have been on the court?

HOUSE: Yes, sir.

STEVENS: Now, it is up to Mr. Jenner, I will ask you if you can speculate as to how it happened, and I would suggest the question is not admissible but I am perfectly willing to have the witness answer it.

At this moment Ochsenschlager stepped in and provided the first indication that he and Jenner were not on the same track, saying: "I would like the record to show we have no objection to the question on behalf of Justices Klingbiel and Solfisburg." In contrast, Jenner held his ground, but to no avail.

JENNER: I object to the witness speculating.

GREENBERG: Gentlemen, [in light of] the extraordinary circumstances of this case, and the fact that Justice House cannot identify just why the assignment of this case was made, the commission is going to permit him to speculate.

Justice House then explained that sometimes he had taken on extra case assignments in the May and September terms, and fewer in the winter terms.

I did that in '66 and I did it in '67, and frankly, my reason is that I love to quail hunt. And I would like to get a little relief after the November term so that I can hunt, and so I am willing to take on a little more in the summer. And that is the possibility, that they skipped me over because [earlier] they could have said, "Well, By"—By, they call me—"By, get a little ahead."

Greenberg confirmed that what House was explaining was simply a possibility. The chairman also emphasized that the commission will "receive this evidence for what it is worth, understanding that it was just a speculation by the witness."

After briefly questioning House about the court's four-to-two vote rejecting the prosecution's petition for rehearing in the *Isaacs* case, Stevens ended his direct examination. House had raised a looming question, and it remained to be seen whether his speculative answer would hold up. Were the commission and the public to believe that Justice Klingbiel wrote the decision in *People v. Isaacs* merely because "By" House loved to hunt quail?

Cross-Examination

It was shortly after eleven o'clock, and time for the cross-examination of House. Ochsenschlager, a tall, hefty, and rumpled man, gave the first sample of the folksy humor he would inject into the hearings:

OCHSENSCHLAGER: Mr. Chairman, do you have any preference as to how we proceed in cross-examination? Shall we go by weight or intelligence?

JENNER: Mr. Ochsenschlager would win on both counts.

The justices' lawyer questioned House briefly, largely in an effort to show the normalcy of what had transpired in the *Isaacs* case. First House confirmed that the justices' impression votes were not binding, and that it was not unusual for votes to change between the impression vote right after oral argument and the final vote on a draft opinion. Next Ochsenschlager posed a series of questions to demonstrate that House recalled nothing unusual in the conduct of any of the members of the court with respect to the *Isaacs* case. House stated, "I have no recollection of anything unusual," but also emphasized that there had been about seven hundred cases decided since that time, so he actually recalled very little about *People v. Isaacs.* When asked whether he remembered any other justice trying to influence his vote in the case, House said he had no such recollection and added, "I think that I would have one if someone did."

House noted that justices usually had better memories of cases in which they had dissented, for "when you write a dissent you remember more about it because you give it two or three studies." When asked more about the justices' practices regarding dissents, he also disclosed that "there are many [decisions] that are not unanimous" but that appear to be unanimous because the dissenting justices choose not to have their contrary votes reported. As House explained these and other practices, he was revealing to the public, and especially to Illinois lawyers, more about the internal customs of the Illinois Supreme Court than had ever been revealed before. In discussing dissent practices in particular, House was opening up questions that later would be of great import for John Paul Stevens.

As the justices' lawyer continued to try to show that there was nothing unusual in the *Isaacs* case, House indicated that he did not recall any effort by Klingbiel to obtain the assignment. House also mentioned two other facts that seemed to support Ochsenschlager's theme. First, the State's Attorney's petition for rehearing, after the Klingbiel opinion had been adopted, asked the court to reconsider its ruling only on count 10. Although Stevens objected to drawing too great an inference from this limited petition, House was able to say, "Normally a lawyer questions everything in the rehearing that he thinks improper." Ochsenschlager obviously was trying to show that the State's Attorney probably thought the Klingbiel opinion was correct in all respects but one.

Second, House testified that Justice Underwood's rejected opinion had found many of the counts of the *Isaacs* indictment legally "bad," and that even under that opinion there would have been very few counts left on which the prosecution of Isaacs could have continued. Although the testimony did not delve into a detailed comparison, the Klingbiel decision did overlap with the Underwood opinion to a great extent.[1] Ochsenschlager plainly was trying to show that the Underwood and Klingbiel opinions were not very different from each other, and that therefore the latter was not suspect. What he was glossing over, of course, was that although the two opinions quantitatively were similar, there was a tremendous difference: Underwood's view would have kept Isaacs under indictment and on trial, while Klingbiel's would not have. There is no such thing as being "a little bit" under indictment, but that was not an observation Ochsenschlager was about to make.

As he was highlighting these points, Ochsenschlager also elicited new information from House adding to the credibility of the justice's speculation about why he had been skipped in the reassignment. In the midst of questions about the justices' practice of trading cases, House volunteered, "I prefer civil cases, and I try to trade off criminal cases every time if I can." Perhaps the skipping of House wasn't so sinister after all.

Jenner's cross-examination of House broke little new ground. Jenner did confirm that House had never had any conversations about the case with anyone outside of the court, a point of considerable importance for Isaacs. When asked whether he had completely forgotten about the case before Skolnick filed his motion with the court, House declared, "I sure had." Similarly, when Jenner asked whether there had been anything "unusual or extraordinary about the case to lead you to think about it after the term of court at which the judgment became final," House said, "Very definitely not."

After a brief redirect examination by Stevens, Ochsenschlager established an obvious, but crucial point. House was one of the justices who consistently voted to affirm the lower court, beginning with the impression vote in September. Thus, even if he had written the decision, he too would have written it in line with the majority view, just as Klingbiel did. It appeared that even though the switch to Klingbiel may have been abnormal and inexplicable, it actually made no difference in the outcome of the case.

Jenner, Stevens, and commission member Edwin Austin each

posed a few more questions to clarify House's testimony, and then the witness was excused. Greenberg announced a short lunch recess. Jenner asked for an additional fifteen minutes so he could make a long-standing engagement. As the first signs of tension between Jenner and Greenberg surfaced, Greenberg said, "Mr. Jenner, you are always a very busy man. We have a terribly tight schedule to meet." Jenner insisted that more time was needed for lunch, and Greenberg relented begrudgingly.

Two Silent Dissenters

By starting with the testimony of Justice House, Stevens had accomplished more than he could have by starting with any of the other justices. Had another justice appeared first and brought to light the skipping over of House, suspense would have mounted as to what House himself later might say about it. Questions even might have arisen as to whether House actually was part of a sinister scheme with Klingbiel and Solfisburg. Stevens was concerned about making House, even temporarily, the victim of an unfair interpretation of the facts.

Instead, Stevens had used a less dramatic, but more effective strategy, presenting through House's testimony both the problem of the out-of-order assignment and an innocent, albeit speculative, explanation. If the facts really showed that there was nothing improper behind the assignment to Klingbiel, the testimony of House's comfort with it was probably the best place to start.

The next logical witnesses to address the court's processes in *Isaacs* were Underwood and Schaefer, the two justices who disagreed with the Klingbiel opinion. They were obviously the ones least likely to have been part of any outside effort to influence the court's outcome, since the result they favored was adverse to Isaacs. What remained to be seen was what these two justices made of the newly revealed fly in the ointment—the irregular reassignment to Klingbiel.

Justice Underwood Testifies

The afternoon session began with Stevens calling Justice Underwood to the witness stand. Underwood had become a McLean County judge in 1946 and an Illinois Supreme Court justice in 1962. He testified first that he had no ownership interests or other connections to the Civic Center Bank, that he had been acquainted with Robert Dolph through political gatherings and two dinners at Dolph's Springfield apartment, and that he had no recollection of ever meeting Isaacs.

Underwood confirmed House's recollection that Underwood's draft opinion in *Isaacs* came in too late in the November term to be voted on, especially because it was a complex case and a lengthy opinion. Stevens embarked on a detailed inquiry into the extensive trading that had gone on among the justices during the first term of 1967, when the Underwood opinion was rejected. Weeks earlier in his deposition, Underwood had explained to Stevens that this term was unusually complicated because of the arrival of the two new justices, a disinclination to assign to them any of the more complex cases coming back on rehearing, and Justice Ward's disqualification from many criminal cases.

Stevens's examination of Underwood about the January case assignments was one of the least lively aspects of the public hearings. It was impossible for a listener to follow the minutiae of the assignments and trades of thirty-two cases. Only the witness, the commissioners, and the lawyers had a chance of understanding what Stevens was getting into, for they had before them the agenda books on which the assignments were listed. Despite the complexity of the testimony, it did clearly emerge that Underwood agreed that House was the one to whom the *Isaacs* case should have been reassigned in the normal order. Underwood also could not explain why House was skipped.

Ochsenschlager's quick cross-examination centered once again on the limited petition for rehearing. Underwood confirmed that the petition had raised only count 10 of the indictment, and that his rejected opinion and the Klingbiel decision had both come out the same way on that count. The justices' lawyer seemed to be making more headway in his attempt to suggest that the Klingbiel opinion was legally sound. Ochsenschlager's pitch was that not only did the State's Attorney find merely one aspect of the decision to complain about, but that this one aspect had been found in Isaacs's favor by both the rejected and the adopted opinions of the court.

Jenner's cross-examination continued on the theme that there was nothing really amiss in the court's work in *Isaacs*. Specifically, Underwood recalled nothing unusual about the reassignment to Klingbiel. Alluding to Justice House's declared aversion to writing decisions in criminal cases, Jenner asked whether Underwood had been aware of it before House testified about it. For unstated reasons—perhaps some resentment toward House's avoidance of criminal cases— Underwood seemed to choose the words of his response very carefully: "I think I may fairly say that I am aware of the fact that he is not enthusiastic about it." Jenner then asked whether Underwood thought it was possible that House's aversion explained his being skipped over for *Isaacs*, but Stevens objected to the attempt to get Underwood to speculate. Greenberg sustained the objection, but Jenner bluntly reminded him that during the morning session Greenberg had allowed House to provide a speculative answer despite Jenner's objection. Greenberg backed down, allowing Jenner to rephrase the question. Ironically, Underwood had no opinion to give.

The questioning of Justice Underwood soon ended. Ochsenschlager finished his questioning with the most blunt, albeit garbled, attempt of the day to talk about what the investigation was coming to be about—not just the "integrity of the judgment," but the integrity of the justices:

> OCHSENSCHLAGER: Did you notice anything unusual about the conduct, and I am going to put it right on the gentlemen who I am here representing, Justice Klingbiel or Justice Solfisburg, about any of their conduct during the time this was being considered, before or after, that would cause you to have any question about their integrity on the court, and particularly in the handling of this one case?
>
> UNDERWOOD: I have no recollection of any such conduct.

A Few Words from the Senior Justice

Stevens called Justice Walter Schaefer as the next witness, but the questioning was done by Jerome Torshen, Stevens's principal assistant. After the extensive detail developed through the testimony of Justices House and Underwood, Torshen sought little more from Schaefer, even though Schaefer—as the first justice whose deposition was taken—had actually been the initial source of much of the evidence thus far.

Torshen quickly covered much the same ground Stevens had covered with the two prior witnesses: Schaefer had no connection to the Civic Center Bank; he knew Isaacs, but could not recall under what circumstances; he knew Dolph; and he confirmed the skip of Justice House, but could not explain it. In the midst of this quick, rather mechanical series of questions and answers, Schaefer twice abruptly made startling revelations.

The first came after Schaefer said he was acquainted with Robert Perbohner:

> TORSHEN: Have you ever received any gifts from Mr. Perbohner?
>
> SCHAEFER: Yes, sir.

Perbohner, of course, was the elusive friend of Isaacs who had given the bank stock to Klingbiel under still unknown circumstances. Had he also made gifts to Justice Schaefer? As the *Sun-Times* wrote, "Spectators leaned forward in their chairs."

> TORSHEN: Will you state the nature of the gifts which you have received?
>
> SCHAEFER: I can demonstrate by these little calendars that are plastic, I think, and you put them on your watchband. I received those from Mr. Perbohner. And I think that possibly in the last year or so he had some sort of plastic fountain pens with his name on them that he sent to me, and I assume to other members of the court.

Stevens and Torshen already had learned during the depositions about these annual gifts from Perbohner to all of the justices. Seemingly implicit in the testimony of the court's most distinguished member about these trinkets was an important message: What might at first look like evidence of grave wrongdoing might prove, upon further inquiry, to be hardly anything at all.

Schaefer's other surprising revelation was more important. Torshen brought out that Schaefer had not only dissented in *People v. Isaacs,* but had actually written a dissenting opinion for one major aspect of the case. He had not told any of the other justices about his draft, nor did he file it as part of the public record of the case. When Torshen asked why the justice had not filed the dissent, Schaefer cited to such luminaries of the law as Justices Oliver Wendell Holmes Jr. and Louis D. Brandeis for the proposition that "often the preparation of a dissenting opinion was foregone waiting for a better opportunity." Schaefer indicated that *Isaacs* was one of the cases in which there wasn't much to be accomplished by publicly dissenting.

> In this case, the problem was basically one of statutory construction. If there was anything wrong with the opinion of the court in the construction of the statute, it was a matter that could readily be clarified by the General Assembly. My dissenting opinion rejects Mr. Justice Underwood's interpretation, as well as Mr. Justice Klingbiel's, as I remember this.
>
> Apparently I was right in my determination not to file it. I was wrong in my appraisal as to what the General Assembly intended, because I think that the statute to this date remains unchanged. And the tenor of this proposed dissent was that the legislature could

hardly have meant the construction that was placed upon the statute by the prevailing opinion.

Stevens would not forget Schaefer's views on the selective filing of dissenting opinions, nor his choice not to file the dissent he prepared in *People v. Isaacs.*

Stevens earlier had heard Schaefer explain this perspective more fully in his deposition. Ironically, Schaefer said more than he thought Stevens would be interested in:

> STEVENS: Are there occasions in which an opinion is distributed to the bar and to the public without either a formal dissenting opinion being appended to it, or any notation of dissent, in which the views of the members of the court were not in fact unanimously in favor of the judgment of the court?
>
> SCHAEFER: Yes, sir. Much more frequently, I would guess, than the bar suspects. . . . It is the sort of philosophical consideration that would probably be irrelevant to your purposes here, but it has been something that has interested me a good deal over the years. That is not a phenomenon peculiar to the Supreme Court of Illinois. The same thing is true of the Supreme Court of the United States, and you find Paul Freund describing Brandeis. Many a time he intended to dissent, but put it aside waiting for another case.[2]

Schaefer, Stevens's former law teacher, could not have known that this "irrelevant" lesson on Justice Brandeis soon would have singular relevance: in a few years, Brandeis's seat on the Supreme Court would be Stevens's.

The full import of Schaefer's testimony was undoubtedly lost on most listeners. Schaefer's dissent would have kept alive two counts of the *Isaacs* indictment that both Underwood and Klingbiel thought should be quashed. If Schaefer had filed his dissent, he would have been disagreeing with Klingbiel's majority on those two counts. Even if the Underwood opinion had been adopted by the court, Schaefer's view logically would have required him to dissent from that part of Underwood's conclusions as well. Underwood would have kept ten counts of the indictment alive against Isaacs; Schaefer would have kept twelve. Only through publication of a combination of the Underwood draft and the Schaefer dissent could the public possibly have known what these two justices thought the correct result in the case should have been.

Of course, this was just a fine legal point, both in the context of the *Isaacs* case itself and in the context of the investigation. What it signified, however, was that the *Isaacs* case had unquestionably been a tough one to decide for all of the justices. Underwood and Schaefer agreed with the majority—Klingbiel, Solfisburg, House, and Kluczynski—on most counts, but not all. The two silent dissenters agreed with each other on a greater number of counts, but still disagreed on a couple. For the critical observer, and especially for a commissioner charged with examining the integrity of the court's judgment, it would be very difficult to find, amidst this shifting lineup of judicial conclusions, that something had definitely gone awry in the decision of Isaacs's case.

Although neither Jenner nor Ochsenschlager cross-examined, the latter made an unsuccessful effort to close this witness's appearance with some levity:

> OCHSENSCHLAGER: I will ask you one question, Justice: Is there anyone on the court, even though you are a senior member, who can beat you in tennis?
>
> SCHAEFER: I don't know. Most anyone can these days.

With the end of Schaefer's testimony, Stevens had completed the promised first phase of his case.

House Committee members and their attorney. *From left:* George Lindberg, William Hundley, Henry Hyde, and Paul Elward. Reprinted by permission of the *Chicago Tribune.*

The Illinois Supreme Court in 1969. *From left:* Justices Kluczynski, House, Schaefer, Solfisburg, Klingbiel, Underwood, and Ward. Reprinted by permission of the *Chicago Tribune.*

The Special Commission. *From left:* Commissioners Bull, Pitts, Greenberg, Austin, and Schuyler. Reprinted by permission of the *Chicago Tribune.*

The Illinois Supreme Court in 1965 taking an impression vote in the court's conference room. *Clockwise from top:* Chief Justice Klingbiel, Justices House, Solfisburg, Underwood, Daily, Schaefer, and Hershey. Reprinted by permission of the *Chicago Tribune.*

John Paul Stevens in 1969. Reprinted with special permission of Chicago Sun-Times, Inc. © 2001.

Sherman Skolnick outside of Judge Healy's courtroom. Reprinted with special permission of Chicago Sun-Times, Inc. © 2001.

From left: Justices Underwood, Schaefer, and House leaving Courtroom 1501 on the first day of hearings. Reprinted by permission of the *Chicago Tribune.*

Albert Jenner. Reprinted with special permission of Chicago Sun-Times, Inc. © 2001.

Chief Justice Solfisburg and Lambert Ochsenschlager arriving at the Civic Center for the evening session. Reprinted with special permission of Chicago Sun-Times, Inc. © 2001.

Justice Klingbiel leaving the Civic Center after testifying before the Special Commission. Reprinted with special permission of Chicago Sun-Times, Inc. © 2001.

Frank Greenberg. Reprinted with
special permission of Chicago Sun-
Times, Inc. © 2001.

Theodore Isaacs at Courtroom
1501. Reprinted with special
permission of Chicago Sun-
Times, Inc. © 2001.

Sherman Skolnick holding a press conference in the Civic Center lobby after release of the Special Commission's report. Reprinted with special permission of Chicago Sun-Times, Inc. © 2001.

John Paul Stevens in 1970. Reprinted with special permission of Chicago Sun-Times, Inc.
© 2001.

Chapter 13

Secrets in the Bank

Monday afternoon, following Justice Schaefer's testimony, Stevens began presenting evidence about the two justices' Civic Center Bank stock transactions. His first witness was Daniel P. Neath, the cashier of the bank, who was called to identify certain bank records that James Nussbaum and I had found. By putting these documents into evidence through a bank functionary who could attest to their authenticity, Stevens set the stage for Nussbaum to explain what the documents showed. Neath's testimony consisted of just the description and marking of documents as trial exhibits, but some eyebrow-raising information emerged.

The testimony showed that the Civic Center Bank was organized in late 1965 and early 1966 and that Isaacs was a key player in its formation. Most significantly, it was noted that 12,850 shares of CCB stock were initially issued to Isaacs and that these shares later were distributed to other people. Neath identified a handwritten four-page list starting with 12,850 in the upper left-hand corner and continuing down to the number 100 as the last entry on the last page. He explained that these sheets showed the distribution of the 12,850 shares issued to Isaacs, and he said the list was prepared when the bank was first organized and was handled by a Mrs. Kegley. Although few people in the courtroom realized it, when the "Kegley list" was identified, one of the most critical pieces of evidence in the investigation was laid on the table.

The questioning of Neath next went to Jenner. As the lawyer for both Isaacs and the bank, Jenner also now was representing Neath, the bank's employee. Jenner's questions aimed at showing that the bank had fully cooperated with the Special Commission, and particularly with Nussbaum and me. Neath testified that the two of us were in the bank pretty much every day for a few weeks, that we were given "a free run of the bank," and that all of the bank's records "were turned over to the gentlemen and reviewed at will."

Ochsenschlager's questioning focused first on the Kegley list. He asked whether the 12,850 shares in Isaacs's name were the same shares that were put up as collateral when approximately $300,000 was borrowed at the First National Bank. Although the witness couldn't answer the question, since he had not been a bank employee at that time, the lawyer's reference to a loan began to paint more of the picture of the bank's organization and Isaacs's multiple roles in it.

Stevens hastened to advise Ochsenschlager that "Mr. Nussbaum will be the next witness, who has made a detailed study of these accounting matters and some of these questions may be appropriately asked of him." Despite this advice, Ochsenschlager made clear what he was trying to accomplish: "With the newspaper people here, I wanted to have them understand as much as they could before we adjourned tonight—that it is, I believe, all of our understanding [that] these [shares] were controlled by the bank. By the bank, rather than Mr. Isaacs." Stevens objected to this "volunteered statement," and Greenberg commented, too. He shared Ochsenschlager's concern that "the press should not go away, so to speak, half-cocked," but he also emphasized that the evidence would have to "come along in a certain order" and that "it will only confuse matters if you volunteer these kinds of descriptive statements."

Lastly, Ochsenschlager tackled the allegation that Chief Justice Solfisburg was secretly an attorney for the bank. He asked Neath whether he had ever seen Solfisburg "in the bank in any capacity at all," "ever seen or heard of him doing any law work for the bank," or "ever seen any evidence of Mr. Solfisburg being an attorney, secret or otherwise, for the bank." To all three inquiries, Neath replied, "No, I haven't." Once again, Ochsenschlager seemed to have defended his client effectively.

Stevens, however, easily rained on Ochsenschlager's parade:

STEVENS: Mr. Neath, you don't know whether Mr. Solfisburg has gone in the bank or not?

NEATH: I haven't seen him.

STEVENS: You wouldn't recognize him if he had been there, would you?

NEATH: No.

With a few more minor questions by Stevens and Jenner, Neath's testimony was concluded. Stevens attempted to complete the introduction into evidence of all the documents Neath had identified, but Jenner objected to admission of the Kegley list. With some frustration, Stevens argued, "The bank, it doesn't seem to me, can in good grace produce this document in response to this subpoena from its own files, and then question its authenticity." After some more tussling, Greenberg postponed ruling on the admissibility of the Kegley list.

It was now late in the afternoon.

JENNER: It is now a quarter after five, which is a normal adjourning time in the trial of cases. An attorney has to get back to his office and get work done. When did you plan the commission would—

GREENBERG: I think the whole proceeding, Mr. Jenner, has a certain abnormality about it, including the time. I had hoped to go until six o'clock. Perhaps this is a good time to announce to counsel and to interested parties that we propose to work tomorrow evening. We will take a dinner recess about 5:30 for one hour and fifteen minutes.

Once again, Jenner and Greenberg disagreed about lawyers' professional and digestive needs:

JENNER: I protest. An hour and fifteen minutes for dinner, to get back to the office, look at some mail, go out and have something to eat?

GREENBERG: I am under a mandate of the Supreme Court of Illinois to finish this investigation and file a report on August 1. I intend to do the best I can with that mandate. Now, I think your objection to the one hour and fifteen minutes may be reasonable. Would you accept one hour and one-half?

JENNER: Yes.

At Counsel Table

While Stevens and Torshen were examining the day's witnesses, McNally and I sat at the counsel table to assist them. Participation from this vantage point was a heady experience for us as young lawyers, but at times it was also nerve-racking. The most alarming moment for me came during Neath's testimony, when the chairman suddenly interrupted:

Mr. Stevens, perhaps you could rest your voice for a moment while the chair makes a statement. Mr. Kenneth Manaster is a young lawyer who has been associate counsel for the commission. He is a very brilliant young man. He has done a very able service. I am told that in the course of his examination of the books of the Civic Center Bank, he ran across the fact that a remote relative of his is a shareholder of the bank. That was duly reported to the commission. The commission considered it to be of absolutely no significance.

Where was Greenberg going with this? Was I about to be criticized, or sacked, in full public view? Some weeks earlier I had discovered a reference to someone with my last name in the bank's records. I found out from my parents that it was indeed a distant relative and reported the information to the Special Commission. During this first day of hearings, however, I learned that Sherman Skolnick had told a reporter about his own discovery of my relative's CCB stock ownership. At least one radio station already had broadcast this news, along with Skolnick's assertion that this was further proof that a whitewash was in the works.

Greenberg continued:

I would not dignify it by referring to it here, except that I am advised somebody made some speech to the television cameras in the corridor about the fact that Mr. Manaster's relative, whoever he is, is a shareholder of the Civic Center Bank, and that this is conclusive evidence that this is a whitewash commission. I can only suggest to the press that it take this matter in the proper perspective. The commission knows about the fact that Mr. Manaster's relative is a shareholder. We do not consider it of any consequence in this investigation.

I nervously rose to thank him and to set the record completely straight: "I want to thank you for clarifying that. I do want to state, however, that according to what I learned in the course of the work I was doing in this investigation, my relative is no longer a shareholder of the bank." Unfortunately, I did not quit while I was ahead. My next statement brought laughter throughout the courtroom: "It is also my understanding, from what my parents inform me, that the relative is no longer alive." With mixed feelings of pride, relief, and embarrassment, I took my seat again.

The Accountant and His Charts

James Nussbaum, the staff's accountant, was the next witness. Stevens took Nussbaum through the identification of a series of charts the accountant had prepared on the basis of documents obtained from the Civic Center Bank, plus some additional documents from the First National Bank of Chicago. Because the hour was late, Stevens's goal was simply to introduce the charts, leaving fuller explanations for Tuesday. The first chart was entitled "Summary of Civic Center Bank capitalization proceeds and loan to T. J. Isaacs covering the period from January 7, 1966, through January 26, 1966." Referring to this summary, Nussbaum explained that the bank's charter was issued on January 21, 1966, on the basis of a capitalization of $2 million, which had been paid in by that date for the issuance of a hundred thousand shares.

Most of the $2 million had come from payments made between January 7 and January 21 by people who earlier had signed subscription agreements to buy the bank's initial stock. Those original subscribers had paid almost $1.7 million by January 21. Nussbaum explained where the remaining money came from:

> The bank had to have on deposit at the First National Bank $2,000,000 in order to obtain its charter from the state. Mr. Isaacs obtained a loan from the First National Bank in the amount of $304,500, which was applied to that $2,000,000 that the Civic Center Bank then had on deposit at the First National Bank on January 21, 1966. For the $304,500 there were 15,225 shares represented by that, that were collateral for the loan.

Stevens then took Nussbaum into further explanation of this loan and its purposes, relying on the minutes of the board of directors meeting of January 21. Isaacs was present at that meeting, both as secretary and as acting cashier. The minutes stated:

> The acting cashier then reported that he had concluded a clearance loan with the First National Bank of Chicago in the amount of approximately $300,000, which loan represented outstanding shares that had not yet been issued to the public. These shares are to be held in reserve to foster new accounts and will be dispensed to new business accounts from time to time until such time as they are all sold. As these shares are picked up from this date henceforth, there will be interest charges to be added to the $20 per share cost.

These avowed objectives for the issuance of these shares—"to foster new accounts" and to be "dispensed to new business accounts"— would be closely examined before the hearings were through.

Nussbaum went on to explain, relying on his chart and various supporting documents, that on January 21 the bank received an addi-

tional batch of payments from original subscribers and that those payments were immediately applied to reduce the clearance loan. Thus
the amount of the outstanding loan when the bank received its charter
actually went down to $257,000, and the number of shares issued in
Isaacs's name as collateral for the loan became 12,850. As of January
21, 1966, these were the only remaining unsold shares in the new Civic
Center Bank—and all of them were in Isaacs's name.

Nussbaum's next chart was a summary of the disposition of Isaacs's
12,850 shares. The accountant testified that he prepared this chart on
the basis of the bank's stock certificate book and stock register sheet,
plus the Kegley list. Two more charts were identified and were described as going into greater detail concerning the 12,850 shares.
Those shares originally had been issued to Isaacs in two different
stock certificates, one for nearly ten thousand shares and the other for
the balance. Nussbaum had traced all of the transfers from each of
these original certificates down to the many smaller certificates issued
to subsequent purchasers, and he identified the exact dollar proceeds
from each sale.

Nussbaum's last chart summarized the disposition of CCB shares
held by two trusts at the Old Second National Bank of Aurora. One of
the trusts, No. 931, had been identified by Solfisburg a few weeks earlier when he publicly disclosed his CCB holdings. His seven hundred
shares had been placed in that trust when he first bought them.

It was now shortly before six o'clock. A few minutes earlier, Greenberg had asked Stevens to find "a convenient place to taper off with
this witness so we can resume in the morning." Stevens now told the
chairman that he had reached a convenient place to stop for the
evening, and the long first day of trial was over.

The Bank Stock Puzzle

The hearings resumed on Tuesday morning with everyone present but
Jenner. Greenberg immediately directed Nussbaum to return to the
witness stand. William C. Murphy, Ochsenschlager's partner, asked
Greenberg to wait since Jenner was late. Greenberg was firm: "No.
We have decided to start at 9:30, and it is now 9:32." The proceedings
began, and Jenner soon arrived.

Nussbaum's testimony concentrated again on the Kegley list, the
four handwritten sheets showing the purchasers of the 12,850 shares
issued to Isaacs as collateral for the clearance loan from the First National Bank. Nussbaum had found that all of the names on the list cor-
responded to the names on the stock certificates issued by the Civic

Center Bank, with a couple of notable exceptions. For example, the last sale, covering the final one hundred shares, was made on October 11, 1966, and the purchaser was Theodore J. Isaacs. Bank records showed that Isaacs personally had paid over $2,000 for those shares. The certificate for those shares was not issued to him, however, but to Robert Perbohner.

Stevens attempted again to have the Kegley list admitted into evidence, this time successfully. Stevens then focused on Solfisburg's stock, and Nussbaum confirmed what by then was obvious: Solfisburg's seven hundred shares had come from the block of 12,850 shares held by Isaacs. Nussbaum pointed out that on the Kegley list "there is an indication, Old Second National Bank of Aurora under its Trust No. 931, and in parentheses, Roy J. Solfisburg Jr., 1412 Downer Place, Aurora, Illinois, alongside the seven hundred shares attributable to Trust 931." Nussbaum also identified two checks drawn by Solfisburg on May 27, 1966, in payment for the stock, one check for the total stock price, and the other for interest charges. The bank's stock certificates for these seven hundred shares were issued on June 16, 1966. The next stock certificate in numerical order was for a hundred shares issued to Robert and Alice Dolph through Trust No. 932 at the Aurora bank. Two more certificates in the sequence covered two hundred shares issued to M. R. Davison. The Dolph and Davison certificates bore the same June 16 date as the certificates issued to Trust No. 931.

Other than the Kegley list and the stock records, there were no other records or correspondence in the bank's files concerning the issuance of stock to Solfisburg's trust. In contrast, Nussbaum explained, many of the other names on the list were supported by correspondence of one form or another. What Nussbaum was highlighting, of course, was the mystery of how Solfisburg had come to purchase these shares. The commissioners already understood that while Solfisburg was buying this stock in May and June—stock that had been first issued to Isaacs—*People v. Isaacs* was pending in the Illinois Supreme Court.

Stevens turned next to a separate set of transactions that seemed at first to have nothing to do with either Solfisburg or Klingbiel. Nussbaum explained that, in addition to the hundred shares Isaacs bought in Perbohner's name, there was another instance in which shares were issued to someone other than the purchaser: Joseph E. Knight bought six hundred shares, but the certificates were issued in the name of Howard M. Hansen.

Knight was well known to many people in the courtroom, for he had been involved in Illinois Democratic politics for years. At the time of the issuance of the bank's charter in January 1966, Knight was the state's Director of Financial Institutions. In that capacity, he issued and signed the bank's charter. In July of that year he bought the six hundred shares of CCB stock with the certificates made out to Hansen. Later on, around the time he left his state position, Knight also became a member of the bank's board of directors in February 1968.

Ochsenschlager and Jenner objected vehemently to this line of questioning, which they called irrelevant. Stevens explained what he was getting at: in August of 1966 there had been extensive correspondence about replacement of one of the stock certificates issued in Hansen's name, as Knight had lost the certificate. The correspondence about how to replace the lost certificate showed that Isaacs, the bank's general counsel, was an active participant in the effort. Stevens argued:

> One of the issues that I believe will be disputed during the course of this hearing is the extent of the participation, if any, of Theodore J. Isaacs in the issuance and distribution of shares in this block of 12,850. I believe this group of documents, together with the testimony that we are in the course of presenting, will be relevant to the issue of what participation, if any, did Mr. Isaacs have in the disposition of these shares.

Ochsenschlager continued to object, saying that proof of Isaacs's involvement in "one isolated instance" proved little, since there had been over a hundred different transfers of stock from the original block of 12,850. Stevens tried to make the relevance of the Hansen-Knight stock even stronger:

> It is true that there are a large number of transactions, most of them for fifty or a hundred shares, and most of them documented. There are a few transactions for large blocks of stock which are not documented.
> The form of this transaction, I think, is even relevant, using a certificate endorsed in blank in the name of a nominee with someone else paying for it, a situation which will be paralleled in later evidence.

Stevens was trying to show a number of things: Isaacs's involvement in the handling of the shares; the undocumented nature of large stock sales such as Knight's six hundred shares and Solfisburg's seven hundred; and the odd instances in which the real owner of CCB stock was not identified on the certificates, as with Isaacs's purchase for Perbohner, and Solfisburg's purchase into Trust No. 931.

Solfisburg Sells Some Stock

The final segment of Stevens's direct examination of Nussbaum concerned Solfisburg's first sale of some of his shares. On June 5, 1967, almost a year after the certificates to Trust No. 931 were issued, three hundred of those shares were transferred to new owners. Nussbaum referred to a trio of letters—dated May 22, 24, and 26, 1967—which identified the new owners and accompanied their payments for the stock. Nussbaum and I had found the letters on July 1, while going through some disorderly files in the bank's conference room. Through them, we learned who had bought Solfisburg's first three hundred shares: there were three purchasers, two of them members of the bank's board of directors. Each of the three purchasers had acquired a hundred shares, and each had paid $2,400.

These transactions at first seemed quite straightforward, until something strange caught my eye. The three purchasers had paid a total of $7,200, but Solfisburg had received more than that. A cashier's check for the shares had been issued to him by the Civic Center Bank on June 1, 1967, in the amount of $7,500. We could find no indication in the bank's files of where the extra $300 had come from, but we had a hunch.

We asked the bank to check the microfilm records of Isaacs's checking account for late May and early June, especially June 1. Descending with bank personnel to a subbasement, we looked on while clerical workers tried repeatedly to produce readable images of canceled checks and bank statements from Isaacs's checking account. After about twenty tense minutes crowded into a small room in the bowels of the bank, after we gave a not very subtle reminder that the commission's subpoena covered our request, and after hovering closely over the machine operator, somehow the microfilm problem suddenly resolved itself. To our amazement, our hunch was right. On May 26, 1967, Isaacs wrote a check for $300 to the Civic Center Bank. The check cleared the bank on June 1 and was grouped with the three $2,400 payments from the purchasers of the stock to produce the $7,500 payment to Solfisburg.

We pressed the bank workers to make legible photocopies of the check and account statement as fast as possible, for it was now approaching two o'clock—when Stevens was scheduled to take Solfisburg's deposition. Earlier I had alerted Stevens by telephone about our hunch. A few minutes before two, I sprinted down La Salle Street to Stevens's office and delivered the photocopies just in time for him to take a quick look at them before entering the deposition, where he would confront Solfisburg with our discovery.

Nussbaum's testimony about Isaacs's $300 contribution to Solfisburg's stock sale did not go into these background details, but the importance of the revelation "seemed to stir the packed hearing room," as one of the many front-page newspaper stories reported. The press did not notice one of the most damning aspects of the $300 payment, however, and that was the date of Isaacs's check. Isaacs wrote it on May 26, 1967. *People v. Isaacs* had finally been concluded in the supreme court with the issuance of the court's mandate on May 25— one day before Isaacs wrote the check.

Stevens's direct examination of Nussbaum ended on this climactic note. Ochsenschlager, however, insisted that the testimony should be viewed with caution:

> This would be immaterial and not admissible here unless it is later tied in with some knowledge on the part of Justice Solfisburg either directly or indirectly, that he had some knowledge of the payment of this money by Mr. Isaacs. This could either be to benefit the buyers or the sellers, and unless it is shown to have been a benefit to Justice Solfisburg that was known by Justice Solfisburg, either then or later, it would be irrelevant in this particular case and would not be within the scope of the inquiry.

Ochsenschlager was not surprised by this disclosure of Isaacs's check, for he had attended Solfisburg's deposition. The lawyer obviously had taken some time to think through the stance he should take toward the check. The possibility he chose to emphasize—remote though it must have seemed to most everyone else in the courtroom—was that Isaacs had chipped in not to benefit Solfisburg, but somehow to help out the purchasers of his stock. The check looked very bad for Isaacs and Solfisburg, but maybe there was more to the story.

Chapter 14

Challenging Witnesses

The last hour of the Tuesday morning session was consumed by Ochsenschlager's cross-examination of Nussbaum—the most confused portion of the proceedings yet, as the lawyer persistently tried to challenge the witness on something he hadn't really said.

Nussbaum had described the clearance loan, and the stock certificates put up as collateral, as being in Isaacs's name. Nussbaum also had said he found no documents indicating that the Civic Center Bank had guaranteed payment of the loan. Ochsenschlager construed this testimony as an assertion that the loan to Isaacs was a personal loan and that the 12,850 shares were purchased and owned personally by him.

The source of the confusion seemed to be that Nussbaum was describing in precise accounting terms the nature of the debt and the identity of the sole debtor, Isaacs. In contrast, Ochsenschlager was trying to fend off an inference he feared that Stevens might try to draw from the debt. Apparently Ochsenschlager thought Stevens would paint Solfisburg's purchase of the bank stock as a purchase from Isaacs, rather than as a purchase from the bank.

Part of Ochsenschlager's difficulty stemmed from the unique nature of the whole proceeding. Stevens had not had to do what lawyers usually do in trials—make an opening statement describing the evidence and crystallizing the specific legal points to be proven. Ochsenschlager knew what Skolnick's motion alleged but couldn't be sure just where Stevens was going with the evidence. In this uncertain position, the justices' lawyer overreacted to Nussbaum's description of the loan.

Greenberg tried to put on the brakes: "Mr. Ochsenschlager, just let me say one thing. I am somewhat disturbed. . . . You said something to the witness about that he was trying to establish an independent loan [to Isaacs]. I have not understood that anybody suggested that this was not related to the bank in some way. I don't think the witness or anybody else has suggested that at all." After this statement, the justices' lawyer moved on to other matters.

In the midst of the confusion, Ochsenschlager nonetheless established a few significant points. Most helpfully for Solfisburg, Ochsenschlager proved through Nussbaum that the justice's stock was bought at the same price—$20 per share—at which all other shares were bought from the block of 12,850 shares. Nussbaum also testified that he had come across no evidence that Solfisburg was a lawyer for the bank.

Inadvertently, Ochsenschlager also triggered a decision about an important aspect of the hearings. Toward the end of Ochsenschlager's questioning of the accountant, Greenberg cautioned the justices' lawyer about some questions that sounded more like legal argument than cross-examination:

> GREENBERG: Mr. Ochsenschlager, there will be plenty of time to argue your case. But you cannot argue it through this witness on cross-examination.
>
> OCHSENSCHLAGER: Mr. Chairman, I have learned for the first time that we are going to have an opportunity for summation or argument. I have asked this of Mr. Stevens, and he didn't know. I am pleased to know that, because that will shorten much of this.
>
> STEVENS: I didn't know it either, Mr. Ochsenschlager.
>
> OCHSENSCHLAGER: I don't know if anyone knew it.
>
> GREENBERG: As a matter of fact, Mr. Ochsenschlager, I didn't know it until now either.

Greenberg had just highlighted, not for the first time, that presiding over a trial was not something he was used to doing. He had accidentally fallen into an important procedural decision. Of course, no one would have known its impromptu nature had he not volunteered—to much laughter in the courtroom—his own surprise. He followed up, slightly more seriously, by indicating that the Special Commission would be "glad to consider setting down some period for summation by both sides, or three sides, or four sides, if there are sides."

Jenner's Offense

After lunch Nussbaum retook the witness stand and Jenner began his cross-examination. Although his questioning did not take as long as

Ochsenschlager's, and covered much the same ground, it produced unexpected fireworks.

Jenner swiftly tried to show that he was taking charge, starting with questions about Nussbaum's credentials. He asked Nussbuam whether, prior to joining Price Waterhouse in 1960, he had gained any experience in the auditing of banks. Nussbaum gave a seemingly innocuous answer, but Jenner saw it differently:

> NUSSBAUM: No, sir. Prior to July 1, 1960, I was in college.
>
> JENNER: You will do better with me, Mr. Nussbaum, if you just answer my questions and not volunteer, especially when the volunteering is not responsive to my question, as with your last answer.
>
> GREENBERG: Mr. Jenner, when you need an admonition to the witness, would you ask the chair to admonish him?
>
> JENNER: Well, I am a little uncertain as to what the chair might do in view of my experience of yesterday and today.
>
> GREENBERG: I ask, nonetheless, that you address the chair on these matters.
>
> JENNER: On occasions when I think it is necessary, I will address the chair.

Although Greenberg gave no indication of flinching at Jenner's brazen responses, Nussbaum was nervous. He sensed that Jenner was about to attack his credentials and his work in this case and was acutely aware of Jenner's prominence as a lawyer, and of his own inexperience as a witness. Nevertheless, Nussbaum was confident in his facts.

After digging into details of the witness's auditing experience, Jenner turned to the same point that Ochsenschlager had already belabored—were the clearance loan and collateral really personal to Isaacs or were they the bank's? Once more, Nussbaum testified that only Isaacs was obligated on the loan, but that the loan was intended to benefit the bank. Nonetheless, Jenner continued to probe into details of the loan and into the bases for Nussbaum's conclusions.

Greenberg eventually announced that the commission had heard enough to warrant admitting into evidence some key documents relating to the loan. He also advised Jenner, "You are rapidly arriving at the limit of what in our discretion we consider to be proper cross-examination of this witness." Jenner objected to the evidentiary ruling and continued to question Nussbaum along the same lines he had been pursuing.

After a few more minutes of this, Greenberg told Jenner that he was repeating what Ochsenschlager had covered. Jenner denied it and kept going. Finally, Stevens offered to stipulate that Nussbaum did not make a full-blown audit of the bank as he might have under ordinary circumstances. Jenner replied: "This witness testified this morning, and he stuck to that testimony despite further examination by Mr. Ochsenschlager, that he found nothing to indicate that the loan was for the benefit of the Civic Center Bank. I am cross-examining him on that question." Greenberg announced another recess so that the parties could try to reach a stipulation.

No stipulation was reached. Greenberg then reviewed the basic aspects of the loan that Nussbaum had described, indicating again that only Isaacs was obligated on the loan, but that he made the loan for the accommodation of the bank. In response, Ochsenschlager said, with refreshing clarity, that the remaining vital part of the inquiry was "to what extent did Mr. Isaacs have control over the distribution of that stock and sale of it." Greenberg's reply was simple: "We haven't gotten to that question yet." Ochsenschlager was reassured, but Jenner was unmollified. He still refused to accept Greenberg's characterizations of the evidence, and he put more questions to Nussbaum about his analysis of the loan and collateral.

Jenner's grilling went on, Nussbaum stayed focused, and finally the commission closed the door, with Greenberg saying:

> Mr. Jenner, I am instructed unanimously by the commission that we exercise our discretion to terminate cross-examination on this point at this time. One of the things which motivates us is that any explanation about this loan is very clearly within the ability of your client Mr. Isaacs, and your client the Civic Center Bank, to bring forward, and there will be ample opportunity afforded to you to explain all of the details. . . . Mr. Nussbaum, you may leave the stand. Mr. Stevens, you will call the next witness.

As Nussbaum left the stand, Jenner protested that he had not had an opportunity to examine the witness about one of the important exhibits in evidence. Greenberg stood firm: "The chair has ruled."

Jenner exploded: "This isn't a commission. It is a kangaroo court!" Many in the courtroom were shocked at this insolence. Even Ochsenschlager, who shared at least some of Jenner's perspective on the proceedings, immediately tried to put distance between himself and Jenner: "Mr. Chairman, I trust you understand that the reference to this commission was the words of the speaker and not of the one who now addresses the commission."

With tension in the air, the lawyers hastily retreated to calmer terrain by concentrating on the marking of more exhibits. In the midst of this sorting out of exhibits, there also was some sorting out of the schedule for the hearings. Ochsenschlager indicated that the two justices "would appreciate it if they could testify today." The reason for their preference was the upcoming oral argument on the constitutionality of the new state income tax. Argument was set for Thursday, and the justices wanted to be in Springfield on Wednesday to prepare. Ochsenschlager emphasized, however, that the justices "will be here whenever they are called."

Greenberg assured the lawyer that the commission hoped somehow to reconcile the scheduling needs of the supreme court and the commission. Nonetheless, he emphasized that the hearings were "running behind schedule," and that Stevens had to be allowed "reasonable discretion as to the order of witnesses." Jenner advised that he had a long-standing commitment to be in Pennsylvania the next day, and he too asked if the justices could be heard "this afternoon or this evening, so that I may be present during their testimony." Stevens, who was trying to present the evidence in as logical a sequence as possible, simply stated: "I will do my best to reach them. I think it would be unfair to either justice to change the order of proof because I think they may want to comment on some of the testimony that will be offered first."

Lawyers from Different Planets

If it was not clear at the outset of the hearings, it certainly was clear to courtroom observers by this point that the lawyers involved in the hearings had very different personalities and courtroom styles. The most stark contrast was between the chief "defense" lawyers, Ochsenschlager and Jenner. As another lawyer in the case later observed, "They came from different planets."[1]

Lambert M. Ochsenschlager seemed a classic incarnation of the folksy, somewhat bumbling country lawyer. He was widely known as "Oxy," a sobriquet that seemed to fit both his size and his manner. As he had already demonstrated in the first two days of hearings, he also brought a good sense of humor—often self-deprecating—to serious moments, although his timing was not always perfect.

Nonetheless, he was not a man to be underestimated. Ochsenschlager had been admitted to the Illinois bar in 1937, after receiving his law degree at John Marshall Law School in Chicago. By 1969 he was the senior partner of a civil litigation firm of about ten lawyers in Aurora. A life-long Republican, he had been very active in party activities both in Kane County and at the state level. He had been a close political ally of Solfisburg for many years and also was friendly with Klingbiel. Frequently he socialized with them, as well as with other Republican justices and officials. Ochsenschlager had been one of the first prominent Republicans to promote Solfisburg as a candidate for the Illinois Supreme Court in 1960. With this shared background between the Aurora lawyer and the Aurora judge, as well as Ochsenschlager's acquaintanceship with Klingbiel, it was not surprising that the two justices chose him to represent them. There was little or no coordination between the justices' lawyers and Isaacs's lawyers. William Murphy, Ochsenschlager's partner, recalls that they saw Jenner and his colleagues—"the big black suits from Chicago"—as pursuing "preposterously complex and ineffectual" strategies. The most obvious indication of the difference between the two teams' approaches was the far greater frequency of Jenner's objections to questions and exhibits, as compared to the relative infrequency of Ochsenschlager's.

By 1969 Albert E. Jenner Jr. was one of the most influential and sought-after lawyers in Chicago. He received his law degree from the University of Illinois in 1930 and in 1933 joined a Chicago law firm that by the 1960s was named Jenner & Block, and had become one of the city's largest. Right out of law school, he teamed up with another young lawyer named Walter V. Schaefer—the future justice—in a number of projects for the drafting of revisions of some important statutes and procedural rules.[2] As a result of this early work and his later participation in federal advisory committees, Jenner was widely known as an expert on the rules of evidence and litigation procedure. He also was known as a man with a distinctive, urbane style, including a courtly demeanor, large ego, custom-made bow ties, and silk-lined suits, all making him something of a local legend in the Chicago legal community. In addition to his principal practice as a litigator in business disputes, Jenner undertook an unusually wide variety of other types of highly publicized cases, including selected criminal defense matters and politically controversial disputes. In 1965, for example, he represented a doctor who was being pursued by the House Un-American Activities Committee, and Jenner prided himself on having fought against what he considered the committee's own "high-handed un-American activities."[3]

Jenner—like Commissioners Bull and Pitts—had been president of the Illinois State Bar Association and continued to be extremely active in state and national bar projects. It may well have seemed to Isaacs that representation by this longtime pillar of the organized bar would be particularly helpful before a commission of men with similar backgrounds.

Jenner also was known for his role in the investigation of the assassination of President Kennedy. He served as one of the assistant counsel to the Warren Commission in 1963–64 and was heavily involved in the investigation of Lee Harvey Oswald.[4] In 1968 President Johnson named Jenner to the National Commission on the Causes and Prevention of Violence.

Jenner's prominence, not surprisingly, often led to his name being mentioned as a possible judicial appointee, even for the U.S. Supreme Court.[5] Many Chicago lawyers knew, however, that Jenner's independent nature and eclectic law practice made it unlikely that he ever would be seriously considered by Illinois Republican politicians for elevation to the Court. What many lawyers also knew was that Jenner relished the talk, and the possibility, of his going to the Supreme Court. Thus, it may well have been that as the commission's hearings unfolded in the summer of 1969, Roy Solfisburg was not the only participant actively indulging the dream of ascending to the bench in Washington.

Although he was a Republican, it was not unusual for Jenner and his firm to represent a Democrat, even one as prominent as Theodore Isaacs. As a longtime partner at Jenner & Block later commented, there was no "holiness test" on the political affiliations of clients. Furthermore, Jenner and his colleagues earlier had represented one of Isaacs's law partners in a criminal matter. Their co-counsel in that proceeding was Harry Busch, Isaacs's lawyer in *People v. Isaacs.*[6]

As everyone in the hearings quickly saw, Jenner's imperious manner was fully in gear. He demonstrated it in part through patronizing comments toward other lawyers and witnesses in the case, as well as toward the chairman. He also intermittently unleashed a flurry of objections to Stevens's questions of witnesses. Jenner was well known among practicing lawyers, including Stevens, for his propensity to exploit his expertise by demonstrating that he knew every conceivable objection that could be raised. Jenner may have felt even more comfortable than usual in objecting to Stevens's questions, since Stevens had been an associate at Jenner's law firm for three years. As Stevens recalls their relationship, in 1969 Jenner still viewed him as a "former employee."

At times during the hearing, Jenner addressed Stevens quite condescendingly, in addition to treating Greenberg with disdain. For example, during Stevens's questioning of Nussbaum, Stevens asked the witness to read the dates on certain documents. Jenner objected:

JENNER: Mr. Chairman, you are interested in expediting this proceeding. So am I, and I am interested in not having counsel ask this witness to read from a document already in evidence that speaks for itself.

GREENBERG: Your objection is overruled.

STEVENS: Certainly it is a lot more rapid to do it this way than for me to take and read it for the record, which I have a perfect right to do.

JENNER: Just as rapid as you were yesterday in not marking exhibits, and taking two hours to mark them when you should have marked them before he came in the courtroom.

GREENBERG: I remind you this is not a moot court exercise in the presentation of evidence.

JENNER: I am aware of what this is, and thank you for telling me.

GREENBERG: Let's get on with the hearing.

JENNER: I would ask you to show respect for counsel also, instead of grimacing every time I make an objection, evidencing your prejudice.

As Jenner voiced these and other biting comments, Jenner the expert litigator was certainly aware that Greenberg, the presiding officer, was not a litigator and had very limited trial experience. Greenberg's expertise instead was in transactional and securities aspects of corporate law. It was probably a difficult pill for Jenner to swallow that these important hearings were being run by a lawyer who seemed far less qualified for the role than Jenner himself would have been. Greenberg, in turn, was skeptical of Jenner's lofty reputation. Greenberg's impression was that there were better lawyers at the Jenner & Block firm, and that Jenner himself often got credit for his colleagues' accomplishments.

With these attitudes in play, tension between the two men flared up sporadically during the hearings, even before the "kangaroo court" outburst. Neither of these strong-willed, talented lawyers was about to be intimidated by the other.

Mrs. Kegley and Her List

After Nussbaum left the witness stand and Jenner vented his anger at the commission, Stevens called his next witness for questioning by Torshen. Jayne W. Kegley was now employed as an administrative assistant at a Chicago company, but previously she worked at the Civic Center Bank. Her responsibilities had included a multitude of duties, including issuance of the initial stock. Mrs. Kegley joined the bank before the charter was issued on January 21, 1966. She explained the tasks she performed in the preparation of lists of original subscribers to the bank's stock and issuance of stock certificates. She worked closely then with Harold Stout, the bank's president, and with David X. Meyers, one of the principal organizers of the bank.

Torshen turned to the heart of Kegley's testimony, her knowledge of the distribution of the 12,850 shares first issued in Isaacs's name. She confirmed that her duties included preparation of the handwritten list of recipients of those shares, that various people told her what names to put on the list, and that most of those instructions were given orally. Kegley identified the six people who instructed her to put names on the list: three bank officers, plus Bailey Howard and David X. Meyers—two of the original directors of the bank—and Isaacs, the bank's lawyer. When asked whether Robert Dolph or Robert Perbohner gave her any such instructions, she said they did not.

Torshen turned Kegley's attention to documents related to issuance of some of the 12,850 shares to potential depositors or to bank employees. The documents all showed that Isaacs was actively involved, or at least had been consulted, in the stock issuance. Nonetheless, Kegley's answers suddenly seemed uncertain about the extent of Isaacs's participation. Concerned, Torshen took an important detour:

> TORSHEN: Mrs. Kegley, do you recall appearing for a deposition on July 5, 1969?
>
> KEGLEY: Yes, sir.
>
> TORSHEN: And that was at 208 South La Salle Street?
>
> KEGLEY: Yes, sir.
>
> TORSHEN: And at that time Mr. Manaster was present and I was present?
>
> KEGLEY: Yes, sir.

Torshen knew, as did Stevens and I, that a few weeks earlier Mrs. Kegley had been extremely firm in her recollections of Isaacs's involvement in the distribution of the 12,850 shares. The deposition now was being brought up to refresh her recollection about what she had told us earlier.

On July 3—a busy day on which Stevens and other staff attorneys took the depositions of five major witnesses—I was trying to track down Kegley. Nussbaum and I had realized the importance of her handwritten list. We knew we had to try to find out from her exactly who told her to put the purchasers' names on the list, especially the names of Trust No. 931 and Solfisburg. Just before dinnertime, I spoke with Kegley by phone. After explaining briefly what the investigation was about and how important it was for me to speak with her as soon as possible, she agreed to meet with me at ten o'clock that night, after she and her husband returned home from some evening plans.

At the agreed hour, I met Mr. and Mrs. Kegley at their small apartment on Chicago's North Side. They were friendly and cooperative, and Mrs. Kegley proved to have an astonishingly good memory. She later testified that people had described her as having a "photographic memory."[7] With her husband sitting with us in their living room, we went step by step through the stock distributions on her list. She remembered an avalanche of details about the organization of the bank, the issuance of the stock, and the people involved in all of it. Slowly and carefully—trying not to call attention to the greater significance of some names on the list as compared to others—I asked who had told her to put each name on the list. For almost every entry, she was firm in her recollection of the source. Finally, as midnight approached, I asked who told her to put Trust No. 931 and Roy Solfisburg on the list. Her answer was unhesitating: Ted Isaacs.

A few minutes later, I left the Kegley apartment. As I started to walk to my car a few blocks away, I realized that I now knew something of tremendous importance to the investigation. I suddenly also realized that I was walking alone on a dark city street late at night with information in my notes, and my thoughts, that could be very damaging to some very powerful people. I looked around quickly and scurried to the car.

As soon as I got home, I telephoned Stevens. He had asked me to call him whenever I finished interviewing Kegley, no matter how late it was. When I told him what I had learned, he insisted that I take her deposition as soon as possible. The obvious purpose was to record her sworn testimony in case we needed later to document what she told me. I was acutely aware, although Stevens probably wasn't, that I had never taken anyone's deposition before.

I spoke with Mrs. Kegley and the court reporter on Friday, the Fourth of July, and arranged for the deposition to be taken at my law firm's offices the next morning. Much to my relief, Torshen agreed to be there to help me.

The deposition went exactly as we hoped it would. Kegley covered the same ground with the same certainty she had displayed during our late night meeting. Once more she went through the names on her list and recalled the sources of most of them. In some instances, our confidence in the accuracy of her memory was strengthened further by documents we found at the bank that corroborated details she re-membered.[8] She also testified to a variety of aspects of Isaacs's per-vasive involvement in the distribution of the 12,850 shares. Three different times she firmly identified Isaacs as the source of the instruc-tions to sell seven hundred shares to Solfisburg. Stevens, Torshen, and I were relieved that Mrs. Kegley's pivotal recollections were now em-bodied in a deposition transcript. What we didn't foresee was just how indispensable that transcript would become.

At the hearing, after showing her a few portions of the questions and answers in the deposition, Torshen asked again about Isaacs's role in the issuance of stock. Kegley still vacillated between vague state-ments about the extent of Isaacs's involvement and more definite statements about exactly what he had done. She also made it a point to add, "My working relationship with him was always open and above-board, and I still consider him a very fine gentleman."

Torshen turned back to the third page of the Kegley list and asked: "Can you look at that page and tell us if there are any persons whose names appear on that page whose names were suggested to you by Mr. Isaacs for inclusion on the list of shareholders receiving shares from this block of 12,850 shares?" Her answer was cautious, saying that "there are names on here that were supplied by Mr. Isaacs," but also saying they may have come from him directly, or through his office, or through correspondence, but "I don't recall." When asked to look down the list and tell which of the names were suggested by Isaacs, Kegley focused on the sixth entry—the entry for Trust No. 931 and Solfisburg—and said, "The sixth entry here I thought perhaps came from Mr. Isaacs, but I cannot say definitely that it did." When asked who had instructed her to write Solfisburg's name and address under the entry for the Old Second National Bank of Aurora, she back-pedaled further: "I couldn't verify who exactly gave me the name, but I know that I did not pick it out of the air. Remember, we are talking about something that took place more than three years ago. I say it may have come from Mr. Isaacs, but I couldn't say definitely. I as-sumed that it was from Mr. Isaacs at this point." This was not the same unequivocal Jayne Kegley I had interviewed and deposed. One of our most critical and helpful witnesses was deserting us.

Torshen tried another approach. He began to ask her whether any of the other five bank officers and directors had given her Trust No. 931 and the justice. With continued uncertainty, she seemed to rule out a few people Torshen asked about one by one. Realizing that this process of elimination was not going to produce anything definite, however, Torshen turned back to the deposition and asked the witness to read certain pages. These pages contained the three firm statements Kegley had made identifying Isaacs as the person who told her to put Solfisburg on the list.

After reading the deposition pages, Kegley continued to say that she couldn't be certain and could only assume that Isaacs was the source. She also hedged on whether reading the pages even refreshed her memory about what she previously had said under oath. Finally, as Torshen continued to jog her recollections, Murphy objected to "the obvious attempt to impeach, with a deposition of which we had no notice and which has first been produced here in court, on his own witness."

Ochsenschlager and Murphy were relying on an old common law rule of evidence that prohibited an attorney from contradicting or impeaching the testimony of his own witness. This rule had long been severely criticized by legal scholars and whittled down in many jurisdictions by a variety of exceptions, but it still retained some "perverse vitality."[9] Torshen, Stevens, and I suddenly feared that the Special Commission would never get to hear the damning testimony we had heard from Mrs. Kegley.

Greenberg quickly recognized that Torshen could proceed only under one of the exceptions to the rule,[10] acknowledging "that counsel is attempting to impeach the witness with the deposition" and suggesting to Torshen that he "first apply for leave of the commission to determine the witness as an adverse witness." Torshen made the prescribed request and Greenberg granted it. It seemed we had dodged the bullet, but Jenner, the evidence expert, had not yet spoken. Jenner must have concluded that Greenberg got it right, however, for he did not object.

Torshen read to Kegley the deposition questions and answers in which she had testified to the link between the Solfisburg entry and Isaacs. She had said, among other things, "This name was submitted by Mr. Isaacs, I recall," and, "I know the source of it initially was Mr. Isaacs." After Torshen finished reading the deposition excerpts, she confirmed that these were indeed the questions and answers from July 5.

Torshen then asked Kegley about the list entries just below the one for Trust No. 931 and Solfisburg: the hundred shares in Trust No. 932 for Robert Dolph and his wife, and the two hundred shares for M. R. Davison. She continued to qualify her answers—saying only "it is very probable" and "it may have been"—and thus avoided a firm response to the question of whether Isaacs had given her these two entries and the Solfisburg entry as a group.

At this juncture Torshen again could have confronted the witness with her contradictory testimony in the deposition. Instead he took a different tack, one less likely to make her resistant to the remainder of his questions, as she might have become if she felt that the staff was now hostile toward her. He simply asked her to go through all four pages of her list and to tell what she recalled as the source of each entry. She again went down the list of nearly one hundred names.

For the great majority of names, she unhesitatingly identified the person who told her to put the name on the list. Torshen let her skip over Solfisburg's entry and did not even try to restore her memory on those shares. He didn't have to. By having her go through each name on the list, he made it clear that Kegley could remember, and did remember, almost everything about how the list was compiled. The difficulties she was having about the Solfisburg shares stood out as either a new and inexplicable memory lapse, or as a selective unwillingness to voice what actually was in her memory.

Why had these gaps in Kegley's memory suddenly appeared? Torshen's final questions suggested the answer:

TORSHEN: When was the last time you talked to Mr. Theodore J. Isaacs?

KEGLEY: Last week.

TORSHEN: Was that after the deposition was taken?

KEGLEY: Yes.

TORSHEN: Did you discuss your testimony with Mr. Isaacs?

KEGLEY: No, I did not.

TORSHEN: Did you advise Mr. Isaacs that a deposition had been taken?

KEGLEY: He asked me if I had been contacted. I truthfully told him that I had been. I did not mention that a deposition had been taken.

It seemed that Mrs. Kegley's conversation with Isaacs—whom she had made it a point today to describe as "a very fine gentleman"—had led her to realize that this investigation was a high-stakes affair for him. It certainly seemed that this recent chat had engendered in her a very cautious approach to voicing what was in her extraordinary memory.

At the conclusion of Kegley's direct testimony, Jenner rose unexpectedly to apologize for the comment he earlier had made about the commission—the "kangaroo court" charge. Greenberg magnanimously said, "In the heat of the kind of dialogue that goes on in this kind of hearing, it is an understandable lapse, and you are quite forgiven."

As the afternoon grew late, Murphy briefly cross-examined Kegley. He obtained the witness's confirmation that everyone on her list paid $20 per share, and most of them paid the small interest charge as well. Kegley also stated that she had not been required to clear every entry on the list, from whatever source, with Isaacs. Although this answer implied a smaller role for Isaacs, she volunteered another comment that suggested otherwise: "There were so many, many days that I would talk to Mr. Isaacs on the phone about stock of the bank, about various other things."

Murphy easily obtained Kegley's assurance that "Solfisburg never appeared in the bank during my employment there." She mentioned a phone call from him, in which he asked about the issuance of his stock, but Murphy quickly got her agreement that this was "for his personal concern" and was not legal advice for the bank.

Murphy attempted to test the significance of Kegley's deposition testimony, and the possibility that we had somehow influenced her statements improperly. He asked whether she had been shown anything other than her own list, "to enable you to identify which of the six gentlemen would suggest a customer to be included." To all of his questions along this line, her answer was the same: No other documents had been shown to her. She stated, a bit modestly but surely to Murphy's disappointment, "This was mostly from my memory."

At about 5:45, just before the dinner recess, Greenberg somewhat extravagantly thanked Kegley, telling her, "You have been very lucid and a very good witness, and we thank you for coming." Stevens and the rest of the staff lawyers also were glad she had come, but were equally thankful that Stevens had made me take her deposition. Ruefully, we wished she would have been as unequivocal a witness now as she had been just ten days ago.

Chapter 15

A Justice's Deals

About seven o'clock that night, the Special Commission reconvened for what Chairman Greenberg described as "an unprecedented night session of this unprecedented hearing." Stevens was about to begin the third phase of his presentation, the testimony of interested parties and others commenting on the evidence from the Illinois Supreme Court and the Civic Center Bank.

Stevens examined the first two witnesses of the evening quickly. The first, Lawrence J. Flynn, was an attorney who lived in Aurora and had a law office there but who mainly practiced in Chicago. His Aurora office was in the same building as Solfisburg's, and his Chicago office was in the same building as Isaacs's. Flynn and Solfisburg had known each other for years, mostly as neighbors and golf partners. They also engaged in some business ventures together, including stock ownership in the same companies, and often exchanged ideas about investments that one or the other thought promising.

Both men had been active in the Financial Security Life Insurance Company, serving as directors and shareholders. Flynn performed legal services for the company, but he testified that on a couple of matters the company also retained one of Isaacs's law partners, J. Richard Bockelman. Flynn acknowledged that he had a nodding acquaintance with Isaacs and knew Isaacs was the Civic Center Bank's attorney.

Flynn testified about two aspects of Solfisburg's ownership of CCB stock. First, Solfisburg had offered him half of the stock he was planning to buy in the bank, but Flynn was wary of new bank stock and declined the offer. Second, and more significantly, in May 1967 Solfisburg asked him to assist in the sale of some CCB stock: "He asked me if I would deliver a letter, an envelope, to the bank in which

three hundred shares of stock of the Civic Center Bank was in the envelope, and I told him I would." These were the three hundred shares Solfisburg sold to the three separate buyers, with Isaacs adding his $300 check. Flynn delivered the stocks in Chicago, but not to the bank.
Instead he delivered them to Isaacs's office.

STEVENS: Did you tell him you delivered it to Mr. Isaacs's office?
FLYNN: I don't ever recall telling him anything.
STEVENS: He knew that you and Mr. Isaacs had offices in the same building, didn't he?
FLYNN: Well, I suppose so, but he didn't know I was taking this up to Isaacs's office. He didn't tell me to take it to Isaacs's office.
STEVENS: What did he tell you to do?
FLYNN: When he gave that to me, he told me to take it to the bank.
STEVENS: But you didn't take it to the bank?
FLYNN: I didn't because I got in there at a quarter of nine, and I went upstairs because I probably had to go to court that morning. And I went over to court, and I didn't think a bank president, that he told me to deliver it to, would be in his office at nine or nine fifteen in the morning. I knew they were representing them. So I took it up there and gave it to them and asked them if they would take it over there, and I assumed they took it over.

Stevens also asked about a receipt Flynn said the receptionist in Isaacs's office typed when he delivered the stock.

Torshen had taken Flynn's deposition two weeks earlier, and Stevens knew the deposition contradicted the testimony he had just given. Once again it became necessary to impeach our own witness. After receiving the chairman's approval to examine Flynn as an adverse witness, Stevens read to him the following exchange from the deposition:

TORSHEN: Did you report back to Justice Solfisburg after you had performed this function for him?
FLYNN: He never asked me, and I don't think I ever told him. He just took it for granted that if he asked me to do it, and being in the same building, I would do it.

Jenner objected that this exchange was not impeachment because it is "absolutely consistent with what the witness said." Jenner had missed the key difference between what Flynn was saying today and what he said in the deposition.

Stevens's final question made the point clearer, although Flynn would not be pinned down:

STEVENS: Mr. Flynn, it is a fact, is it not, that the reason Justice Solfisburg "took it for granted" was that he knew that you and Mr. Isaacs had offices in the same building?
FLYNN: I wouldn't know what he took for granted. I am not Mr. Solfisburg. I don't try to read minds.

During his deposition, Flynn had also admitted to delivering another two hundred shares of Solfisburg's stock for sale in 1968, again taking the shares to Isaacs's office.[1]

After minimal cross-examination by Murphy and Jenner, Flynn was excused. A few hours earlier, when Ochsenschlager asked whether the justices could testify soon, Stevens cautioned that the justices "may want to comment on some of the testimony that will be offered first." Now what he meant was becoming clearer. Through Flynn's testimony, Stevens had raised the possibility that when Solfisburg sold CCB stock, he purposely went through Isaacs.

The next witness was M. R. Davison, an officer of the St. Charles National Bank, a few miles north of Aurora. This was the bank from which Solfisburg had borrowed the $14,000 he used to buy his seven hundred shares of CCB stock. Solfisburg also was a director of the St. Charles bank. Although Davison played no part in that loan, he bought two hundred shares for himself at about the same time the justice made his purchase. In fact, Mrs. Kegley's deposition testimony indicated that Solfisburg's seven hundred shares, Davison's two hundred, and the Dolph trust's one hundred probably all came in as a group, submitted by Isaacs.

Stevens's questioning concentrated on Davison's decision to buy the stock. Davison testified that in May 1966, Robert Dolph mentioned that he was buying some stock and thought it would be a good investment. Davison asked if he could buy some too, and "on June 1, Dolph called me and said that he had two hundred shares of stock for me and to send the check for the stock to him." According to Davison, he never talked with Solfisburg about the investment and Dolph did not mention Solfisburg's stock purchase, although Davison later found out about it.

Finally, Davison testified that before he made this investment of over $4,000 in the Civic Center Bank, he made no investigation of the bank, did not know who was associated with it, did no business with it, and had no understanding that he was expected to become a depositor or other type of customer. With that, Davison's appearance ended, and it was time for the main event.

On the Stand

At eight o'clock Chief Justice Roy J. Solfisburg Jr. took the witness stand. A *Chicago Today* report described Solfisburg's "wavy white hair and chiseled face making him look like a judge from Central Casting." After a few preliminary questions, Stevens turned to Solfisburg's familiarity with Financial Security Life Insurance Company, as well as with Isaacs and his law firm. The justice acknowledged that he was one of the incorporators of the company, its first board chairman, and a director from 1960 to 1964. When abruptly asked whether he had ever had dinner with Isaacs, Solfisburg answered, "Not that I recall." This was the kind of answer that would be heard from him with astonishing frequency.

On his relationship with Robert Dolph, the justice's memory was stronger. He recounted that Dolph had been his campaign manager in 1960, they had offices in the same Aurora building, and he frequently dined at Dolph's apartment in Springfield. In his deposition, Solfisburg had commented that he often took his widowed mother with him to Springfield "to get her out of the house." He also said that Dolph always invited his mother over when she was in Springfield, and other justices' depositions confirmed that she was present at Dolph's dinners on occasion.[2]

About 1963 Dolph introduced Solfisburg to his fellow commerce commissioner, Robert Perbohner, and the justice occasionally saw Perbohner at Dolph's apartment and other gatherings elsewhere. The justice also said, "I believe I had dinner with him once in Rockford," but could not recall whether anyone else was present then or even what year the dinner took place.

Stevens probed Solfisburg's purchase of the CCB stock. The justice stated that either Perbohner or Dolph—probably Dolph—recommended the investment to him. Emphasizing repeatedly that his recollection of all this was limited, the justice said he probably first heard of the investment in September or November 1965 in a conversation at Dolph's apartment with both Perbohner and Dolph present:

> Well, they said there was a subscription out for original issue stock for a new bank in Chicago, Civic Center Bank, and they asked me, one or the other of them, I don't know which—generally I think

Dolph did most of the talking but I am not saying Perbohner didn't do any of the talking. Just that there was a new bank, was I interested, did I want to subscribe to some stock in the bank? I said I was interested, and I was asked how much I wanted. And roughly in my mind, I knew it was $20 a share, and I said seven hundred shares.

And again, either Dolph or Perbohner—I don't know which—said he would protect me on it. In other words, I would be counted in. I never did sign a written stock subscription agreement.

Solfisburg said that he made no inquiry about who was associated with the new bank.

Solfisburg also said that he heard nothing further about the bank until late May 1966, when he was told by "either Dolph or Perbohner, most likely Dolph," that it was time to submit his money for the stock. Stevens asked again whether he might have been told this by Perbohner in "the luncheon meeting" in Rockford that May, but the justice insisted, "I don't even remember the year that I had lunch with Perbohner." Ochsenschlager and Jenner objected to Stevens's focus on just Perbohner. Greenberg reminded Stevens that "the witness said it was either Mr. Perbohner or Mr. Dolph," but the chairman added, "I am sure that Justice Solfisburg is quite able to protect himself on that type of question." The justice replied, "I hope so."

Solfisburg explained that on May 27, 1966, he borrowed the $14,000 from the St. Charles National Bank, wrote a personal check for that amount to the Civic Center Bank, and wrote an additional $350 check for the interest. Stevens also asked about steps the justice began to take around that time to take out a loan on his life insurance to be used to repay the St. Charles loan. Before obtaining the loans, Solfisburg made no investigation into whether the CCB stock would be a desirable investment. He explained simply that he had previously owned different bank stocks and knew "just enough to know that I have never seen an original issue of a bank stock go down." He also indicated that he had no clear recollection of talking with Flynn or Davison about investing in CCB stock, although he added that he thought Flynn "just didn't want to split it with me."

Stevens also called the witness's attention to his May 27, 1966, letter transmitting the $14,350. In that letter, Solfisburg specifically asked that the stock certificates for the seven hundred shares be issued in denominations of one hundred shares in his name and sent to his home address. Solfisburg's request for issuance of stock certificates in his own name obviously raised an interesting point. Previous witnesses had already established that the certificates were issued not in his name, but instead to Trust No. 931 at the Old Second National Bank of Aurora.

The trust was created on June 15, 1966, and the only assets it ever contained were the seven hundred CCB shares. Stevens asked the key question:

> STEVENS: For what purpose was that trust created?
>
> SOLFISBURG: Well, I have created a lot of trusts, my father and his partner created many, many trusts. I just decided I wanted to go into a trust, and you note that originally I applied for this personally, my check was personal for the 14,000 and also for the 350. Thereafter I got the loan from the Northwestern Mutual, and I considered life insurance pretty much belonging to my family, and this is one of the reasons I put it in trust, not only for myself but my wife and children.

Although rambling, the answer at first seemed plausible. The justice apparently had created a trust in order to set aside the assets for his family's benefit, since to pay for them he used some of the cash value of the life insurance he maintained for their protection.

Stevens immediately showed that the justice's later actions were flatly inconsistent with this purpose for the trust:

> STEVENS: But, of course, as soon as you sold the stock, you took the proceeds of the sale out of the trust, did you not?
>
> SOLFISBURG: I think it went for their education. I had three of them in college.
>
> STEVENS: But it is a fact, is it not, that the proceeds of sale of the seven hundred shares were withdrawn from the trust promptly after the sales were concluded?
>
> SOLFISBURG: Except $100. I wanted to keep the trust open.

Obviously the justice had not used the trust for the claimed purpose.

Stevens changed the subject, asking the justice whether he was aware when he made his investment that Isaacs had been indicted and that his case was being appealed to the supreme court. The justice went on for at least a minute and a half, acknowledging that "perhaps" he had read about the case in a newspaper, but mostly giving a meandering explanation of the court's practices for the setting of cases and distribution of the agenda for each term. At the end, realizing he had gone astray, he said, "Did I answer the question?" Stevens asked the court reporter to read it back.

While the question was being read back, Solfisburg's discomfort as a witness was suddenly and vividly emphasized. At the beginning of the chief justice's testimony, Greenberg and others pointed out that Solfisburg was speaking too softly to be heard well. Solfisburg explained, "I have a postnasal drip that isn't helping me any." After his faltering attempt to explain the trust and the long, disjointed answer about Isaacs's appeal, Solfisburg tried to pour himself a glass of water from the pitcher at the front of the witness stand, perhaps to ease his throat problem or just to collect himself. According to Stevens, Solfisburg was "so upset because he realized his testimony was flatly inconsistent with what he said earlier" about the trust. The *Daily News'* account of the evening described the chief justice's "increasing irritation" with the "barrage of questions," as he shook "his head of wavy, grey-blonde hair, displayed facial twitches, and attributed repeated coughing to a post-nasal drip."

When Solfisburg leaned forward and started to pour from the pitcher, he suddenly and noisily knocked it over, spilling the water. The water covered the ledge in front of him, dribbled down the marble facade of the witness stand, and may even have gone into his lap. As others scrambled to clean up, Solfisburg looked helpless and bereft: a stark reversal of the picture of confidence the chief justice presented earlier. Solfisburg, suddenly and for the first time, just looked like an ordinary man in a lot of trouble.

Stevens Restrained

After the spill was taken care of, Stevens decided to restate the question. As he did so, there was a change in his tone. In both the aggressiveness of his phrasing for the rest of the evening and in the depth of his probing, Stevens backed off by a perceptible degree.

Stevens softened his questioning of the chief justice in part because, as he later explained, "I thought that I had made the point that his credibility was seriously to be questioned." In part, too, the sad sight the justice had just presented on the witness stand aroused sympathy in Stevens, as it did in many people in the courtroom.

Solfisburg's answer to the rephrased question about his awareness of the *People v. Isaacs* appeal was tentative. He "may have" heard about the case before it came to the supreme court. He stated with more certainty that he previously had known that Isaacs was state director of revenue, and that Isaacs's law partner Bockelman had done work for Financial Security Life. Stevens asked whether Solfisburg knew at the time *Isaacs* was argued, in September 1966, that Isaacs was associated with the Civic Center Bank, and the answer was a firm no. Solfisburg conceded, however, that in December of that year he received, signed, and returned a CCB proxy notice bearing the names of Bockelman and Isaacs. Although he claimed that it "didn't particularly register with me" then that Isaacs was associated with the bank, he also said, "I suppose I am charged with having read it."

Stevens moved on to questions about the justice's sale of his seven hundred shares, beginning with the sale of three hundred in 1967 for $25 per share. In 1968 he sold the rest, in two blocks of two hundred shares at $27 each. Stevens showed Solfisburg a May 23, 1967, letter in which the justice directed the Aurora bank to sell three hundred shares from Trust No. 931, by delivering the shares to Harold Stout at the Civic Center Bank. Solfisburg recalled talking about the sale before then with Stout, the bank president, who told the justice he could get $25 a share.

On another letter about the shares, from the Aurora bank to the Civic Center Bank, an additional typed notation and the justice's signature made clear that on May 25 he personally received the certificates for the three hundred shares, "For Delivery" to the bank in Chicago. Once again, Solfisburg's memory was poor, for he said he did not recall picking up the certificates. Stevens asked Solfisburg why he chose not to have the certificates mailed from one bank to the other, but instead picked them up himself for personal delivery. He had no recollection of his reasoning, saying, "except I have given things to various people to take in or bring out of Chicago for me."

The Commission's Frustrations

As nine o'clock approached, Greenberg interrupted Stevens to say that he wanted to ask several questions and to propose that the commission then resume in the morning. Stevens replied that he had only a very few questions left. Greenberg replied, "I think that there may be further questions on other examination." From the outset of the hearings, Greenberg had been trying harder than anyone to move the proceedings along quickly. Now he seemed to be resisting Stevens's desire to finish with this witness tonight. Both Murphy and Ochsenschlager assured the chairman that they had no questions for Solfisburg, but Greenberg put them off too.

Greenberg was reflecting two frustrations building in the commissioners. The first concerned Solfisburg, as Henry Pitts later recollected: "We all felt Solfisburg was not being truthful, and his explanation of why he suddenly decided to have the stock put in a trust, rather than his own name, was little short of preposterous." The second frustration was Stevens's failure to maintain a more aggressive stance in questioning Solfisburg.

Greenberg began to pepper the chief justice with a series of pointed questions. Greenberg asked him whether Dolph and Perbohner were members of the Illinois Commerce Commission when they undertook to "protect you" for the seven hundred CCB shares, and the justice said they were. Greenberg developed more about the justice's understanding that he would be able to buy the shares later on, but still at the initial subscription price, even though he hadn't signed any subscription agreement. When asked whether he considered that Dolph or Perbohner was doing him a favor, Solfisburg said: "No. As a matter of fact—I guess I shouldn't volunteer—but I wasn't too happy about paying interest." Greenberg asked whether Solfisburg had ever before committed $14,000 to a stock investment with no more investigation into the company than he had made into the Civic Center Bank. Once again, Solfisburg expounded his theory that "whether original issue or not, bank stocks are a good buy."

Greenberg homed in on a few important facts about Trust No. 931. The trust was fully revocable by Solfisburg and had no income tax consequences. Solfisburg had never before created this type of trust for himself. Greenberg then got directly to the point:

GREENBERG: Mr. Justice Solfisburg, let me ask you directly, did you cause the seven hundred shares of stock of the Civic Center Bank to be transferred into the name of Trust No. 931 for the purpose of concealing from the public your ownership of those shares?

SOLFISBURG: No, I did not. Number one, there is this letter. If I intended to create a secret trust, there never would have been that letter from me to the bank. Furthermore, it is my personal check to the bank, and even though the stock was issued in the name of the trust, I am sure the bank records will reflect that it was my check they got.

GREENBERG: Well, Judge, I don't want to seem argumentative about it, but could one put the construction on this that you were not concerned with concealing the ownership of the shares from the bank, but were interested in not having it reflected in the transfer records which were required to be filed in the Recorder's Office?

SOLFISBURG: I don't know about that. The bank records must show that I sent in my check personally. I also wish to state one thing I don't want overlooked, if I may.

The "one thing" was the fact that Solfisburg had indeed listed the CCB stock on his ethics statement, the declaration of financial interests that judges had to file. Greenberg tackled this point, too.

GREENBERG: The ethics statement is not, however, open to the public, is it?

SOLFISBURG: Well, it turned out to be opened. And mind you, that was at my request, and not my objection. It was to make it known.

Greenberg continued, explaining that the charges that the Special Commission had been called on to investigate included charges of impropriety and the appearance of impropriety. He asked Solfisburg if he would like to comment on the suggestion "that causing these shares to be taken in the name of a trust would thus, although not concealing the fact from the bank, remove it from the possibility of public scrutiny in the Recorder's Office" and thus give the transaction an appearance of impropriety.

Solfisburg's response sidestepped the question, and Greenberg's quick rejoinder showed that he knew it:

SOLFISBURG: Well, I am sure every member sitting up here of this commission has drawn a number of trusts, and you have drawn them for a variety of reasons. Hindsight is a wonderful thing, but I would say in any trust you drew like mine, for whatever reason you drew it, the same thing could be said. The only difference is, I am a judge.

GREENBERG: That is a difference.

This exchange ended Greenberg's unexpected series of questions. He then suggested that perhaps it was time to stop for the night. Ochsenschlager and Stevens indicated that they each had very few final questions for the justice, but Greenberg still didn't seem inclined to go on. He asked whether Stevens intended to question Solfisburg about another issue, the assignment of the *Isaacs* opinion. Stevens said he could do that quickly, and Greenberg agreed to let the questioning proceed until 9:30. Stevens asked Solfisburg about the skipping over of Justice House for the writing of the opinion. Solfisburg was unable to explain why the case went to Klingbiel.

The last series of Stevens's questions was different from all that had preceded it. Stevens showed the witness a January 1968 *Chicago Tribune* article and asked whether as a result of reading it Solfisburg had a conversation with Isaacs. Ochsenschlager objected that events in 1968 were too remote to be admissible, but Stevens argued that a conversation then "might be relevant in connection with determining the extent of the relationship between the judge and Mr. Isaacs." Greenberg allowed the question.

In an unusual effort for someone on the witness stand, Solfisburg tried to persuade Stevens not to pursue the question:

> SOLFISBURG: You know what that conversation is, Mr. Stevens. Do you think it has any relevancy to this case?
>
> STEVENS: Judge, I wouldn't ask the question if I didn't think so. I should also like to state for the record that prior to the judge's telling us about this conversation in his deposition, I had no knowledge of it. But he did volunteer it, and I do believe it to be relevant.

The justice explained that, after seeing a newspaper article about Isaacs's retirement from his position as a brigadier general in the Illinois National Guard, he called Isaacs. Solfisburg's oldest son was about to graduate from college, and his draft classification was about to change to 1A, the most vulnerable status for induction into military service.[3] Solfisburg spoke with Isaacs a few times to obtain guidance on how his son could get into the National Guard. After the chief justice explained this interaction, Stevens had no more questions.

The session was not quite over yet, for the commissioners, still frustrated, had more questions. Schuyler and Greenberg asked whether Solfisburg had received anyone's guarantee of an opportunity "to sell those shares at a profit after a period of one year." Solfisburg said no. Vice Chairman Pitts zeroed in on the creation of Trust No. 931, and Solfisburg reiterated his weak linkage between the trust, his life insurance, and his children's school expenses. Greenberg and Pitts continued questioning briefly in an obviously unsuccessful attempt to understand the justice's rationale for the trust.

Greenberg then commented that he and others were getting tired, and he reminded Stevens that he had not yet asked Solfisburg about the charge that the justice was a secret lawyer for the bank. Greenberg asked Solfisburg to return in the morning. The justice, while reiterating his need to get to Springfield by Thursday, reluctantly indicated he would attend. He and Ochsenschlager still tried to get the commission to finish with him tonight, emphasizing that during the deposition there had only been about two questions on the accusation that he was the bank's lawyer.

Greenberg persisted. Citing fatigue, and blaming himself for going this late, he asked Solfisburg to return on Wednesday morning "with the understanding that we will get finished with the justice as quickly as we can after the opening of the hearing."

The Night Goes On

Although the hearing ended at 9:30 P.M., the work of the commission and staff was not over yet. Stevens realized, with some dejection, that he had not done a complete job in questioning Solfisburg. The commissioners definitely believed that Stevens needed to be "more searching in his questions," since "Solfisburg was being less than forthcoming in his responses."[4] The principal reason Greenberg had been so persistent about finding a reason to have Solfisburg return on Wednesday was that the commission wanted Stevens to question him much more intensively.

Perhaps Stevens would do this on his own initiative. Greenberg and Pitts did not leave it up to Stevens's own judgment, however. They talked with Stevens at length that night, expressing their frustrations and identifying some of the specific points they wanted him to pursue more fully. As Torshen recalls the meeting, Greenberg told Stevens, with a dose of irony, "We're not getting our money's worth."

Greenberg was especially concerned that if Stevens went into no greater depth with Solfisburg, the "whitewash" charge would gain renewed strength. It might be said that the commission had let the chief justice testify weakly and inconclusively in the dark of night. The commissioners feared that this session might be portrayed as a cover-up, and they wanted Stevens to do much more with Solfisburg.

In directing Stevens, the commissioners were blurring the normal line between a prosecuting attorney and a judge. Stevens felt uncomfortable about the conversation, thinking, "It was a little unfair to the witness." As he later described it, the commission had given him a second chance of the sort lawyers usually don't get when they have failed to do a good job with a witness. Nonetheless, this was not a normal proceeding, he was not a prosecutor, and the commissioners were not judges. Technically it was only an investigatory hearing, with the staff assigned to assist the commission. Despite the vigorous advocacy of Ochsenschlager and Jenner, it was not even formally an adversarial dispute. If the commissioners wanted more information from the witness, and there was any more to be had, Stevens's responsibility was to try to get it.

Another Morning

On Wednesday, Stevens woke up at 4 A.M. and immediately started getting ready to face the chief justice one last time. In fact, many Chicagoans got up earlier than usual that morning, gathering in front of television sets to watch the blastoff of the Apollo 11 mission to the moon at 8:32 A.M. Stevens was far too busy to watch.

The Special Commission hearings reconvened at 9:30. Stevens immediately resumed questioning Solfisburg. The justice's expectation, on the basis of the discussion at the end of Tuesday night's session, was that he would be mainly, and briefly, asked whether he had been a lawyer for the bank. Solfisburg was visibly surprised, then, when Stevens began probing more deeply into matters that had been touched on the previous night. The justice asked, "Are we going over yesterday's testimony again?" Stevens replied, "To a certain extent we are, Judge."

Stevens starting by asking about the justice's two later sales of his CCB stock. Stevens pinned down the dates of those sales, in March and November 1968, and tried to link them to the justice's talks with Isaacs about getting his son into the National Guard. Stevens, now reverting to more aggressive phrasing, asked: "Now going back to March of 1968, it is correct, is it not, that you might have talked to Mr. Isaacs about the sale of two hundred shares of Civic Center Bank at that time?" When Solfisburg flatly denied this, Stevens turned to the justice's deposition of July 1, "to refresh the judge's recollection." The deposition showed that Solfisburg had then said he indeed might have spoken to Isaacs about the sale in early 1968.

This first series of questions was just the beginning of a string of inquiries Stevens pressed on the justice. In no apparent order, they covered about a dozen different aspects of the transactions the witness had described the night before. In fact, very little new information emerged from this questioning. Instead, what was repeatedly revealed was that there were large gaps in the credibility of the justice's explanations.

Stevens's overnight homework was evident. Over and over, he confronted the justice with contradictions between his testimony and his deposition, and between his testimony and other documents. Recalling the justice's claim that he sold the three hundred shares in 1967 because he needed the money to pay for his children's college expenses,

Stevens relied on Solfisburg's 1967 tax return to show that in the same year he had realized a large amount of money from the sale of his stock in Financial Security Life Insurance Company. The justice admitted that the proceeds of this other sale were "much more than adequate to discharge the obligations" he then faced.

Many other problems with the justice's claims were revealed. For example, although Solfisburg had characterized the $14,000 stock purchase as not an unusually large acquisition for him, Stevens brought out tax returns showing that the justice had many investments, but only two for larger amounts than this. Furthermore, his $14,000 loan was shown to be the largest loan he had taken out for investment purposes since the 1950s. The insurance policy loan he obtained in connection with this transaction was shown to be the first time Solfisburg borrowed money on his life insurance policies for any purpose. Clearly this investment was anything but the run-of-the-mill addition to his portfolio that the justice had tried to portray.

During intensive questioning about the witness's use of Flynn to deliver the CCB shares to Chicago, he testified that use of a courier was his normal practice, but in the deposition he had said the opposite. On Tuesday he had offered the "speculative guess" that he might have picked up the three hundred shares in person from the bank in Aurora because he might be able to sell them there. Wednesday morning he reiterated this possibility with more certainty. In contradiction, Stevens brought out that before the justice retrieved the shares, he claimed to have already spoken with Harold Stout, the CCB president, and reached a firm agreement to sell the shares at $25. Solfisburg denied that the timing of his May 23, 1967, decision to sell three hundred shares had any connection with the end of the *Isaacs* case that week. Nonetheless, his deposition suggested more knowledge of Isaacs's links to the bank than his hearing testimony offered.

On some key points, Solfisburg was firm and consistent. During the deposition, Stevens had showed him the photocopy of Isaacs's $300 check. At that time, the justice and Ochsenschlager registered genuine surprise. Solfisburg insisted then that he knew "nothing about it."[5] In his testimony now, he reiterated, "Until my deposition was taken, I knew nothing about it." Similarly, in both the deposition and the hearing, Solfisburg insisted that he had not known that even before his three hundred shares were delivered for sale on May 26, 1967, the three purchasers for that stock had already been found and had sent in their payments.

As Stevens went through this testing of the justice's statements, Solfisburg occasionally protested. He insisted that he thought Stevens had rested his case the night before and was only supposed to ask to-day about whether he had ever been the bank's attorney. Greenberg set him straight:

> Well, I don't think, Mr. Justice Solfisburg, that is quite correct that Mr. Stevens rested. He had indicated that he was very close to the close of his examination. However, the commissioners had a large number of questions and this morning, I may say, that we instructed Mr. Stevens to continue his examination to cover the questions that we desired to ask, as well as further questions that he apparently still had to ask. And that is why the examination is going on.

Theory and Practice

In one important area of inquiry, Stevens got nowhere, but in the attempt he illuminated a theory about Solfisburg's purchase of the CCB stock. Stevens asked Solfisburg again about when Dolph or Perbohner first mentioned the CCB investment. Solfisburg insisted the conversation was in September or November 1965, but Stevens asked whether it might have been in early May 1966 and brought out the justice's travel vouchers for the May 1966 term. Stevens attempted to link the justice's time in Springfield in early May with a possible luncheon with Perbohner and others in Rockford later that month. Solfisburg, however, consistently was unable to recall the details and timing of his "lunch or dinner" with Perbohner. Try as Stevens might to fit these pieces of the puzzle together in a way that Solfisburg would acknowledge, the justice gave no useful answers.

Stevens's theory posited the following chain of events: Dolph or Perbohner first mentioned the CCB stock to Solfisburg in Springfield in early May 1966 while the *Isaacs* case was pending. On May 26 Solfisburg was told in Rockford by Perbohner and others, perhaps even Isaacs, to get the money in right away for the stock. On May 27 the justice in some haste borrowed the money and sent it to the bank. Soon after that he took steps to borrow on his life insurance to pay off most of the May 27 loan and finance the purchase at a lower interest rate. After first directing the bank in writing to have the stock certificates sent to him, he "reflected on the matter and decided to take the stock in a different way." Although the theory had coherence, and Stevens and his private investigator had fragmentary evidence of a Rockford meeting, Solfisburg said nothing to confirm the scenario.

Toward the end of his examination, Stevens pursued questions that he said the chairman had directed him to pose and that related to the appearance of impropriety. Just as on Tuesday night Greenberg had asked the chief justice to comment on whether his use of the trust gave rise to an appearance of impropriety, Stevens now raised the same inquiry with regard to a variety of other facts. Solfisburg deflected all of these questions by either focusing on just a specific factual detail or pointing out that the commission itself would have to determine the answers, but did offer one broad comment in his own defense: "I will say I wouldn't be here today if I thought I did something wrong."

Before this exploration ended, Greenberg asked Solfisburg whether he thought certain American Bar Association statements on judicial ethics "represent an acceptable guideline for your life as a judge." During a lengthy, inconclusive dialogue between the chairman and the chief justice, Solfisburg emphasized that a practical difficulty would arise from some of the guidelines about appearances of impropriety: "If you want to go to the fact that because four of us [on the court] know Mr. Isaacs, we should disqualify ourselves, there isn't a quorum left. His lower court opinion couldn't have been reversed if we had disqualified ourselves."

In making this last statement, and the statement that he didn't think he had done "something wrong," Solfisburg conveyed two important messages. First, he was unwilling to engage in the awkward exercise Greenberg was inviting him to participate in. The commissioners obviously were curious about Solfisburg's ethical perspectives, and they probably wanted to test out publicly the legal standards they were thinking of applying, including the appearance of impropriety concept. Nonetheless, Solfisburg's resistance to these questions seemed to be a sensible stance, for he really was being asked about the ultimate legal questions under investigation.

Solfisburg's second message clearly was that he did not believe he had done anything wrong. As his lawyer William Murphy later recalled, both Solfisburg and Klingbiel found it startling that anyone would suspect any relationship between their dealings with Isaacs and their ruling in his criminal case. They thought that an illogical and unwarranted link was being made, and that the CCB stock had no influence at all on their decision in the *Isaacs* case. In his deposition some weeks earlier, Solfisburg said, "I think I have been libeled, and I don't like it."[6]

At least in part because of Solfisburg's inability to grasp the precariousness of his situation, he gave little information or strategy suggestions to his attorneys. Murphy recalls that he and Ochsenschlager had trouble convincing both justices that the investigation was serious business.

Earlier in Stevens's questioning of the chief justice on Wednesday morning, a simple question was posed, but Solfisburg had trouble understanding it. "Judge, if you knew during the *Isaacs* litigation what you know today about Mr. Isaacs's association with the Civic Center Bank, would you have participated in the decision of the *Isaacs* case?" After two lengthy, irrelevant replies, Solfisburg finally answered, "Well, I spent a long time saying no." Even in this exchange, which got considerable attention in newspaper reports of the day, Solfisburg did not seem to understand that there was anything questionable about his conduct. One newspaper even quoted a whispered comment made by a lawyer among the spectators after Solfisburg finally answered the question: "He'd reverse a case for answers like that."

Late in the morning, Solfisburg was excused. Despite the fusillade of questions and the array of contradictions exposed, he left the courtroom somewhat battered but seemingly unbowed. Still, the intensity of the questioning was evident and was widely noted in the press reports of Solfisburg's testimony, along with his evasiveness on many points. Jack Mabley, the reporter who first investigated Isaacs, described Stevens's performance of the "vocationally unenviable" task of interrogating the chief justice as "relentless."

Stevens remembers this Wednesday morning session as a very significant episode in the investigation. Henry Pitts goes further, describing it as "one of the defining moments—when the justices and others came to the realization that this was not to be a whitewash."

Chapter 16

The Gift

Toward the end of the Wednesday morning hearing, after Solfisburg's testimony ended, it was time to hear from Klingbiel. Coincidentally, newspapers that day were reporting Klingbiel's resignation as chairman of the Illinois Courts Commission, the ordinary mechanism for investigation of judicial misconduct. Klingbiel had quietly resigned at the end of the previous week, before the Special Commission's hearings began. Although no official explanation was given, it seemed that Klingbiel was clearing the way for possible Courts Commission action after the Special Commission made its report at the end of July.

Klingbiel took the stand for questioning by Stevens. It soon became clear that he was going to be a far more compliant witness than Solfisburg had been. In part this reflected Klingbiel's physical and intellectual weakening in recent years. As his family and many lawyers already knew, by 1969 the justice was slowing down. Furthermore, Klingbiel simply appeared ready to speak without evasion. As one reporter wrote, "Klingbiel's straightforward, terse presentation contrasted sharply to Justice Solfisburg's rambling responses."[1]

After establishing the justice's tenure on the Illinois Supreme Court since 1953, Stevens explored Klingbiel's relationships with Dolph, Perbohner, and Isaacs. Klingbiel acknowledged a close friendship with Dolph, going back about ten years and including vacation trips they and their families had taken together. Klingbiel identified himself as one of the justices who frequently dined at Dolph's apartment in Springfield. He noted, in passing, that although Justice Schaefer was often invited, he never accepted Dolph's invitations. Dolph also occasionally sent Klingbiel small gifts, such as specialty foods at Christmas, and Klingbiel usually sent thank-you notes.

Stevens suggested that Klingbiel had only a casual acquaintanceship with Perbohner, but Klingbiel volunteered that it was more than
that. In this answer, as in many others, Klingbiel seemed fully candid,
even when he easily could have shaded his responses to minimize incriminating implications. Klingbiel went on to note that, like the other
justices, he too received the little watchband calendars each year from
Perbohner, and sent thank-you letters for these as well.

Klingbiel was emphatic that he barely knew Isaacs, having only
been introduced to him in passing early in the 1960s "in Springfield at
some affair" for government officials. Nonetheless, Klingbiel readily
admitted that even before *People v. Isaacs* was argued in September
1966, the justice knew Isaacs had been indicted.

Stevens turned to the main subject, Klingbiel's receipt of the hundred shares of CCB stock registered in Perbohner's name on October
11, 1966. These already had been shown to be the last one hundred
shares out of the large block controlled by Isaacs, and it had been
proven that Isaacs, not Perbohner, paid for them. Stevens asked the justice how the certificate in Perbohner's name came into his possession.

Klingbiel explained what happened on an evening in Springfield
during the November 1966 term, shortly after he had been retained by
the voters in his district for ten more years in office:

> It was at one of the dinners that Bob Dolph had invited me to
> along with, I know, one or other members of our court, because I
> never went over alone. After the dinner, if I recall, Bob called me
> into, I believe, the bedroom and said, "Ray, as you recall sometime
> ago during the summer or early fall I told you that Bob Perbohner
> and I wanted to make a contribution to your campaign fund."
>
> And he said, "We didn't get around to doing that as I indicated I
> would, and now that your election is over, I would like to give you
> this certificate of stock for one hundred shares of this Civic Center
> Bank."
>
> Well, first of all I think I inquired, I said, "What is it worth?" He
> said, "Well, it has sold for $20 a share." And I said, "Oh goodness, I
> don't think I spent that much money on my campaign."
>
> "Well," he said, "I don't care." He said, "If you want to sell it and
> recoup what you have spent, all right. If you just wish to keep it, do
> that." He said, "I think the stock is going to increase in value. It
> looks like it is a good going bank." It was then handed to me, and I
> put it in my pocket.

Klingbiel stated that Perbohner was probably also there when
Dolph gave him the stock. He confirmed that the election was already

over, that even before the election he had collected about $6,500 in contributions, and that he only spent about $2,000 on the whole campaign.

When the stock was given to him in Dolph's bedroom, Klingbiel made no inquiry about the bank and who was associated with it. Klingbiel testified that he had never heard of the Civic Center Bank before this occasion, and no one made any reference to the *Isaacs* litigation at the time. The case, of course, had been argued two months earlier and was still going through the court's decision-making process.

The stock certificate Klingbiel received was endorsed in blank, for Perbohner had already signed it and Dolph had signed as a witness, but no transferee's name was inserted. In this form, the certificate was fully negotiable. When asked whether Solfisburg was present at this dinner at Dolph's, Klingbiel replied, "I can't say positively." After Stevens refreshed Klingbiel's recollection by reference to his deposition answers, Klingbiel agreed that Solfisburg probably was there, although in the living room and not as part of the discussion in the bedroom.

The testimony next turned to what Klingbiel did with the stock. One thing he did not do was send Dolph or Perbohner a thank-you note of any sort. In the deposition he had explained that he simply took the stock certificate home, probably told only his wife about it, and put it in the top drawer of his bedroom dresser.[2] He did nothing with it until January 2, 1968, when he wrote that date on it as the date of the transfer from Perbohner. He still did not fill in the name of a transferee. Klingbiel explained: "I had determined that I would give that stock to either my daughter or to her children, and I think the [January 2, 1968] date on there indicates that that possibly was the time that I had determined that, and the reason for that is that just two days prior thereto I had deeded property to my son as a gift." His idea was to equalize the gifts he was giving to his daughter and her family with those he was giving to his son.

The transfer to his grandchildren was not completed until September 5, 1968, when the certificate in Perbohner's name was canceled and a new certificate was issued in the grandchildren's names, in care of the justice. Why the delay? Klingbiel explained more:

> Well, for a long time after I deeded this, I kept thinking sometime I
> would go in and deliver it and have it transferred, and apparently I
> just put it off, or just didn't get around to doing it. So I think the lat-
> ter part of August I decided to do it, and I came into Chicago and I
> had lunch with George Bieber, whom I had known for a number of

years. And it was getting late, and I asked him if he would take care
of it for me.

Stevens had taken the deposition of Bieber, a Chicago criminal lawyer,
a few weeks earlier. Bieber's description of his friendship with Klingbiel and of his delivery of the stock at Klingbiel's request coincided
with Klingbiel's. Bieber also stated that his visit to the bank to deliver
Klingbiel's envelope to the appropriate transfer agent was the first
time he was ever there. When asked whether he knew Isaacs, Bieber
replied, "I don't know the man from a bale of hay."[3]

Stevens turned to more recent events, asking Klingbiel about a telephone call the justice received in early May from a *New York Times* reporter after Skolnick had expressed his suspicions about Klingbiel to
the reporter.

> KLINGBIEL: Well, he said, "It has come to our attention that you
> own stock in the Civic Center Bank in Chicago." And I think he
> made inquiry where I got it and so forth. That is about all I can
> remember.
> STEVENS: Judge, didn't you tell him that you purchased the
> stock?
> KLINGBIEL: I did.
> STEVENS: And, of course, that was not an accurate statement, is
> that correct?
> KLINGBIEL: That's correct.

Stevens then asked about a conversation later in May with another reporter, one from the *Daily Calumet,* who called the justice in Springfield:

> STEVENS: Do you recall saying to him that you had purchased
> the stock?
> KLINGBIEL: I think so.
> STEVENS: And again that was not an accurate statement.
> KLINGBIEL: That's correct.

Klingbiel also acknowledged a third deceptive conversation about the
stock, this time with another member of the supreme court:

> KLINGBIEL: I talked with Judge Kluczynski during the May
> term. I think just casually I mentioned that I had received calls
> with reference to acquiring this stock, and that I told the persons
> that called that I had purchased it.

STEVENS: Did you tell Justice Kluczynski that that had not been an accurate statement?

KLINGBIEL: I did not.

STEVENS: So would it be a fair inference that Justice Kluczynski would have drawn the conclusion that you had purchased the stock?

KLINGBIEL: I would think so, yes.

Klingbiel's candor and lack of resistance as a witness were evident by this point, especially to Stevens and the commissioners who had read his deposition. During the deposition, Klingbiel had explained these three conversations but insisted that at least he had a reason for lying to the reporters:

STEVENS: Was there any particular reason why you made reference to purchase of the stock?

KLINGBIEL: Nothing except that I felt it was my business whether I bought it or it was given to me.[4]

Now, on the witness stand, Klingbiel didn't even try to present this excuse.

Klingbiel's concern about the reporters' calls also led him into two other conversations before he left in late May on his vacation to Morocco and Spain. One of these was with Chief Justice Solfisburg, who earlier had also testified about this conversation. In their discussion, Klingbiel confirmed his ownership of CCB stock, and Solfisburg replied that he formerly had also owned the stock but already had sold it. About that time, Klingbiel also called Perbohner and asked to see him. According to Klingbiel:

I then told him about these telephone calls, and that there was some insinuation that this stock had come from Isaacs and that he had only been a conduit for it from Isaacs to me and, of course, he denied it.

He said, "Why Ray, that isn't so. I bought that stock." And he said, "I wanted to give it to you for campaign purposes." And he says, "I don't know why I haven't any right to do that."

Stevens asked a few more questions, emphasizing Perbohner's statement that he had purchased the stock. Prior testimony of Nussbaum and Kegley, of course, already had shown that Isaacs paid for the stock. Stevens's last question was whether Dolph, Perbohner, or anyone else ever suggested "that Justice Solfisburg had in turn suggested to those gentlemen that you be given this stock." Klingbiel's reply: "Never."

After a lunch break, Stevens tried to obtain the witness's recollections about what he said to Charles Nicodemus and Ed Pound when they each called him in early June. Although Klingbiel's memory was very confused, he conceded that in his first conversation with Nicodemus he described his acquisition of the stock as a purchase, but in the second as a campaign contribution.

Chairman Greenberg then posed some questions, focusing on the fact that "the Illinois Commerce Commission is very often a litigant before your court." Dolph and Perbohner were members of the ICC when they gave the stock to the justice. In fact, the *Daily News* had quoted Perbohner in its very first story on the stock as saying, "In my position, one needs to have an 'in' with the Court." Klingbiel agreed that the ICC was frequently before the court, and Greenberg mentioned that the staff had found that three cases involving the ICC "were pending before your court at the time you received the gift of stock from Mr. Perbohner." Klingbiel did not remember the cases.

Greenberg covered the same judicial ethics material that he had discussed with Solfisburg. Quoting various standards relating to a judge's responsibility to be free from impropriety and the appearance of impropriety and to avoid gifts or favors from litigants, he asked whether the justice accepted the standards. Klingbiel emphatically responded that he did. He did not avoid answering, as Solfisburg had, but still it appeared, as it had for the chief justice, that he did not perceive that he had violated ethical standards in any way.

Ochsenschlager's cross-examination was brief. With respect to the suspicious inconsistency between Klingbiel's customary thank-you notes for small gifts from Dolph and Perbohner and the absence of a thank-you for the larger stock gift, Ochsenschlager brought out that none of the small gifts had been personally delivered. In contrast, the stock was handed to the justice, and he expressed his appreciation on the spot.

With regard to the status of the ICC in cases before the court, Klingbiel stated, "I never considered them litigants at all. I thought they were in the nature of judges or quasi judges." He analogized the ICC to a court whose decisions were being reviewed by the supreme court. Greenberg followed up on this, getting Klingbiel to agree that, even under this analogy, ICC members still might be quite interested in not having their decisions reversed by a reviewing court.

As Klingbiel's testimony drew to a close, Commissioner Edwin Austin initiated an unusual dialogue. Austin said:

> There is a good deal of suspicion in the air that surrounds this case, and it is directed in part at you and some of the judges, and in part at this commission. You are suspected of failing to avoid the appearance of impropriety, and our commission is suspected of accepting appointment merely with a view to whitewashing the court and its members.

According to Austin, one theory behind suspicion of the Special Commission was that "the judges in effect are sitting in judgment on themselves." Klingbiel, of course, rejected that notion, adding, "As to that whitewashing, I just don't understand that at all. It just strikes me as being nonsense, like a lot of other matters I have heard from the petitioner in this case."

Austin asked Klingbiel about another theory, the view that attorneys could not form an unbiased judgment for fear of having to argue cases before the court after having criticized it. Klingbiel's response largely missed the point. First he doubted that "any member [of this commission] would be fearful of incurring the wrath of the supreme court." Then he emphasized that few cases reach the court anyhow and offered other tangential comments. What he didn't offer was any assurance that the court respected the Special Commission and its function, and thus would have no inclination to retaliate in any way against a commissioner, which was probably the kind of statement Austin was seeking.

Austin's last question was a reprise of the question Stevens put to Solfisburg earlier in the day. If Klingbiel had known in 1966 what he knew now, would he have disqualified himself from the *Isaacs* case? Klingbiel answered unequivocally: "Had I known that there was any information that Isaacs was connected in any way with the passing of the stock to me, I sure would have."

After a few more questions from Ochsenschlager and Schuyler, Greenberg asked the justice if there was anything else he would like to say. Klingbiel's response was poignant: "This is a very sad affair for me, as you can well realize, at sixty-eight years of age, having the esteem of all my many, many friends at home and elsewhere in the state."

As Justice Klingbiel's testimony ended, he looked like "a man out of tune with the events whirling around him," but plainly he was suffering over the harm to his reputation.[5]

The Sixth Justice

Thomas E. Kluczynski was the sixth and last justice to testify in the hearings, as well as the sixth and last of the justices to participate in the decision of *People v. Isaacs*. The January 1967 term was the first he attended. In that term, Justice Underwood's opinion was rejected and Klingbiel received the reassignment. When Klingbiel submitted his opinion in March, Kluczynski joined with him, Solfisburg, and House to make up the majority that quashed all counts against Isaacs.

Under questioning by Torshen, Kluczynski reviewed his many years of service as a trial and appellate judge in Cook County before coming to the supreme court. Torshen then asked a series of questions producing confirmation that neither Kluczynski nor any of his relatives had any interest in the Civic Center Bank. These questions were being asked in great detail in response to Skolnick's complaint on the first day of the hearings that the justices were not being asked fully enough about their interests in the bank.

Torshen next took Kluczynski on a detour, but one the justice wanted. He asked Kluczynski whether he owned stock in another bank that had not been mentioned in the hearings, not even in Skolnick's motion. Torshen asked the commission's indulgence "for a few questions which might not be wholly relevant," and then proceeded:

TORSHEN: A charge has been made that you own stock in the Archer National Bank.

KLUCZYNSKI: It is not true.

A few more questions established that neither the justice nor his family had any present interests at all in Archer.

The detour was a response to more recent accusations by Skolnick. As earlier noted, during Skolnick's strange deposition on July 10, with the press in attendance, Skolnick had vaguely implicated Kluczynski in more alleged chicanery with Isaacs.[6] Skolnick had claimed that this "third judge" was part of "the fixing of the Isaacs case" and was financially entangled with Isaacs through the Archer Bank.

By asking the justice about this other bank, Torshen was allowing him to use this public forum to clear his name. On Saturday, July 12— two days after Skolnick's deposition and two days before the hearings were to begin—Stevens received a telephone call from Kluczynski's attorney, calling from the justice's home in suburban Wilmette. The most remarkable thing about this call was the identity of the justice's attorney. It was John Joseph Sullivan, Greenberg's predecessor as head of the Chicago Bar Association. Joe Sullivan was the man— along with then Illinois State Bar president Alfred Kirkland—whom the Illinois Supreme Court first had intended to lead the Special Commission.[7]

Sullivan was calling to express his client's distress at the newspaper publicity about Skolnick's accusation of Kluczynski's involvement with Isaacs and this other bank. The justice and his lawyer wanted Stevens to investigate the matter and clear Kluczynski. Stevens agreed to send Torshen out to Wilmette to discuss the problem later that afternoon.

At the Kluczynski home, Torshen heard their plea and suggested a solution. He told the justice that he could offer him an opportunity to set the record straight during his testimony in the hearings. Kluczynski's surprised response essentially was, "What testimony?" Although his deposition had been taken by Torshen on July 3, apparently the justice had not realized that he would be called to repeat his testimony in public.

After Torshen clarified that the testimony was needed, Kluczynski agreed to the offer. They also decided to hold an impromptu rehearsal. Then and there—late on Saturday afternoon in the justice's home—Torshen questioned him as he had done earlier in the deposition, but now emphasizing the portions of his testimony that would be revisited on the witness stand. On a most important point, a problem suddenly appeared. In Klingbiel's deposition, he had recounted the conversation with Kluczynski in late May concerning the telephone calls Klingbiel had received from the *New York Times* and *Daily Calumet*. In Kluczynski's deposition three days later, Torshen also asked him about the conversation:

TORSHEN: Did Justice Klingbiel at that time tell you how he obtained the stock?

KLUCZYNSKI: My recollection was that he said he bought it.[8]

If Kluczynski was right about this statement, it appeared that Klingbiel had lied to a fellow justice.

When Torshen reached this question during the rehearsal at Kluczynski's home, the justice's answer was much more equivocal about what he had heard from Klingbiel. Torshen mentioned that if the justice described the conversation with Klingbiel differently on the stand from what he said in the deposition, it might be necessary to impeach his testimony. Torshen went home that afternoon uncertain about what the justice would say.

In the hearing, Torshen first clarified that the justice had never had any business dealings with Isaacs. Torshen then got into Kluczynski's conversation with Klingbiel and specifically into the key question:

TORSHEN: Did Justice Klingbiel tell you how he acquired the stock?

KLUCZYNSKI: He said he bought it.

A few minutes later, Ochsenschlager probed this answer on cross-examination. Kluczynski conceded that he wasn't entirely certain about whether Klingbiel told him directly that he bought the stock, or instead told him that he had told the *New York Times* reporter that he bought it. Ochsenschlager seemed to be shaking Kluczynski's recollection, suggesting that "now you are uncertain as to just how [the statement] developed." Kluczynski agreed, although he phrased his answer oddly for a judge, especially one now testifying under oath: "I can't swear to it."

Ochsenschlager took his questioning a step further, but it backfired:

> OCHSENSCHLAGER: But you did learn that he had told the *New York Times* reporter that he had purchased the stock?
>
> KLUCZYNSKI: I couldn't swear to it, except I know this: that the impression was that he bought the stock.

Kluczynski had stayed on course, and his statement dovetailed perfectly with Klingbiel's earlier testimony. Joe Sullivan, Kluczynski's lawyer, later told Torshen that there had been a lot of outside pressure on Kluczynski to weaken his testimony, but the justice had stood up to it.

The last portion of Kluczynski's testimony concerned the court's decision-making process in the *Isaacs* case. Nothing new emerged from the questioning by Commissioners Austin, Greenberg, and Pitts, but Kluczynski did explain one of the justices' little-known practices. In contrast with procedure in the U.S. Supreme Court—where the absence of a majority of votes for resolving a case affirms the lower court's decision—the Illinois Supreme Court, Kluczynski explained, "hold[s] the tie until a judge changes his vote and there is a decision." The lawyers, the press, and the public were still getting an unusual education in the inner workings of the state's highest court.

The Perbohner Puzzle

Two principal witnesses remained this afternoon, one in person and the other in absentia. The first was J. Richard Bockelman, Isaacs's law partner. Both Solfisburg and his friend Lawrence Flynn had already testified that Bockelman did legal work for Financial Security Life Insurance, the company Solfisburg helped to create and direct. Bockelman's brief testimony was mostly a description of the legal projects he had undertaken for Financial Security. Bockelman also testified to his belief that Solfisburg was aware during this period that Bockelman and the Isaacs firm were doing work for Financial Security.

Stevens's next live witness would have been Robert Perbohner, but he wasn't there. Instead Stevens wanted to have Perbohner's deposition read aloud.[9] Robert Hanley, Jenner's partner, objected both on technical grounds and more emphatically because "this deposition has no probative value." He called attention to the uncertainty surrounding Perbohner's medical condition at the time and said the deposition showed "an inability to handle these questions." Greenberg replied that the commissioners were sophisticated enough to judge the deposition's probative value. After some further haggling, Greenberg ruled that the deposition could be read.

The reading was complicated by the large cast of characters in the Wisconsin episode. Each of Stevens's staff lawyers was assigned a role to read. I heard Torshen announce, "Mr. Manaster will read those portions of the deposition in which the record was made by Mrs. Perbohner or the nurse." Rubbing salt in this small wound, Greenberg asked, "Who is acting the part of the females?" Torshen reiterated, "Mr. Manaster," and the courtroom erupted in laughter.

The reading proceeded for quite a while without interruption. Occasionally it provoked more laughter, resulting from the poor casting, the confusion among the assembled participants at the hospital, and the strangeness of the deposition statements themselves. The commissioners and the audience now heard Perbohner's baffling, fragmentary, and even self-contradictory statements about his involvement with the bank, the justices, and the newspaper investigators who telephoned him in early June.

When the reading ended, Greenberg announced a ten-minute recess, commenting, "I don't think this is ever going to take the place of *Bonanza,* or Shakespeare for that matter. Time out for a commercial." After the recess, Greenberg stated that the commission did indeed have some problem about the probative value of the deposition, as well as specific concerns about certain questions. He invited the lawyers for the interested parties to move to strike the deposition, which they then did, and he set up a schedule for written briefs to be filed on the motions over the next few days.

After some discussion, Greenberg allowed the depositions of Dr. Farrington, Dr. Ashe, and Mrs. Steigberg to be read aloud as well. After the readings, the Special Commission adjourned until Monday.

Chapter 17

Intermission and Jail

The Special Commission's four-day break from hearings was not an opportunity for Stevens to relax. He needed to prepare for next week's witnesses, and he and I took two more depositions of Civic Center Bank officers. Stevens also directed some intriguing work by the staff's private investigator, Ed Power.

Stevens sent Power out to Aurora with a subpoena to try to find the typewriter used to prepare the documents and correspondence involved in Solfisburg's sale of the three hundred shares of CCB stock in May 1967. Stevens's hunch was that a typewriter in Aurora, either at the Old Second National Bank or at Solfisburg's office, had been used in preparation of the documents, including the receipt that Lawrence Flynn claimed was typed in Isaacs's office. If that theory was correct and the typewriter could be found, it would prove that Solfisburg had intended for the shares to be delivered to Isaacs's office, and not to the Civic Center Bank as the justice and his friend Flynn had claimed.

Power served the subpoena at the Aurora bank to obtain access to typewriters there. Ochsenschlager was outraged that he was not given advance notice of the subpoena. In retrospect, Stevens thinks Ochsenschlager's anger may have been justified, and that "maybe we were too aggressive" in the handling of this aspect of the investigation. In any event, despite scrambling around the town quite a bit, Power never found the typewriter.

Three Problem Witnesses

When Stevens took Sherman Skolnick's deposition a week earlier, Skolnick claimed to have informants with important information, but he refused to identify them. By the end of the deposition, Stevens had declared his intention to get a court order requiring Skolnick to provide this information, but Skolnick remained defiant, proclaiming that even if sent to prison, he would not name his "sensitive witnesses."[1]

Over the first three days of the hearings, Skolnick still refused to cooperate with the Special Commission. During a morning recess on Wednesday, Chairman Greenberg called an impromptu press conference in which, as the newspapers described it, he blasted Skolnick in a scathing attack. He described Skolnick's deposition testimony as "evasive, secretive, and sometimes just plain contemptuous." Greenberg complained, "I can't turn on the radio without being treated to some variation of Mr. Skolnick's charges that this is a whitewash commission." Greenberg insisted, "I have no ambition to compete with Mr. Skolnick, but I'm tired of the steady obbligato being played [by him] outside in the corridors." Greenberg invited the news media to "join with the commission in asking that Mr. Skolnick 'put up or shut up.'"

Greenberg's denunciation of Skolnick coincided with the delivery to Skolnick of a notice to appear again before Judge Healy in circuit court the following day. As Stevens had promised, the staff was going to request a court order to compel him to answer the deposition questions.

Skolnick was not the only disobedient witness about to be brought to Judge Healy's attention. Stevens also filed a petition to compel further answers from Doris Steigberg, Perbohner's secretary. In her deposition at the end of the previous week, she stated that Perbohner told her he wanted to help Isaacs at the time of his indictment, but when Stevens pressed for more information, she clammed up.

A court order was being sought against Howard Hansen, too. A former Chicago police officer, Hansen had become the chief security officer of the state Department of Revenue, a position he obtained when Isaacs ran the department. Hansen's name first surfaced in the hearings when James Nussbaum described bank records showing that six hundred shares of stock issued in Hansen's name were actually bought by Joseph E. Knight, the state official who issued the bank's charter. Stevens had zeroed in on the Hansen-Knight holdings as another example of the issuance of CCB stock with Isaacs's involvement and in a manner that hid the real owner's identity.

In his deposition on July 9, Hansen confirmed a friendship with Perbohner going back to the 1930s. He also described a complex chain of events in which Perbohner supposedly gave Hansen $2,100 in cash early in 1965 to be used to help Isaacs with his legal fees in *People v.*

Isaacs. Isaacs had told a similar story in his deposition on July 3. Additionally, Hansen provided details of his acquisition of the six hundred shares of stock. Although he said he did not know who paid for them, he acknowledged that within ten days of receiving the certificates, he endorsed them in blank and gave them to Knight.

During the deposition, when Stevens asked Hansen whether he had recently spoken to Isaacs and told him the deposition was going to be taken, Hansen refused to answer on the advice of his attorney. Stevens tried without success to persuade the lawyer of the relevance of the questions, and then said he would seek a court order to require Hansen to answer.

Both Hansen and Steigberg seemed to possess valuable inside information about the dealings in CCB stock and about possible efforts by Isaacs, Perbohner, and others to prevent the full facts from being revealed. Skolnick, on the other hand, was harder to gauge. It was virtually impossible to predict whether he really had any solid evidence, but Stevens felt obligated to find out.

On Friday, staff lawyers Torshen and Sack, accompanied by lawyers for Steigberg and Hansen, appeared before Judge Healy. Steigberg's lawyer announced that an agreement had been reached with Stevens for her deposition to resume. Hansen's lawyer stated that his client was fishing in Wisconsin or Canada and might be difficult to locate, but would appear for his deposition as soon as possible.

Showdown with Skolnick

In contrast with these small steps forward, the effort to overcome Skolnick's recalcitrance did not go well at all. On Thursday morning he appeared in Judge Healy's courtroom with a large audience in attendance, and with Torshen and Sack there for the Special Commission. Once again, Skolnick moved for a change of venue, repeating his charge of close ties among Cook County judges, the "Chicago Crime Cartel," and the Civic Center Bank. Healy denied the motion.

Torshen summarized Skolnick's refusal to answer certain questions at the deposition a week earlier, and the judge told Skolnick that the issue now was whether those questions were pertinent to the investigation, "and if they are pertinent, then I will order you to go back there and answer them." Skolnick asserted that while observing the commission's hearings, "I saw and heard, with my own eyes and ears, them torpedo the testimony of two key witnesses." He said the staff "bollixed up the testimony" of Kegley and Flynn, and said he would not allow this to happen "with the witnesses that we have gotten by our own methods." He claimed that he was cooperating with eleven other state and federal agencies investigating "the supreme court matter," and would make "our witnesses available to these other groups, but they will not be made available for the whitewash commission." Skolnick insisted that the Special Commission was unconstitutional and that, therefore, he would not comply with any order to answer the commission's questions.

Hearing this, Judge Healy declared Skolnick in contempt of court and sentenced him to four months in the county jail. The judge indicated that if Skolnick decided to answer the questions, Healy might entertain a motion to vacate the contempt order. Skolnick responded that he was going to send a telegram to the U.S. Department of Justice regarding this deprivation of his federal constitutional rights.

Judge Healy set Skolnick's bond at $1,000. Only $100 was actually needed to secure the bond, but Skolnick said he did not have that much money with him. The judge indicated that he would be available to release Skolnick from the custody order that afternoon if Skolnick posted the bond. Still defiant, Skolnick shook his finger at the judge and insisted that he should be let out on his own recognizance. When the judge responded that even lawyers in contempt of court were not let out on recognizance, Skolnick, ever disdainful of the legal profession, didn't skip a beat: "Don't put me in the same category with the Bar Association."

The judge allowed Skolnick to remain free until early afternoon, to give him time to get the bond money. At 1:30 P.M. Skolnick returned to court and told Healy: "I'm not going to make bond. I have asked the United States Department of Justice to investigate you and Chief Justice Roy J. Solfisburg Jr., since I accuse both of you of conspiring to put me in prison." The judge, observing that "there is nothing else for me to do if you want to be a martyr," directed the bailiffs to take Skolnick to the county jail.

The Citizen in Jail

Skolnick was taken into custody and held in a small cell in the Civic Center lockup for transfer to the county jail. The citizen whose suspicions had given rise to the entire investigation, and whom many people regarded as a brave little David challenging the Goliath of the Illinois judiciary, was in jail. The New York Times summed up this shocking development: "The first person punished as a result of the investigation was the man who started it."

Stevens viewed the newspaper photos of Skolnick behind bars as "the most unsympathetic thing in the world, in his wheelchair and all. We were blasted in the press because we were picking on the guy who started it all." Clearly the staff could not have planned worse publicity, and it almost appeared "as if we were trying to sabotage everything" the commission had accomplished so far.

Skolnick, in contrast, seemed to be enjoying himself. For about an hour and a half, he sat in the lockup cell, where he was interviewed and photographed by reporters. Next he was lifted in his wheelchair from the Civic Center loading dock into a paddy wagon to take him to the jail at 26th Street and California Avenue. At the county jail, as Skolnick recalls the day, the warden said that he and the sheriff were prepared to let Skolnick wait in a nearby restaurant until bail money arrived. Skolnick, however, insisted on being held in the jail in the normal fashion.

Around 6:30 P.M. a friend put up the $100 bail and Skolnick was released. The friend was Dick Gregory, a prominent civil rights activist and leader of some of the protests during the previous summer's Democratic Convention. Gregory and Skolnick had been friendly for a few years, having worked together on electoral reapportionment lawsuits. Gregory had attended portions of the commission's hearings earlier in the week.

According to newspaper reports, Gregory convinced Skolnick that he was "more useful to the public on the outside than in jail." Gregory did not want to see Skolnick "rotting in jail," and Gregory thought Skolnick's continued presence at the hearings was important "to keep things straight." According to Skolnick's later account, there also was a bit of theater involved with the bail money. Despite having told the judge he didn't have the $100, Skolnick says he actually did have the money with him and later simply gave it to Gregory to post on his behalf: "I wanted to give him the honor." When a reporter asked Gregory where he got the $100, the former comedian tossed off a line: "I borrowed it from the Civic Center Bank." Skolnick's final flourish for the day was his appearance on a popular late-night television show, with fingerprint ink still on his hands, to recount his few hours of martyrdom.

Amidst Stevens's embarrassment and Skolnick's enjoyment, Torshen was contacted by two other men who were deeply distressed about these events:

> Immediately after court adjourned, Judge Healy telephoned me and said I had to do something to get him off the hook. Skolnick had

insulted the court. However, Healy did not want to be responsible
for jailing someone in Skolnick's physical condition. I told Healy I
would do what I could.

Almost immediately thereafter, I received a call from Skolnick's
father, who said that it would be terrible if his son had to go to jail.
He said that physically Sherman probably couldn't do this.

Torshen told Skolnick's father that he would try to find a way to avoid
having Skolnick serve the contempt sentence. Torshen soon met with
Judge Healy, who said that an apology from Skolnick would put an
end to it.[2]

Torshen reported this back to the Skolnicks, but Sherman was not
yet ready for apologies to anyone. Quite to the contrary, he had telephoned the U.S. Attorney's Office in Chicago right after Healy issued
the contempt citation. Skolnick spoke with the head of the criminal division there and demanded a federal investigation of the alleged judicial conspiracy to violate his constitutional rights. Even as he left the
county jail, Skolnick vowed that he would "never reveal the names of
my witnesses no matter how long they keep me in jail."

Coming into Focus

Skolnick's brief incarceration continued to fuel newspaper interest in
the investigation. The publicity Skolnick was getting, however, was
becoming less favorable. Newspaper reporters and columnists who at
first applauded his courage and tenacity were becoming skeptical of
his motives and critical of his actions. In the Thursday edition of
Chicago Today, Jack Mabley described Skolnick as "the plain citizen"
who found the evidence "that led to the *Alton Telegraph*'s disclosure
of the bank stock" owned by Solfisburg and Klingbiel. Mabley's column was written before the contempt citation against Skolnick, and
Mabley was simply giving fair credit to Skolnick for what he had accomplished. Mabley artfully acknowledged Skolnick's abrasiveness,
noting that he "is not a lovable person, at least to the legal profession."

An editorial in Friday's *Chicago Today* painted a much harsher
view of Skolnick's behavior. It described his tactics as "absurdly and
tragically self-defeating, virtually forcing the court to punish him."
The paper urged him to cooperate fully, by giving the investigators all
the evidence of wrongdoing he could produce and challenging them to
try to cover it up. Finally, the editorial emphasized that, even though it
would be incorrect, the conclusion that would be drawn elsewhere in
the country is that "anyone who dares stand up for the public against
finagling by the powerful can expect to be penalized for it." Casting

blame equally on Skolnick and the Special Commission, the paper lamented that "both sides now seem more interested in discrediting each other than in establishing the facts about Klingbiel and Solfisburg."

A few days later, another *Chicago Today* reporter wrote a bitter commentary on Skolnick. Don Sullivan—in a piece entitled "Mourn the Loss of Sherman Skolnick!"—condemned the gadfly's destruction of his own credibility:

> This city—any big city—needs a little guy with brains and guts and the courage to expose the big special-interest boys and the Establishment phonies and the too-frequent high officials who use their power to fill their pockets. But Skolnick is dead, and he did it to himself. With his irrational, abrasive, unwise, and contemptuous behavior, he eliminated himself from serious consideration by any reasonable person.

Other, similar newspaper commentaries also struggled to bring Skolnick into focus and joined in Greenberg's call for the citizen to "put up or shut up."

Of greater importance than the newspapers' reactions to Skolnick were their diverse reactions to the evidence coming out at the hearings. At one end of the spectrum was a mild commentary in the *Aurora Beacon-News* praising the talent of the attorneys in the hearings. Similarly, the *New York Times'* account of the hearings merely emphasized that in its investigation of the appearance of impropriety by the justices, the Special Commission "is developing plenty of material to work with."

At the other extreme was a surprisingly blunt editorial in *Chicago Today* on Thursday, headed "Klingbiel Should Resign." This piece focused on Klingbiel's admissions concerning both the campaign gift of stock he received after the 1966 election and his lies to reporters about the stock. The newspaper stated:

> These admissions not only discredit Klingbiel as a man of impartiality and integrity. Thru [*sic*] him they cast doubt on the impartiality of the state Supreme Court. And that is something Illinois cannot afford. . . .
>
> A justice whose integrity and impartiality have been shown to be less than complete has no business on the Illinois Supreme Court. Justice Klingbiel should recognize that fact, and act on it.

With this, the first public call for a justice's resignation, the potential impact of the investigation suddenly seemed greater than ever.

The Stature of Greenberg

As reporters, lawyers, judges, and others digested the first week's hearings, another participant also came into sharper focus. Frank Greenberg suddenly began to get a great deal of publicity, most of it complimentary.

Greenberg was a native Chicagoan, fifty-eight years old, and the son of Russian immigrants. He worked his way through the University of Chicago, earning his law degree there in 1932. He then joined the law firm where he stayed for his entire career. By 1969 the firm, with about a dozen lawyers, was named Peebles, Greenberg, Keele, Lunn & Ford, and he had a thriving tax and corporate law practice there. He had long been active in Chicago Bar Association activities, serving on numerous committees over the years and becoming its president just as the Special Commission was being created.

A newspaper profile of Greenberg, published after the first days of hearings, was entitled "Hearings Boss Emerges as Man to Watch." A similar article by Charles Nicodemus in the *Daily News* was headed "Greenberg Lays Down Law to Illinois Justices." It referred to the portion of Solfisburg's testimony during which Greenberg read aloud various ethical standards and asked Solfisburg whether he accepted them as guides to his conduct. Nicodemus noted, "Frank Greenberg sounded almost like a judge passing sentence." The article also reflected growing recognition that the original skepticism about the commission was misplaced: "The Special Commission of five prominent attorneys, that is investigating the very court that appointed it, is 'for real.'"

Greenberg was a man of considerable self-confidence and pride in his talents and his eloquence. He had a deep and resonant voice, and at times he seemed to enjoy the sound of it to a great degree. A colleague noted that he was "often stern and forbidding in his insistence on excellence,"[3] and some in the Chicago bar thought him arrogant.

The flattering newspaper commentaries, and the increasingly favorable talk among lawyers about the job Greenberg was doing, appealed to his ego. Some people even were saying that he seemed eminently suited to be a supreme court justice himself. Greenberg was not displeased by the notion.

The investigation "officially was known as the Special Commission of the Supreme Court of Illinois, but most lawyers and the news media called it the Greenberg Commission."[4] Greenberg surely liked that name, and the spotlight he was in. He was ready to serve as "the guardian of the profession against breaches of faith by every other lawyer"[5]—and by judges, too.

Chapter 18

After the Landing

The weekend was historic, beginning with the drowning on Friday night of a young woman in Senator Edward Kennedy's car at Chappaquidick. Sunday night saw the landing of American astronauts on the moon. President Nixon declared Monday "a national day of participation" in honor of the event, and most government offices in Chicago were closed for the day. The Illinois courts were in session, however, and so was the Special Commission. Greenberg reconvened the hearings at 9:30 that morning.

Somewhat to the surprise of the lawyers and audience, he solemnly took note of the moon landing and declared: "I ask you to rise and observe a moment of silence in affirmation of the common hope, in which we all share, that our astronauts will be safely returned to Earth, and that their courage and the fantastic technological development they have so dramatically climaxed will be turned to the service of mankind." Everyone at the hearing rose for a moment of silence. This brief transformation of the courtroom from a legal proceeding to something like a religious assembly felt inspiring to some, but awkward for others.

When everyone was seated, the work of the commission went on, and the elevated mood was soon gone. Ochsenschlager asked whether the commission intended to rule on the pending motions to strike the Perbohner deposition, which had been read aloud at the last session. Greenberg proceeded to explain the rulings.

The commission rejected Isaacs's objections about technical violations of certain court rules on advance notice of different types of depositions. On the bigger question of whether Perbohner, when questioned in the Wisconsin hospital, had the ability "to observe, to recollect, and to communicate," the commission saw "some obvious problems with the weight to be given to the testimony." Nonetheless, the commission would allow the deposition into evidence "for what it is worth and will accord it such weight as the commission may deem proper in the circumstances." The commission upheld the justices' motion to strike from Perbohner's deposition all of the questions and answers pertaining to his telephone conversations with the *Daily News* in early June.

Ochsenschlager then asked that he and Jenner be given advance notice of any depositions yet to be taken by Stevens, but this request was denied. Greenberg emphasized again that, despite the trappings of the courtroom and the appearance of an adversary proceeding, this was still an investigation and thus not covered by procedural rules applicable to trials. He stressed that the Special Commission would base its findings and report on the "testimony when everybody is present."

Solfisburg and Financial Security

Before getting to the main witness of the day, Stevens briefly presented another witness, Emil R. Christofferson, a former executive vice president of Financial Security Life Insurance Company, the business that Solfisburg helped to organize in the early 1960s. Stevens presented this testimony principally to show that Solfisburg had been actively involved in Financial Security and was fully aware of which law firms the company used, including Theodore Isaacs's firm. Stevens wanted to prove that Solfisburg and Isaacs were far better known to each other before *People v. Isaacs* than Solfisburg had indicated in his testimony.

Stevens first tried to question Christofferson about statements in the minutes of a Financial Security stockholders meeting in March 1964, two months before Christofferson joined the company. The statements strongly suggested that Solfisburg was heavily involved in the company's operations, including its selection of outside law firms. Because Christofferson had not attended the meeting, however, and could not vouch for the authenticity of the document, Stevens was unable to persuade Greenberg that a foundation had been proven for the admissibility of the minutes into evidence.

Stevens was frustrated by Greenberg's ruling but was still determined to get the minutes before the commission. Stevens boldly asked permission to recall Solfisburg. Stevens apparently was prepared to insist that the chief justice of the Illinois Supreme Court be required to return to Chicago and the witness stand simply to prove that the minutes of the shareholder meeting really were what they appeared to be. Once again, it was made apparent that Stevens was taking this search for the facts very seriously. The sound of whitewashing was nowhere to be heard.

Pragmatically, Stevens also mentioned that Ochsenschlager might want to stipulate to the authenticity of the minutes. Greenberg agreed to Stevens's request to have the chief justice recalled as a witness if no stipulation were reached. Ochsenschlager obviously realized that Stevens was not bluffing and that only a stipulation would save Solfisburg from a trip back to the witness stand. Ochsenschlager said he needed time to study the minutes, and the status of the document was left unresolved.

Greenberg's adverse ruling on the minutes prevented Stevens from exploring Solfisburg's specific knowledge of the Isaacs firm. Nonetheless, Christofferson's brief testimony still painted a picture of Solfisburg's extensive involvement in the company on a variety of occasions.

The Banker

Stevens's principal witness on Monday was Harold H. Stout, president of the Civic Center Bank. Having held that position since the bank was organized in late 1965, presumably he knew a lot about the stock transactions and Isaacs's roles in the bank. After reviewing Stout's many years of experience as a banker, Stevens turned to the loan from the First National Bank and the block of 12,850 shares issued to Isaacs and put up as collateral for that loan. Stout confirmed that the stock was to be reserved for people interested in the bank other than just as investors, and who could help it to obtain new business.

Stevens showed Stout letters indicating that some people who wanted to buy stock were falsely informed that none was available because all the stock was subscribed and paid for by January 21, 1966. Stout acknowledged that people who could not help the bank's business were disregarded. Not just anybody could buy the bank's stock, and the 12,850 shares were distributed selectively.

Stevens asked Stout about the Kegley list and whether he had participated in its preparation. Surprisingly, Stout answered, "Until you subpoenaed our records, I didn't know that it was in existence." Stevens asked how Trust No. 931 and Solfisburg got on the list, and Stout had nothing to offer: "Who saw to it that that name got on there, I have no knowledge. I never heard of him until this case developed."

This statement was of tremendous importance. Solfisburg had claimed that he spoke with Stout in May 1967, before he sold his first three hundred shares of CCB stock, and that Stout had quoted the price of $25 per share then. Now Stout was saying he had never heard of him until this case developed in June 1969.

Stout also testified that he knew of nothing Solfisburg had done to foster new accounts or other business for the bank. Although Stout had just said he didn't know which of the bank's initial organizers had put Solfisburg's name on the list, he did confirm that none of the 12,850 shares could be sold without Isaacs's signature because the shares were all issued in his name.

Stevens returned to the theory that just before Solfisburg bought his seven hundred shares in late May 1966, he met in Rockford with Perbohner, Isaacs, and others, including Stout.[1] On May 10 of that year, Stout wrote a letter to Mark Waggoner, a director of the bank who lived in Rockford. Among other things, the letter said that Stout, Isaacs, and another bank officer planned to be in Rockford on May 26. Stout wrote that he would phone Waggoner "next week to determine if it is all right for us to stop and see you at that time" to discuss the bank's loan policies.

As Stevens described it, Stout's letter implied that Stout and the others already were planning on going to Rockford for some purpose other than to talk to Mr. Waggoner. Stout's daily calendar also contained notations of a meeting with Waggoner and Isaacs on May 24 to discuss the bank's loan policy. There was another similar calendar entry for two days later, May 26, mentioning "Rockford, Ted, loan policy." When asked about this evidence, Stout's memory was fuzzy. Despite the letter, he acknowledged no possible purpose for a Rockford trip other than to talk to Waggoner and insisted that he never went to Rockford on bank matters. Once again, as in the questioning of Solfisburg, the suspicion that there had been a Rockford meeting right before Solfisburg bought his shares was not borne out.

Stevens turned to another, seemingly innocuous aspect of Stout's letter to Waggoner. Early in the letter, Stout wrote, "Bob Perbohner said you sounded very cheerful on the phone when he last talked to you the other day."

> STEVENS: Directing your attention to the second sentence of the letter, do you have any recollection, having read that sentence, of any discussions with Mr. Robert Perbohner?
>
> STOUT: I don't know Mr. Perbohner.

These answers were not a surprise to Stevens, for in our first conversation with Stout the day we began our work at the bank, Stout told us that he had never even heard of Perbohner before the newspaper stories mentioned him.[2] Stevens asked Stout how he "happened to make a reference to Bob Perbohner in that letter." Stout said, "I don't know."

This was strange. Stout's letter seemed to be based on a previously planned meeting in Rockford with someone other than Waggoner, but Stout had nothing to say about such a plan. The letter also referred to a conversation with Perbohner, but Stout didn't know Perbohner and couldn't account for that reference, either. With these mysteries unexplained, Stevens ended his direct examination.

Questions from Everyone

Before cross-examination began, Greenberg asked a few questions. In fact, before Stout was through on the witness stand, all five of the commissioners would question him, the first time this had happened with a witness. The commissioners generally took the view that since Greenberg was acting as a kind of presiding judge, the other commissioners' questions should either go through him or be given in advance to Stevens for him to ask. By this stage in the hearings, however, and in view of Stout's key role at the bank, the commissioners were ready to question actively.

Greenberg probed Isaacs's role at the bank, noting that Isaacs had a personal interest in it as an organizer. Stout enthusiastically agreed that Isaacs was "an important man" in the bank: "Oh, yes. No question about it. That's right." This aggrandizing statement about Isaacs probably was the kind of thing the amiable Stout often said about Isaacs and other major figures in the bank. It probably was the kind of statement Isaacs ordinarily liked to hear too, but in the midst of this investigation, anything that highlighted or magnified Isaacs's status at the Civic Center Bank surely was not what he wanted anyone to hear.

Before giving Ochsenschlager the go-ahead for cross-examination, Greenberg asked Stevens whether he planned to ask Stout "about certain communications made to him or to the bank by Mr. Justice Solfisburg in connection with the sale of Mr. Solfisburg's shares." Obviously the commissioners were interested in the glaring contradiction between Solfisburg and Stout about when they first had any dealings with each other. Stevens crisply replied that Stout earlier stated that he never heard of Mr. Justice Solfisburg until this matter arose.

Stevens believed that Stout's statement was damning enough on its own. As an experienced trial lawyer, Stevens saw no need to run the risk that, under further questioning, Stout might soften his firm statement that he never heard of Solfisburg until 1969. Commissioner Mason Bull, however, did what Stevens was disinclined to do and revisited the issue:

> BULL: Did you have any conversation by telephone or otherwise with Justice Solfisburg about a sale of the stock?
>
> STOUT: I heard him testify that he called me on, I think, two or three occasions. I do remember that name as of last fall when he called about two hundred shares. The name I remember, but prior to that I do not remember; no, sir.

Stout now was saying he first learned of Solfisburg earlier, in the fall of 1968. Despite this change, the critical contradiction between Stout's testimony and Solfisburg's remained, for the justice had tried to put Stout in a pivotal role in the May 1967 transactions.

Perhaps inspired by the realization that Stout obviously was not going to bat for Solfisburg, Greenberg jumped in on another point. He asked Stout, as an expert in banking, "Is it true that all stock in new banks goes up?" That theory, of course, was Solfisburg's explanation for putting $14,000 into Civic Center Bank stock with no advance investigation. Stout answered that he would not buy stock in a new bank unless he had made some investigation into the bank's location, organizers, and directors. He thus matter-of-factly discredited Solfisburg's investment theory.

Ochsenschlager had few questions for Stout, most of them just touching on themes he had emphasized with earlier witnesses. He obtained Stout's agreement that in Solfisburg's stock purchase he got no better treatment than everyone else on the Kegley list. Additionally, Stout confirmed that Solfisburg was never a lawyer for the bank.

Daniel Schuyler then asked who decided on the distribution of the 12,850 shares. Stout described the informal committee of bank organizers, directors, and officers, more or less as other witnesses such as Kegley had done. Asked whether Isaacs was the one who permitted Solfisburg to buy his shares, Stout had no recollection. When Schuyler asked whether it was possible that Isaacs did so, Stout said, "He could have, I presume."

Henry Pitts came back to Stout's knowledge of Solfisburg: "When did you first hear of Judge Solfisburg?" Stout answered again as he had when Bull inquired: the fall of 1968. Ochsenschlager tried to undercut this testimony by referring to correspondence and documents relating to Solfisburg's first sale of CCB stock in May 1967. He quickly got into difficulty, however, for he could not find the exhibits he needed. With the lunch hour approaching and Ochsenschlager needing some time to review exhibits, the midday recess was called.

When Ochsenschlager resumed questioning after lunch, he seemed to have given up the effort to prove that Stout knew of Solfisburg in 1967. Instead he focused on details of the original clearance loan and the 12,850 shares. Stout's answers clarified that Isaacs had signed blank stock transfer forms to enable the bank to issue stock to new purchasers. This information undercut Stevens's earlier implication that Isaacs constantly held the reins on issuance of those shares.

Next it was Jenner's turn. His questions focused heavily on the role of his client, Isaacs, in the formation and operation of the bank. Stout pointed out that Isaacs's function was purely that of an attorney for the bank, and that Isaacs had little prior knowledge about banking. Stout noted that Isaacs briefly held the position of acting cashier before the Civic Center Bank received its charter, but Stout emphasized that this assignment was just a technicality and involved no real banking duties. Isaacs's other bank position, secretary of the board, imposed on him merely the duty to record the proceedings of board meetings. Jenner's themes appeared to be that the bank was organized and run in a thoroughly ordinary fashion, and Isaacs performed only the limited functions that a lawyer for a new bank would ordinarily perform. Stout also said: "The distribution of stock in this bank was very unusual in that the organizers were trying to accomplish as broad a base as possible, rather than to allow a large block of stock to fall in anyone's hands."

No one commented on the irony of the "broad a base as possible" notion, which plainly contradicted what Stout earlier said about rejecting potential buyers who couldn't help the bank's business. Stout went on to explain that directors were limited to fifteen hundred shares each, and other people were limited to a thousand. Although Stout did not say it, and Jenner surely did not intend to highlight it, this testimony implicitly emphasized that Solfisburg's seven hundred shares were an unusually large purchase, especially for someone who, as Stout already had noted, was not doing any other business with the bank.

As Jenner and Stout plodded through details of the bank's organization and the issuance of its stock, no major point was being made, but a lot of time was being consumed. As Jenner quizzed Stout about details of a shareholders meeting, Stevens tried to speed things up by suggesting, "in the interest of expedition," that Jenner "confine the examination to matters not shown by the minutes" of the meeting. Shortly after that, Greenberg said: "Mr. Jenner, I don't want to be misunderstood by you, and I don't want to inhibit your questions at all. The commission is haunted by the specter of midnight, July 31, 1969, and anything that you can do to help expedite the matter on things that are not terribly important, we would be very grateful." Jenner said he would do his best.

The mild phrasing of both Greenberg's statement and Jenner's reply stood in sharp contrast to the combativeness of their earlier exchanges. The change in tone was probably the result of a variety of factors: Greenberg now was more at home in his presiding role; he and the other commissioners knew the tide had turned favorable in the press's evaluations of their work; Jenner was resolved to avoid another embarrassing moment like his "kangaroo court" outburst; and Jenner probably was beginning to realize that the evidence against the justices and Isaacs was mounting and he had little to offer in rebuttal.

Another half an hour or so of testimony about the bank produced hardly any significant information. Stout was asked about Jayne Kegley, whom he described as "a fine person, very efficient, almost a little bit too much after a while." He reported that Kegley had been fired from the bank because of a tendency to "sort of take over" work from others inappropriately. The last straw leading to her dismissal was her refusal to wear the required uniform for women employees at the bank. Jenner asked, "Did she undertake to do things on her own?" Stout replied, "Yes, this was her basic problem." Apparently seeing an opening to undermine the Kegley list, Jenner established that Stout had never instructed her to prepare the list, but Stout also said, "Someone must have told her, but it wasn't me." Finally, but delicately, Greenberg told Jenner that his questioning seemed to be getting very close to being too extensive. Jenner soon ended his cross-examination.

Stevens's redirect examination mostly just tied up loose ends. On a couple of points, however, he took an aggressive, even argumentative, stance. When Jenner had asked Stout whether Isaacs took an active role in the allocation of stock, Stout had replied, "Not to my knowledge." Stevens, however, pointed Stout to a series of Stout's diary entries between February and May 1966 that clearly indicated that Stout had met with Isaacs "re: stock."

Stevens also took on Ochsenschlager's theme that Solfisburg got no "better treatment" than other stock purchasers. Stevens seemed particularly angered by that refrain. Stevens's questions now directly contrasted the chief justice's treatment with the treatment received by people who were falsely told there was no stock available, people who were only allowed to buy fifty or a hundred shares even though they wanted more, and people who were not allowed to buy and sell their

stock directly through the bank but instead were referred to brokerage firms where commissions and fees had to be paid. Stevens's dan-
der was up. It was clear to him that Solfisburg had gotten exceptionally
good treatment from the bank, and no witness had yet offered a good
explanation for it.

After a few questions from Greenberg, Ochsenschlager forged
ahead to show that Solfisburg paid more interest than he should have
when he bought his seven hundred shares. The difference was only
about $80, so Stevens still had made his point. Ochsenschlager seemed
to be grasping at straws.

Mason Bull posed the final questions for Stout. He began by stating
his recollection that Stout had said that he was not acquainted with
Robert Perbohner. Calling Stout's attention to his May 10, 1966, letter
to Mark Waggoner in Rockford, Bull finally got part of the explanation for the letter's statement that "Bob Perbohner" had said Waggoner sounded cheerful on the phone:

> BULL: To whom did Bob Perbohner say that?
>
> STOUT: I had some help apparently from somebody within the
> organization who knew of this letter being written, that added
> that with the thought that it might be helpful to Mark Waggoner.
>
> BULL: What do you mean it would be helpful?
>
> STOUT: He suggested that I put that in there.
>
> BULL: And who was that?
>
> STOUT: I'm not certain.

The witness explained that an effort was under way to persuade Waggoner to stay on the bank's board of directors, despite ill health. Bull
pressed ahead to the conclusion of the jovial bank president's testimony:

> BULL: Although you did not know Mr. Perbohner, you were re-
> ferring to him as "Bob"?
>
> STOUT: Yes. I still don't know him.
>
> BULL: Are you still referring to him as "Bob"?
>
> STOUT: That's good public relations. Yes, sir.

Night and Day Witnesses

The last two witnesses on Monday were a study in contrasts. The first,
Joseph E. Knight, was a man in his late fifties, a wily veteran Democratic politician now weakened by poor health. He had seen it all in the

rough world of Illinois politics and appeared to be no longer surprised by anything. The second witness was Ed Pound, the twenty-five-year-old reporter from the *Alton Evening Telegraph* who broke the Klingbiel story. Energetic, naive, and a bit hotheaded, Pound was very different from the world-weary, cynical, imperturbable Knight.

Before the questioning of Knight began, William Murphy questioned what relevance his testimony might have to the two justices and the integrity of the *Isaacs* judgment. Stevens explained that Knight was expected to testify about Isaacs's activities at the Civic Center Bank. Greenberg allowed Knight to be heard, and Jerome Torshen began the questioning.

It was quickly established that Knight had served as the state's Director of Financial Institutions under Governor Kerner from 1961 until early 1968. In that position, he supervised about seven thousand state-chartered banks, savings and loans, and other institutions, and he signed the Civic Center Bank's charter. Knight said that he had known Isaacs since 1960 and also knew that Isaacs was a figure in the organization of the bank, but not a predominant one. In February 1968 Knight was elected to the bank's board of directors.

On the witness stand, Knight seemed the most relaxed, unflappable witness the Special Commission had heard. When Torshen asked him about the clearance loan from the First National Bank, he said he knew nothing about it. Torshen pressed him on this, and Knight blithely said, "You can probe for an hour, and I still don't know anything about it."

Torshen asked whether Knight had ever acquired CCB stock, and he answered that his mother had done so. He said, "She is a woman of means and asked me to get her some of it. So we ordered six hundred shares. I paid for it off of her account." Torshen asked from whom he ordered the stock, and Knight answered, "I presume somebody in the bank. Four years having elapsed, my memory fails me." He said the stock was held in "a street name, Howard Hansen," because his mother had "an estate problem in the future" and "didn't want it in her name at the time."

Torshen inquired about the use of Hansen, the elusive Department of Revenue employee who had refused to answer deposition questions about recent conversations with Isaacs. Stevens was still trying to complete that deposition.

TORSHEN: Who asked Mr. Hansen to hold the stock in his name?
KNIGHT: I don't know.
TORSHEN: Did you ever make inquiry?

KNIGHT: No. He delivered the stock to me, and I have known him. He is a man of good reputation. My mother had all the certificates. He kept nothing.

TORSHEN: Did he have any position in the state government at that time?

KNIGHT: I think he did.

TORSHEN: In what department?

KNIGHT: Department of Revenue, I think.

TORSHEN: Who was the director of revenue at that time?

KNIGHT: Mr. Isaacs.

Knight was wrong, of course, in believing that Isaacs still was in state government in mid-1966 when this stock was purchased, but clearly Knight knew of Hansen's connection to Isaacs.

What Knight didn't know, or so he said, was whom he dealt with in ordering the six hundred shares and who called on Hansen to serve as owner of record of the shares and to deliver them to Knight fully endorsed and negotiable. Knight said he didn't even question the name of the nominee: "The certificate was there. If it was in Al Capone's name, it still was a good certificate."

Torshen asked Knight about a conversation the witness had on Friday, July 18—just three days earlier—with Ed Pound of the Alton paper. Torshen posed hard questions, and Knight tried to dodge them:

TORSHEN: Do you further recall in that conversation, Mr. Knight, stating to Mr. Pound that for purposes of acquisition of the stock you went to Theodore Isaacs because Theodore Isaacs was handling the disposition of the stock?

KNIGHT: I don't recall saying that. But my mother got on the phone and told Mr. Pound that it was her stock, . . . she's going to keep it.

TORSHEN: Do you recall during the course of that conversation, Mr. Knight, your telling Mr. Pound that you presumed that Theodore Isaacs asked Mr. Hansen to act as the nominee for that stock?

KNIGHT: I may have said that. I don't know who did. I'm honest. I don't know.

Greenberg interrupted to tell the witness that it was the chairman's "responsibility to suggest to you that obviously counsel is going to call Mr. Pound to testify to these conversations which took place last Friday." Knight simply said, "Well, that's all right."

After establishing that Knight had known Perbohner for many years, and that he presumed Isaacs knew him also, Torshen asked about the incident in August 1966 when one of the CCB stock certificates in his home was accidentally destroyed. Nussbaum had testified about this early on, and correspondence was in evidence showing Isaacs's heavy involvement in the efforts to replace the lost certificate.[3] Asked about those efforts now, Knight would only say he talked to Hansen about it but disavowed any knowledge of Isaacs's participation.

There was no cross-examination of Knight, only a few questions from Greenberg and Schuyler. Schuyler, not only a practicing lawyer but also a Northwestern University law professor and a nationally prominent expert in the law of future interests, asked about the "future estate problem" that Knight said motivated his mother to acquire the stock in someone else's name. Specifically, Schuyler asked how the registration of the stock in Mr. Hansen's name would avoid an estate problem. After some fumbling, Knight simply said, "We thought there was at the time an advantage," but he couldn't say what it was.

This ended Knight's testimony. A week earlier, when Nussbaum first described the Knight-Hansen stock, Stevens had emphasized that this was one of "a few transactions for large blocks of stock which are not documented." Obviously Solfisburg's purchase was another.

Stevens also then had called attention to the "form of this transaction," involving a certificate "endorsed in blank in the name of a nominee with someone else paying for it, a situation which will be paralleled in later evidence." It was now clear that the parallel situation was Klingbiel's stock, issued in Perbohner's name with Isaacs paying for it. There also were other parallels with the Klingbiel situation, although Stevens did not mention them yet. In both instances the person in whose name the stock was issued was a close associate of Isaacs, and in both instances the person who received the stock was a high state official whose goodwill would be of interest to Isaacs. In 1966 Knight was the Director of Financial Institutions with power over the new bank. Although Knight claimed the stock was his mother's, he also told the *Chicago Sun-Times* that the stock was purchased in Hansen's name "because I didn't think it would look right for me to own stock in a bank I was supervising." Klingbiel, of course, was a justice of the supreme court, in the midst of deciding *People v. Isaacs*.

At about five o'clock, Ed Pound took the witness stand. He had never before testified in a legal proceeding, and he was nervous. Torshen began to ask him about the telephone conversation with Knight, but Jenner and Ochsenschlager objected that the answers would be hearsay. Torshen stated that the purpose of Pound's testimony was to impeach Knight's statements, and a lengthy colloquy developed among the three lawyers and Greenberg. Pound sat and anxiously listened, waiting to tell more about his call to Knight.

Unfortunately, Pound misunderstood something Ochsenschlager said, and the young reporter reacted in a manner that immediately got him in hot water with the commission and compounded his own bad case of nerves. Ochsenschlager, referring to Stevens's calling of Knight as a witness, said, "He called him for the purpose of setting up for impeachment." Pound mistakenly thought Ochsenschlager was talking about the purpose of Pound's own telephone call to Knight and was casting aspersions on him. Pound interrupted and angrily took umbrage:

POUND: That's a lie, sir. And I don't appreciate that. That's a lie. That is, sir. Now, look, I have agreed to testify, but that's baloney.

GREENBERG: You are out of order.

JENNER: May that be stricken?

GREENBERG: You will strike that.

POUND: I don't like it if he's going to assume things.

GREENBERG: Mr. Pound!

POUND: I'm sorry, sir.

Greenberg ruled that Pound's testimony could be received "only for the purpose of impeaching the testimony of Mr. Knight."

Torshen attempted to have Pound recount what was said in the conversation on July 18 with Knight. Pound repeatedly fell into characterizing and summarizing what was said, rather than stating his best recollection of exactly what was said. After repeated objections by Jenner, Pound finally explained the phone call in the proper manner.

Pound said that Knight described the six hundred shares as belonging to his mother. More importantly, Pound quoted Knight as saying that he had gone to Isaacs to get the shares, and that he knew Isaacs was disposing of the CCB stock connected to the clearance loan. Although it was not mentioned at this time, Knight had also told other newspaper reporters that he acquired the stock through Isaacs. With regard to the question of how Hansen's name got on the stock certificates, Pound testified that Knight said he didn't know but presumed that Isaacs had placed the name on them. The thrust of Pound's testimony was clear: Knight had gone to Isaacs for the six hundred shares, and Isaacs had picked Hansen as the nominee and courier.

There was one other important area of questioning for Pound. Before he put together his breaking story in early June, he made a series of phone calls to Isaacs, Perbohner, and Klingbiel.[4] Stevens wanted to get these calls, and others made by the *Daily News,* into evidence before the commission, but he already had run into trouble. The commission had ruled earlier in the day that the portions of Perbohner's deposition denying conversations with the *Daily News* could not go into evidence. Stevens and Torshen expected that Jenner and Ochsenschlager would try again to prevent Pound, or any other newsmen, from testifying to these conversations, but the staff lawyers had a plan.

Torshen asked Pound about his telephone call to Klingbiel in Spain on June 9. Ochsenschlager objected: "Unless this is for the purpose of impeaching Justice Klingbiel, I certainly want to object to it." Ochsenschlager noted that Klingbiel already had admitted falsely telling reporters that he had purchased the stock, so there was no dispute on that point and no need for this testimony. Greenberg ruled that the evidence could come in for the purpose of impeachment and also as an "extrajudicial admission by an interested party." Greenberg noted, to Jenner's satisfaction, that hearsay statements that were out-of-court admissions of facts by Klingbiel would only be binding on him, but not on any other interested party.

At that point, Stevens made the move he and Torshen had planned: "Mr. Chairman, I would mislead the Special Commission and Mr. Jenner if we let that stand, because we believe the testimony is also admissible as a statement in furtherance of a joint activity of some kind and may therefore be admissible." Jenner took the bait, offering another lesson on the law of evidence and bringing the word "conspiracy" into the heart of the proceedings:

> If Mr. Stevens is now arguing that he is going to . . . establish a conspiracy, and under the doctrine of conspiracy, acts by conspirators while the conspiracy was still in effect in furtherance of that conspiracy are admissible against all of the parties to the conspiracy, that is one thing. But that hasn't been established, and a basis to that rule is that conspiracy must first be established before that evidence is permitted.

Greenberg stated that over the weekend he had been trying "to prepare myself for this" by reading evidence law treatises and cases. He stated his understanding that under Illinois law in a criminal case the conspiracy would have to be proven first before hearsay evidence could be used against a party. In a civil case, however, there is discretion to proceed more flexibly, allowing the hearsay evidence in "subject to a motion to strike and subject to being tied up" by subsequent proof of a conspiracy. Greenberg said the commission would follow the civil case approach.

Jenner, who must have realized Greenberg was right, left it at that. Stevens and Torshen had hoped that Jenner would raise the hearsay objection so that they could present the commission with their theory that Isaacs, Perbohner, Klingbiel, and others had conspired to prevent the true facts from being disclosed. Jenner not only had made the anticipated objection, but he had spelled out the law almost exactly as Stevens and Torshen saw it.

Pound was still nervous and bedeviled by difficulty in laying out the conversation with Klingbiel systematically. He was also plagued by uncertainty, borne of inexperience, about whether a journalist really should be testifying in a court proceeding like this at all. Nonetheless, he testified that Klingbiel said he got the stock from Dolph and Perbohner as a campaign contribution prior to the date of his reelection to the court in 1966. Klingbiel had admitted in his testimony before the commission, of course, that he received the stock after election day.

Pound described two telephone conversations with Perbohner on the same day, June 9, while Perbohner was in the Wisconsin hospital. One conversation preceded Pound's talk with Klingbiel, and the other followed it. In the first conversation, Perbohner told Pound that he bought the stock from Isaacs, paying for it with a check made out to the bank, and that Klingbiel then paid Perbohner for it. In the second conversation an hour later, Pound told Perbohner that Klingbiel had said the stock was a campaign contribution, and Perbohner said, "If he says I gave it to him, I guess I did."

Finally, Pound recounted an earlier call he placed to Isaacs, late on Sunday night, June 8. Isaacs told Pound that he had not given stock to Klingbiel or anyone else, and Isaacs explained the clearance loan and the stock issued in his name as collateral. This ended Pound's testimony. As Stevens recalls the testimony, Pound was nearly a "disaster witness," but Torshen still was able to get into evidence through him the link between Knight's stock and Isaacs, and some of the falsehoods uttered by Isaacs, Perbohner, and Klingbiel as the scandal was first coming to light. Pound's testimony wasn't smooth, but it was helpful.

When Pound was through, Stevens realized that nothing had been said to contradict Klingbiel's testimony, so Stevens advised the Special Commission that he wished to withdraw an earlier comment about impeaching the justice's statements. Stevens said, "I thought the testimony would impeach Justice Klingbiel, and it did not." It was now a little after 5:30. Greenberg adjourned the hearing until Tuesday, and told Pound he was excused from the witness stand. The harried and embarrassed Pound made his last, and simplest, statement of the day: "Thank God."

Chapter 19

Alibis

On Monday night Stevens and William McNally resumed the deposition of Doris Steigberg, Perbohner's secretary. With Perbohner still out of reach, perhaps useful details about his activities could be extracted from this witness, who was closely involved with his business and political affairs. Unfortunately, it quickly became evident that Steigberg was unlikely to say anything damaging to Perbohner or Isaacs.

She explained that she was very close to Perbohner and his family, having been a friend, houseguest, and part-time employee even before becoming his full-time "chauffeur, nurse, secretary, bookkeeper, what have you."[1] She explained that after her husband died in 1959, "I started doing Girl Friday–type things for Mr. Perbohner on occasion, and then Mrs. P. and I became very good friends, my family adopted their family, their family adopted my family."[2]

Stevens's earlier attempt to take her deposition in Wisconsin had foundered when Perbohner's lawyer, Sam Adam, encouraged her to hire an attorney before answering any more questions. She had followed Adam's advice and chosen a lawyer: him. Also attending the deposition was Patrick A. Tuite, a Chicago criminal lawyer associated with Harry Busch who had attended the Wisconsin depositions, representing Isaacs. Steigberg and Adam had invited Busch to attend Monday night's continuation of her deposition, and Busch had asked Tuite to cover it for him. This cooperation among Isaacs's lawyers and the lawyer now shared by Perbohner and Steigberg also suggested that her testimony was unlikely to be adverse to her boss and his friend Isaacs.

Skolnick's Secret

Earlier on Monday Skolnick finally gave the Special Commission some cooperation. As the newspapers described the event, he "quietly brought" one of his "sensitive witnesses" to the Civic Center to meet briefly with Stevens and Torshen. Stevens found the person's information totally useless, but at least the Skolnick fracas finally was settling down. By cooperating with the investigators, Skolnick had removed the basis for Judge Healy's contempt order.

On earlier occasions such as his deposition, Skolnick had claimed to have a few "strategically placed" informants. Even after the investigation was over, he still claimed to have had an anonymous source for his initial suspicions.[3] Many years later, however, Skolnick acknowledged that there never really were any secret informants. He had begun looking at Civic Center Bank records in early 1969 not because of any inside tip, but simply because of a hunch by Harriet Sherman, his associate in the Citizens' Committee to Clean Up the Courts. Harriet Sherman called him one day from a pay phone in downtown Chicago to report that she had just happened to walk by the bank, looked in the window, and noticed hardly any customers or visible activity going on there. Here was a new bank located at the vortex of so much political and business activity, yet it looked so dormant.

She and Skolnick began to suspect that the bank might be "a shuttle bus to Switzerland" for politicians' ill-gotten gains. The two of them agreed that she should look through the CCB stockholder lists in the Cook County Recorder's Office, and from there the scandal emerged. The whole chain of events, in Skolnick's appreciative words, "came from Harriet's intuition."[4]

Another Loan to Isaacs

When the hearings resumed on Tuesday morning, July 22, Ochsenschlager stipulated to the admissibility of the 1964 shareholder meeting minutes of Financial Security Life Insurance, the minutes Stevens had tried to ask Christofferson about on Monday morning. Ochsenschlager reported that Solfisburg had confirmed the correctness of the minutes. Solfisburg would not have to be called back to testify on this small point. The minutes were further evidence that Solfisburg was heavily involved in the insurance company and was aware of the Isaacs firm's involvement with it as early as 1964.

Stevens next called Theodore J. Isaacs to the witness stand. Some newspapers had speculated about when or whether Stevens would question Isaacs and had wondered if "clever cross-examination by his attorney, Albert Jenner, might cancel out anything Isaacs might say to help prove the charges of impropriety." For the commission to do its job with any semblance of thoroughness, however, there could be no doubt about the necessity of hearing what Isaacs had to say. Stevens had taken Isaacs's deposition two and a half weeks earlier, and he already had a pretty good idea of what Isaacs would tell the commission.

According to the *Daily News,* Isaacs, as his testimony began, "was smiling and cordial. He was consistently soft-spoken, and his answers to Stevens were brief." The reason many of his answers were brief was that he often gave the same uninformative reply about transactions and events: he just didn't recall. Other answers were much longer, however, as he offered a series of explanations for dealings that looked suspicious, but that he claimed were entirely wholesome. Stevens already had heard these explanations three times, first in Isaacs's deposition on July 3; again on July 9 in the truncated deposition of Howard Hansen, the Department of Revenue employee; and finally from Doris Steigberg in her deposition on Monday night.

Stevens began by briefly covering Isaacs's legal, political, and military career. Then he focused on the January 10, 1968, newspaper article concerning Isaacs's resignation from the Illinois National Guard. Stevens asked about Solfisburg's telephone call seeking guidance in getting the justice's son into the National Guard. Stevens emphasized the timing of the call, for Solfisburg had said it occurred in the summer of 1968. Stevens was trying to show that the series of conversations between the two men occurred much earlier than that.

When Stevens asked if the initial conversation was soon after the newspaper announcement, Isaacs couldn't recall. This memory gap contradicted his deposition statement that Solfisburg called him shortly after the article appeared. For the first of many times, Stevens confronted Isaacs with his contrary deposition statement. Isaacs then acknowledged his earlier answer, and—with a suddenly improved memory—went on to recount another conversation with Solfisburg in March or April 1968, as well as a meeting with the justice's son. When asked whether he had ever talked by phone with Solfisburg before 1968, Isaacs didn't recall.

Isaacs described an active friendship with Perbohner going back to 1960 and involving frequent telephone conversations. He said they seldom met in person because Isaacs was based in Chicago and Perbohner was usually either in Rockford or Springfield. This description of a long-distance friendship carried an unnoticed irony: although the two men seldom saw each other in Illinois, just a few weeks earlier

Isaacs suddenly had flown up to a small town in northern Wisconsin to see Perbohner in the hospital. That trip was made the day after the Klingbiel stock story first made headlines. If Isaacs's characterization of the friendship now was accurate, that visit was even more unusual and suspicious than it had seemed at the time.[5]

Stevens asked about exchanges of gifts between Isaacs and Perbohner, and Isaacs said they only exchanged small items such as cigars, at least up to the time of Isaacs's indictment in late 1964. Isaacs told of something quite different after the indictment:

> In March of 1965, I received a sum of money from him indirectly, but I didn't consider it as a gift. My best recollection is I had a telephone call, and this is some time in March of 1965, from a Mr. Hansen, Howard Hansen. I don't recall whether he came to my office, or continued to tell me over the telephone that Mr. Perbohner had stopped and given him a sum of money to assist me in my legal expenses, together with a small amount for personal expenses. . . . My best recollection is Mr. Hansen said, "Mr. Perbohner stopped by, gave me an envelope with $2,000 in it, added another $100. He said, 'Give this to Ted for his legal expenses. I know he is undergoing heavy obligations now, and give him the $100 for his own personal use.'"

Isaacs explained that he asked Hansen to take the money to Harry Busch, Isaacs's criminal defense attorney, to apply against his legal fees.

Stevens had heard this same story in Isaacs's deposition, but this time Isaacs added another ingredient, almost as an afterthought: "Mr. Hansen did say one more thing. 'Bob said when you get around to it, at any time you get around to it, you can pay it back to him,' or words to that effect." Even though Stevens had asked Isaacs about the $2,100 payment three separate times during the deposition and had asked him to explain any conversations with Perbohner about it, Isaacs did not mention this last statement then at all.

Stevens now suggested that Isaacs had regarded the money as a gift, but Isaacs insisted he did not, instead considering it a contribution toward his expenses. Stevens pressed the point, and Isaacs labored to preserve the distinction he was making:

> ISAACS: I think an outright gift is something given with no expectation of return. In my particular case, with contributions being made from several sources, most of which were unknown to me, I hoped to be able to accommodate these people and pay them back some day.

STEVENS: I am curious, Mr. Isaacs, how was it that you planned to make a return to these unknown sources if you didn't know the source?

ISAACS: I say, if I didn't know, I couldn't do it. There were many unknown. Those were gifts.

STEVENS: They were gifts if you didn't know who they were from, and they were contributions if you did, that is the distinction?

ISAACS: Partially.

Isaacs did not recall any written documents as part of this transaction, but he did remember that the transfer of funds was by cash rather than check.

The Special Commission and public had just heard the first link in the chain of Isaacs's alibi: Perbohner had loaned him $2,100 for his legal fees, using Howard Hansen as a messenger. Hansen had explained the same transaction in his deposition. He had known Perbohner since 1936 "through politics," and he testified that Perbohner gave him an envelope with $2,000 in cash for Isaacs's lawyer, plus another $100 for Isaacs's personal expenses.[6] Perbohner didn't explain, however, why he was using Hansen as an intermediary, instead of giving the money to Isaacs himself.

Hansen said he converted the cash into a certified check at a currency exchange—a small store offering check-cashing and other monetary services—and brought it to Harry Busch's office. Hansen explained that he got the check because he had called that office and found that Busch was not there, so "this way there was a record as to how much I turned over to Mr. Busch." Nonetheless, Hansen did not ask for a receipt from Busch's secretary. He also never reported back to Perbohner that he had made the delivery.

These descriptions of Perbohner's contribution to Isaacs obviously could not be verified, and Stevens was suspicious of the story. Doris Steigberg's deposition on Monday night also added pieces to Isaacs's puzzle. She stated that Perbohner had told her he wanted to help Isaacs with his legal fees and expenses and had directed her to take some cash from the office vault for this purpose. Having heard about this from Isaacs and Hansen already, Stevens asked, almost facetiously, "I suppose it was $2,100?" Steigberg said it was.

The most credible information tending to corroborate this transaction was a statement made by Harry Busch during Isaacs's deposition. Busch confirmed that his office had received a cashier's check or money order from Hansen for $2,100 to be applied to Isaacs's fees.

Busch, however, had no knowledge of the real source of the money Hansen delivered.[7]

Paying It Back

Stevens moved on to the subject of Perbohner's CCB stock. Isaacs said he probably talked with Perbohner in late 1965 about the organization of the new bank, but he denied any involvement in Perbohner's original subscription purchase of two hundred shares. Stevens asked whether Isaacs recalled any discussion at the time of Perbohner's initial stock purchase "about the possibility of making him either a gift or repayment of value roughly comparable to the $2,100 that he had given to Mr. Hansen that you referred to earlier." Isaacs had no recollection of a conversation about repayment then.

Later on, however, in the fall of 1966—about the time of oral argument in the Supreme Court in *People v. Isaacs*—Perbohner and Isaacs talked again:

> ISAACS: During the course of this conversation with Mr. Perbohner, he stated that he would like to have an additional or some more, as I recall, shares in the Civic Center Bank. The number finally resolved by him in that conversation was one hundred more shares. My best recollection is that I told him that there might not be any more of the original issue shares, but I would inquire, and if there were, I would undertake to secure them for him. And this would give me also an opportunity to repay finally this loan or this contribution he made toward my legal expenses. I would proceed immediately to do the best I could. . . .
>
> STEVENS: Then what did you do?
>
> ISAACS: I called somebody at the bank. I can't recall whether it was the cashier or one of two ladies who were working I think at that time, and asked them to secure a hundred shares for me. I would pay for them. They were to be issued to Mr. Robert Perbohner. . . .
>
> STEVENS: And then what happened?
>
> ISAACS: Subsequently it turned out there were a hundred shares available. The transaction was completed, and I paid for the shares . . . then, I gave the shares to Mr. Perbohner.

Isaacs had now provided the second link in his version of the chain of events: his purchase of the hundred shares that went to Perbohner in

October 1966—and then to Klingbiel a few weeks later—was simply repayment of a debt incurred in March 1965 when Perbohner contributed $2,100 for Isaacs's legal fees. Isaacs's check for these one hundred shares, including interest, totaled exactly $2,081.84.

Stevens zeroed in on one more aspect of this repayment. Had Isaacs obtained the approval of anyone else in the bank before directing the issuance of these shares to Perbohner? Isaacs was sure he hadn't cleared it with the bank's president or key organizers of the bank, but his recollection was hazy about other people he might have spoken with. He was fairly sure that the mechanics of the stock issuance went through Jayne Kegley. Once again, Stevens refreshed Isaacs's recollection with his deposition answers. Isaacs had to admit that Stevens asked him about the transaction three times during the deposition, and each time Kegley was the only person he recalled talking with about this.

Stevens asked, "As you sit here today, do you recall asking anybody's approval with respect to having a hundred shares issued to Mr. Robert Perbohner in October 1966?" Isaacs replied, "No, I don't recall asking for approval." After all the questioning of various witnesses about Isaacs's participation in the stock distribution, this single transaction spoke volumes about what he had the power to do. These were not just any one hundred shares—they were the last hundred shares. With people clamoring to buy more CCB stock, Isaacs decided—entirely on his own—that Robert Perbohner would receive the final hundred.

The Other Deals

The questioning next turned to Solfisburg's seven hundred shares. Isaacs's recollection now was unclear about when he first learned that Solfisburg owned CCB stock. During his deposition, Isaacs had stated that he learned on May 26, 1967, that Solfisburg was the seller of the three hundred shares delivered to his law office that day by Lawrence Flynn. Now he backtracked, saying he instead found out during a meeting with Harold Stout two months later.

Stevens showed Isaacs the receipt signed by Isaacs's secretary on May 26, acknowledging Flynn's delivery of the three hundred shares. Isaacs testified, as he had during his deposition, that this receipt was not typed in his office. The typeface on the receipt was plainly not the sort used on his firm's typewriters. Additionally, the typed signature line read "Theodore Isaacs," but his secretaries almost invariably included his middle initial.

Isaacs was confirming the strong, yet still unexplained, evidence that before the Solfisburg shares were delivered to Isaacs's office, someone in Aurora had decided they should go there. This, of course, contradicted Flynn's and Solfisburg's testimony that Flynn was asked by the justice to bring the shares to the bank but instead suddenly decided on his own to just drop them off at Isaacs's office. Isaacs was conceding a damaging point.

Isaacs next explained his actions in lining up purchasers for the Solfisburg shares even before May 26, the date they were delivered to Chicago by Flynn and the date of Isaacs's $300 check. First, he described a conversation a week or so before that date with C. E. McKittrick, one of the bank's organizers. According to Isaacs, McKittrick mentioned during a meeting at the bank that he and his wife wanted to buy more shares and that somebody at that meeting had stated that there were going to be some shares available at $24 each. McKittrick asked Isaacs for his advice, and Isaacs told him he couldn't go wrong at that price. On May 22 McKittrick bought a hundred shares, mailing in his check for $2,400 to the bank.

Second, Isaacs said he telephoned a friend, James Pelts, to tell him about the availability of the shares he had heard about from McKittrick. Pelts sent in his $2,400 on May 26, with a cover letter indicating he was doing so per his conversation with Isaacs. The third purchaser, Ronald Landsman, was an accountant who also had been active in founding the bank. Landsman authorized payment of $2,400 on May 24. Isaacs did not remember talking to him about these shares at all.

Isaacs now had his chance to explain the most baffling aspect of this sale of Solfisburg's stock. Stevens asked how it happened that Isaacs wrote the $300 check on May 26 that became part of the sale proceeds received by Solfisburg. Isaacs answered that the bank's cashier, Harry Mertz, called him that day and said that "there was a discrepancy between an acquisition and sale of shares, and it looked like the bank was going to get stuck." Isaacs went to the bank, and Mertz told him that there was a commitment to acquire three hundred shares for $25 a share, but the bank had received payments at $24 a share.

Isaacs testified that when Mertz asked him what to do, "I recognized that Mr. Pelts and Mr. McKittrick were involved, and I told Mr. Mertz that I was responsible for both of them in particular ordering and paying $24 per share." Since the bank had no account to use to fix the error, he said, "I would consider it my obligation to make up the difference and not to bother Pelts, McKittrick, or the others about it, and let the transaction go through." Isaacs explained his fondness for the elderly McKittrick and the young Pelts, and said he would have been terribly embarrassed to go back to them and admit his blunder.

Isaacs said he didn't know why Mertz called him, rather than calling the purchasers or the seller. Stevens asked whether Mertz had first called the bank president or vice president before calling Isaacs, and Isaacs didn't recall. Stevens asked whether Isaacs inquired about who had made the commitment to $25 a share. Isaacs didn't recall. Stevens asked why, when Isaacs's secretary sent the three hundred shares to the bank, she included a note indicating her assumption that Flynn was handling them for Solfisburg. Isaacs didn't recall, although he emphasized that he was not concerned about the seller, but rather about his friends, the purchasers.

Stevens asked about Landsman, the third buyer, to whom Isaacs had made no commitment. Isaacs noted that he and Landsman were very close, but that he didn't recall whether he had talked to him at all. Stevens asked whether it had occurred to Isaacs to solve the problem by telling the seller that the price was $24, not $25. It hadn't occurred to Isaacs. Stevens noted that both McKittrick and Landsman were active directors of the bank, but Isaacs insisted he still felt a personal obligation to make up the $100 deficiency for each of them. He also did not ask Harold Stout or anyone else at the bank to make up the difference. After probing a few more details of the sale of Solfisburg's three hundred shares, Stevens ended his questioning on these transactions. Isaacs now had presented his innocent explanation of the $300 check: he had made a mistake and rectified it.

Two weeks earlier Stevens and Nathaniel Sack had taken James Pelts's deposition. Pelts testified that he bought his first hundred CCB shares as part of the original subscription; Isaacs was the only bank representative he discussed it with at that time. Later, in May 1967, Pelts expressed to Isaacs an interest in buying more shares. Isaacs suggested he buy directly from the bank to avoid brokerage fees, and it was agreed that Pelts would buy another hundred shares at $24 per share. Stevens asked Pelts whether a price of $25, rather than $24, would have prevented him from buying the shares. Pelts assured Stevens that this small increment would not have made any difference in his decision to buy, even if Isaacs had later called and said he made a mistake in quoting the lower price.[8]

McKittrick was a pivotal part of Isaacs's innocent account of these transactions, but he had since died. Nonetheless, there did seem to be at least one other person who could corroborate Isaacs's story. Isaacs had said in his deposition that he learned of the availability of the three hundred shares "from Mr. Stout, I believe, maybe others." He also stated that Stout made the commitment to the seller to buy the shares at $25 each.[9] Solfisburg similarly testified, both in his deposition and in the hearings, that he spoke with Stout in May 1967 before sending in his three hundred shares.

Stout's agreement on these points would have given great support to Isaacs's and Solfisburg's explanations, but he didn't agree. His testimony on Monday, the day before Isaacs took the stand, made clear that he never even heard of Solfisburg, much less had a conversation with him, until the fall of 1968. As Isaacs testified now, he simply sidestepped this contradiction by omitting references to Stout. Now it was McKittrick, not Stout, who brought the $24 shares to Isaacs's attention. Isaacs no longer said that Stout made the $25 commitment to Solfisburg; now he just didn't know.

Before the commission recessed for lunch, Stevens explored with Isaacs, as he had with Stout, the letter and other evidence of a planned meeting in Rockford in late May 1966, right before Solfisburg bought his seven hundred shares. Once again, the questioning was unproductive. Isaacs remembered being asked to join in a meeting on loan policy in Rockford with Mark Waggoner, but also remembered that the meeting never occurred. He knew of no other purpose for a meeting there and said he "would have written this letter differently" to make clear that the only purpose was to see Waggoner. Isaacs also had no explanation for the reference to Bob Perbohner in Stout's letter, saying, "I had nothing to do with the letter."

Many More Witnesses?

After lunch Greenberg asked the lawyers about their plans for the remainder of the hearings. Stevens said he planned to finish presenting evidence on Wednesday. Ochsenschlager and Jenner each said they probably would call no witnesses. Hearing this, Stevens informed the other lawyers that he did not intend to call either Doris Steigberg or Howard Hansen as witnesses.

Both Steigberg's deposition and Hansen's still uncompleted deposition contained statements supportive of Isaacs's claim of the Perbohner loan and the repayment with CCB stock. Stevens now was signaling that he didn't give much credence to those two witnesses. If Ochsenschlager or Jenner thought the Special Commission should hear from them, those lawyers would have to call them.

Jenner responded by asking to see those depositions. Stevens pointed out that Patrick Tuite, one of the lawyers for Isaacs, had attended Steigberg's deposition just the previous night. An astonishing exchange followed:

JENNER: If he is an attorney for Mr. Isaacs, this instant is the first time I have known that.

BUSCH: Mr. Chairman, Mr. Tuite is one of my associates and was present at the investigation preliminarily at the Woodruff, Wisconsin, area.

STEVENS: And last night.

There had been confusion from the beginning about whether Isaacs was represented by Busch, Jenner, or both. Even Jenner was still somewhat in the dark.

Stevens readily agreed to turn over copies of the Hansen and Steigberg depositions, provided each of the witnesses consented to the disclosure. He plainly believed that these two witnesses would consent, since they were very much in Isaacs's and the justices' corner.

In fact, Steigberg had not only supported Isaacs's loan and repayment alibi, but on Monday night she even gave a convoluted explanation of Perbohner and Dolph's gift of stock to Klingbiel. The gist of it was that Dolph had committed himself and Perbohner to contribute $1,000 each to Klingbiel's campaign. When Dolph told him about the commitment, Perbohner was unhappy that Dolph had promised on behalf of both of them. He was especially distressed because Dolph couldn't come up with $1,000, and Perbohner didn't have money available either. Perbohner realized—coincidentally—that he had just received the repayment from Isaacs in CCB stock worth a little over $2,000. Steigberg explained, "Rather than have the two of them embarrassed, [Perbohner] said that he was going to take that stock and use that" as their joint contribution to Klingbiel.[10]

At one point in her garbled explanation, Steigberg actually seemed to say that Perbohner told Isaacs about Dolph's promise to Klingbiel. Nonetheless, Stevens did not find her testimony credible enough on this and many other points to be worth presenting. If her stories were to be brought into evidence, the initiative would have to come from Ochsenschlager or Jenner.

Chipping and Hammering

Stevens resumed questioning Isaacs, chipping away at Isaacs's assertions that he had only a limited role at the bank and no knowledge of the transactions by which Solfisburg and Klingbiel acquired their stock. Isaacs agreed with Stout's description of the bank organizers' commitment to avoiding the concentration of too many shares in any one owner. Isaacs admitted, however, that there were no procedures established to make sure that the ceilings on stock purchases—fifteen hundred shares for directors and a thousand for others—wouldn't be circumvented by individuals buying stock in their children's names, street names, or the names of brokerage firms or trusts. Stevens asked whether, for example, the issuance of the seven hundred shares to Trust No. 931 at the Aurora bank had been checked, to see whether the beneficial owner of the trust actually might have more shares than the bank's purchase limitations allowed. Isaacs said the subject never came to his attention.

Stevens pressed Isaacs hard about the clearance loan and the 12,850 shares. Stevens emphasized Isaacs's sole, legal responsibility for payment of the loan, and Isaacs's "legal right, if you had the money available, to take the money which was required, pay off the loan, and obtain the stock for yourself." Isaacs denied that he had such extensive power over the stock.

The commission's counsel went on the offensive, tightening the net he had been casting over Isaacs:

STEVENS: But, Mr. Isaacs, that is exactly what you did with the hundred shares for Mr. Perbohner, wasn't it? . . . You just ordered Mrs. Kegley to send them out, didn't you?

ISAACS: Now we are back to the subject we talked about this morning. I said I called and asked if they were available.

STEVENS: Well, what if six months earlier you had called and said, how many shares were available, and she said four thousand, and you had sent in a check for the four thousand and ordered them out?

ISAACS: No, you know I wouldn't have done that. . . .

STEVENS: You had the legal right to do that, though, didn't you, Mr. Isaacs?

ISAACS: I don't think so. I don't think so.

STEVENS: What was the difference in the legal situation with respect to one hundred shares and with respect to 12,850 shares?

ISAACS: Well, first of all, the requirements upon me were not any more than one thousand to begin with, and I certainly wouldn't have gone beyond that no matter what.

STEVENS: Well, but you could have taken them in the name of a trust, couldn't you, Mr. Isaacs?

ISAACS: No, sir.

STEVENS: Nobody would have looked?

ISAACS: No, sir, that isn't true.

Stevens continued to hammer away, establishing that all that was needed to have stock issued from that block was a good check and a stock transfer signed by Isaacs himself. Isaacs insisted that he couldn't have acted for his own interest as Stevens was describing because it would have violated "an agreement among the directors." Jenner angrily joined in, supporting his client's refrain.

Stevens was unrelenting, and Isaacs began to show his frustration:

STEVENS: But you did it with respect to Mr. Perbohner's stock, didn't you, Mr. Isaacs?

ISAACS: Oh, come on. I asked for one hundred shares if they were available, and I purchased a hundred shares, and as of this point I myself was a small owner. I wasn't even up to the thousand shares in my own name, if you want to put it that way.

STEVENS: But you didn't have to ask anybody's okay to do it, did you?

Stevens then linked this small purchase with a bigger one:

STEVENS: Couldn't you have ordered seven hundred shares for the Old Second National Bank of Aurora if you had $14,350 of good money with which to pay for them? . . .

ISAACS: I don't know Old Second National Bank of Aurora, and, therefore, I couldn't order anything out for them.

STEVENS: Well, apparently somebody could, Mr. Isaacs.

Stevens's sarcasm triggered objections from Jenner and Ochsenschlager, and Greenberg ordered the comment stricken.

Isaacs denied having anything to do with the distribution of stock to Solfisburg, Joseph Knight, or Howard Hansen. He disavowed knowledge of how Hansen happened to become the nominee for Knight's mother's stock, and he didn't recall how he first learned about the stock certificate lost at Knight's home. The only name Isaacs was sure he had suggested for the distribution of some of the 12,850 shares was that of his own son.

Finally, Stevens returned to the supposed $2,100 advance from Perbohner and repayment with a hundred shares of CCB stock. Stevens asked about Isaacs's financial status when the money came in and later when he bought the stock. Isaacs explained that he had lost income in 1965. He had begun to reestablish himself, however, by the fall of 1966, but he denied that his improving financial condition had any bearing on his decision to repay Perbohner then. Stevens asked whether, as of September and October 1966, Isaacs might still have

faced the prospect of heavy legal expenses in his criminal case, especially since he then had no way of knowing the outcome of the litigation. Isaacs agreed, saying, "I would handle that as it came along."
Stevens had no more questions for Isaacs.

Chairman Greenberg posed a few questions. His most surprising
query came when he asked Isaacs if he knew, "in the parlance of La
Salle Street and Randolph, in Chicago, what is meant by 'clout.'"
Isaacs said, "I think the common definition would be the ability of
someone to have favors done." Greenberg asked whether he thought
the bank organizers wanted him not because of his legal ability, but instead because of his "clout." Isaacs said, "If they did, then they were
sadly mistaken, because I don't use clout." Greenberg made his question more specific, asking whether Isaacs's influence with Joseph
Knight, then the Director of Financial Institutions, might have been
the reason he was brought in to help start the bank. Isaacs conceded
that it had occurred to him that this might have been the organizers'
motivation but emphasized that what he did was standard legal work.

Greenberg then asked if Isaacs could explain why the bank would
have regarded Justice Solfisburg as a valuable shareholder to the tune
of seven hundred shares. Isaacs insisted, "I had no connection with the
issuance of any of the shares or with the transfers." Isaacs also couldn't
identify anybody else at the bank who had anything to do with allocat-
ing seven hundred shares to the chief justice.

Henry Pitts asked why Isaacs felt obligated to cover the $1 per share
difference between McKittrick's payment of $24 and the sale price of
$25, especially in view of McKittrick's presence at an earlier meeting
at which Stout expressly quoted the higher price. Isaacs said he didn't
know at the time that McKittrick previously had heard the higher
price. Edwin Austin asked about Isaacs's failure to investigate who
made the commitment to sell at $25. Isaacs said he simply relied on the
word of the cashier, Harry Mertz, that a commitment had been made.

Greenberg turned Isaacs's attention to the three hundred shares
owned by Otto Kerner. Isaacs was asked whether he had anything to
do with the placement of those shares to Kerner. Isaacs had surprising
difficulty giving a clear answer, but eventually indicated that Kerner
bought on the basis of a conversation with Isaacs a week or two before
the purchase in September 1966.

Ochsenschlager's brief examination of Isaacs focused mainly on
Bailey Howard's association with the bank. Isaacs also emphatically
denied that Solfisburg had ever been an attorney for the bank. Jenner
questioned more extensively, largely to emphasize Isaacs's limited involvement in the stock distribution and to reiterate the normalcy of

the clearance loan. Jenner secured Isaacs's assurance that neither Robert Dolph, Robert Perbohner, nor anyone else ever spoke to him about guaranteeing or protecting Solfisburg in his acquisition of CCB shares. Isaacs also said that he did not know until this investigation arose that Klingbiel or his relatives owned CCB stock.

When Isaacs left the witness stand about 4:30, he had testified for more than six hours, but not much new information had emerged. I found Isaacs's testimony disturbing. I was struck by his repeated, seemingly studied inability to recall information on many important points. It appeared to me, as it had during Solfisburg's testimony, that the witness often claimed not to remember things he probably remembered quite well.

During the morning session, when Isaacs talked about the $2,100 loan from Perbohner, Stevens skeptically asked, "So there is really no possible way to verify the details of this transaction except by the recollection of the persons involved?" Isaacs replied, "Yes, sir, that is right." With this answer, and many others, Isaacs seemed to take smug pleasure in the impenetrability of his alibis. He seemed to view his and his friends' activities—whether in government service or outside ventures—as akin to participation in an exclusive private club.

Chapter 20

Testing the Stories

Stevens had four witnesses left. Most of what they had to say challenged Isaacs's versions of the facts. Late Tuesday afternoon Stevens called Harry Mertz, who had been the cashier at the Civic Center Bank when Solfisburg's three hundred shares were sold. Isaacs had testified to a phone call from Mertz about the $300 discrepancy between what the three purchasers paid and what the seller was promised. Isaacs also described meeting with Mertz at the bank to solve the problem.

Mertz now remembered only "a sale about that time" and "some minor discussion" about "somebody who was shorted." Beyond that, Mertz had no specific recollections. His answer to one of Stevens's final questions, however, produced the most solid of his answers, one not helpful to Isaacs. Stevens asked whom Mertz would consult regarding a shortage such as the $300 disparity. Mertz unhesitatingly replied: "Mr. Stout."

Next on the stand was Max Sonderby, a veteran reporter for the *Chicago Sun-Times*. Sonderby testified about a conversation on July 2 with Stout and Isaacs at the Civic Center Bank. At that time, Sonderby asked the two men about the organization of the bank and the selection of its shareholders. Stout and Isaacs described the informal committee of five or six original organizers of the bank, including David and Edward Meyers. Isaacs said he was not on the committee. Stout said the bank stock was oversubscribed. Sonderby continued:

> I asked Mr. Isaacs, "Well, if you weren't on the committee, how did your friends get stock?"

He said, "I had to be very careful not to hurt their feelings. It was a problem."

I said, "So you took care of them, did you?"

And he said, "They knew who they were," meaning the committee or the Meyers brothers.

The next day Stout explained again to Sonderby by phone that the bank originally had far more requests for stock than it could satisfy. Sonderby testified that Stout said the committee sometimes would call in others to settle who should get stock when a dispute arose. Isaacs was one of those called in. Ochsenschlager clarified the dates of the conversations, but otherwise, for the first time, no one other than Stevens had questions for the witness.

Stevens's last witness for the day was Robert J. Seltzner, executive editor of the *Daily Calumet,* who had two months earlier first dug into Skolnick's suspicions about Klingbiel. Seltzner testified about his telephone conversation with Justice Klingbiel on May 20, when he asked Klingbiel about the Cook County listing of a transfer of a hundred shares from Perbohner to Thomas and Anne Simpson in care of Judge Klingbiel.

Klingbiel said that he bought the stock from Perbohner for his grandchildren, Thomas and Anne, about the time that the bank was organized in January 1966. Klingbiel denied knowing Isaacs, other than having met him once at a bar association meeting, and said he felt there was no conflict of interest in having stock in a bank in which Isaacs was involved.

Jenner ended the day by putting Isaacs back on the stand and asking him about the conversation with Sonderby. Isaacs denied ever being part of any discussion by any bank committee regarding issuance of stock. He said he told Sonderby that he had to be "terribly careful" toward his friends who wanted shares in the bank, but also that he therefore had nothing to do with the sale of shares. Isaacs labeled Sonderby's additional statement—that Isaacs had said the committee dealing with the stock knew who Isaacs's friends were—"absolutely incorrect." With this answer, the Tuesday session was over.

The Editor Tells All

On Wednesday morning Stevens brought Roy Fisher, editor of the *Chicago Daily News,* to the witness stand for questioning by Torshen. Daniel Feldman, the newspaper's lawyer, was there to represent

Fisher. As with Mertz and Sonderby, Stevens's principal purpose in calling Fisher was to undercut Isaacs's testimony.

Torshen asked Fisher about his telephone conversations with Isaacs on June 9 and 10, just before the *Daily News* printed its first story on Klingbiel and the CCB stock. Fisher recounted Isaacs's telling him, in their first conversation, that Perbohner's shares had come from the block of stock being held in connection with the clearance loan for distribution to "friends of the bank." Fisher continued: "Mr. Isaacs did say that Mr. Perbohner's stock was acquired in a normal business transaction that he, Mr. Isaacs, had nothing to do with." Isaacs agreed to go over to the bank right away to find records "that show that this was handled in the same fashion that the other stock was handled and that I had nothing to do with it."

In the second conversation, the next afternoon, Fisher asked Isaacs if he had found these records. Isaacs said he had not, claiming that "the records of the bank leave something to be desired," but agreed to look further. Isaacs also denied knowing the stock was going to Klingbiel and asserted that the transfer to Perbohner had nothing to do with Isaacs's case in the supreme court. Fisher testified that he never heard from Isaacs again.

Fisher said he had known Perbohner for about twenty years. After the calls to Isaacs, he called Perbohner in the Wisconsin hospital to ask about the stock transfer to Klingbiel. Perbohner told Fisher the stock was a gift to Klingbiel to express his appreciation for Klingbiel as he ended his service as chief justice. Perbohner also said, "In my position, one needs to have an 'in' with the Court." Fisher asked Perbohner if Isaacs had given him the shares, and Perbohner said, "Oh, I paid him," specifically by a check to the bank. Fisher explained further:

> I said to Bob Perbohner, "Now, let's see if I have this straight. You bought the stock from Ted Isaacs, and you paid him by check, is that right?" He said, "That is right."
> "The check was made out to the Civic Center Bank?" He said, "That is right."
> "You got the stock, Bob, and then you gave it to Justice Klingbiel?" He said, "Oh, no. I didn't give it to Justice Klingbiel. . . . I gave it to Roy Solfisburg."
> I said, "Roy Solfisburg? Why did you give it to Roy Solfisburg?" He said, "Because he asked me to do it. It was his idea. . . . It was his idea that we should do something nice for Judge Klingbiel."

This was the conversation Fisher had edited with dubious selectivity in the paper's first story and had failed to investigate further at the time.[1]

Now Fisher had finally and publicly revealed the full details of what Perbohner told him. Perbohner's inconsistent explanations of his role were revealed, and a shocking link between Solfisburg and the gift to Klingbiel was declared.

As Ochsenschlager readied himself to cross-examine, he was plainly aghast at what he had just heard about his client Solfisburg. Greenberg realized this and declared a ten-minute recess.

After the recess, the justices' lawyer concentrated first on Fisher's duties at the *Daily News* and on the prominence of Bailey Howard in the parent corporation. Ochsenschlager's tone was hostile as he asked Fisher why he telephoned Perbohner. Fisher emphasized that "the importance of the story was such that I wanted to be completely satisfied that what we had would stand up."

Ochsenschlager probed for the sources of Fisher's information before he called Perbohner. Fisher listed five staff members who worked on the story, including Nicodemus, and then Ochsenschlager charged that "there was much communication between your staff members and Mr. Skolnick in the early days of this investigation." Torshen objected that this questioning exceeded the scope of the direct examination. Ochsenschlager fiercely made clear what his examination was about:

OCHSENSCHLAGER: Mr. Chairman, I certainly have a right to show the bias of this newspaper about their relationship with Justice Solfisburg. This dates back many years, and I think I have a right to show this to test the credibility of his testimony of the conversation over the telephone.

GREENBERG: Are you suggesting that this line of questioning goes to the credibility of—

OCHSENSCHLAGER: Of the witness.

Greenberg, plainly skeptical, allowed the inquiry to proceed.

Fisher explained that one or two of the reporters had talked with Skolnick, who had provided some of the original leads. Fisher said he only spoke to Skolnick once by telephone and had never met him. Ochsenschlager asked whether the *Daily News* had ever compensated Skolnick for any purpose, but Fisher knew of no such payments. By this point, Ochsenschlager seemed to lack both any definite strategy to undercut Fisher's testimony and any real evidence of the *Daily News*' bias against Solfisburg.

The irony of the bias accusation was surely lost on most everyone in the courtroom, except Fisher, who knew that over a year earlier his superiors had killed the intensive investigation of Solfisburg by Donald Barlett and the Better Government Association. Fisher had also been extraordinarily cautious in his handling of the information from Perbohner for many reasons, including the bigger conflict he was engaged in with the paper's management and Bailey Howard.[2] Fisher actually had been a participant, albeit a reluctant one, in the shielding of Solfisburg from adverse publicity for almost a year and a half. Now Ochsenschlager, knowing little or none of this history, was charging that Fisher and his paper had long been out to damage the chief justice.

Ochsenschlager moved on to other angles in a meandering attempt to discredit Fisher. He asked whether Nicodemus might have been in a position to pay Skolnick for his information, and Fisher said he didn't know of any way the reporter could do that. Fisher lightly added, "We don't pay them well enough." To laughter from the audience, Ochsenschlager professed to be "sorry to hear that" and, turning to the reporters in the jury box, added, "If I haven't got you all a raise, it isn't my fault." After a few more questions, he was through.

Jenner did not share Ochsenschlager's good humor or his unfocused manner of questioning this witness. His cross-examination was aggressive and intense. He examined in detail the timing of Fisher's conversations with Isaacs and Perbohner, and the preparation of Fisher's written notes of these conversations, including a typed transcription prepared with the help of Feldman. Jenner was at his most haughty, chiding Fisher whenever the witness's answer strayed from the precise focus of the question.

After highlighting Fisher's confusion on a couple of dates, Jenner moved to the substance of Fisher's conversations with Isaacs. Jenner probably was hoping to find similar confusion in Fisher's recollections of what was said, but didn't. Fisher recited once again, nearly identically, the conversations he had testified about on direct examination. As he began this recitation, Fisher stopped to ask Jenner, "Do you want me to go on with what I repeated before?" Jenner answered, "I want all the conversation." This was a mistake.

Jenner apparently didn't anticipate that Fisher, an experienced newsman, had a great command of facts and details. Jenner was unable to find any inconsistencies or gaps in Fisher's memory of the calls, and by going through "all the conversation" again, Fisher simply reinforced his earlier testimony. Jenner—like Ochsenschlager before him—had nothing to work with to undercut Fisher. A newspaper account even reported that "Isaacs was hurriedly brought into the courtroom by his attorneys, presumably to rebut [Fisher], but left later without testifying."

Throughout Fisher's testimony, Jenner remained on the offensive, seeking to dominate this witness just as he had tried to do days earlier with James Nussbaum. Greenberg advised Jenner not to interrupt Fisher so frequently, and Stevens jumped in to restrain Jenner when he misstated facts, admonishing, "Let's be precise, Mr. Jenner." Earlier in the hearings, Jenner had taken every opportunity to correct his former employee on minor misstatements. Stevens now reversed the roles.

After Fisher explained the Isaacs conversations, Jenner asked him about his call to Perbohner. Jenner focused on Fisher's failure to call Solfisburg afterward to inquire about Perbohner's comment that Solfisburg had suggested the gift of stock to Klingbiel. Fisher explained that he did not do so because "we only had Perbohner's statement about that." Fisher continued: "We did not think that it was necessary at that point to go beyond what we could absolutely prove documentarily and with open admissions from all parties involved. But if you took the lid off this story, the rest of it would come crawling out." Fisher seemed to imply that there was other damaging information about Solfisburg that he had decided not to pursue at that time.[3]

Jenner asked whether Fisher had ever tried to verify Perbohner's statement about Solfisburg with Klingbiel, and Fisher explained that "this is the first time I have told anybody about it." After a few more questions by Jenner and Ochsenschlager, the hearing recessed for lunch. The editor who had been unwilling or unable to tell all that he knew through his newspaper now had told it—probably with greater impact—from the witness stand.

The End of Testimony

At two o'clock James Nussbaum, the staff accountant, returned to the witness stand. At Stevens's request, he had prepared another chart, this one summarizing activity in all of Perbohner's bank accounts from 1964 through 1966. Stevens explained that the summary was relevant to the weight to be given Isaacs's testimony about "a purported transfer of $2,100 by Mr. Perbohner via Mr. Hansen to Mr. Isaacs." Stevens asserted that if Isaacs's story was in fact correct, an examination of Perbohner's accounts should reveal a withdrawal at or about the date of the alleged transfer of funds, thus substantiating the story.

Stevens pointed out that Nussbaum's analysis showed no such withdrawal, and thus tended to refute Isaacs's claim. Robert Hanley and William Murphy objected to the speculative nature of this testimony, saying, quite sensibly, that it would simply be "an inference on an inference." Greenberg nonetheless allowed it. Nussbaum stated that during February and March 1965, "there were no checks which cleared these accounts in the amount of $2,000 or $2,100." Ochsenschlager's questions quickly established the limited force of this testimony. Nussbaum was not eliminating the possibility that the payment had been made in cash or through a number of smaller checks. In fact, in Howard Hansen's deposition—which Ochsenschlager had been given the previous evening—Hansen said that Perbohner gave him twenty-one $100 bills.

When Ochsenschlager asked whether Stevens had told Nussbaum how the payment was made, Stevens objected, and suddenly the Special Commission's counsel's strategy became clear:

> STEVENS: I object to this as beyond the scope of the direct examination. If the other side wants to call Mr. Hansen to testify as to this rather improbable set of circumstances, they are free to do so.
>
> OCHSENSCHLAGER: Would you be willing to stipulate whether he said that it was paid in cash or by check?
>
> STEVENS: Not unless he gets on the witness stand.

At this moment, it must have dawned on Ochsenschlager and his colleagues that Stevens had an ulterior motive in offering Nussbaum's inconclusive analysis. Stevens was daring them to call Hansen as a witness.

Stevens knew Hansen had said Perbohner gave him cash, but Stevens also didn't believe Hansen's whole story about the loan and supposed repayment, just as he didn't believe Isaacs's and Steigberg's renditions of it. If Ochsenschlager and Jenner wanted to correct the implication of Nussbaum's analysis—that the absence of checks or withdrawals showed there had been no loan by Perbohner—they would have to put Hansen on the stand. Stevens would then finally get the opportunity he had been trying to get for weeks, to examine the elusive fisherman in full about his part in the conspiracy to cover up the facts.

Ochsenschlager quickly ended his questioning. Stevens then announced, "Mr. Chairman, this is the extent of the evidence which we propose to offer." He was through presenting his case. Stevens added that two or three more depositions were still to be taken, and that he might find it necessary later to ask to reopen the record if new evidence were found. Hanley asked for information about the depositions, but, as before, Stevens declined to provide it.

Ochsenschlager spoke of the difficulty he faced in trying to decide whether to call witnesses before Stevens had finished deciding if he would offer more evidence. Greenberg stated the commission's assumption that Stevens had completed his proof, "subject to something extraordinary that may arise." Greenberg then asked whether witnesses would be called on behalf of either the justices or Isaacs, and Ochsenschlager and Hanley each said no. They had apparently decided not to accept Stevens's dare to call either Isaacs's friend Howard Hansen or Perbohner's friend Doris Steigberg.

Greenberg announced that Stevens would be allowed one and a half hours for an oral summation of the evidence. An hour each also would be allowed for oral presentations by the justices' lawyer and Isaacs's. The oral summations were scheduled for the following afternoon. Jenner, however, earlier had stated his preference to make a written presentation instead. Ochsenschlager now asked whether he might combine a brief oral summation with a written submission, and Greenberg allowed this, setting a Friday deadline.

Greenberg noted that it "has been a long six days" and thanked all of the attorneys "for your help and for the way in which you have assisted in carrying out this investigation with what we hope has been a degree of decorum and order." With that, he adjourned the proceedings until Thursday.

Chapter 21

Summing Up

Shortly after two o'clock Thursday afternoon, the Special Commission began its final public session, with oral summations as the main order of business. Five weeks had passed since the Thursday evening when John Paul Stevens was playing with his children and received the call from Henry Pitts that began this whirlwind. For over three weeks he had dug for the facts, and for almost two weeks now he had publicly presented his findings and prodded witnesses for more. Now it was time for him to pull the evidence together, but he had to do so in a way that respected some important constraints. As had been said repeatedly by the chairman and others, this was an investigation, not an adversary proceeding. Stevens did not have a specific client whose interests were to be protected or advanced. Furthermore, the applicable legal standards for evaluating the "integrity of the judgment" in *People v. Isaacs* remained unclear. As Stevens recognized when he began the investigation, his task was to help the Special Commission find the facts. His job now was to summarize those facts, leaving it to the commission to articulate their ultimate legal significance.

The courtroom was full, with people waiting in the hallway to be admitted as others occasionally left. Stevens began by noting the Special Commission's responsibility to investigate Skolnick's accusations insofar as they related to the integrity of the judgment. He also noted that the court itself had stressed that it was of "paramount importance" that the confidence of the bar and the public in the integrity of the court not be further impaired.

Before setting out on his main trail, Stevens cleared away some underbrush. He assured the commission that each charge in Skolnick's petition had been investigated. He stated that the staff had found no evidence to support the charges that Klingbiel's daughter and other persons held CCB stock as nominees for him, and that Solfisburg was secretly an attorney for the bank. He said that in investigating the integrity of the *Isaacs* judgment, the exploration covered all of the supreme court's members, not just Klingbiel and Solfisburg. On this basis, the staff "did not offer any evidence which might imply impropriety or appearance of impropriety on the part of any other member of the court, because we found none."

Similarly, the staff did not find anything in the internal deliberations of the court to put any other justice on notice of possible improprieties by the two accused members. In this regard, the irregularity in the assignment of the *Isaacs* opinion to Klingbiel in the January 1967 term was susceptible to various reasonable explanations, including the fact that in the prior term four justices other than Klingbiel had taken extra cases from the two new members, Ward and Kluczynski. Furthermore, he stated that the staff had examined the reasoning of the opinion itself and found nothing to put "members of the court who disagreed with the opinion on notice that there may or may not have been anything improper about the deliberations within the court itself."

With this preliminary statement behind him, Stevens went on to his primary task of reviewing the facts that had been put in the public record of the hearings. He proceeded in chronological order to place the entire matter in perspective, despite the jumping back and forth, both in time and among documents, that had characterized the presentation of evidence. He first reminded the commissioners of key dates in the *Isaacs* litigation: the December 1965 notice of appeal; the September 1966 oral argument; and the May 1967 conclusion.

His review began in 1963 and ended in June 1969. As he went over major pieces of evidence, he linked them together to highlight their implications. The first implication was that early on Solfisburg and Isaacs were acquainted with each other and Solfisburg knew of Isaacs's association with the Civic Center Bank. Stevens pointed to the work Isaacs's law firm did for Financial Security Life Insurance Company, beginning in 1963. Further support for this implication was the December 1966 CCB proxy notice, and Solfisburg's calls to Isaacs beginning in January 1968, seeking assistance with the National Guard for his son.

As he finished addressing the relationship between Isaacs and the chief justice, Stevens elaborated on the nature of the evidence:

One thing is of interest. There is no correspondence between Mr. Isaacs and Mr. Solfisburg on any subject at any time that we have found or has been produced for us. There is also no correspondence with respect to many of these transactions, though one would normally expect there to be correspondence if they were "ordinary business transactions," as the principals involved would have us believe.

Stevens was voicing two interrelated themes that would dominate much of his summation: There frequently were no records, correspondence, or other documents to corroborate alleged transactions and events, and what Isaacs and others repeatedly tried to characterize as "ordinary" or "normal" business transactions were instead quite extraordinary and abnormal. Stevens's broader implication, of course, was that a wholly undocumented, supposed transaction that sounds quite out of the ordinary probably didn't happen.

Stevens returned frequently to these themes, as well as two others. He emphasized the absence of explanations for developments that should logically not be difficult to explain. Isaacs, for example, "did not undertake to explain" how Financial Security came to be a client of his firm:

> I think it is reasonable to infer that a prominent member of a law firm, knowing that a relationship with a particular client was under discussion in a hearing of this kind, would have explained the source of that client, had he not himself been the source. This is a matter of inference and, I submit, it is a reasonable inference.

More generally, Stevens emphasized the decision by Ochsenschlager and Jenner to call no witnesses. Stevens noted that the interested parties had the power to subpoena witnesses, and that they had "fair notice of basically what the evidence would be." He observed: "It is of some significance, I respectfully suggest, that no evidence has been put in by any one of the interested parties, notwithstanding their opportunity to do so."

The fourth of Stevens's refrains was the suspicious frequency and convenience of memory lapses by key witnesses. He pointed to failures of memory on the witness stand, and also to memory problems displayed by participants—such as Perbohner, Isaacs, and Klingbiel—who contradicted themselves and one another in various critical assertions outside of the hearings. Throughout his chronology of facts, Stevens continued to build on these four themes: absence of documentation, abnormality of transactions, failure to explain, and frequency of memory lapses.

Turning to Isaacs's claim of a loan from Perbohner, via Hansen, in

March 1965, Stevens emphasized "that nobody has any piece of paper of any kind tending to corroborate this rather improbable event." He noted the absence of any evidence of a receipt from Hansen to Perbohner, a withdrawal by Perbohner from a bank account, a money order purchase, a receipt from Harry Busch, a thank-you letter from Isaacs, or any other correspondence. Stevens continued:

> I submit that at the inception of this suggested transaction, it is not an ordinary business transaction. . . . No note was signed. If this was to be a loan, no evidence of indebtedness. No request for repayment. No thanks for repayment. No thanks for the gift. There is no corroboration of any kind, and this is characteristic of so many of the circumstances in the series of events that we are considering.

Stevens, speaking with intense seriousness, had begun to convey his suspicion about the alibis the commission had heard. In the same vein, he turned to Solfisburg's testimony about a late 1965 conversation with Dolph and Perbohner during which supposedly they recommended CCB stock to him and he suddenly decided to invest $14,000. Stevens elucidated the circumstances making this conversation improbable. He said, "First, again there is no document to corroborate it," such as a subscription agreement. Second, he referred to the unequivocal testimony of Civic Center Bank representatives that neither Dolph nor Perbohner had any right to allocate CCB shares to anyone. Third, he noted the added improbability that Solfisburg "would merely say, 'I'd like seven hundred shares,'" and those two men would get it for him from "this oversubscribed issue."

Stevens summarized the basic facts of the January 1966 clearance loan and the 12,850 shares held as collateral. He emphasized the absence of evidence that anyone other than Isaacs had legal control over the shares, and he detailed "considerable evidence in the record which contradicts Mr. Isaacs's testimony that he had virtually nothing to do with what happened to these shares." Stevens explained:

> The most dramatic example is Mr. Isaacs's own testimony with respect to the hundred shares that went to Mr. Perbohner. He simply called Mrs. Kegley and ordered them out. . . . He got no approval from any committee or anything else.

Stevens also referred to Jayne Kegley's testimony, in which she several times specifically identified Isaacs as the source of her instructions with respect to the list.

Stevens mentioned Stout's diary entries, and various letters and memoranda, that implicated Isaacs in the stock issuance. Stevens referred to Isaacs's memorandum reporting on the loss of Joseph Knight's stock certificate, asking: "Is it not reasonable to take this document as corroboration of Mrs. Kegley's recollection that Mr. Isaacs was the one responsible for the issuance of these shares and the way in which they were issued?" He also commented on Knight's loss of memory on the witness stand. Stevens understated his inference: "Mr. Isaacs had something to do with the disposition of these shares."

Moving on to Solfisburg's May 1966 stock purchase, Stevens conceded that it was difficult to ascertain how the arrangements for the purchase were made. Solfisburg hadn't been able to recall who requested him to submit his payment. Stevens recounted the correspondence about a planned meeting in Rockford and reminded the commission that Solfisburg, after repeated questioning, eventually remembered a luncheon meeting with Perbohner in Rockford at some time or other. Stevens now said: "It is possible—who knows, because he does not recall—that he was there the day before he wrote the check, and that is why he got the money in the next day." Stevens acknowledged the absence of direct evidence of such a meeting.

Stevens commented on the strange reference to "Bob Perbohner" in Harold Stout's letter about a Rockford meeting, even though Stout didn't know Perbohner. Stevens noted Perbohner's prominence in this correspondence, as well as in the supposed loan to Isaacs in March 1965: "Mr. Perbohner, of course, is the key figure all through these events."

Stevens listed various oddities of Solfisburg's purchase: the absence of an address on his letter to the bank; his written request for the shares to be issued in his name, and the later undocumented change to a trust; and the absence of his transmittal letter in the bank's files. Stevens speculated:

> There is no way of knowing whether or not this letter was actually sent or, if it was sent, whether it was delivered by courier perhaps to Mr. Isaacs, who then perhaps said—this is merely a matter of supposition and inference—"It would be preferable not to have the shares issued in your name because they must be recorded with the Recorder of Deeds of Cook County."
>
> By Mr. Isaacs's testimony, he knew this was a procedure that had to be followed, but Mr. Justice Solfisburg testified it was a matter with which he was unfamiliar.

Stevens went on to highlight the justice's unprecedented life insurance loans to finance most of the stock purchase. Stevens observed, with facetious understatement, that "apparently he was quite confident in

the desirability of this investment, notwithstanding the fact that his investigation had been somewhat less than thorough."

Solfisburg's trust for the seven hundred shares was now described
as serving only one actual function: to conceal from public record the
fact that he was the beneficial owner. Stevens suggested, "There is an
inference one can draw that his motive was to do exactly what was accomplished, namely to conceal the fact that he was becoming the beneficial owner of seven hundred shares of Civic Center Bank stock
while the *Isaacs* case was pending before the Supreme Court of Illinois." Stevens also noted that the seven hundred shares could well
form part of a block of a thousand shares, when matched with Dolph's
and Davison's.

More firmly, Stevens noted that the justice promptly withdrew from
the trust all proceeds from sales of the stock: "There was no continuing purpose in creating this trust. The inference of an intent to conceal
is inescapable." Stevens's last comment on Solfisburg's seven hundred
shares reprised Kegley's testimony that her instructions to issue those
shares to the justice came from Isaacs.

Stevens moved on to two more factual areas: Klingbiel's CCB
stock, and the sale of Solfisburg's. He turned to Klingbiel's testimony
about a conversation with Dolph and Perbohner in the late summer or
early fall of 1966 about their intention to contribute to the justice's reelection campaign. Stevens reiterated his earlier themes as they fit
both the campaign contribution and the transfer of the hundred shares
from Isaacs to Perbohner:

> There is no correspondence to confirm what was said or any rea-
> son for a campaign contribution. It is an improbable campaign con-
> tribution from the outset. . . .
>
> Mr. Isaacs, when queried by Mr. Fisher, tried to discuss this as an
> ordinary business transaction. It is not ordinary even if one accepts
> his entire description of the events involving the alleged, antecedent
> gift. . . . I respectfully submit to the commission that the charges
> made here are of grave public importance. They involve questions
> as to the integrity of a former member of the governor's cabinet, of
> two members of the Illinois Commerce Commission, and two mem-
> bers of the Supreme Court of Illinois. Mr. Isaacs knew the matter
> was under investigation. He knew—he certainly is presumed to
> have known—that he wrote this check, and presumably it was avail-
> able, but did he bring these facts forward when asked by Mr. Fisher
> for them? The answer is no. He gave answers which tended to con-
> ceal the true nature of the transaction.

Stevens emphasized the complete absence of documentation of the supposed repayment to Perbohner, as well as of the campaign contribution to Klingbiel. Stevens described Klingbiel as "a courteous gentleman" who wrote thank-you letters to Perbohner and Dolph on other occasions for much less valuable gifts, but there was no written acknowledgment of this one.

Stevens speculated that Isaacs "at that time was more concerned about what the Supreme Court of Illinois would do with his litigation, which was recently argued, than with any other matter." He added another critical inference: "Isaacs knew Mr. Perbohner well enough so he must have known that Mr. Perbohner on frequent occasions met in Mr. Dolph's apartment with members of the supreme court." Stevens highlighted the abnormal actions of Klingbiel at the time of his receipt of the stock:

> When Mr. Justice Klingbiel received this extraordinary amount from the persons from whom he got it, in extraordinary form—a certificate endorsed in blank—what he did with it was extraordinary in the sense he put the certificate in his pocket, failed to have it registered in the name of anyone else other than Mr. Perbohner for almost two years, goes back into the social gathering in the living room, and says nothing about this rather delightful occurrence, if it is a normal bona fide matter.

Stevens also mentioned Klingbiel's belated and unusual method of transferring the shares to his grandchildren, using a Chicago attorney to handle the matter personally.

Stevens noted that "over and over again in this record, transactions are handled in a way that is not the normal way to handle them" and that concealed their true nature. Concealment also was shown by Klingbiel's conduct as recently as May, lying to the newspaper reporters and deluding Justice Kluczynski about the acquisition of the stock. Stevens summarized: "The only explanation must be that he was deliberately desirous of concealing the transaction because he had guilty knowledge with respect to the true nature of the transaction. No other reasonable inference can be drawn."

Next Stevens reviewed the facts of Solfisburg's sale of the first three hundred shares, just as the *Isaacs* litigation terminated in May 1967. Stevens structured his comments around the testimony of Isaacs that he did not know Solfisburg was the seller, and the testimony of Solfisburg that he did not know Isaacs had anything to do with the transaction. Stevens said that pertinent documents "shed considerable doubt on the credibility of both sides of this testimony." He reviewed Solfisburg's conduct in personally picking up the certificates from the Aurora bank, his use of Flynn rather than the mail to get them to Chicago, Flynn's familiarity with the bank and Isaacs's association with it, Solfisburg's invitation to Flynn to participate in the justice's original acquisition of CCB shares, Flynn's delivery of the certificates to Isaacs's office, and the receipt signed by Isaacs's secretary but typed earlier on a typewriter somewhere else.

Stevens homed in on two parts of the record. The first was Flynn's statement that he obtained a receipt in order to be ready in case Solfisburg were later to say, "I never brought it up to Isaacs." The second was Flynn's statement that he didn't report back to Solfisburg about the delivery because Solfisburg "just took it for granted that if he asked me to do it, and being in the same building, I would do it." Stevens summed up the point: "I respectfully submit the only reasonable inference from the testimony in the entire transaction is that Mr. Flynn took these certificates to Mr. Isaacs's office because that is exactly what Judge Solfisburg asked him to do."

Stevens attacked Isaacs's claim of ignorance that Solfisburg was the seller when Isaacs made up the $300 shortage. Stevens mentioned Isaacs's vague testimony about when he first learned Solfisburg was a CCB stockholder. Stevens surmised that if Isaacs really didn't already know of Solfisburg's ownership of CCB stock by May 1967, "whenever that came to his attention it would have been an event which he would remember with clarity and distinctness, in view of the importance of the litigation and the judge's position with the Supreme Court of Illinois." Also, Isaacs's secretary knew the shares were delivered by Flynn on behalf of Solfisburg, for she wrote that in a note to Stout when she took the certificates to the bank. Stevens queried, "Is it reasonable to assume, in view of the fact she too was aware of the importance of the *Isaacs* litigation, she made no mention of this fact to her employer, Mr. Isaacs?"

As for Isaacs's $300 check, if Isaacs actually had to make an emergency trip to the bank on May 26 and cover the shortfall on the spot, Stevens asked, "Why didn't they send the check out right away?" Instead the bank's check for the total sale proceeds did not go to Solfisburg until June 1. Stevens said it seemed more reasonable to infer that Isaacs sent his check over with the certificates themselves. He suggested, "Mr. Isaacs's explanation for his contribution of $300 to the transaction is less probable than another explanation the commission may wish to draw."

The last angle Stevens touched on relative to the Solfisburg shares was the later sales, beginning in March 1968 after Solfisburg had called

Isaacs about the National Guard. Stevens, with a touch of sarcasm, noted Flynn's testimony that "the same scenic route was taken for delivery of the shares, by way of Mr. Isaacs's office and ultimately to the bank."

Stevens concluded the chronology by suggesting two legal principles the commission should consider in determining whether these transactions were isolated events. The first principle was the well-settled rule "that affirmative acts of concealment are evidence of consciousness of guilt." He declared, "The evidence here establishes unquestionably, on behalf of each principal, affirmative acts of concealment."

The second principle was "that it is not necessary to prove an unlawful agreement by direct evidence," but instead such an agreement, or conspiracy, may be inferred "from the evidence of more than a coincidental sequence of events." Stevens read a lengthy quotation from a ten-year-old Illinois Supreme Court decision that stated, among other things:

> A conspiracy is rarely susceptible of direct proof, but must very nearly always, from the nature of things, be established by circumstantial evidence and legitimate inferences arising therefrom. The inferences depend largely upon the commonsense knowledge of the motives and intentions of men in like circumstances.

The quotation had special ironic force because of its author: Justice Klingbiel.[1]

Stevens invited the commissioners to consider "what possible explanation will account for the parallel threads that run through the facts which I have described." Again, Stevens emphasized Perbohner, "a central figure throughout this picture," as the man with whom Isaacs dealt and "the man from whom Mr. Justice Solfisburg and Mr. Justice Klingbiel received their Civic Center Bank stock directly or were advised to get it." It was abundantly clear, Stevens argued, that Perbohner's "primary motivation was to prevent the full facts from coming into public view."

Stevens reiterated that both Klingbiel and Solfisburg got stock in the bank while the *Isaacs* litigation was pending and both voted consistently in Isaacs's favor. Both received significant and immediate economic benefit from the stock. Neither justice, he said, "made any reasonable inquiry as to the source of the benefits they were receiving, took any precautions to protect them against the danger of having received benefits from a litigant who then had a case pending before them. . . . Both of them, I respectfully submit, are guilty of affirmative acts of concealment." Again, he spoke of the hidden ownership, one justice through a trust and the other through a certificate endorsed in blank. He spoke again of the use of couriers and of the absence of "any correspondence which would reasonably explain the situation in which they find themselves involved, where one would expect correspondence to exist."

Finally, Stevens again mentioned the failure of the justices "to bring forth any action which will help explain these transactions in a satisfactory, normal, business way." Stevens said of the justices, "They are fiduciaries, each one of these individuals, to the people of the state of Illinois, who have a duty to account clearly and unequivocally for what they have done." He finished sharply:

> I respectfully submit to the commission that there is a substantial basis in this record for finding that these, the following persons— Theodore J. Isaacs, Robert M. Perbohner, Ray I. Klingbiel, and Roy Solfisburg—are each guilty of gross impropriety.

Stevens's Choice

Stevens's summation thus ended abruptly, without the type of statement that usually completes a lawyer's courtroom argument. He finished with the assertion of gross impropriety, but didn't go on to say what the Special Commission should do about it. The omission was Stevens's deliberate choice, although not one he had made easily.

When testimony ended on Wednesday afternoon, Stevens was convinced that Solfisburg and Klingbiel were so tainted by their improper conduct and falsehoods that they should resign from the Illinois Supreme Court. He told all the staff lawyers in his office that afternoon that he was planning to end his summation by urging the commissioners to demand the justices' resignation. Most of the staff members initially agreed that Stevens's plan was justified and appropriate. Although these lawyers had no specific client in this proceeding, in a broad sense they felt accountable to the public and the legal profession. From this perspective, it seemed entirely suitable for Stevens to express the conclusion that the justices had forfeited the privilege of serving on the state's highest court.

The newspapers at this time were speculating about what Stevens would say. *Chicago Today* reported that Stevens "will not recommend what action the Commission should take." In contrast, the *Rockford Register-Republic* quoted an unnamed source on the commission staff as saying that the staff was unanimous in believing the justices should leave the court, and also that Stevens "will recommend that the justices resign or be removed from the high court bench."

During the Wednesday afternoon meeting, Nathaniel Sack quoted a pertinent aphorism—"If you shoot at the king, you should shoot to kill." Stevens remembers the aphorism as phrased a bit differently during the intense discussion: "If you shoot at the king, don't miss."[2] Either way, the point was the same: If Stevens was going to condemn the justices' behavior and credibility as strongly as he believed the evidence warranted, he might as well go all the way and urge that they leave the court.

I saw things differently. I said that we really had no way of knowing what the commissioners would do in their final report a week later. We didn't know for certain that the commissioners considered it within their authority to ask for the justices' resignations, nor did we even know whether the commissioners would conclude the evidence was strong enough to warrant their departure. I wasn't sure the commissioners had the authority to demand this result, and I was even less sure it was proper for the commission's counsel to urge them to do so. His principal function now, I suggested, was to summarize the facts and offer his perspective but leave the identification of outcomes entirely in the hands of the Special Commission.

I especially feared that if Stevens urged the commissioners to demand resignations, the staff would be putting them in an unfair bind. If they followed his recommendation, they might be criticized by the justices' supporters for simply deferring to Stevens's view, rather than making up their own minds. If they rejected the recommendation, they would certainly be criticized harshly in some quarters for their weakness in failing to follow the more aggressive, principled position of their own counsel. Undoubtedly Sherman Skolnick would revive the "whitewash" charge, and newspapers that already had called for the justices to resign would chastise the commission for its failure to join in that call. Finally, after further debate, Stevens decided that the summation should omit any recommendation.[3]

When Stevens finished his presentation on Thursday afternoon with the assertion of gross impropriety, Greenberg took a moment to remind the press of the significance of Stevens's presentation: "It remains the personal responsibility of this commission to decide this matter, and to accept or reject the appraisal in whole or in part of the evidence which Mr. Stevens has submitted to us." Greenberg added that, even though the press might judge Stevens's statement "to be an able argument from a very able advocate," Greenberg wanted the news media, and through them the public, to remember that in the end the Special Commission would make up its own mind.

Mutual Indignation

Because Isaacs's lawyers wanted to present their closing remarks in written form, only the justices' attorneys remained to be heard. William Murphy went first to give their affirmative view of the evidence, and Lambert Ochsenschlager followed to reply to Stevens. Murphy asserted that the sole issue was whether judges "are chargeable with conduct which has the appearance of impropriety or, in the words of Mr. Stevens, guilty of gross impropriety," when each judge owns only a tiny percentage of a corporation's stock and participates in the decision of a criminal case concerning a defendant who, "without the actual knowledge of the judges concerned, and without knowledge on their part of facts that would put an ordinarily prudent judge on inquiry," is also a small shareholder and officer of the same corporation.

Central to this statement was Murphy's view that the justices lacked any knowledge, or any reason to inquire, about any connection between Isaacs and the Civic Center Bank: "There is no issue here as to what the answer would be if the judges knew then what they know now. Both judges stated without equivocation that they would not have participated in this decision had they known then what has now come into the record." Murphy's point echoed the indignant perspective Ochsenschlager had repeatedly pursued during the hearings. If the justices were unaware of Isaacs's connection to the stock, and if there was "no knowledge of facts which would put a reasonably prudent man on inquiry," then the justices simply could not have done anything wrong.

From this central theme, Murphy offered his analysis of some parts of the evidentiary record. He attacked Stevens's suggestion that the justices had actively tried to conceal their stock transactions. He noted that Solfisburg had written his own check to the bank, and that both justices were forthcoming in producing their documentary records and giving their testimony. He offered the somewhat counterproductive opinion that "had it been their desire to conceal, the evidence that has come out in this case reveals that they were absolutely and totally inept in concealment."

Murphy emphasized the ordinariness of the gift to Klingbiel in fulfillment of a promise by old friends. He argued that Klingbiel's receipt of more than he spent on his campaign should not be held against him any more than it would be against anyone else running for office.

As for Isaacs's explanation of the Perbohner loan and repayment, Murphy returned to his main point:

Justice Klingbiel knew none of this. He did not know that Isaacs had
received a contribution from Perbohner or that Isaacs had transferred stock back to Perbohner in payment, or whatever the testimony was. Knowing none of this, and having knowledge of no facts
that would put him on notice to inquire into it, he was in the most
honorable sense a politician receiving a gift, and Mr. Stevens would
have us believe that the politician receiving the gift should not only
look the gift horse in the mouth, but make a complete investigation
of the stable boys and former owners. That is not the law with
horses. It is not good sense with stock.

As for Solfisburg's stock acquisition, Murphy argued that "he received the same treatment as one hundred other people received." If
it was desired to make him a stockholder because of his office, that was
"not a dishonorable desire." It would only be wrong for a judge to become a bank stockholder if he knew that someone associated with the
bank was before him as a litigant.

Murphy reminded the commission that Solfisburg testified he put
the stock into the trust to protect his family, because he had used insurance funds to buy the stock. The trust was not part of a plan for concealment, for if it were, "Why did Solfisburg send in his own check?"
If he wanted to conceal the purchase, the simplest thing would have
been to give the money to the Aurora bank and have its check sent instead.

Murphy explained Flynn's delivery of Solfisburg's stock by saying
that "when a neighbor is asked to do something, he does it." Again,
Murphy emphasized, "none of this has any import unless you attribute
to Justice Solfisburg actual knowledge of Isaacs's connection or facts
which should have put him on notice of such connection. And there
are no such facts." In framing the issue this way, Murphy was probably
in fundamental agreement with Stevens. The profound difference, of
course, was that Murphy saw no such facts, while Stevens found ample
evidence from which to draw precisely the opposite conclusion.

As he approached the end of his argument, Murphy made two of his
strongest points. First, he referred to Stevens's statement that nothing
occurred during the decision of *People v. Isaacs* that would have put
any of the other justices on notice of improper conduct. Murphy asserted that the judgment itself was thus not tainted. Ultimately the
only disagreement within the court, he said, was over a few counts on
which the Underwood and Klingbiel opinions differed. Even then, the
State's Attorney sought rehearing on only one count, and there was no
disagreement among the justices on that count at all.

Murphy's other concluding point was based on Klingbiel's impression vote in favor of Isaacs on September 15, 1966, almost a month before he received the CCB stock. Murphy asked, "What possible explanation can there be for the fact that Mr. Justice Klingbiel, before he got the stock or knew he was going to get the stock, would have voted at the impression vote to affirm? Now that is . . . evidence that cannot be explained away." After a few final comments, Murphy sat down and Ochsenschlager rose to reply to Stevens.

With his usual homespun, rambling style, Ochsenschlager did not make as methodical a presentation as those of Stevens and Murphy. He declared his confidence in the justices' full disclosure of their files, minds, and memories, and expressed his disagreement with Stevens's insistence on the importance of documentation to corroborate the justices' testimony. He emphasized that much of Stevens's case rested on circumstantial evidence and the drawing of inferences.

Ochsenschlager reiterated his earlier view that the Illinois Commerce Commission came before the supreme court not as a litigant but instead as an appellate or trial court whose decisions were under review. Acknowledging ethical constraints on a judge's acceptance of campaign contributions from a lawyer "who is apt to be practicing in your court," Ochsenschlager emphasized that Perbohner was not a lawyer and Dolph had abandoned his private law practice when he joined the Commerce Commission.

Returning to the campaign contribution to Klingbiel, Ochsenschlager expressed his view that such contributions are "as common as rain in the spring." Somewhat prophetically, Ochsenschlager stated that perhaps in the future there might be a law requiring any elected official to publicly report "each and every gift that he might receive above a certain value," and he observed that such a requirement would be "fine with me." Of course, he added, there was not yet a law declaring improper "this practice which has gone on from time immemorial."

As he finished, Ochsenschlager touched briefly on a variety of other points, including Isaacs's $300 check, Klingbiel's conversation with Kluczynski, other financial advice Isaacs might have given Solfisburg if they really were friends, and the practical problems the court would face in mustering a quorum for decisions if justices always had to disqualify themselves whenever they had any acquaintance with a litigant.

In the end, as at the beginning of the hearings, Ochsenschlager brought to bear his folksy manner. He invited the news media to drop in if they came out to Aurora to investigate him. Referring to Stevens, he said, "I have had my differences with my good friend here, but I will tell you one thing, I have gotten to know him this way, and this has been great."

"Permit Us to Go in Peace"

The final questions of the hearings were posed by Daniel Schuyler. He asked Ochsenschlager to comment on how Solfisburg came to be allocated seven hundred shares. The lawyer emphasized his belief that Solfisburg acted solely on the advice of Dolph, and his opinion that almost anyone with some stature who wanted stock probably could have gotten it. He noted the presence of many prominent persons on the CCB stockholder list: "It looks like the roll call in Springfield."

After this exchange, Henry Pitts made some closing remarks. He stated that from the time five weeks earlier when he and Greenberg suddenly were asked to serve on the Special Commission, they and the other commissioners were determined to conduct this proceeding with decorum and dignity, rather than as "a scramble for a place on the five o'clock news." He emphasized that the court expected "a prompt, impartial, and effective investigation" and that there has not been "the slightest doubt in the minds of any member of this commission or of the staff" about meeting that expectation. Alluding to the political tumult of the late 1960s, Pitts concluded: "I admit it may be strange to some in this period—when it often appears more fashionable to jeer than to cheer—[but] an unflinching quest for truth of this character is not something unusual to those who are familiar with the history and traditions of an independent bar in Anglo-American jurisprudence."

The final words were Greenberg's, and they were mostly compliments. Emphasizing that he was not intimating either agreement or disagreement with Stevens's summation, he nonetheless described the work of Stevens and the staff as a "moment when one detects again the nobility and pride which good lawyers have in their profession." Characteristically, he spoke as though pronouncing a benediction:

> Now the commission has ended its hearings. Our job is to begin to reflect, to think, to write our report, and to file it in a very short period of time.
>
> I hope that the press and the news media, with whom we have tried to be as open as circumstances and our tradition permit, will understand that when we have something to say that can be properly said publicly, we will say it. Until then, I trust that they will permit us to go in peace.

Chapter 22

Meeting the Deadline

The Special Commission had one week until the August 1 deadline set by the Illinois Supreme Court for completion of the investigation. The commissioners promptly met to discuss the evidence, formulate their conclusions, and write their report. To assist them, Stevens provided a detailed set of "Proposed Findings of Fact."

Greenberg took the lead role in writing the report, particularly since he was, in Henry Pitts's understatement, "a pretty good wordsmith." Greenberg's secretary, Catherine Delaney, recalls doing "one hell of a lot of typing."

Still Searching

Although the commission was now in its final phase, the staff's fact-finding job was still not quite over. Stevens was quoted as saying a few more depositions were needed to try to "unravel the mystery of how Mr. Justice Solfisburg got his stock." Thus, on Friday afternoon at one o'clock, I took the deposition of a former secretary to David X. Meyers. David and his brother Edward were two of the prime movers in creating the Civic Center Bank. At two o'clock Torshen and I took David's deposition, and on Monday McNally and I took Edward's.

The secretary confirmed much of what we already knew about the organization of the bank in 1965, but she knew little about later events. In contrast, David Meyers declared that even though Isaacs wasn't on the informal committee that controlled the distribution of stock, "if he wanted to buy some stock or had somebody that was interested in buying the stock, we would lean toward him, the same way you would do that to your friends."[1] He remembered that Isaacs submitted names to the committee, although he couldn't remember which.

Meyers testified that he had been aware that Jayne Kegley was keeping track of the issuance of shares. Torshen and I asked Meyers whether he had selected certain people to receive shares, and in every instance he denied any knowledge or involvement. His brother Edward made a similar denial. The brothers didn't know that the names we asked them about had been identified by Kegley as coming from Isaacs. The brothers' denials were thus consistent with Kegley's testimony.

Stevens took two more depositions. On Tuesday afternoon, July 29, he deposed the manager of the currency exchange that had issued a $2,100 money order in March 1965 cashed by Harry Busch. The manager produced the canceled money order, which appeared to be the one Isaacs had testified about and Howard Hansen had discussed in his still uncompleted deposition. Unfortunately, neither the currency exchange manager's memory nor his records offered firm information about who actually bought the money order. There was only a puzzling indication that the purchaser was "D. C. Evans," a name new to the manager and to us.

Stevens's last deposition began at two o'clock on Thursday, July 31, a few hours before the deadline for finishing the commission's work. The deponent was Howard Hansen, who had finally been located and induced to appear. Stevens immediately asked him to identify the last time he had talked to Isaacs. Hansen's lawyer objected, insisting that Hansen had only been ordered by Judge Healy to answer the questions asked by Stevens on July 9. Now Stevens was asking about possible conversations with Isaacs after that date.

Stevens quoted from the transcript of Judge Healy's rulings, which indicated that the questioning could go beyond the earlier questions. Hansen's lawyer was unpersuaded, and Stevens upped the ante: "We have information that we feel in fairness to your client, he should be given an opportunity to answer. If he chooses not to, we will take appropriate steps." Stevens tried to break the impasse by giving Hansen an opportunity then and there to read the answers he gave at the July 9 deposition and to change the substance of his testimony if he wished. Hansen's lawyer rejected this procedure because it didn't give the witness enough time to read the prior answers carefully. Stevens and the commission, of course, were virtually out of time for this witness or anything else.

The dialogue between the lawyers grew heated, with accusations exchanged about who was responsible for the lateness of Hansen's appearance. In the end, Stevens reiterated his threat, although he still did not put all his cards on the table:

> We have reason to believe that the substance of Mr. Hansen's testimony is false, and that he may have been guilty of perjury and we, therefore, want to give him the opportunity here and now to change that testimony if he desires. If he doesn't, why we will have to refer the record to whatever authorities would take whatever action they desire.[2]

Hansen continued to decline the opportunity, and the questioning was over. Stevens had finished his last, and least useful, deposition.

Barely in Peace

Greenberg had asked the press to allow the Special Commission to go off and complete its work in peace. He didn't quite get his wish, for developments continued to swirl around the commission, and the newspapers continued to give them prominent attention.[3] On Monday, July 28, there suddenly was a dramatic, highly publicized interference with the quiet that the commission had hoped for. Ochsenschlager filed with the Illinois Supreme Court a "Motion for Clarification of Prior Court Order and for Instructions to Special Commission." He asserted:

> It has come to the undersigned [counsel's] attention that John Paul Stevens, counsel for the Special Commission, has contended and continues to contend that the Special Commission is empowered to make and in fact is considering the making of conclusions and the recommending of sanctions regarding one or more of the Interested Parties.

It was unclear how Ochsenschlager came to believe he knew what Stevens was thinking. One newspaper later commented, "There had been no hint that the Commission might go so far as to recommend resignation by one or both of the justices until Monday," when Ochsenschlager himself made the assertion. What had become clear over the weekend, however, was that there was an upsurge of opinion around the state that the justices should leave the court.

On Sunday the Lindsay-Schaub chain of downstate newspapers— in East St. Louis, Carbondale, Champaign-Urbana, Decatur, and Edwardsville—published an editorial in each of its papers calling for Klingbiel's resignation. The editorial also said that Solfisburg should either resign or withhold participation in any court decisions "until further evidence of his 'non-involvement' is presented." Also on Sunday *Chicago Today* reported that it had surveyed "many legal experts across the state" who opined that the two justices probably would resign even before the deadline for the commission's report. The article noted that the commission's hearings, which "opened amid suspicions they would be a 'whitewash,'" were now given "rave reviews" by these same unnamed legal experts. Even Sherman Skolnick now conceded that the panel "did a pretty good job."

Ochsenschlager's motion, however, suggested that the justices still were prepared to fight. The motion argued that under the court's order creating the Special Commission, as well as under the Illinois Constitution's provisions on the Illinois Courts Commission, the Special Commission lacked authority to make conclusions or recommend sanctions. Ochsenschlager also charged that a supreme court rule required the Special Commission to keep its findings confidential "until a complaint, if any, is filed" before the Courts Commission. This last point was the same one that Isaacs had urged, and the court had rejected, just a few days before the public hearings began.[4] Now Ochsenschlager was asking the court to order the Special Commission both "to avoid conclusions and the recommendation of sanctions," and to keep its report confidential.

Stevens fired back the Special Commission's answer on the same day with two blunt points. First, it noted that the rule argument had been made by Isaacs before and rejected by the court. Second, the answer asked that the commission "be permitted to make its own determination as to the proper scope and content of the report which it is now preparing." The answer, signed by each of the five commissioners, urged the court to deny the motion. On Tuesday the court did so, without comment.

The *Daily News* reported this result in a front-page story and noted, as did other papers, that the court's brief order "did not indicate the vote or whether Solfisburg and Klingbiel had taken part in the decision." This comment highlighted how extraordinary the Special Commission's investigation had become, and just how strange Ochsenschlager's motion was. The chief justice and another justice of the Illinois Supreme Court had just filed a motion with the very court on which they sat. It is difficult to believe that they would have participated in the decision of their own motion, but at least some experienced reporters seemed to consider that a possibility. On Wednesday, however, the *Daily News* reported that the two justices did not participate, and that the other justices ruled on the motion.

Another, collateral development on Tuesday was the announcement by Illinois Attorney General William J. Scott of an investigation into the granting of the state charter for the Civic Center Bank. Scott said his investigation was an offshoot of a broader investigation of Joseph Knight and would look into possible conflicts of interest and other irregularities in the establishment of the bank. Scott's office had asked for a full transcript of the Special Commission's hearings. It was also reported that Illinois law prohibited a state bank from borrowing money using its own stock as collateral. If that were correct, new questions would arise about the legality of Isaacs's clearance loan from the First National Bank.

On Wednesday Skolnick filed yet another motion with the supreme court, this time charging Solfisburg and Klingbiel with misconduct and conflicts of interest in three cases involving property taxes owed by a railroad. Skolnick alleged a web of connections among the railroad, the two justices, Financial Security Life Insurance, and various banks. He also told reporters he planned to file over twenty more motions relating to the two justices. Ochsenschlager and the railroad quickly issued angry statements, denying the charges and pointing out factual contradictions and misunderstandings in Skolnick's latest barrage.

Jenner's Parting Shots

Amidst these distractions, and while Stevens finished the depositions, the commissioners labored to write their report. As they approached the end of their task late on Wednesday afternoon, July 30, they finally received Jenner's closing submission, a thirty-eight-page "Statement" on Isaacs's behalf. The statement began with mild criticism of the investigative process, particularly the closed depositions. It described Stevens's conduct and summation as characteristic of "a public prosecutor rather than an impartial investigator." The statement asserted that "it was not a summation of the evidence or lack thereof in the record." Instead, it claimed to be something more modest: "We shall dwell solely upon principles of proof and inferences fairly to be drawn from that proof, and supply examples of claims made by Mr. Stevens in his summation that are at odds with those principles." The bulk of the statement then followed an unusual methodology. It listed and numbered seventy-seven "Asserted Facts" from Stevens's oral argument, and then listed "Inferences Drawn by Counsel from His Asserted Facts." The stated purpose was "to show that counsel, in his summation, made inferences from facts which do not support those inferences, and in some cases he has made inferences from other inferences."

Following roughly the same chronological progression Stevens had followed, the statement chipped away, one by one, at a selection of "examples of claims made by Mr. Stevens in his summation that are at odds" with principles of circumstantial evidence. In a brief conclusion, the statement again expressed dissatisfaction with the investigative process, emphasized how cooperative Isaacs and the bank had been during the investigation, recited the various charges Stevens had conceded were unproven, and ended by saying: "When stripped of [Stevens's] innuendo and cynical hindsight moralizing, the eight-volume, 133-exhibit record contains nothing which will justify vilification of Mr. Isaacs."

The statement was notable for its shrill tone, lack of cohesiveness, and misstatement of key facts.[5] In place of an accurate and cogent synthesis of evidence, as would be expected from as accomplished a litigator as Jenner, the statement read more like a list of factual quibbles and expressions of pique. The statement was first submitted very late on Tuesday but was replaced on Wednesday afternoon by an "As Amended and Corrected" version containing a large number of changes. The clumsiness of this filing, and the statement's amateurish content, suggested that it probably was drafted by junior lawyers in Jenner's office without close supervision by him or Robert Hanley.

By this time, of course, Jenner apparently had concluded that he had no facts available with which to fashion a strong response for Isaacs. Jenner's defense of Isaacs may have faced other problems, too, stemming from an excessively high level of client participation in the effort. Isaacs, after all, was a lawyer himself, and a man with lots of experience as a high-level strategist. In marked contrast with the two justices, who provided their lawyers with too little direction, Isaacs may have tried to give his lawyers—and maybe even friendly witnesses like Hansen and Steigberg—too much. Don Reuben later observed that by the end of the proceedings, Jenner probably had become embarrassed about being in the case. Reuben had been approached early on by Klingbiel for legal representation but had declined the justice's request. Reuben recalls Jenner later telling him, "You were smart to stay out of it."[6]

The Report

The Special Commission finished its report late Wednesday night. Thursday morning Henry Pitts drove to Springfield and delivered it to the supreme court and to the Courts Commission's secretary, Roy

Gulley. The court made the report public immediately. It was also delivered in Chicago to a representative of the House Committee.

Lawyers, litigants, and reporters invariably begin the reading of a decisive legal document at the end, to see who wins and who loses. Certainly most readers of the "Report of Special Commission of the Supreme Court of Illinois" approached this document in the same way, turning immediately to the last of the sixty-one pages of the report. They found strong words:

> The Commission believes that the confidence of the public and the Bar in the Court is a most essential foundation of our society. It has been severely shaken by the facts disclosed in this record. The Commission believes that such confidence can best be restored by the prompt resignation of the two Justices.*

The asterisk led to a footnote declaring that Commissioner Bull "dissents from the view of the other four members of the Commission that this statement is properly within the province of the Commission." Although Bull agreed with all of the other findings and conclusions in the report, he felt that the commission would exceed its mandate were it to call for resignations.

The sixty pages preceding the resignation demand presented a carefully crafted and detailed statement of the Special Commission's view of the facts and pertinent law. The commission emphasized, as Stevens had done in his summation, both its duty to investigate the integrity of the judgment in *People v. Isaacs* and the court's additional expression of concern "that the confidence of the Bar and the public in the integrity of the Court not be further impaired." The report then made a critical link:

> We deem the Commission's function to be investigatory and not adjudicatory. Therefore we do not intend that this Report be interpreted as a determination of the rights or liabilities of any person. However, we consider that the thrust of the charges we have been called upon to investigate is that Justice Solfisburg and/or Justice Klingbiel were guilty of such acts of impropriety, or gave such an appearance of impropriety, as to create a substantial doubt of their impartiality, fairness and integrity in the decision in the *Isaacs* case; and that their conduct was such as to seriously compromise the confidence of the public in the integrity of the decision. In that sense, the integrity of the judgment in the *Isaacs* case is inseparable from the question of whether Justice Solfisburg and/or Justice Klingbiel

have so conducted themselves as to raise substantial doubt of their own impartiality, fairness and integrity in participating in the decision.

The Findings

The heart of the report was thirty-five pages of "Findings of Fact." To a large extent these findings accepted Stevens's view of the evidence and the staff's "Proposed Findings of Fact," but it was clear the commissioners had gone through our submission with surgical precision—deleting, adding, and modifying so that the findings stated exactly what they wanted to say. Furthermore, the staff's proposal had described facts but not elaborated on their significance. The commissioners frequently took that important additional step.

The report reiterated the chronology of events, although in much greater detail than Stevens had given orally. Starting with the *Isaacs* decision itself, the commissioners addressed the unexplained, irregular assignment of the opinion to Klingbiel. They summarily concluded, "We do not attribute any particular significance to this circumstance." Describing the organization of the Civic Center Bank, the report found that Isaacs was "unquestionably an influential and important person in the organization of the bank and has continued to be so," adding that "he did not limit his activity in the management of the bank to purely legal services." This finding, like almost all others in the report, was supported by numerous citations to the hearings transcript and documentary exhibits.

The commissioners found that "Isaacs and a number of other persons who were members of the organizing group or importantly associated with the bank" controlled the disposition of the 12,850 shares held by Isaacs. These shares were to be sold to persons "in a position to help the bank or who, for other reasons, might be favored by Isaacs" and the others. Isaacs "had an apparent legal right to direct the issuance of shares," and he exercised that right "without the approval or consent of any other official or organizer of the bank." It was also noted that of the approximately one hundred people who bought shares out of Isaacs's block, only five purchased more than five hundred shares. Three of those were bank officers or organizers, and the other two were Solfisburg and Howard Hansen, both of whom "received their shares through the influence of Isaacs."

The report described Solfisburg's acquisition of his shares, focusing on his own assertions and memory gaps regarding the transaction. It noted Solfisburg's inability to recall how his desire to have the shares put into Trust No. 931 was communicated to the bank. The commissioners contrasted this gap with Kegley's testimony that she "received her instructions to issue the 700 shares to Trust 931 from Isaacs or Isaacs's office." Regarding the purpose of the trust—a point that the commissioners had probed intensively during Solfisburg's testimony—they found that "the only function served by Trust No. 931 and the issuance of the 700 shares in the name of the Trust was to conceal Justice Solfisburg's acquisition and ownership of said shares."

Solfisburg was found to have known that the Isaacs law firm performed services for Financial Security Life Insurance Company. The report also cited Flynn's knowledge of Isaacs's association with the new bank, Solfisburg's close relationship with Flynn, and Solfisburg's discussion of the bank stock purchase with Flynn. It concluded that Solfisburg "had ample opportunity to learn of Isaacs's association with the bank at the time he acquired the shares."

The commission recounted Flynn's testimony that Solfisburg asked him to deliver to Stout—at the bank—the first three hundred shares the justice sold. The report bluntly declared, "The Commission does not credit this testimony." It then explained in full detail the facts suggesting instead that Solfisburg requested Flynn to make the delivery to Isaacs's office, not to the bank. These included the previously prepared receipt with Isaacs's name typed on it, the improbability of Flynn's supposed decision to depart from the justice's instructions, the greater probability that Solfisburg would ask a senior practicing attorney to make a delivery in his own office building rather than at a bank four blocks away, Flynn's two statements indicating that Solfisburg knew the delivery would be made to Isaacs and in the same building, and "Justice Solfisburg's demeanor on the witness stand during questioning about his use of a personal courier to effect the delivery."

Turning to Klingbiel, the report reviewed the chain of events by which the last hundred shares of CCB stock were bought by Isaacs, given to Perbohner, and then given to the justice. The commissioners observed that "if he did not in fact already know it, Justice Klingbiel could readily have learned that Isaacs was closely associated with, and an important figure in, the Civic Center Bank upon making even a casual inquiry." Klingbiel was found to have given "no satisfactory explanation for the rather extraordinary fact that he retained the shares in negotiable form, registered in the name of Robert M. Perbohner," for over a year and a half. He, Isaacs, and Perbohner also were found to have made false statements to the press about Klingbiel's acquisition of the shares. Finally, the commission described Perbohner:

[He] was a central figure in the transactions pursuant to which Justices Klingbiel and Solfisburg acquired Civic Center Bank stock while the litigation in *People v. Isaacs* was pending. Perbohner, notwithstanding the recent operation on his hip, was, in the opinion of his attending physician, competent to testify in this investigation. He was instructed and advised by his counsel not to answer a number of questions, truthful answers to which would greatly have aided this investigation, and he did refuse to answer such questions.

A Justice's Duty

The report's next section was headed "The Duty and Obligation of the Justices of the Supreme Court." It detailed approximately a dozen different formulations of the ethical responsibilities of judges. At the most general level, the report relied on proscriptions such as Canon 4 of the Illinois Judicial Conference's Canons of Ethics, which read:

> A judge's official conduct should be free from impropriety and the appearance of impropriety; he should avoid infractions of law; and his personal behavior, not only upon the Bench and in the performance of judicial duties, but also in his everyday life, should be beyond reproach.

Other, more specific canons included the prohibition of a judge's acceptance of "presents or favors from litigants, lawyers practicing before him, or others whose causes are likely to be submitted to him for judgment."

The commission emphasized its unequivocal readiness to apply these standards: "The canons to which we have referred are not abstract statements of ethical considerations but are firmly grounded in the long history of Anglo-American jurisprudence." The commission also reiterated the importance of the standards, particularly amidst the turmoil of the 1960s:

> We do not regard these canons as quaint moral precepts, derived from an outmoded age of innocence. They are intensely practical and necessary statements as to the conduct required of judges. . . . There is nothing which is in our judgment so fundamental to the maintenance of a government based upon the Rule of Law, as the need of the public to understand that the decisions of our courts, often unpopular and seemingly contrary to prevailing public sentiment, are impartially and fairly arrived at and that the judges responsible for the decisions are above reproach. Adherence to the

principles expressed in the canons seems to us particularly necessary in an age when authority is increasingly threatened and the traditional concepts of law and order are under attack.

Having made its factual findings and summarized the applicable
standards for judges, the commission turned to its "Conclusions." The
commission declared itself bound by a requirement "that our conclusions must be based upon clear and convincing evidence—a standard
more rigorous than that which would normally prevail in a civil case."
It then rendered the first part of its verdict:

> We do not believe that any elaboration of our findings of fact is re-
> quired to demonstrate conclusively that the conduct of Justice Sol-
> fisburg and Justice Klingbiel presents precisely the *appearance of
> impropriety* to which Canon 4 is addressed. The appearance of im-
> propriety is so substantial and pervasive in the case of both Justices
> that they must, without more, be held clearly to have violated the
> Canons of Ethics of the Illinois Judicial Conference.

Without linking this conclusion to specific factual findings, the commissioners rendered the damning opinion that this "substantial and
pervasive" appearance of impropriety "resulted from acts and conduct in which Justice Solfisburg and Justice Klingbiel were knowing
and willing participants." Neither was "an innocent victim of circumstance."

The second part of the conclusions established "certain positive
acts of impropriety" in violation of the Canons of Ethics of the Illinois
Judicial Conference. Three such acts were linked to Klingbiel, and
two to Solfisburg. Klingbiel's first act of impropriety was acceptance
of the stock gift from "Perbohner and/or Dolph," both of whom were
members of the Illinois Commerce Commission at the time of the gift.
The Commerce Commission was then a litigant in at least three pending cases.

Next, Klingbiel's attempt to characterize the stock as a campaign
contribution, rather than a gift, was addressed. Since the stock was
given after Klingbiel's election to a new ten-year term in office, "and
he already had collected more than three times as much in contributions as he spent, . . . the acceptance of a gift of this amount and under
the circumstances was an act of impropriety." Lastly, Klingbiel's pattern of concealment of ownership of the stock, including his lies to the
press and misleading of Justice Kluczynski, was found to be another
violation of the Canons of Ethics.

None of these three conclusions about Klingbiel's acts of impropriety mentioned Isaacs or the *Isaacs* case. Although the appearance of impropriety conclusion had encompassed a finding that Klingbiel could readily have learned of Isaacs's importance in the Civic Center Bank, the commissioners were ultimately unable to decide that Klingbiel actually knew the CCB stock gift had anything to do with that litigant.

In contrast, the two acts of impropriety by Solfisburg had a lot to do with Isaacs and were spelled out with greater force and detail than the conclusions on Klingbiel. The first act focused on the acquisition of his seven hundred CCB shares:

> At a time when he knew Isaacs was a litigant before the Court in a case that had attracted much public attention, Justice Solfisburg accepted a valuable favor which he knew, or in fulfilling the obligation of one in his position to avoid impropriety and appearance of impropriety could readily have determined, was attributable in substantial measure to the influence of Isaacs.

The commission cited Solfisburg's own testimony that he considered himself an original subscriber of the bank stock and expected Dolph and Perbohner to "protect" him by seeing that he got the seven hundred shares even though he never signed a subscription agreement. This testimony "manifested his awareness that he was to be the recipient of preferential treatment." In this first conclusion on Solfisburg, the commission plainly was linking the chief justice's stock purchase to the ethical prohibition on a judge's receipt of favors from a litigant.

The conclusion on Solfisburg's second act of impropriety was carefully phrased and heavily documented. It echoed the conclusion on his first improper act but focused more sharply on his knowledge of Isaacs's influence:

> We believe that a strong inference could be drawn from this record that Justice Solfisburg knew, at the time he acquired the 700 shares of CCB stock, that he was afforded the opportunity to make this purchase (which he obviously regarded as a favorable and potentially profitable one) through the influence of Isaacs, who was at the time a litigant before the Supreme Court.

The report then listed fifteen separate facts, including Isaacs's role as a "prime mover" in the bank and the distribution of its stock; the close relationships among Isaacs, Perbohner, and Dolph; Perbohner's desire to help Isaacs in defending himself against the indictment; Solfisburg's acquisition of seven hundred shares without any expectation that he would assist the bank in any way; Solfisburg's interaction with

Flynn regarding the purchase and sale of the stock; the concealment of the shares in a trust; the request from Isaacs or his office for issuance of these shares to the trust; Solfisburg's commencement of liquidation of "his investment (at a 25% profit) immediately after termination of the *Isaacs* litigation"; and the "extraordinary manner" in which this first sale was handled, including the delivery by courier to Isaacs's office, the receipt by Solfisburg of a higher price than the purchasers paid, and Isaacs's payment out of his own pocket to make up the difference.

The commission also made two other forceful observations about what it believed the record established:

> Justice Solfisburg's account of having invested $14,000 of borrowed money in the stock of an enterprise about which he made no inquiry whatsoever is, tested by what a reasonable and prudent man would do in like circumstances, wholly incredible.

> The whole series of events was characterized by an air of furtiveness and concealment.

The Special Commission, in lawyerly but stinging prose, was calling the chief justice a liar.

The commission finished its lengthy explanation of Solfisburg's second impropriety:

> [I]t is evident that he violated the Canons of Ethics of the Illinois Judicial Conference by engaging in a pattern of concealment of his ownership of 700 shares of CCB stock, in furtherance of which he caused the stock certificates to be issued in Trust 931. The uncontroverted evidence concerning the use of the revocable trust device established that the only actual function served by Trust 931 was to conceal from the public the identity of the true owner of the stock.

The "pattern of concealment" thus was Solfisburg's second act of impropriety. These five experienced lawyers not only hadn't bought Solfisburg's weak attempt to justify the use of Trust No. 931, but had also been offended by the dishonesty of the attempt.

Finishing the Job

In the penultimate section of the report, the Special Commission declared that there was no evidence to support the charges that Solfisburg had been an attorney for the bank and that Klingbiel's daughter or other persons had held CCB stock as nominees for him. The commissioners also absolved the other members of the supreme court from having any knowledge or reason to believe that Klingbiel or Solfisburg "was subject to any undue influence or had any disqualifying interest in the decision in the *Isaacs* case." Broadly, the report also announced that all of Skolnick's other charges, other than those set forth in the report, were unsupported by any credible evidence.

Of the five questions the commission and staff had been looking into since June, three had now been disposed of as lacking any merit. Nothing was suspect in the *Isaacs* opinion itself, or in the decisional process in that case, and Solfisburg had never acted as an attorney for the bank. The two areas of inquiry where wrongdoing was found related directly to CCB stock: the purchase by Solfisburg and—as Skolnick suspected from the beginning—the gift to Klingbiel, both of which occurred while the *Isaacs* case was pending before the supreme court.

Finally, the commission returned to the main focus of its mandate, the linkage between the two justices' conduct in these transactions and the *Isaacs* judgment. The commission did so in three, succinct paragraphs, harking back to its earlier statement of the inseparability of the justices' and the judgment's integrity:

> The integrity of the judgment in the *Isaacs* case is affected by what we have found to be the appearance of impropriety on the part of two of the Justices, Solfisburg and Klingbiel, who participated in the decision.
>
> The correctness of a judgment or its legal soundness cannot, in the eyes of the Bar or the public, save it from taint if it appears that a judge or judges who participated in rendering the judgment had disqualifying interests or were themselves guilty of such conduct as to raise a reasonable suspicion as to their impartiality, fairness, and integrity.
>
> However, the question whether the judgment in the *Isaacs* case should now be vacated or reopened by the Court is one which is beyond our proper province and should be left for adjudication by the Court.

With these words, the Special Commission discharged its duty under the court's order creating the commission.

The last paragraph of the report was the three-sentence statement emphasizing that the public's and the bar's confidence in the supreme court had been "severely shaken." All the commissioners joined in this statement, a clear response to the court's own expression of concern that confidence "in the integrity of the Court not be further impaired." Toward that end, four of the commissioners took the next fateful step, believing it their responsibility to tell the court, the public, and the two justices what needed to be done:

> The Commission believes that such confidence can best be restored by the prompt resignation of the two Justices.

IMPACT

August and Beyond

Chapter 23

A Sad Affair

Sherman Skolnick held a press conference in the lobby of the Civic Center early Thursday afternoon, about an hour after the Special Commission's Report was released. He described himself as "shocked and astonished" that the commissioners "did a pretty good job," especially since they acted "at great risk to themselves." Now, at last, he offered his highest compliment: "It wasn't a whitewash."

Skolnick proclaimed that his own pressure on the commission and publicity from the news media "made it impossible to do anything but the right thing." Described now by the *Chicago Tribune* as the "winner in the first round of his battle with the Illinois Supreme Court," he vowed to continue with further investigation of Solfisburg, Klingbiel, and other judges. In Skolnick's view, the commission still had not gone "far enough to get to the real bottom of corruption in the courts."

A little later Greenberg met with reporters at the Chicago Bar Association office. Before speaking with them, he asked two "uninvited guests"—Skolnick and his associate Harriet Sherman—to leave, and they quietly did so. Greenberg commented on the limited authority of the commission. The report, he said, "simply tried to state what we believe is evidenced by our investigation," and he emphasized that "what the court or Mr. Solfisburg or Mr. Klingbiel do . . . must be left entirely to them." He gave credit to Skolnick for starting the inquiry, but added that Skolnick "occasionally had difficulty separating reality from fantasy" and declared that the commission was not influenced either by his prodding or the press.

The only other commissioner to speak publicly now was Henry Pitts. He held a brief press conference in Springfield after delivering the report to the Illinois Supreme Court and the Courts Commission.

As the press conference was ending, a reporter asked, with friendly sarcasm, "Where do you intend to practice law now?" Pitts, and the other reporters, just laughed.

Would They Resign?

Klingbiel issued a statement Thursday night saying he had read the report and did not "personally feel that I have been guilty of any impropriety or appearance of impropriety whatsoever" in the *Isaacs* case or any other. He said that in twenty-four years on the bench, including sixteen on the Illinois Supreme Court, his integrity had never before been questioned. He ended, "I am proud of my record, and I do not intend to resign."

On Friday morning *Daily News* reporters went to the justices' homes, seeking further comments. In Moline, Klingbiel was intercepted in his bathrobe as he went outside to bring in the garbage can. He declined to talk. Solfisburg, who had made no public statement yet, remained closeted at his home in Aurora. His wife answered the door Friday morning and said that the chief justice was not talking with reporters. Asked when he would make a statement, Mrs. Solfisburg replied, "I don't know. We don't like you people. We're mad at you."

While the two justices were saying very little, their lawyers were speaking more fully on their behalf. On Thursday afternoon Lambert Ochsenschlager and William Murphy said they were "deeply disappointed, but not surprised" by the report. For the first and only time during the summer, Ochsenschlager found himself in some agreement with Skolnick: "The constant outcry of 'whitewash' by Sherman Skolnick, and the reporting of these charges in the press and over the air, subconsciously placed the commission under such pressure that it caused them to violate their own rules of procedure in an effort to prove Skolnick wrong in his whitewash charge." Ochsenschlager opined that the commissioners submitted their harsh report because of this pressure and because they "wanted to come out of this as heroes."

Ochsenschlager disagreed with the Special Commission's findings "1,000 percent." He complained that what started as an investigation had turned into a prosecution, and he expressed confidence that "when the Illinois Courts Commission calmly, soberly, and objectively views this matter, a finding exonerating the justices will be returned." In the meantime, he insisted, the justices would not resign. He added, "I have never seen them more determined than now."

Ochsenschlager emphasized that a hearing before the Courts Commission was constitutionally required before the justices could be removed from office. He insisted, "The full story isn't out," and he claimed, "I'll bring in some witnesses, if it ever comes to a trial, whom the Special Commission interviewed and kept secret." This last statement plainly—and misleadingly—ignored his repeated opportunities to call additional witnesses in the hearings, particularly the two alibi witnesses Stevens pointedly refused to present—Howard Hansen and Doris Steigberg.

Among the other voices raised in response to the report were the newspapers'. On Friday a *Chicago Tribune* editorial called for the justices to resign, and *Chicago Today* expanded its resignation demand of two weeks earlier. That newspaper at first had only insisted that Klingbiel should go, but now it targeted both justices. *Chicago Today* also congratulated the commission "for a thorough and conscientious job" and even applauded Skolnick: "We've bawled out Mr. Skolnick for tactics and statements that seemed to us irresponsible, but his work has been a great service to the state, and we hope he keeps it up."

The *Chicago Daily News* weighed in with an editorial on Friday. The paper observed that "no scandal of such proportions" had ever touched the court before, and that the two justices' departure "would mark the first time that any member of the tribunal had stepped down in such circumstances." Nonetheless, the *Daily News* said there could be no public confidence in the court so long as Solfisburg and Klingbiel were on it. Additionally, Saturday's *Daily News* carried a column by Roy Fisher, naming all of the paper's reporters who had worked on the story and recounting, quite defensively, the paper's handling of the scandal.

In a follow-up editorial on Saturday, *Chicago Today* quoted a statement by William Murphy lamenting that the Special Commission's report would put a great burden on all judges. Murphy had claimed it would require them to review all their investments and social contacts or else be "wide open to a Sherman Skolnick." The newspaper noted that Murphy found this burden "a distasteful imposition," but the editors found it "an absolutely great idea."

The *Chicago Sun-Times* also joined the chorus, asserting that the justices' refusal to step down was "incredible" and had the effect of "damaging public esteem for the court and compounding public indignation toward them individually." The *Sun-Times* compared the two Illinois justices to U.S. Supreme Court Justice Abe Fortas. Noting that Fortas had resigned in May in the face of alleged appearances of impropriety, the paper emphasized that Solfisburg and Klingbiel "stand accused of more than the mere 'appearance' of impropriety," for the Special Commission had found "certain positive acts of impropriety" as well.

Additionally, the newspapers carried stories about the commissioners and the staff. Greenberg was quoted as saying that Stevens did "a marvelous job . . . just marvelous." Greenberg also mentioned his desire to get back to his law practice. A *Sun-Times* profile of the legal team described Stevens as "a soft-spoken, low-key lawyer who mostly handles antitrust cases and flies his own airplane for recreation." Stevens was quoted as saying the task he had just finished for the commission was "one of the hardest, but most satisfying," of his career.

The article remarked that Stevens was not only unpaid as counsel to the Special Commission, but might even lose money from taking so much time away from his regular law practice. Stevens observed that since late June the team had worked ten to twelve hours a day, seven days a week, and he said, "Our work probably would have cost a couple of hundred thousand dollars if it were billed on an hourly basis." Although the young lawyers on the staff continued to draw salaries from their firms, Stevens noted that Jerome Torshen—a sole practitioner—received no such salary, making "a sacrifice that few lawyers have ever made before."

Other Questions

The newspapers also addressed a handful of other questions being asked in various forums. First, would the Courts Commission now begin its own inquiry and remove the justices from the court, as it had the power to do under the Illinois Constitution? Roy Gulley, the Courts Commission's secretary, transmitted the report to Justice Daniel Ward, its new chairman since Klingbiel had quietly left the post two weeks earlier. Gulley was treating the report as a complaint against the two justices, and he said the Courts Commission would meet in mid-August to consider the case. Justice Ward said that he and the four other judges on that commission had begun studying the report and the hearings transcripts. Under the supreme court's recently amended rule, the Courts Commission no longer needed the court's permission before convening to consider a complaint.[1] The Courts Commission looked to be the most likely forum in which the justices' fate would be decided.

Another question was whether the House Committee chaired by Representative Lindberg would revive its pending investigation of the two justices and the rest of the Illinois judiciary. The committee was scheduled to meet on Tuesday, August 5, to plan its next steps. One possibility was that the committee would recommend to the House that the justices be impeached. A few state legislators, both Democrats and Republicans, already promised to pursue impeachment if the Lindberg Committee found the justices had acted improperly. The full legislature was scheduled to return for a brief session in October, with a longer session the following year, and impeachment proceedings might be initiated at either of those times.

State Senator Alan J. Dixon—later to be a United States senator—suggested that the creation of the Courts Commission in the 1964 Judicial Article had eliminated the House's power to impeach, but Lindberg disagreed. As this debate heated up, some legislators echoed the Special Commission's demand for the justices' resignations. Henry Hyde, a member of the House Committee, insisted: "I think it is an intolerable situation when the very commission set up by the court tells two justices to resign and they refuse to do so."

Would Isaacs be disbarred? The Chicago Bar Association announced that appropriate committees would begin investigating whether Isaacs was guilty of misconduct in the bank stock deals and should therefore be recommended for disbarment by the supreme court. Albert Jenner scoffed at the idea, saying there was nothing in the hearings or the report "that would lead me to believe there is a cause for disbarment." One legislator also suggested that the possible disbarment of Solfisburg and Klingbiel should be examined.

Would Governor Richard Ogilvie remove Robert Perbohner from the Illinois Commerce Commission? The governor said he wanted "to be brought fully up-to-date on all aspects of Mr. Perbohner's involvement" in the scandal and for this purpose would take a close look at the Special Commission's report.

The question of a possible perjury prosecution against Howard Hansen also made headlines. On Thursday, July 31, the day Stevens took his last stab at getting answers from Howard Hansen, the Special Commission's staff contacted Edward Hanrahan, the State's Attorney of Cook County. In a report to Hanrahan, delivered shortly before the commission expired, Stevens asked the State's Attorney to investigate possible perjury charges against Hansen. During that final deposition attempt, Stevens had warned Hansen that the staff had information that Hansen's testimony about a $2,100 loan from Perbohner to Isaacs in March 1965 was false. Hanrahan's office now made clear just what the incriminating information was:

Hansen told the Special Commission he received the $2100 from Perbohner in Hansen's Chicago office March 16, 1965, and converted the cash—21 $100 bills—into a money order that same day. Illinois Commerce Commission records, however, show that the Commission met that day in Springfield, 200 miles away, and that Perbohner was in Springfield most of that week. He billed the state in his expense account for meals and lodging from March 14 through March 19.[2]

Another big question was how vacancies on the supreme court would be filled if the justices resigned. There appeared to be no provision in Illinois law for special elections to fill supreme court vacancies or for the governor to make interim appointments. If the two resigned, the court would have only five members until the next regular election, in November 1970. If Solfisburg did not resign, he would still face a regular retention vote in that election, but Klingbiel was not due to come before the voters again until 1976.

Finally, there was the question of *People v. Isaacs*. The Special Commission had left it to the court to decide what to do about the tainted judgment. The newspapers paid little attention to this obvious question, but there was probably a good reason for their silence. No one was saying much about what the court might do, and the only people who might actually know—the seven justices themselves— were not talking.

Resignation

On Saturday afternoon, August 2, Murphy went to a country club in Aurora for a round of golf. He had spent most of Friday evening with Solfisburg, who told him he was not going to resign but instead would stand for election in 1970 and let the people then decide if he should still be on the court.

A day earlier, however, there was a quiet signal that the justices were thinking of resigning, even while Ochsenschlager was publicly declaring otherwise. Henry Pitts received a telephone call at a friend's home in Rockford, where he had gone to attend the annual Winnebago County Bar Association clambake. The caller was the ubiquitous Joe Sullivan, the Chicago Bar Association's ex-president who nearly served on the Special Commission and then showed up as Justice Kluczynski's lawyer.

Sullivan seemed to be calling on behalf of the two beleaguered justices, although he didn't come right out and say so. Pitts recalls the conversation:

Joe Sullivan tracked me down and asked whether the Illinois State Bar Association (which in those days handled disciplinary proceedings as commissioners of the supreme court for all downstate lawyers) intended to initiate disbarment proceedings against the two justices. I was offended by his call and responded by saying the work of the commission was over, that I personally did not intend to push for disbarment, but obviously I did not know what others would do and that it was inappropriate for me to discuss the matter further.

Pitts surmised that Solfisburg or Ochsenschlager had asked Sullivan to call, for "Solfisburg was not an old man and wanted to continue to practice law."[3]

As Murphy played the third hole, someone suddenly brought him the news: Solfisburg had resigned. An hour or so later, he learned that Klingbiel had just announced that he too was leaving the court, although his departure was a "retirement," not a resignation.

The two justices reached their decisions on Saturday independently of one another. Ochsenschlager was quoted in the *New York Times* and other papers as saying the decisions had been reached separately and against his advice. Klingbiel's wife also denied any "deal that if one resigned, the other would too."

Solfisburg's decision was communicated to Chicago newspapers around noon. A *Sun-Times* reporter reached Klingbiel by telephone in Moline shortly before one o'clock. Klingbiel said that this was the first he had heard of Solfisburg's resignation, and that he would probably reach a decision during the next week. Within an hour, however, his resignation statement was also announced by Ochsenschlager. The justices gave very different reasons for their departures, but both asserted their innocence of any wrongdoing and their conviction that the Special Commission's treatment of them was unfair.

Solfisburg's statement was described by *Chicago Today* as "angry and eloquent." He asked that the statement be reported in its entirety, which many newspapers did. He implored the media to grant to "my wife, my children, and to me the personal privacy and solitude that we so dearly need at this particular hour." He described his many years as a lawyer and judge and declared:

At no time during my entire career have I ever done anything unprofessional or in any way wrong. Specifically, the *Isaacs* case was correctly decided on the law and was decided in an objective and proper judicial manner. . . . No decision of mine and no decision of the Supreme Court of Illinois during my service was the product of

anything less; none is tainted with impropriety or the appearance
of impropriety.

I am deeply wedded and devoted to the law, the court system of
Illinois, and especially to our supreme court and my fellow justices.
I am now compelled because of this total commitment to resign
from the supreme court and the bench and thus from the work that I
so deeply love.

Solfisburg described the Special Commission as intended by him and
the other justices "to investigate, to protect, and to preserve the reputation and integrity of the supreme court." Although the commission
"was composed of thoroughly honorable men, I do not and cannot
agree with—nor do I accept the correctness of—the findings of fact of
the commission." Then he blasted it:

> The commission did not observe the rules of evidence or the court's
> mandate to it. . . . Its findings are not based upon the weight of the
> evidence adduced. . . . The Special Commission from the beginning
> was the constant target of the irresponsible charge that it was going
> to "whitewash." Such a widespread and continued accusation, I
> think, must have subconsciously affected the commission's deliber-
> ations and report, for I know as a judge that such a climate could
> never be conducive to thoroughly reflective and objective decision
> making.

Solfisburg affirmed his belief that if the matter were to go before the
Courts Commission, he would be vindicated completely, and that if he
were to go before the voters in 1970, he could be retained in office.

Nonetheless, while insisting he was not leaving because of the Special Commission's findings or the evidence it heard, he would resign.
The finding of the appearance of impropriety, "and the massive publicity of that finding," would make it difficult, he said, to give "the diligent judicial service I have rendered previously. . . . The Special
Commission has obviously precluded me from sitting with the same
public confidence I previously enjoyed." He concluded: "I am also
deeply grateful for the years of judicial service that I have been allowed to devote to this state, and I regret not one day of that service."

Klingbiel's statement was shorter. He too summarized his years of
public service and added that he had only intended to remain on the
court for a year or two more because he was already sixty-eight years
old. Now things had changed:

> However, in view of the report of the Special Commission—and the
> fact that four members of it decided to go beyond their authority

and assume the prerogative of the constitutionally created Illinois
Courts Commission—it would place such pressure upon the health
and happiness of my family, as well as myself, that in consultation
within our own household, I have decided to retire from the Illinois
Supreme Court.

He emphasized that he felt no guilt and maintained that he was not
guilty of "even the appearance of impropriety." He offered his respect
for the commissioners but insisted that he fully disagreed with their report.

Klingbiel thanked "the hundreds of lawyers, judges, and people
generally who urged me not to take this step but to see it through the
Illinois Courts Commission." He said: "At first I felt I could do so—
but the pressure upon my loved ones and myself—and the certainty of
continued pressure makes necessary this decision."

Shame and Fatigue

The departing justices' criticism of the Special Commission was certainly not surprising. Solfisburg and Klingbiel were not the only justices, however, who were dissatisfied with the Special Commission.
Alfred Kirkland had been the outgoing Illinois State Bar president
back in June, when he was asked first by the court to head the Special
Commission.[4] Weeks later Kirkland happened to run into Justice
Kluczynski. Kluczynski had been a forthright witness during the hearings, resisting outside pressure and steadfastly confirming Klingbiel's
deceptiveness. Nonetheless, the justice complained bitterly about
Kirkland's failure to embrace the invitation to serve on the commission: "You had a chance to help Roy Solfisburg, and you let him
down."[5]

When the Special Commission was created, the court had acknowledged "the inevitability of criticism of any course it chose." By the end
of its work, the Special Commission was receiving far more praise than
criticism, but at least three of the supreme court justices who had
formed the commission—Solfisburg and Klingbiel, of course, and
Kluczynski as well—were among its critics.

The supreme court also had emphasized in June the importance of
making sure that public confidence in the court's integrity "not be further impaired." Instead, the Special Commission concluded that confidence in the court "has been severely shaken by the facts disclosed in
this record" and that the best way to restore it would be for the chief
justice and Klingbiel to resign. All seven of the justices had surely
hoped for a report that assured the public that the court deserved un-

questioning, high regard. All seven of the justices now felt the pain and frustration of being part of a sullied institution.

Solfisburg must have felt this most acutely. His resignation statement focused on the loss of public confidence, and he could not have failed to recognize that the commission's findings, the newspaper editorials, and the time it would take for the Courts Commission and the legislature to come to any resolution all added up to an irreversible extinguishing of the public esteem he had enjoyed for years. His dream of going to the United States Supreme Court was shattered.

Despite the blame Solfisburg placed on the Special Commission, he must have felt profound regret, for he had to realize that in many ways his own conduct had led to this blight on himself and the court. His colleagues had joined with him in trying to find a mechanism for getting through this scandal with the court's reputation preserved, but his own dealings and evasions had prevented that. For him to continue as chief justice, or even as a member of the court, would obstruct the path toward restoration of the court's good name. As one editorial later observed, and as he surely knew, his continued presence on the court "could have had no other effect than to weaken public confidence in it."

In the aftermath of Solfisburg's resignation, rumors circulated that newsmen had called and threatened to reveal other alleged misconduct by him, and that he resigned rather than subject his family and himself to additional humiliation. There is no evidence of any such threats, however, and none was needed.

For Klingbiel as well, it would be an uphill battle to regain the approbation of the bar, the press, and the public. In contrast with Solfisburg, however, Klingbiel probably felt more fatigue than embarrassment or regret. Klingbiel gave little evidence of grasping just how ethically offensive his conduct had been. In contrast with Solfisburg's evasiveness on the witness stand, Klingbiel had been candid, unhesitatingly admitting his earlier falsehoods. Nonetheless, and although he wanted to make it "absolutely clear that I possess no sense of guilt," he knew it was time to end the ordeal. He was just too tired to fight this battle anymore.

When asked by reporters to comment on the resignations, Frank Greenberg simply said, "This has been a difficult and very painful business, and I believe it would be inappropriate for me to say anything." John Paul Stevens's reaction was similar. When a reporter reached him at his summer home on Saturday and told him of the justices' decisions, he too said little: "Nobody has enjoyed this. It has been . . . a sad affair."

Chapter 24

Loose Ends

The scandal was over, but important loose ends remained. One was the status of Sherman Skolnick. He remained subject to Judge Healy's contempt order and the four-month jail sentence. A sudden, more urgent problem for Skolnick arose on Saturday when, shortly after the resignations were announced, he received telephoned threats on his life. Chicago police officers were stationed outside his home by Saturday night. The police also provided a squad car to take him to his various appointments for the next few days, and nothing untoward happened.

The resolution of the contempt order looked fairly simple, since Skolnick had already talked with Stevens and Torshen and given them some names of his sources. Also, Torshen knew of Judge Healy's eagerness to vacate the contempt order, provided Skolnick apologized. As with many of the events involving Skolnick this summer, however, this last step got complicated, as well as a bit comical. Torshen later described the denouement:

> Judge Healy's courtroom was packed with onlookers and the press. Skolnick was wheeled up before the bench. Healy asked him if he had anything to say. Skolnick said, "No." Healy said, "Are you sure you don't want to say anything?" Skolnick repeated that he didn't want to say anything. Healy said, "Are you sure?" Skolnick said, "What do you want me to say?" Healy said, "What do you want to say?" Skolnick said, "I don't want to say anything."
>
> Ultimately, Healy said, "Don't you even want to say you're sorry?" Skolnick said, "If you want me to say I'm sorry, I will say I'm sorry." Healy almost shouted, "Your apology is accepted. Case dismissed," and ran off the bench.[1]

With that, Skolnick's formal involvement in the chain of events he had started months earlier was finished. Skolnick continued to sound off about the need for further investigation of the two justices' involvement in other deals and cases, and about alleged misdeeds of other judges. Years later he declared without hesitation that what was revealed in the summer of 1969 "wasn't even the moisture on the iceberg," let alone the tip.

Skolnick was enjoying a greater measure of celebrity than ever before. *Time* magazine published a long article extolling his success in exposing the scandal and calling him "a sort of modern day Robin Hood for the law's many losers." The article also mentioned that Skolnick promised more revelations, saying, "We have angles on top of angles."[2] Skolnick did quickly move on to other controversies. Before the end of August he was probing potential scandals involving federal court administrators, and in mid-September he was arrested, along with ten newsmen, for violating an order banning cameras and recording equipment from the federal court building where the Chicago 8 conspiracy trial was starting.

More Departures

The status of other key figures was also being sorted out. On Saturday, August 9, the Civic Center Bank announced that Theodore Isaacs had been "temporarily" relieved of his duties at the bank. The bank stated that Isaacs had asked for this change until "the air has been cleared of any innuendoes that could lead to derogatory, false statements . . . which could in turn tend to reflect unfavorably on the bank."

A new element was added to the cloud over Isaacs. The Chicago office of the Internal Revenue Service announced that it was looking into possible federal tax violations and criminal fraud by Isaacs, as well as by Perbohner, Joseph Knight, Howard Hansen, Solfisburg, Klingbiel, and others. This announcement was particularly portentous for Isaacs and Knight. They would meet up with the IRS soon again, on other serious matters.

Perbohner found himself in hot water with Governor Ogilvie. Ogilvie had studied the Special Commission's report, and on August 6 publicly demanded that Perbohner resign from the Illinois Commerce Commission. Ogilvie declared that Perbohner "has failed in his duty to the people of Illinois" by refusing to cooperate with the Special Commission and to give full and truthful answers to questions "involving his acts as a public official." The governor added a lawyerly, alternative reason for Perbohner to leave the commission: "If, in fact, his health is so poor as to justify his failure to appear before the Special Commission and to warrant his continued absence from the state and from his official duties, he is then additionally disqualified from further tenure in his state position." If Perbohner did not resign, Ogilvie would fire him.

Perbohner was still hospitalized in Wisconsin, although it was predicted he would return to Illinois soon. Once again, as with everything involving Perbohner, the picture got muddled. First he was quoted as saying he would resign because he had no choice in view of the governor's powers, then it appeared that he had resigned, and then his wife denied that he had. A couple of days after the governor's announcement, Perbohner even told a Chicago reporter that he couldn't remember giving any bank stock to Klingbiel!

Finally, on August 14, Perbohner sent the governor a letter from Rockford, declaring his refusal to resign. The next day Ogilvie removed him from office "for incompetence and neglect of duty." Perbohner's public service to Illinois was over.

The Legislature's Power

The Lindberg Committee met on August 5 to begin what one of its members called "a top-to-bottom inquiry into the entire judiciary in Illinois," taking up where the Greenberg Commission left off. William Hundley, the committee's outside counsel from Washington, declared that the Special Commission had done an outstanding job and that the House Committee would profit from its work. The committee decided to try to obtain access to the confidential, annual financial statements of all of the six hundred or so judges in Illinois. George Lindberg stated that the objective was to get "a composite picture of the financial dealings of Illinois judges and their employment in addition to their judgeship." The committee, with a $100,000 budget, intended to hire more investigators.

The committee's announcement was timely. Not only had Solfisburg and Klingbiel just resigned, but on the day of the committee's meeting, a former Cook County circuit judge, Louis W. Kizas, pleaded guilty to fifteen charges of official misconduct for accepting payoffs to release defendants on recognizance bonds. The Illinois public had probably never before been made so aware of judicial corruption.

On August 6 Lindberg wrote to Stevens, conveying the House Committee's commendation for his work as counsel to the Special Commission. The letter also invited Stevens and Torshen to attend the committee's next meeting, on August 12, to give the legislators "the

benefit of your experienced opinions and recommendations as we begin our work."[3] Before that meeting was held, however, five Chicago
lawyers filed a taxpayers suit in Cook County Circuit Court to stop the
House Committee's work. Much later, William Hundley wondered
about the strategic wisdom of the committee's expansion of its inquiry
to include all Illinois judges. It was not surprising that lawyers who
were friendly with judges, or wanted to curry favor with them, would
go to bat for judges who resented the committee's prying into their finances.

The suit, *Cusack v. Howlett,* claimed that through the committee
the legislature was attempting an unconstitutional exercise of authority vested in the judicial branch of government. For the legislature to
investigate the judiciary would violate the separation of powers provision of the Illinois Constitution. The committee vowed to fight the
lawsuit. The members also went ahead and held their planned de-
briefing with Stevens and Torshen.

On August 29 a Cook County judge issued a permanent injunction,
barring the committee from expending any state funds in pursuit of
the House resolution. The committee appealed to the Illinois
Supreme Court. The case was argued on October 20, with Hundley arguing for the committee and Leonard Ring, a prominent Chicago trial
lawyer, appearing for the plaintiffs.

On November 26, in an opinion written by Justice Schaefer, the
supreme court affirmed the injunction. The court found that the committee lacked constitutional support for its intended investigation of
the state judiciary. The court emphasized Hundley's concession during
oral argument that realistically the investigation had no relationship
to impeachment of any judges.

The justices saw the committee's main objective as being at best "to
acquire information necessary for informed legislative action in the
field of judicial ethics." Nonetheless, Schaefer wrote that the 1964 Judicial Article, which established the Courts Commission, eliminated
the legislature's power to remove judges from office, "and it is the
supreme court which is now authorized to prescribe standards of judicial conduct." Accordingly, there was no valid legislative purpose
supporting the House resolution, and the committee's intended investigation was in violation of the constitutional separation of powers.[4]

The decision made it impossible for the House Committee to conduct its investigation or hold any hearings. Committee members could
only offer their individual perspectives in other forums where issues
related to the judiciary were being aired. There also was no longer any
need for Hundley's services. Feeling that he had not really accom-

plished much of anything, in the end he never even submitted a bill for his work.[5]

Eventually, the committee submitted a final report to the full legislature in November 1970. It complimented the Special Commission for performing its "difficult task with dispatch, fairness, and precision." The committee's report mostly just described what had developed elsewhere, such as the report of the Special Commission and proposed amendments to the Illinois Constitution. Only with considerable humility could Lindberg, Hyde, and the other members describe what they had accomplished: "Indeed the committee, having been frustrated in performing its legislative purpose, can only claim that many changes have occurred since the committee came into existence, and perhaps because the committee was in existence."

Years later, however, George Lindberg described the committee's contributions as more significant, pointing to the ensuing ethics legislation promoted by himself and other committee members, and to changes in the Illinois Constitution made in response to *Cusack v. Howlett.* In retrospect, he claimed the House Committee had more impact "as a result of being throttled" than it would have had if permitted to run its originally intended course.

The Court Goes On

The supreme court regrouped, with its numbers severely depleted. On September 8, the first day of the new term, only four justices were present. Solfisburg and Klingbiel were gone, and Justice Byron House was in a hospital in Clayton, Missouri, where he had suffered a stroke in mid-August. Because the constitution required four members to agree in order for a case to be decided, and because Justice Ward was still disqualified from Cook County criminal cases, one of the court's first actions was to postpone the scheduled hearing of twelve such cases.

On the first day back, the four justices in attendance elected Robert Underwood as the new chief justice. This choice was widely predicted, especially since Underwood had not previously served in that role. From one perspective, however, the choice of Underwood was surprising. When the court last met in July, its membership consisted of four Republicans and three Democrats. Underwood was now the only Republican left, yet he still was chosen to head the court. A newspaper editorial commented, "That the Democrats voted to place Judge Underwood in so important a post illustrates the high regard in which he is held."

The court took other actions in September in response to the summer's events. On September 9 it appointed a Committee on Judicial Ethics, chaired by the dean of the University of Illinois College of Law and also including former bar presidents Alfred Kirkland and John Joseph Sullivan. The ethics committee was charged to formulate standards "regarding nonjudicial activities of judges" and to suggest possible revisions to the court's requirements for judges' statements of economic interests.

On December 4, 1969, the committee recommended that the court adopt as Standards of Judicial Conduct most of the Canons of Ethics adopted by the Illinois Judicial Conference ten years earlier. The committee also urged the court to adopt a companion set of Rules for the Regulation of Judicial Conduct. With these in place, the committee believed Illinois would have "the most up-to-date and workable code of judicial ethics in the United States." Lastly, the committee called for some tightening up of the requirements for financial disclosure by judges.

The court promptly incorporated the committee's recommendations into new supreme court rules, most of which took effect on March 15, 1970. Also, as of January 1971, judges were barred from assuming "an active role in the management of any business." Clearly the court was trying to rebuild public confidence in the judiciary. This was the first time ever that the Illinois Supreme Court had asserted the power to set ethical standards for judges.[6] The court also made changes in its rule governing procedures of the Illinois Courts Commission. These changes clarified and strengthened the Courts Commission's power to inquire into alleged instances of judicial misconduct.

Before the end of its September term, the court's quorum quandary became much more serious, for Justice House passed away on September 27. The court now faced a grave constitutional crisis, since the election of new justices was more than a year away. Fortunately, the Judicial Article of the Constitution offered a solution. The supreme court could assign any retired judge, with his consent, to judicial service. By October 9 the court had obtained the agreement of three retired circuit court judges—one from each of the districts in which there was a vacancy—to serve temporarily on the supreme court.[7] The court was back to a full complement.

"Finally Disposed Of"—Again

Two years earlier, the State's Attorney of Sangamon County, Raymond Terrell, had commented that *People v. Isaacs* was "finally disposed of," but later events proved him wrong. Now, in September

1969, the supreme court still faced the thorny question of how to respond to the Special Commission's finding that the court's judgment had been tainted.

On September 25 the court ordered Isaacs to file suggestions and a memorandum of law on whether the judgment should be reopened or vacated. Isaacs's lawyers, Albert Jenner and Robert Hanley, promptly filed a lengthy legal memorandum, arguing that "the judgment in *People v. Isaacs* must remain in repose." Once again, they attacked various aspects of the Special Commission's procedures and findings. Their principal points were that the commission had not found clear and convincing evidence that a fraud was committed on the court in that case, and that although the appearance of impropriety might warrant the resignation of judges, it would not justify upsetting a prior judgment.

A reply was filed by Attorney General William Scott and the new State's Attorney of Sangamon County, Richard Hollis. They argued that, even in the absence of a specific finding of fraud, the *Isaacs* decision was "void or voidable" because Solfisburg and Klingbiel should have disqualified themselves from the case and because of the appearance of impropriety in their conduct.

On January 24, 1970, the Supreme Court of Illinois ruled in *People v. Isaacs* for the last time. It construed the Attorney General's and State's Attorney's position as a motion to vacate the judgment, and the court denied it, with Justice Ward again not participating.

Just as the Special Commission had done, the court focused on the differences between the Underwood and Klingbiel opinions, saying, "The essential difference between the two opinions was in their interpretation of the statutory provisions involved." The court also observed that several sessions of the legislature had intervened since the case was decided, "and the statutes involved have not been amended." The court cited precedents to the effect that the absence of amendments to a judicially construed statute was considered indicative that the judicial interpretation "correctly reflected the legislative intent." With this perspective, the court finished *People v. Isaacs:*

> The construction adopted in the prevailing opinion is thus reinforced by legislative acquiescence. Accordingly, we have concluded that the opinion originally adopted in this case would again be adopted by the court, and the motion to vacate the judgment is therefore denied.

The court's position was virtually the same perspective that Justice Schaefer had expressed when he testified during the Special Commission hearings.[8]

As they brought down the final curtain, Schaefer and the others undoubtedly knew that reliance on legislative silence is a very debatable
judicial rationale.[9] Nonetheless, over five years had passed since
Isaacs was indicted. His original challenges to the myriad of counts in
the indictment had been technically complicated and invited many
differences of opinion among the justices. The case had been controversial when it began in 1964, and had only become more so through
the revelations of 1969.

Facing a second chance to decide this nettlesome matter, the three
new justices, the two silent dissenters—Schaefer and Underwood—
and Kluczynski as the only surviving member of the original majority,
unanimously found a way out. Whether or not any of them thought the
Klingbiel opinion was wrong when it was issued in 1967, it would now
be considered right. The legislature's subsequent inaction and silence
were taken to mean that the majority had understood the statutes correctly. The court indulged the dubious assumption that in the interim
the legislature had studied the *Isaacs* decision, understood it, and con-
sciously decided that the court, speaking through Klingbiel, got it right
the first time. For better or worse, the court would pass up the opportunity to decide the case again. *People v. Isaacs* was finally, and now ir-
revocably, disposed of.

Chapter 25

Legacies and Echoes

Soon after the justices left the court, signs of the scandal's long-lasting impact on Illinois law and politics appeared. The scandal also had lingering effects in the world of journalism. On August 4 the *Chicago Daily News* printed a lengthy retrospective piece on the scandal and investigation subtitled "Skolnick, *Daily News* Started It." Later in September, the *Alton Evening Telegraph* published its own account, emphasizing that it broke the story a few hours ahead of the *Daily News* and with a more informative, forthright article.[1] The rivalry between the papers that had fueled the scandal at the beginning was continuing in the competition for credit at the end. The managing editor of the *Telegraph* wrote to the *Chicago Journalism Review,* responding to published claims by Roy Fisher that the *Daily News,* "alone of all newspapers," aggressively pursued the scandal and "brought about a historic purging of the Supreme Court." The *Telegraph* editor recited the exact timing of the papers' respective stories on June 11, 1969, in order "to bury forever the myth that the *Daily News* broke the Solfisburg-Klingbiel story."[2]

The dispute spilled over into the awarding of prizes. On September 30, 1969, the Associated Press Managing Editors Association awarded a Citation for Exceptional Cooperation to the *Alton Evening Telegraph.* The citation described the *Telegraph*'s sharing of its story with the AP even before the *Telegraph* could publish the story in its own regular edition. The AP observed that the *Telegraph* story "launched" the ensuing investigation. Six months later, the *Daily News* received an Award for Newspaper Public Service from Sigma Delta Chi, a national journalism organization. The paper was found to have demonstrated in this instance "that journalistic enterprise of a high order can go hand in hand with a sense of civic responsibility of an even more commendable character." The *Daily News* nominated itself for this award, but the less sophisticated *Telegraph* reporters failed to make a nomination on their own behalf. Two weeks after the Sigma Delta Chi award, Skolnick, speaking at a journalism conference sponsored by that organization, argued that Sigma Delta Chi had made an error. Any journalism awards for exposing the conflicts of interest on the Illinois Supreme Court, he thought, should be given to Ed Pound and Ande Yakstis of the *Alton Telegraph,* and not to the *Daily News.*

The *Columbia Journalism Review* also delved into the rivalry. In April it received a written explanation of the *Daily News'* work from Charles Nicodemus, and then an angry ten-page rebuttal from Ed Pound. In its summer 1970 issue, the *Journalism Review* published a commentary on the papers' competing claims and came down on the *Telegraph*'s side. The *Columbia* article characterized the *Daily News'* first story as "far less comprehensive and conspicuously more vague" than the *Telegraph*'s report. It also mentioned Donald Barlett's work at the *Daily News* investigating Solfisburg in 1968 and observed that "the paper—for what Barlett decided were questionable policy reasons—spiked the story."

The *Journalism Review* acknowledged that after the *Telegraph* first broke the story, the *Daily News* "indisputably distinguished itself in the depth and continuity of stories and editorials." Nonetheless, the *Journalism Review* awarded "a special double Laurel" to Pound and Yakstis both "for breaking an important exposé" and for "prodding a large metropolitan daily into the kind of action that large metropolitan dailies should take without having to be prodded."[3]

In Pound's letter to the *Columbia Journalism Review,* he scathingly criticized Nicodemus and the *Daily News* for their version of the summer's events, saying that they "want the Pulitzer Prize so badly they will lie for it." In fact, the *Alton Telegraph*'s publisher, Paul Cousley, nominated Pound and Yakstis for a Pulitzer Prize in local investigative or specialized reporting. Additionally, the *Telegraph* itself was nominated for a Pulitzer by the editor of another small Illinois paper. Skolnick, too, wrote the administrator of Pulitzer Prizes at Columbia University to recommend Pound and Yakstis.[4]

Ultimately, no Pulitzer Prizes were awarded for the work of any of the newspapers involved in the summer's scandal. Years later, there is still lingering bitterness over this result. Charles Nicodemus believes that the work he and a few other *Daily News* reporters did throughout the investigation warranted more acclaim, but that the hesitancy of the newspaper's leadership prevented full recognition of their investigative breakthroughs.

Ed Pound believes the *Daily News'* boasting unfairly obscured the credit that the *Alton Telegraph* rightly deserved. Pound still feels his work on this scandal was "the best story I've ever done." He feels even more strongly that Paul Cousley, the *Telegraph* publisher, deserved recognition for his courage in giving his young reporters the freedom to follow their investigative instincts. Pound doubts that many small-town publishers "would have had his kind of guts" to allow the story to be pursued "full bore." Pound proudly reflects, "There were no lawyers, no nervous nellie editors and fixers standing in the way. We did not pull our punches."[5]

Most bitter of all are the journalists who worked at the *Daily Calumet* when it was ready to scoop all the other papers. Jameson Campaigne remembers his anger at the killing of their early story by James Linen, his business partner, and Don Reuben, their lawyer. Robert Seltzner, who wrote the doomed story, remains even more embittered. He says the episode "will always be a black period for me. It hurt. I had the son of a bitch in my hand, and then was forbidden to play that hand."[6]

The New Constitution

By coincidence, the Illinois Supreme Court scandal erupted on the eve of another historic episode for Illinois. On December 8, 1969, a Constitutional Convention convened in Springfield to begin drafting a new charter to replace the Constitution of 1870. Because the Judicial Article of the old constitution had been amended as recently as 1962, it originally was expected that the Constitutional Convention—widely known as "Con Con"—would focus little attention on the state's judicial system. The summer's scandal abruptly changed the situation.

The Special Commission and its report convinced the Con Con delegates, as well as many other people around the state, that at least two core aspects of the state's judicial system had to be addressed in the new draft constitution. One was the method of selecting judges, and the other was the method of investigating and punishing judicial misconduct. Judicial reform, it was observed at the time, "has suddenly become the dominant issue for the forthcoming Illinois Constitutional Convention."[7]

Among the most vocal advocates of putting judicial reform on the Con Con agenda were Henry Pitts and Frank Greenberg. Not only as

bar association presidents, but now also as the highly publicized leaders of the Special Commission, they spoke out on the scandal's implications for constitutional reform. On September 9 a luncheon
attended by a few hundred people was held at the Union League Club
in Chicago in honor of the Special Commission and its staff. In a prepared speech, Greenberg urged a rejection of the traditional Illinois
system of partisan election of judges, and the adoption instead of an
appointive system based on the concept of merit selection.

This was by no means the first time a bar president in Illinois had argued for merit selection. This time, however, Greenberg appeared to
be seizing an unprecedented opportunity for the appointive system—
"no panacea, but an infinitely better system than we have now"—to
be adopted through constitutional revision at a time of extraordinary
public displeasure with the character of the judiciary. Indeed, Greenberg was building on a widely publicized speech five days earlier in
which Governor Ogilvie declared "a crisis of confidence" in the Illinois courts and strongly advocated merit selection.

Henry Pitts's remarks focused on the other judicial reform issue,
"the constitutional framework for retirement, suspension, and removal of judges in office." Although he recognized that the Illinois
Supreme Court had recently made constructive changes in its rules for
Illinois Courts Commission proceedings, he argued that a more effective disciplinary system still was needed. In part, Pitts was reacting to
the obvious uselessness of the Illinois Courts Commission during the
summer's scandal and to the widespread sense that judges could not be
trusted to find and punish the indiscretions of their own colleagues.[8]

With salvos from the governor and the major bar association presidents, but with opposition from powerful political interests and many
judges, the stage was set for a momentous battle on judicial selection
and discipline. This was a battle that simply would not have been
fought as part of the Con Con process had the scandal of that summer
not occurred. It was also a battle that the bar associations approached
with greater fervor, and hope for success, than ever before.[9]

The complete history of this battle has been written elsewhere. It
amply explains the complex political process through which the judicial reform proponents eventually achieved only very limited success
when the voters considered the new constitution in December of
1970.[10] The merit selection proposal that emerged out of Con Con was
separated out to be voted on independently of the main body of the
proposed constitution. Bar leaders described the presence of merit selection on the ballot as "the most significant accomplishment in the
20-year effort for court reform in Illinois."[11] When the votes were

counted, however, the new constitution was adopted, but the merit selection proposal was defeated.

In what was described as "the election's biggest surprise," the proposal garnered a majority of the votes cast in Cook County, "despite all-out opposition by Mayor Richard J. Daley and his Democratic machine."[12] However, even with this accomplishment, the statewide result was a rejection of the change. Postmortems suggested that the merit selection forces had underestimated the depth of public preference elsewhere in the state for the election of judges.

Had merit selection been adopted into the new constitution, it could plausibly have been claimed that its acceptance was in great measure a public reaction to the Solfisburg-Klingbiel scandal. With its defeat, it starkly appeared that if merit selection could not be accepted during an extreme crisis in the judiciary, it would be a long time before such a change would ever be accepted in Illinois.

The other prong of the judicial reform campaign met with some success. The bar associations had formed a fourteen-member Joint Committee on the Judicial Article, which included Mason Bull as one of its senior members and myself as one of its most junior, appointed by Greenberg. The proposed Judicial Article the committee drafted included not only the merit selection system, but also a vast overhaul of the Courts Commission. We proposed that the Courts Commission be made up of four lawyers and three nonlawyers, but no judges. The commission also would have its own investigative staff and broader procedural and punitive powers. This proposal was altered considerably in Con Con, through political dynamics that Frank Greenberg later summarized:

> It was quickly evident that the system of exclusive judicial control of judicial discipline had lost the confidence of the organized bar, the people, and a substantial majority of the delegates to the Convention. But it was equally evident that the judiciary was implacably opposed to any change that would accord to anybody but judges a significant role in the disciplinary process.[13]

A compromise evolved, retaining the Courts Commission's prior structure as a panel of five judges with the ultimate decision power in cases of alleged judicial misconduct. What was new, however, was a first level of action, a Judicial Inquiry Board of nine members with the authority to receive or initiate complaints against judges, to conduct investigations, and then to file formal complaints for the imposition of disciplinary sanctions by the Courts Commission. The Judicial Inquiry Board was to have a membership of two circuit judges selected by the supreme court, and three lawyers and four nonlawyers appointed by the governor. This novel approach, it was hoped, would provide a more effective and credible system for investigating and punishing judicial misdeeds, and for rebuilding public trust in the judiciary.

The new system went into effect on July 1, 1971. Prominent among the initial members of the first Judicial Inquiry Board that Governor Ogilvie selected was Frank Greenberg. Although Greenberg did not serve at any time as chairman, his highly publicized, passionate commitment to judicial integrity made him one of the most visible symbols of the new, more aggressive disciplinary system.

Under this new constitutional scheme, which is still in place, there has been considerably more activity than would have been feasible under the Courts Commission arrangement as of 1969.[14] Unfortunately, there also have been criticisms that the scheme has not accomplished much, and there have been conflicts over the scope of both the board's investigatory powers and the commission's disciplinary authority.[15]

Even more regrettably, major judicial scandals in Illinois have continued. The best known and most extensive, of course, was Operation Greylord, the massive federal investigation and sting operation of the 1980s. Aimed at widespread corruption in the Cook County courts, Operation Greylord produced indictments of almost ninety judges, lawyers, clerks, and police officers, and the convictions of eighty-one.[16]

Scandal did not touch the Illinois Supreme Court again until 1997, when accusations were brought against Chief Justice James D. Heiple, principally relating to the justice's offensive responses to being stopped by police for traffic violations. The Judicial Inquiry Board filed a complaint with the Courts Commission, and the commission censured Heiple, who then resigned as chief justice but stayed on the court. In response to skepticism about the Courts Commission's action, a legislative committee investigated possible impeachment proceedings against Heiple.[17] Although Justice Heiple's misconduct was very different from that of his accused predecessors in 1969, it sadly appeared that arrogant behavior on the state's highest court was not yet a thing of the past. It also seemed that the judicial disciplinary system had not yet evolved to the point of being itself unimpeachable.

United States v. Isaacs and Kerner

A few years after the Solfisburg-Klingbiel affair, there was another blockbuster scandal in Illinois involving a judge: Otto Kerner of the

federal Court of Appeals for the Seventh Circuit. The scandal concerned events that occurred while he was the governor of Illinois and
was dealing extensively with his close friend and adviser, Theodore
Isaacs. This later scandal not only carries strong echoes of the earlier
one, but it also sheds surprising light on what was revealed during the
summer of 1969.

Right after Solfisburg and Klingbiel resigned, the Internal Revenue
Service publicly announced that it was looking into possible federal
law violations by them, Isaacs, Joseph Knight, and others. A few
months later, the IRS also began looking at Isaacs and Knight for entirely different reasons. This investigation was secret, however, for at
the heart of it was Kerner, a man of far more prominence, and a far
loftier reputation, than Isaacs or Knight ever had.

The crux of the case was bribery. In contrast with the 1969 scandal,
this time Isaacs was not the person who seemed to be offering bribes.
Instead he was a recipient, as well as the intermediary for the other
recipient, Kerner. Now the booty was not bank stock, but stock in
companies conducting horse racing in Illinois. In the fall of 1969 Marjorie Lindheimer Everett, the most prominent owner of racetracks in
Illinois, began to tell IRS agents about a complex scheme through
which she claimed to have been pressured to make stock in her companies available to Kerner and Isaacs at bargain prices. In return, they
would provide various forms of official assistance to her business interests.

The IRS and the Department of Justice probed this sensational
charge and brought Kerner, Isaacs, and many other witnesses before a
federal grand jury. On December 15, 1971, Attorney General John
Mitchell and the new U.S. Attorney in Chicago, James R. Thompson,
announced an indictment against Kerner, Isaacs, Knight, and two
other individuals. They were charged with a variety of crimes related
to the bribery scheme, including tax evasion, mail fraud, conspiracy,
and perjury. On January 3, 1973, the trial began in Chicago against
Kerner and Isaacs. Knight, whose health was deteriorating, was not included in the trial, and he died four months later. The two other defendants were given immunity in exchange for their testimony against
Kerner and Isaacs.

On February 19, 1973, the jury brought in guilty verdicts on all
counts, and one year later the court of appeals upheld most of those
findings. The appeals panel consisted of three judges from elsewhere
in the country. All of Kerner's colleagues on the federal appeals court
in Chicago had disqualified themselves, because they could not rule
on his case with any appearance of objectivity. Included in that group

was John Paul Stevens, who by then was a member of that court. Unlike the other judges on the Seventh Circuit, however, Stevens had an added reason for not hearing Kerner's case. Because of his work in the summer of 1969, he had the dubious distinction of knowing a lot about Isaacs and his ways.

The full and controversial story of *United States v. Isaacs* has been told in great detail elsewhere.[18] Whatever history's ultimate verdict on that case, the evidence against Kerner, Isaacs, and Knight in the 1973 trial provides added insight into the misconduct exposed by the Special Commission four years earlier.

A comparison between the report of the Special Commission on *People v. Isaacs* and the decision of the court of appeals in *United States v. Isaacs* reveals strong parallels between the two scandals. In both cases, there was a pattern of financial favors given by persons in need of official assistance to those in a position to provide it. In both cases, the principal financial favors offered were opportunities to purchase privately controlled stock at bargain prices.[19]

In both cases, the financial transactions had common characteristics: the use of nominees to hide stock ownership, fictitious loans to give seeming credibility to later dealings, and personal selection of purchasers for the resale of stock. In both cases, the transactions were complicated, although the racetrack deals were much more intricate—and involved much more money—than the Civic Center Bank deals. The Kerner bribery, for example, involved a shifting array of at least four different corporate entities, in contrast with the relative simplicity of the CCB stock structure. Nonetheless, the federal prosecutors faced the same difficult task Stevens confronted in trying to piece together Isaacs's tangled web of secret transactions, which often were lacking in documentation and involved many different people as lead actors and bit part players.

Isaacs's and Kerner's lawyers also argued—just as Isaacs's lawyers and the two justices' lawyers had—"that the stock acquisitions were legitimate business transactions unrelated to any attempt to influence official conduct and that their conduct was within the realm of propriety."[20] Similarly, just as Stevens had argued in his summation, the court of appeals found "frail support" for the claim of "ordinary business transactions" and also found evidence that strongly "discredits the claim of a legitimate business transaction." Just as Stevens insisted that Solfisburg had acted as though he knew there were no risks in his unusually large, wholly unexamined investment in the Civic Center Bank, so too did the court of appeals find that "Isaacs and Kerner ran none of the risks inherent in ordinary business affairs."

In the end, the court of appeals found that Kerner and Isaacs had each invested a little over $15,000 in the racetrack stock, yet each gained almost $160,000. Apparently the price others had to pay to influence Isaacs and his friend Kerner was a lot higher than the price Isaacs and his friend Perbohner thought they needed to pay in order to influence the supreme court justices.

There are other, even more specific parallels between the two sets of events. The critical stock deals in both cases occurred during the same time period, from late 1965 to early 1968. Isaacs was the key player in all the transactions in both cases, and Knight figured prominently in both as well. Many of the racetrack stock transactions involved use of the Civic Center Bank, usually with Isaacs's participation.

Most strikingly, such a comparison provides strong evidence that Knight and Isaacs perjured themselves during the Special Commission hearings. The chronology of transactions underlying each case tells the tale. On July 12, 1966, Knight submitted payment of $12,000 plus interest for the six hundred shares of CCB stock for his mother or himself. Isaacs directed that Knight's stock should be issued in the name of Howard Hansen, and on July 13 this was done. Knight testified that he didn't remember from whom he had ordered the CCB stock, nor did he know who arranged for Hansen to be his nominee. Isaacs similarly testified that he had "nothing to do" with Knight getting his shares.

Also on July 13, Knight paid over $11,000 for 28,000 shares of Chicago Harness Racing stock. This stock was issued in two 14,000-share certificates, one destined for Isaacs and one for Kerner. These shares ultimately made up what the court of appeals called "the smaller part of the bribery." These certificates were issued in Knight's name, and a few months later Knight arranged for one of Everett's lawyers to be substituted for him as nominee. Thus, on the very same day, Isaacs helped Knight buy a block of bank stock in the name of a nominee, and Knight helped Isaacs buy a block of racetrack stock in the name of a nominee.

The Kerner case makes clear that Isaacs knew full well what Knight was doing on his behalf on July 13. By the same token, it is nearly impossible to believe that Knight did not know what Isaacs was doing for him at the exact same time. The two men were working together on a complex array of checks, "loans," deposits, purchases, and transfers related to the racing stock around this time. Certainly they must also have talked about Knight's purchase of the CCB stock and the use of Isaacs's close friend Hansen as the nominee for Knight. Although

Knight told the Special Commission there were no such contacts with Isaacs, he admitted them to Ed Pound just a few days before he testified.[21]

The dealings in CCB stock and racetrack stock involving Isaacs, Knight, and Kerner continued actively over the next several weeks. For example, on August 10 there was a pivotal meeting between Isaacs, Knight, and others to transact an additional, much larger purchase of Everett's stock for Kerner and Isaacs. This stock became the major component of the bribery scheme. One week later Kerner bought his three hundred shares of Civic Center Bank stock. About this time, Isaacs reported the loss of Knight's stock certificate for a hundred shares.

These and other developments in the two investment arenas indicate that Isaacs, Knight, and Kerner were actively in communication with each other during this period. Isaacs's testimony before the commission that he was only minimally involved in Kerner's CCB stock purchase thus is barely credible. Furthermore, Kerner's own testimony during his trial emphasized that he left the details of stock transactions to Isaacs and followed his advice on when and how to submit payment for stock purchases. When pressed for details on the racing stock transactions, Kerner repeatedly testified that he "let Ted do it."[22] If that were true for the racing stock, it must have been even more true for the CCB stock, given Isaacs's position as an insider at the bank.

Similarly, the credibility of Isaacs's and Knight's testimony that Isaacs was only peripherally involved with the lost CCB stock certificate is weakened, since the two men both attended the critical August meeting in Chicago and were still working together then on the complicated racing stock transactions. Indeed, the extensive financial entanglements between Isaacs and Knight raise a question as to whether Isaacs was truthful when he told Frank Greenberg that his friendship with Knight was not a factor in the bank organizers' selection of him as the bank's lawyer. A subsequent commentary on the 1969 scandal suggested that Isaacs was hired by the bank precisely because of his relationship with Knight, since the bank "previously had been unable to obtain a charter" from Knight.[23] Although evidence to support this claim is lacking, the Kerner case facts do suggest much closer ties between Knight and Isaacs than were revealed in 1969. It begins to look more plausible that Isaacs helped Knight to buy the six hundred shares in the Civic Center Bank as part of a calculated effort to make sure that Knight looked favorably on the bank from his official perch in the Department of Financial Institutions.

On March 26, 1968—coincidentally about the same day as Solfis-burg's second sale of CCB stock through Isaacs—the Kerner bribery came to full fruition. The proceeds from resale of Kerner's and Isaacs's major racing stock holdings were distributed to them. Once again, Knight was the intermediary. A $300,000 check was issued to him by the purchaser, and he endorsed it in blank and gave it to Isaacs. Isaacs then took actions only possible for someone with considerable lever-age over the way the bank operated:

> Isaacs arranged with the Civic Center Bank, whose attorney he was, to negotiate [the check] without an endorsement, although this was contrary to normal bank procedures. Isaacs deposited $135,000 in his checking account and a similar amount in a new checking ac-count opened for Kerner. Then he deposited $15,000 each in two new savings accounts, which he had opened for himself and Kerner.[24]

Once again, something other than "ordinary business transactions" was taking place, and Isaacs was acting as something other than an or-dinary lawyer for an ordinary bank.

In these and other ways, the stock transactions in *United States v. Isaacs* undercut the protestations of innocence the Special Commis-sion heard from Isaacs, Knight, and others. In one ironic respect, how-ever, the evidence of the Kerner case bribery supports Isaacs's 1969 testimony. Isaacs told the commission that in 1965 he had experienced financial problems, but by the fall of 1966, he stated, "I had begun to reestablish myself again." In view of the tremendous profits he had positioned himself to make through the secret, bargain purchases of racing stock in the summer of 1966, it is no wonder he felt his financial picture had brightened by that fall.

In 1969, when Solfisburg and Klingbiel resigned, many people no-ticed that Isaacs came out of the scandal unpunished for anything he had done. The justices had to leave the court, but he was "home free."[25] In the federal case four years later, things were different. Isaacs and Kerner were each sentenced to pay a $50,000 fine and serve three years in prison. On July 29, 1974, after the U.S. Supreme Court declined to review the case, Kerner entered a federal prison in Lex-ington, Kentucky. When he was diagnosed with lung cancer in March 1975, Kerner was quickly released on parole. He died fourteen months later.

Isaacs was disbarred on July 1, 1974. A few weeks later, on the same day Kerner went to prison, Isaacs began his sentence at a federal insti-tution in Terre Haute, Indiana. He was later transferred to Lexington and served one year in prison before being paroled and returning to Chicago.

While the Kerner case was under way and afterward, many people blamed Isaacs for Kerner's downfall. In a letter written two weeks into the trial, Edwin Austin—the Sidley & Austin senior partner who served on the Special Commission—wrote: "The current trial of Otto Kerner and Isaacs brings back vivid memories of Mr. Isaacs' methods. Without intending to comment on a pending trial, I have a feeling that whatever facts are brought out will show that Mr. Isaacs rather than Otto was the real mastermind of the situation."[26]

Not everyone took such a charitable view of Kerner. The day after the guilty verdicts were rendered against him and Isaacs, Mike Royko, the famed *Chicago Daily News* columnist, expressed doubt that Kerner was simply manipulated by Isaacs. Royko emphasized that Kerner was a product of the Chicago Democratic Machine and had grown up observing the machine first created by Mayor Cermak. Kerner's father, of course, had been one of Cermak's closest advisers, and Kerner's wife was Cermak's daughter. Royko observed:

> It is hard to believe that someone with Kerner's background wouldn't have had some idea of what Isaacs was up to. For all of his suave manner, Kerner grew up among people who knew first-hand that Chicago politics is a gold mine, and exactly where to start digging. . . .
>
> There are many tears being shed, some of them by naive journalists, about the "tragedy" of Otto Kerner and his shattered career. And his friends are explaining that poor Otto just isn't very bright. In fairness, there is some evidence of that. He didn't show much brains in getting tied in with Isaacs, who has to be one of the all-time bungling bagmen.[27]

Royko's cynical view of Kerner seems justified. As Kerner's biographers later put it, "Several of his undisputed actions were clearly uncharacteristic of straightforward, legitimate investing and were tragically contrary to the expected behavior of an honest public official."[28] Royko's description of Isaacs as "bungling," however, is harder to agree with. There was no indication of bungling by Isaacs with regard to the Kerner bribes. His scheme there, as in the supreme court scandal, was multilayered and cunning. Nonetheless, in both instances, intense investigative efforts uncovered his machinations. Isaacs wasn't bungling—he was just caught.

Chapter 26

Stevens to the Bench

When his work as counsel to the Special Commission ended, John Paul Stevens went back to practicing law. His name was now much more widely known. As Henry Pitts later wrote, "John Paul Stevens's performance in the hearings drew much applause."[1] Conspicuously silent, however, were the members of the Illinois Supreme Court. Not a word of appreciation came from them toward Stevens or any of the commissioners.

Stevens's sudden notoriety did not translate into any significant change in his work as a lawyer. It brought him no new clients or new types of cases. His relationship to the Chicago Bar Association changed a bit, for he soon was named as the group's second vice president, in recognition of both his prior Bar Association work and the Special Commission investigation. He was thus on track to become the association's president.

Otherwise, Stevens's life and law practice returned pretty much to normal. The summer's events were still very much with him, of course, even when he least expected it. In September he drove his eldest daughter, Kathryn, down to Quincy, Illinois, to begin the school year at college. Along the way they stopped at a restaurant for lunch. Coincidentally, seated at another table in the room was Roy Solfisburg with his family. The two men did not speak to each other.

The Senator's Committee

In 1966 Republican Charles H. Percy—whom Otto Kerner had defeated for governor in 1964—was elected as the junior U.S. senator from Illinois. When Everett Dirksen died in 1969, Percy became se-

nior senator and succeeded to the dominant role in recommending
nominees for federal court vacancies in Illinois. Actually Percy's participation in the selection process already had become substantial.
Shortly after Percy entered the Senate, Dirksen spoke to him about
their responsibility to submit names and indicated his preference that
both senators should agree on the recommendations.

As a freshman senator, Percy made a decision—a decision that was
quite unusual for an Illinois politician—to recommend judicial nominees with little regard for their political service and much greater
regard for their real competence to serve on the bench. To aid him,
Percy assembled an informal screening committee of about ten prominent lawyers. He proudly remembers that neither Dirksen, the White
House, nor the Senate ever turned down a nominee Percy identified
through his screening system. Even though Percy was one of the mod-
erate Republicans in the Senate whom President Nixon privately condemned, those strains seemed to have no effect on Nixon's deference
to the senator's judicial choices.[2]

Although Percy's screening committee never held meetings, he and
his staff would receive advice from various members whenever federal court vacancies arose. The people he consulted included such pillars of the legal community as Justin A. Stanley of the Mayer, Brown,
& Platt firm, Professor Philip Kurland of the University of Chicago
Law School, Edward H. McDermott of McDermott, Will, & Emery,
and Albert Jenner. Additionally, soon after the Chicago Council of
Lawyers formed in mid-1969, it reached agreement with the senator
that he would make no nominations of individuals the council found
unqualified.

By early 1970 Percy had established an unprecedented network of
Illinois lawyers from various political sectors, and different genera-
tions, to advise him on judicial nominations. He also touched base
with his political allies, such as Governor Richard Ogilvie and Attorney General William Scott. Percy was actively committed to getting
the best people on the bench, almost regardless of their politics. Once
a promising candidate was identified through his network, Percy himself would interview the individual.[3]

Judge Stevens

With the death of Judge Elmer J. Schnackenberg in 1968, a vacancy
arose on the Seventh Circuit Court of Appeals. In early 1970 this position remained open, and there were other federal court vacancies in

Chicago as well.[4] Senator Percy's staff and screening group were hard at work trying to identify qualified lawyers to fill these positions.

Because of his recent prominence in the Special Commission investigation, Stevens's name readily surfaced. With his long-standing reputation as a fine trial lawyer, his consistent participation in Chicago Bar Association projects over many years, and now his widely heralded service as counsel to the Special Commission, Stevens appeared as an obvious choice. Some people, however, thought there was another reason why Stevens was an obvious selection for Percy to make: The two had known each other as college classmates at the University of Chicago.

In fact, their prior acquaintance played only a minor role in Stevens's selection. It was the independent work of Percy's staff and committee that brought Stevens's name to the senator's attention. As the senator prepared to interview three candidates at the Ambassador East Hotel in Chicago, he reviewed their names, one of which was John Paul Stevens, a name Percy didn't recognize at first. Probably Stevens's practice of using his middle name professionally had caused Percy not to realize that this was the same John Stevens he had known some thirty years earlier as a classmate.

Percy says that this pleasant surprise was accompanied by the memory that Stevens was "the smartest guy I knew at the university." As the selection process progressed, Percy's positive recollection of Stevens and their college friendship "didn't hurt any," as Stevens later put it, but it was not determinative in Stevens's elevation to the bench. This favorable factor entered into the equation only late in the game and helped only to seal Percy's resolve to make a nomination justified on the merits. Nonetheless, the friendship may have had some influence on Stevens's placement on the court of appeals, rather than in one of the district court vacancies.

Once Percy decided to proceed with the recommendation, he felt it necessary to be extra careful to make sure that Stevens was a meritorious candidate. Having established his screening system in part to avoid cronyism, Percy was sensitive to the possible charge that he was reverting to the old ways of Illinois politics and selecting Stevens because he was a friend, rather than because he was qualified. The glowing endorsement by his committee and the Chicago Council of Lawyers, and later by the American Bar Association, allayed the senator's concern.

When Percy and Stevens met at the Ambassador East to discuss the possible judgeship, Stevens at first expressed qualms about leaving his law practice. He was worried about making enough money to complete his children's education. He asked Percy to give him five or six more years before nominating him for a judgeship, and Percy forcefully replied that by then he might no longer be in the Senate and there might no longer be a Republican in the White House. Percy also told Stevens—in an effort at flattery that turned out to be prophesy—that if he became an appellate judge now, in about five years he ought to be on the U.S. Supreme Court. As Stevens later described, somehow Percy just "happened to hit it right!"[5]

In early April 1970, reports began to appear in the press that Percy was going to recommend Stevens for the Seventh Circuit. In the following weeks, other potential nominees also were rumored to be under consideration. On June 24 Senator Percy and the new senator, Ralph Smith, announced that they had submitted a package of five recommendations to Attorney General Mitchell for filling the federal court openings. John Paul Stevens was proposed for the court of appeals.

Stevens's nomination was lauded in the press, with references to his work for the Special Commission figuring prominently. A couple of the other nominees were more controversial, or at least carried problematic political freight. The nomination of state Judge Thomas J. Moran attracted special attention because of his links to Solfisburg. When Solfisburg first sought election to the Illinois Supreme Court in 1960, he secured the Republican Party's nomination at a contentious nominating convention in his district by defeating Charles H. Davis, an incumbent member of the court and former chief justice. With Solfisburg gone, Davis—now an appellate court judge—wanted to return to the supreme court, but Moran seemed likely to challenge him for the nomination in the heavily Republican district. According to press reports, in the background supporting Moran against Davis was none other than Roy Solfisburg. In the words of Charles Nicodemus of the *Daily News,* Solfisburg was "out to regain some of the dominant influence over that tribunal which was stripped from him last year when he was forced to resign," and Moran was "the chosen instrument for Solfisburg's return to statewide influence." With the recommendation of Moran for the federal court—apparently with Senator Smith's urging as he prepared for his own election battle—a divisive conflict for the Republican nomination for Solfisburg's vacancy would be avoided in what the *Chicago Tribune* called "the Republican Party's best vote-producing territory" in the state.

Amidst these machinations, and criticisms of some of the other proposed nominees, it began to seem likely that the five recommendations might not be successful. Although Stevens now was second vice president of the Chicago Bar Association, the association weighed in against the package. Its new president condemned the method of judicial selection embodied in the package. Taking pains to emphasize that the association was not commenting on the qualifications of the candidates, he emphasized that in the senators' recommendations, "political leverage rather than merit is what controls."

The purpose of the Chicago Bar Association statement was obviously not to jeopardize Stevens's prospects. Instead it was to highlight the need for Con Con to adopt a merit selection plan for judicial selection, for it seemed that even Senator Percy's bold effort to raise the selection process for federal judgeships to a more elevated level was being dragged down by party politics.[6] On the other hand, Percy clearly was not doing business completely as usual for his party. In recommending Stevens, he was promoting the lawyer who had played a major role in ending the judicial careers of two politically prominent Republicans. It was rumored that party leaders, especially in Solfisburg's area, were quite displeased at Percy's effrontery. In retrospect, Percy recalls no backlash from Republicans for his nomination of Stevens, but he adds, quite plausibly, that he wouldn't have let it stop him anyway.

Three months after it was announced, the full package deal was dead. On September 22 only two of the five candidates were nominated by President Nixon for confirmation by the Senate. John Paul Stevens was nominated to fill Judge Schnackenberg's seat on the court of appeals, and Frank J. McGarr was named to fill a newly created position on the district court.

The summer had been an anxious time for Stevens. Not knowing whether he would be going on the bench or staying in practice, he was particularly frustrated when a few promising new clients decided to take their business elsewhere, rather than risk having their lawyer leave for a judgeship. Happily, once the nomination was submitted to the Senate, the confirmation process was quick and uneventful. On October 14 the Senate confirmed Stevens's nomination, and he was sworn in as a judge of the court of appeals on November 2, 1970.

As Stevens assumed his new position, he had no doubt about "the causal connection between the investigation and my ultimate appointment to the bench."[7] In 1992 Stevens spoke to the American Bar Association about how important it is for lawyers to do pro bono work, taking on cases in the public interest without compensation. He described pro bono cases he had worked on, including the Special Commission investigation, and noted its impact on his career:

If you do stumble into a high visibility, pro bono case, sometimes it just happens that it works out well, and it may be there's a vacancy on a court at the time it works out well. And the publicity may be favorable, as it happened to be in that instance. And all I can say is had I not participated in that particular pro bono matter, I'm sure I would not be occupying the position I occupy today.[8]

At the Seventh Circuit

Among the new colleagues Stevens gained at the court of appeals was Otto Kerner. In light of the 1969 investigation, there might have been some awkwardness between the two judges. Fortunately, Stevens found Kerner "totally courteous and friendly." They never talked about the investigation or Isaacs.

A year after Stevens joined the court, Kerner was indicted and immediately suspended his participation in cases there. After speaking with Kerner, Stevens also wrote to him: "I deeply regret this development and wish there were some meaningful way in which I could be of assistance to you. . . . I shall miss your valuable and honorable participation in our work, but am sure that temporary difficulties will not diminish our friendship."[9] Clearly Stevens was pained by the Kerner case, both what it was doing to the man and what it might ultimately say about the man.

Another echo of 1969 heard by Stevens on the Seventh Circuit was the voice of Sherman Skolnick. Stevens participated in a few appeals in cases initiated by Skolnick[10] and remembers Skolnick beginning his argument in one case by saying, in essence, "I know I can't get a fair hearing from this tribunal. The judges on this court are just as bad as the rest of the judges in Cook County." Stevens and the other members of the judicial panel just let Skolnick "get it off his chest," although Stevens notes, "Some judges would have had him hauled off in contempt right away."

Justice Stevens

On November 28, 1975, the day after Thanksgiving, President Gerald Ford announced his nomination of Stevens for the U.S. Supreme Court. Stevens would succeed Justice William O. Douglas in the seat earlier held by Justice Brandeis.

Press reports noted that Stevens "first earned general public attention in 1969" when he served as counsel to the Special Commission. It also was observed that Stevens's nomination "came as somewhat of a surprise, as he is relatively unknown outside of Illinois legal circles." Stevens himself was rather shocked by the nomination. Responding to a congratulatory note from Otto Kerner, Stevens added, "It is a little difficult to realize what seems to be happening."[11]

On December 11 the Senate Judiciary Committee unanimously voted to recommend confirmation, and on December 17 the full Senate unanimously confirmed the nomination. Stevens was sworn in at the Court on December 19. Senator Percy's prediction had come true.[12]

The full story of Stevens's nomination has been told elsewhere and includes the pivotal roles of Stevens's old friend Edward Levi, then the U.S. Attorney General, and again of Senator Percy. A dominant factor in Stevens's confirmation was the extraordinary scope and caliber of the judicial opinions he had written during his five years on the Seventh Circuit. President Ford later wrote that he pored over these opinions himself and found them "concise, persuasive and legally sound."[13]

Ford's selection of Stevens was motivated in large part by the president's desire to "restore confidence in government in the wake of the Watergate scandals" and the embarrassments the two previous presidents had encountered with some of their Supreme Court nominations.[14] Ford was determined to present a candidate of unquestioned integrity and talent "whose professional reputation put him outside the pale of partisan political controversy."[15] Stevens fit the bill.

Although the confirmation process took less than three weeks and the Senate Judiciary Committee's hearings took only three days, the committee did spend some time on issues related to Stevens's conduct of the Special Commission investigation. As the hearings began, the American Bar Association submitted a glowing report on Stevens that included a brief description of his work as counsel in 1969.[16] As the hearings progressed, there were additional references to that work, though not all of them were favorable.

Late in the morning of the second day of hearings, Senator Charles Mathias of Maryland advised Stevens that the committee had received an affidavit and a press release from a Chicagoan named Anthony R. Martin-Trigona containing two serious allegations. First, Martin-Trigona was suggesting, based on articles then appearing in the *Chicago Daily News,* that Stevens may have been the secret beneficiary of a Chicago-area land trust about ten years earlier that allegedly involved Tom Keane, the former Chicago political powerhouse, and one of Stevens's law partners, Edward Rothschild. Martin-Trigona called attention to Stevens's publicly disclosed net worth of only about $170,000 and made a leap of suspicion that Stevens secretly must have had other undisclosed financial interests such as the land trust. In language reminiscent of Sherman Skolnick, Martin-Trigona claimed that the *Daily News'* disclosures "are being ignored in an attempt by the Ford Administration to steamroller the nomination of John Stevens without adequate disclosure and examination."

In the hearings, Stevens confirmed that he had no undisclosed assets of any sort, that he had no interest in the land trust deal, that his partner was involved only in a limited professional capacity, and that he was informed that Tom Keane actually had no interest in the venture anyway. Stevens conceded that "it is somewhat embarrassing to have to acknowledge that one's net worth is as small as it is."

Stevens addressed one other aspect of the innuendos being raised about his finances. Speaking about Martin-Trigona's statement that Rothschild might have been a secret nominee for Stevens, he said:

> I certainly had no occasion at that time to have a nominee serve for me in any capacity. It is a particularly sensitive area because the investigation that I ran emphasized certain judicial conduct where nominees did hold interests for judges, and I am conscious of the fact that that is a method of concealment that has been used by others in the past. It has never been used by me, and it never will be used by me.

Stevens remembered what he learned about the Civic Center Bank transactions, and he was not about to imitate them.

A more troublesome issue raised by Martin-Trigona's lengthy affidavit was his suspicion that Stevens had covered up incriminating information about two more Illinois Supreme Court justices during the Special Commission work. In 1970 Martin-Trigona had retained Torshen to assist him in securing admission to the Illinois bar. He had passed the bar exam but ran into trouble obtaining clearance from the Committee on Character and Fitness for admission to practice. Martin-Trigona now claimed that Torshen had made statements to him indicating that "the complete truth concerning the discoveries of the Special Commission had not reached the public." The affidavit noted that Martin-Trigona also filed an unsuccessful lawsuit in 1972 against the Illinois Supreme Court and Stevens related to his suspicions. By that time, he and Torshen had parted company.

In response to this serious charge, an affidavit submitted by Torshen unequivocally denied that he had made the alleged statements in the first place, affirmed that the 1969 investigation uncovered no impropriety by Illinois justices other than the two who resigned, and attested to Stevens's worthiness. Similar forceful affidavits were submitted by Frank Greenberg and Henry Pitts, both praising Stevens's performance in 1969 and describing the investigative process that made it "inconceivable that any evidence could have been suppressed" without their knowing about it.

On the third and final day of the hearings, Martin-Trigona appeared before the Judiciary Committee and repeated his allegations. He said he had no personal animosity toward Stevens but merely wanted to raise information helpful to the committee's inquiry. He then reiterated his suspicions at great length. As he went on, the senators became increasingly frustrated with the lack of any hard evidence. Senator Quentin Burdick at one point insisted, "I am trying to be fair with you, but I want some evidence pretty soon." In the end, Senator Burdick and Senator Strom Thurmond simply concluded that the witness had none to offer.

With the submission of the affidavits from Torshen, Pitts, and Greenberg, plus Martin-Trigona's own meandering and speculative testimony, the flap over his allegations evaporated. Stevens, who emphatically denied the alleged cover-up, also commented on the irony of a charge that he had acted dishonestly in the very case that had done the most to establish his public reputation for integrity and led him to a judgeship:

> It is sort of ironic because I am inclined to think that the performance of the work of that Special Commission is the real reason why the course of events developed to bring me here today. That happened shortly before my original appointment, and I think it was because of a good deal of public attention that my name came to the attention of the people who were trying to find people who might fill a vacancy. . . .
>
> I think that the commission, and I say this as a member of a team, did a magnificent job which I regard as one of the principal, important professional achievements of my life.

Legacies to the Justice

The scandal that helped make Stevens a judge also shaped some of the ways in which he has performed his judicial duties over the years. As he told the Judiciary Committee, the investigation gave him a heightened sensitivity to the use of nominees and other methods by which judges may try to conceal their financial holdings. The 1969 experience left even more of its mark on Justice Stevens in other, unstated ways.

The old evidentiary rule against impeaching one's own witness does not frequently arise as an issue before federal appellate courts, much less the U.S. Supreme Court. Nonetheless, Stevens says, "whenever we get a case in which the lawyer has been unable to impeach his own witness, I think of Mrs. Kegley. I remember that so well."

More significantly, Stevens also hasn't forgotten Sherman Skolnick. The Illinois gadfly particularly comes to mind when the justice wrestles with his colleagues' impatience with individuals who persistently file numerous merit-less petitions with the Court. In recent years, a majority of the Court has tightened its procedure on "in forma pauperis" filings, petitions for relief submitted by persons who cannot afford to pay the usual filing fees.[17] The majority has streamlined its review of "frivolous or malicious" filings by such persons, and in a number of cases the Court has directed the clerk not to accept any further petitions from "prolific filers" unless regular fees are paid.

In each of these numerous rulings, Justice Stevens has dissented, first along with other justices such as Brennan, Blackmun, and Marshall, and more recently on his own. His view is that each petition's merit should be considered individually, rather than automatically presumed unworthy of the Court's attention. He has made the reasons for his disagreement clear, principally emphasizing the Court's "great tradition of open access" and the importance of "the symbolic interest in preserving equal access to the Court for both the rich and the poor." Contrary to the majority, he asserts that he has not "detected any significant burden on the Court, or threat to the integrity of its processes, caused by the filing of frivolous petitions."

Stevens believes, as his fellow dissenter Justice Marshall stated, that "we should not presume in advance that prolific indigent litigants will never bring a meritorious claim." Recognizing that even the frequent and vexatious litigant sometimes can hit pay dirt, Stevens remembers Sherman Skolnick: "I've always objected to those rules, and Sherman is the one who's responsible."

Finally, there is Stevens's well-known practice of writing separate opinions, either concurrences or dissents, much more frequently than the other justices. He earlier evidenced this tendency during his five years on the court of appeals. In the hearings on his nomination to the Supreme Court, Senator Robert Byrd asked Stevens for his perspective on unanimity of decisions. Stevens explained:

> It has been my practice to dissent whenever I disagreed with the majority. . . . I know there is one school of thought that the appearance of unanimity tends to add stability and respect to the law. My own

view is that it actually facilitates the fair adjudication process if everyone states his own conclusion as frankly as he can. I think it also serves the purpose to let the litigants know that . . . their arguments were understood and they were persuasive to some, even though not to all. And I found in my court, although I did dissent a great deal, that if it is done in a forthright way, it does not stimulate dissension within the court.

A bit later Stevens added: "I think preserving in the record of the opinion of the case itself, the fact that there was a diverse point of view . . . may make a record that will help at a future date when the same issue may be again presented for reexamination."

Legal scholars have chronicled, and statistically analyzed, Justice Stevens's propensity to write plentiful concurrences and dissents.[18] Despite his explanation, some scholars have continued to be puzzled by it. Even an admiring Justice Brennan observed, "I cannot pretend to know exactly why Justice Stevens has chosen so often to explain why his colleagues were marching in the wrong direction, but I have some ideas." Brennan suggested that Stevens writes separately because "he can," describing Stevens as "a person of extraordinary intelligence who can produce thorough and finely reasoned opinions on very short notice." As to why Stevens so frequently chooses to exercise this ability, Brennan simply observed "that he takes seriously the duty upon judges to explain their decisions."[19] This was precisely the point Stevens made during his confirmation hearings.

What Stevens has not had earlier occasion to explain, however, is how the Illinois Supreme Court scandal cemented this commitment. The decision in *People v. Isaacs* was initially reported as unanimous. Two years later, through a unique investigation, it came out that it actually was a four-to-two decision, but neither Justice Underwood nor Justice Schaefer publicly recorded their dissenting votes on various counts of the indictment against Isaacs.

In Schaefer's deposition and again on the witness stand, he offered a concise lecture to his former student Stevens on the reasons why even eminent jurists were selective about voicing their disagreements.[20] Stevens was unpersuaded by what he heard from Schaefer and offended by what he observed in *People v. Isaacs*. When he became a judge, he remembered those reactions: "At that time, among appellate judges, dissenting was something you didn't do unless you really felt compelled to do it. This experience is what persuaded me, when I became an appellate judge, that it's not for me to decide: If I don't agree, I should record the fact, and that's what I've always done."

Stevens also had seen that the cloud of suspicion over the Illinois Supreme Court initially enveloped *all* the justices, including Schaefer and Underwood, because no one knew they were not actually part of the majority that had thrown out the whole case against Isaacs. Stevens felt that had Schaefer made his dissent known, "there would have been no possibility that he would have been guilty by association." That possibility, however, was not what ultimately shaped Stevens's perspective on writing separate opinions:

> My reasoning was just a little different. My reasoning was that the public should have known about this. The fact that a justice disagrees with his colleagues is a matter of sufficient importance that the public is entitled to know it. I don't think a justice should decide some are sufficiently more important than others. I just think it's part of the process that should be in the public domain, so that's why I've followed that practice ever since. It's because of this incident.

In retrospect, it is tempting to speculate as to the impact a published dissent in the *Isaacs* case might have had on later events. If Schaefer or Underwood had expressed the view that at least some of the statutes under which Isaacs was indicted actually did apply to his conduct, might the State's Attorney have been emboldened to seek rehearing on more counts than just one? Might one of the other justices have changed his mind in response to such a rehearing petition? Might a dissent have prompted some legislators to seek amendment of the statutes to make clear that the dissenters correctly understood the legislative intention but the majority had gotten it wrong? Might future cases have been decided differently, building on the dissenters' explanation of their thinking?

Finally, and most ironically, what if the dissenting views had been made public, and the legislature had still done nothing to change the statutes? Then the basis for the court's ultimate conclusion not to reopen the *Isaacs* case—purportedly because legislative inaction signified agreement with the majority decision—would have had much more credibility. As it was, the court rationalized—in an echo of Schaefer's own testimony before the Special Commission—that the legislature must have silently decided that the supposedly unanimous decision was right. This rationalization had a hollow ring to it, for neither Schaefer nor Underwood had given the legislators or anyone else the benefit of their careful, but contrary thinking. John Paul Stevens could never be charged with a default like that. *People v. Isaacs* had put him on a very different path.

Chapter 27

Integrity of the Judgments

Stevens was not the only person whose life was changed by the events of the summer of 1969. Roy Solfisburg fell the furthest, with his position on the state supreme court gone and his dream of going to the national Supreme Court demolished. Quickly, however, he picked himself up and went back to work as a lawyer. Within less than a month, a circuit court judge in Kane County appointed him to defend an indigent young man challenging his conviction for burglary.[1]

According to William Murphy, his former lawyer, Solfisburg never expressed bitterness over what had happened or discussed the events that had forced him from the judiciary. Over the next few years, he built a private practice in Aurora, in association with his son-in-law. With remarkable aplomb, he even took on a few cases that brought him back before the Illinois Supreme Court.

Early in 1971 he went to Springfield to argue the first of these cases, in what must have been an emotional return to the scene of his former eminence. The night before the scheduled argument, Solfisburg suffered a heart attack in his hotel. He was hospitalized but recovered quickly. He subsequently returned to Springfield, argued the case, and won it. In 1984 he again presented and won a case before the supreme court.[2] He died in Fort Myers, Florida, in April 1991.

Ray Klingbiel's final years were fewer and sadder than Solfisburg's. He remained bitter about what he derided as the "political push" that took him from the court. He was shaken and sorrowful, telling Mason Bull on one occasion that deep in his heart he knew he was not a crook, "but I was a damn fool." Klingbiel's son succinctly describes how the justice spent much of his time after leaving the bench: "He baby-sat my children." Klingbiel passed away in January 1973.

After being fired from the Illinois Commerce Commission, Robert Perbohner also faced an unhappy future. His health continued to fail, depriving him of the ability to walk. With dwindling finances, and with both his mental and physical faculties deserting him, he spent his final years in a veterans hospital and died in the early 1970s.

Theodore Isaacs suffered no real change in his career as a result of the Special Commission. Once the Illinois Supreme Court closed the book on *People v. Isaacs* early in 1970, his legal status was also secure, at least for a while. In December 1971, when he and Kerner were indicted, his life turned the corner that led to prison. Following his parole in mid-1975, he returned to Chicago, worked in the insurance business, and died in 1998 at age eighty-six.

The members of the Special Commission returned to their law practices. Frank Greenberg and Henry Pitts each completed his term as bar president, with heavy involvement in the battle over judicial reform in the 1970 Constitution. Pitts practiced actively until 1982.

Greenberg, as earlier noted, was appointed in September 1971 to the new Judicial Inquiry Board, where he served for eight years. As a well-known champion of judicial reform, with growing involvement in national judicial conduct organizations, he was seen as "one of the prime movers in getting the board off the ground." In the eyes of many people, "the board was the Greenberg Board, just as the supreme court commission had been the Greenberg Commission."[3]

In the early 1980s, Greenberg suffered a debilitating stroke but still maintained his law practice, albeit at a reduced level. He died in 1984 at the age of seventy-three. At a memorial service at the University of Chicago, he was lauded as a "unique and compelling" man. Greenberg and his wife left most of their estate to the university's law school, where Greenberg had studied, for the endowment of a professorship in their name.

Watergate found Albert Jenner in an important role. In January 1974 he became counsel to the Republican members of the House Judiciary Committee, which was considering impeachment of President Nixon.[4] Jenner once again displayed his professional versatility and readiness for public service. Before he died in 1988, he endowed a professorship in his name at the law school he had attended, the University of Illinois College of Law. Coincidentally, the Jenner professorship at Illinois and the Greenberg professorship at Chicago later were joined by a Stevens professorship at Northwestern, established by the justice's former law school classmates.

The 1969 scandal altered the careers of some journalists, too. As a result of the attention Ed Pound's work received around the state, he was offered a job at the *Chicago Today* newspaper. Realizing that he had the ability to "play with the big boys," he left the *Alton Evening Telegraph* and began work as an investigative reporter in Chicago in May 1970, later working in Washington, including eleven years as chief investigative reporter for the *Wall Street Journal.* With a string of major exposés and awards behind him, in 1997 he became the senior investigative reporter at *USA Today.* Pound's colleague Ande Yakstis has stayed on as a reporter at the *Alton Telegraph.* The *Telegraph* is the only one of the newspapers principally involved in the 1969 affair still in business.

In 1978 the *Chicago Daily News* succumbed to the market forces and internal difficulties that had been troubling it for at least a decade. Roy Fisher, its editor, had found himself increasingly embroiled in battles with upper management, and he finally threw in the towel in 1971. He soon became dean of the University of Missouri School of Journalism, where he served until 1982. He died in 1999.

Charles Nicodemus has remained an active, award-winning investigative reporter in Chicago, principally with the *Chicago Sun-Times* after the demise of the *Daily News.* He worked on a variety of stories on corruption in Illinois during the 1970s, as well as in subsequent years.

The *Daily Calumet* changed ownership and was merged into other small papers. Robert Seltzner, the editor who had put together the first stories about Klingbiel, stayed in journalism, most recently as publisher of a small weekly newspaper in Wisconsin.

Donald Barlett would have broken the story about Solfisburg's financial dealings in 1968, had the *Daily News* allowed him and Roy Fisher to proceed with the investigation they had begun then. In 1969 he was at the Cleveland newspaper and could play only a minor part in bringing facts about Solfisburg to light. Subsequently, Barlett went on to become one of the country's premier investigative journalists. From 1971 to 1997, he and fellow reporter James B. Steele were at the *Philadelphia Inquirer* and since then at *Time* magazine. They have conducted a host of powerful investigations, published five books, and received most major journalism awards, including two Pulitzer Prizes. Because Barlett was on the sidelines in 1969, his work on Solfisburg obviously did not advance his career. It is equally obvious, however, that the *Daily News'* rejection of his work was not much of a career setback either.

Sherman Skolnick lives in the same home on the South Side of Chicago that he has occupied for decades. He is still chairman of the Citizens' Committee to Clean Up the Courts. The extraordinary range of governmental wrongdoing and conspiracies Skolnick pursues is now electronically showcased through his "hotline news" recorded telephone messages, his weekly community access cable television show, and his extensive Internet site. Although the Solfisburg-Klingbiel scandal is regarded as Skolnick's most concrete achievement, he has never given signs of resting on his laurels or restraining his investigative zeal.

Finally, there is the Civic Center Bank, its reputation sullied by the scandal in 1969. In December 1971 the bank merged with the South East National Bank to form the Chicago Bank of Commerce. Later it became the Associated Bank of Chicago, one of a network of banks owned by a Wisconsin holding company. The local, political Civic Center Bank is long gone.

Meanings of Corruption

Corruption in Illinois government was not a new or surprising phenomenon around the time of the Solfisburg-Klingbiel scandal. One of the most prominent state officials of that era, Paul Powell, became the stuff of legend when it was discovered after his death in 1970 that he had well over $500,000 in cash shoved into shoe boxes in his Springfield hotel suite. Powell had been quoted as saying of government service, "We take care of the people's business first and then we take care of ourselves."

Mike Royko suggested in 1967 that Chicago's official motto should be changed from "Urbs in Horto"—meaning "City in a Garden"—to "Ubi Est Mea": "Where's Mine?" Another writer, Nelson Algren, observed that in Chicago, "What can I do for you?" means "What can you do for me?" Others have recognized in Illinois more generally "a point of view that takes as a given the rigged, crooked nature of power and authority."[5]

This was the culture on display, and under assault, in Courtroom 1501 in the summer of 1969. Isaacs, Knight, Perbohner, and others exemplified traditional Illinois politics—pride in cunning, acceptance of rigged power, and enthusiastic participation in opportunities to get "mine." Theirs was a culture that thrived on the fruits of influence and the enjoyment of clout. Perbohner's son recalls that his father "just used to do things for people," especially favors for important people. This time, though, the favors Robert Perbohner did for Isaacs "were the favors that got him screwed."

What was new and shocking was that Solfisburg and Klingbiel were so much a part of this culture. Despite general cynicism about self-dealing by politicians, occasional rumors about the fixing of cases, and widespread understanding of the vices of a system of political election of judges, with the involvement of two supreme court justices, a basic article of public faith had been breached. That summer, alongside their ingrained pride in the coarseness, strength, and cunning of Illinois politicians, people knew that something was wrong when a criminal case against an influential man like Isaacs was thrown out by the supreme court under circumstances suggesting that an ordinary person could not be certain of receiving the same consideration and the same chance of a favorable outcome. In fact, as only a few people remembered that summer, a relatively unknown man named John J. Lang was branded a criminal for participating in the very same scheme for which Isaacs was indicted but never tried.

Although he didn't admit it, Roy Solfisburg probably knew he had crossed an ethical line. His involvement with the stock was complicated, his holdings were relatively large, and his efforts at subterfuge were studied and repeated. His protestations of innocence before the Special Commission had too many holes, too many contradictions, and too little conviction to be credible. He seemed to have known from the beginning of his involvement with the CCB stock that he was doing something wrong. As Stevens recited in his closing summation, "Affirmative acts of concealment are evidence of consciousness of guilt."

At best, Solfisburg simply knew he was profiting from his position at the court, enjoying favors from whatever source they might come. At worst, he knew that the bargain stock he was getting was offered as a bribe to vote in Isaacs's favor.

The truth probably lay somewhere in between, perhaps in a way of thinking that both men were familiar with. They both had worked with insurance matters, and perhaps Isaacs was simply buying something akin to insurance for the right outcome in his case. Insurance proceeds, of course, never have to be paid out unless a loss is actually suffered. Solfisburg may have sensed that if Isaacs wasn't going to lose his case anyhow, there would never be a need to provide him any added protection, any extra efforts to bring about the "right" result. Isaacs was offering a favor, but maybe Solfisburg convinced himself that no return favor would be needed. Maybe Isaacs just wanted to buy some peace of mind. What harm could there be in Solfisburg's selling it to him?

It was never proven that the stock Solfisburg bought—or the stock Klingbiel was given—made any actual difference in the outcome of *People v. Isaacs.* There is no way to know whether either justice would have viewed the close legal questions in the case differently had he not gotten the bargain purchase or gift. This uncertainty condemned the two justices. As the Special Commission forcefully concluded, public trust and confidence in the courts are deeply corroded when a judge's financial well-being derives from a litigant's favors.

Solfisburg may have believed the stock had no bearing on his thinking and voting in the *Isaacs* case. He seemed to subscribe to the philosophy of taking care of the people's business first, and then separately taking care of himself. His furtiveness and evasiveness, however, telegraphed that he didn't fully believe the separation could be made. At the least, he seemed to sense that it was unseemly for a judge to be so financially entangled with a litigant. He was smart enough to know that "What can I do for you?" probably meant—and would certainly look like it meant—"What can you do for me?"

The Special Commission drew from the evidence a strong inference that Isaacs was involved with Solfisburg's stock purchase and that Solfisburg knew of Isaacs's influence in it. The source of Solfisburg's stock thus was a man who was before the court accused under "the traditional notion of corruption—a public servant using his position to enrich himself personally."[6] Ironically, this was the same basic accusation Skolnick would later launch against Solfisburg and Klingbiel. If the justice had any inkling at all that Isaacs—a man facing charges like that—was connected to the Civic Center Bank, then he must have suspected that what he was getting had strings attached. When Isaacs testified before the commission, he defined clout as "the ability of someone to have favors done." Solfisburg must have known that he was in a position to do Isaacs a big favor, and that Isaacs knew it too.

As with anyone who succumbs to the temptations of a corrupt environment, what prompted Solfisburg to risk his judicial stature was probably a blend of motivations, ambitions, and needs that were his own secret, hidden perhaps even from himself. Nonetheless, by the time he faced the Special Commission, and most likely long before then, Solfisburg probably knew that his judgment in getting involved with the stock and Isaacs at the outset was fatally flawed.

Klingbiel was a little different. He seemed ready to tell all to the commission, with no apparent recognition that there was anything ethically suspect in his receipt and handling of the stock gift. He was, in a word, oblivious. Unlike Solfisburg, Klingbiel's sequestering of his stock, and his falsehoods to the press and his fellow justice, seemed motivated more by confusion, inattention, and irritation than by a desire to cover up improper activities.

Solfisburg put a lot of thought and effort into how he bought and sold his stock. Klingbiel put very little into the stock he received. Paradoxically, he thus appeared to be even more deeply submerged in the "Where's mine?" culture than Solfisburg was. Even assuming he knew nothing of Isaacs's link to the bank, Klingbiel admitted to accepting a gift of valuable stock in an unknown business from friends who also were litigants before his court. The gift was purportedly for a political campaign that already was over and for which he previously had collected far more money than he needed to cover his campaign expenses. His unhesitating, automatic receipt of this strange gift bespoke a blind acceptance of the notion that public position is an entitlement to private benefit.

Meanings of Integrity

An observer of the 1969 episode later described it as "a moment of vulnerability in which the system could not protect itself."[7] The circumstances that created this rare vulnerability concomitantly created an unusual moment of strength for forces committed to protecting the legal process from corruption.

The Illinois Supreme Court invited the full exercise of this strength, not just by the court's formation of the Special Commission, but also by the specific mandate the court gave it. The court ordered the commission to report on "the integrity of the judgment" in *Isaacs* and expressed its concern that "the integrity of this Court" not be further impaired. The court seemed to be employing the two different common meanings of "integrity." The first usage focused on the wholeness or structural soundness of the actual decision in the case, while the second related more broadly to the moral soundness and probity of the court and its members.[8] By using one word for both concepts, the court, perhaps unwittingly, invited the commission to link the decision in *Isaacs* to the conduct and character of the two accused justices. Had the court instead just asked the commission to investigate the "legal correctness" of the judgment, the commission might have found itself compelled to reach a much narrower and different outcome.

Integrity of the Commission

Beyond the court's semantic contribution, the structure of the Special Commission and the character of the lawyers who led it were also critical to the breadth and force of its work. Once again, the two meanings of "integrity" help to explain what happened. First, elements of structural integrity increased the likelihood that the investigation would be honest and thorough. Although the combination of these elements in

1969 was unique, some of them still may be worthy of consideration in the ongoing national debate about the use of independent prosecutors and special tribunals for investigation of official corruption.

One important element was the clear, firm deadline for the entire effort. The powers of the "prosecutor" and his staff, and of the commission, would expire on August 1, and no one had an interest in trying to extend them. The commissioners had their own separate bases of support and stature, yet they could not linger in the investigation without neglecting other professional responsibilities and losing income. These pressures also faced Stevens and his chief assistant, Torshen, and to a lesser degree the other staff members as well.

Additionally, the eleven lawyers comprising the commission and staff were not all adherents to the same political party. Similarly, Solfisburg, Klingbiel, Isaacs, and their associates were a bipartisan conglomeration too. Plainly the investigation could not be seen as a partisan attack. There also were other competing forums—most notably the legislature and criminal prosecutors—whose potential investigative powers were available but held in abeyance while the Special Commission worked toward its deadline. If the commission were seen in the end to have done its job poorly, others would step in.

The public hearings were integral to the growth of the commission's credibility. Had the commission not opened the evidence to public view, and enabled the public to see the commissioners wrestling with the facts and their implications, there could not have been such widespread acceptance of its report. There would probably also not have been such prompt acquiescence by the two justices to the call for their resignations.

Conversely, Stevens's determination to keep the prehearing discovery process confidential, and to prevent leaks of information to the press, was also important. As Stevens later observed, "Our opportunity to sift through the facts before organizing a public hearing contributed both to the persuasiveness of our final presentation and fairness to judges who were in fact blameless but at first blush might have appeared otherwise."[9] The best example of this beneficial effect was in the shocking discovery that the assignment of Klingbiel to write the *Isaacs* decision was out of the normal rotation. After exhaustive, quiet probing of this oddity, Stevens was able to conclude "that what at first appeared to be evidence of wrongdoing really had no probative effect." Had this discovery been made public before it was fully understood, it would only have diverted time and attention from the real misconduct.

These were the principal aspects of the investigatory process that helped keep it focused and honest, that gave it a structure with integrity. Of course, there were other, more fortuitous contributions as well, particularly the informed and active role of the press from start to finish. There also was Sherman Skolnick. Although the citizen gadfly wasted a lot of the commission's time, he still made valuable contributions. Not only did he publicize his suspicious hunch that began the entire investigation, but through his continued needling, he challenged the commission to make sure that its methods, questioning, and results were beyond reproach.

There is no way to know whether the process ultimately would have had the same integrity without Skolnick's carping, but certainly he didn't hurt in this respect. Indeed, by initially helping to incite public skepticism about the commission, he paradoxically bolstered the credibility of its final report at the end. If even Skolnick could say the Special Commission had done an honest job, its work must have been pure.

Integrity of the Lawyers

The final and perhaps most important ingredient was the personal integrity of the lawyers who led the effort. The five commissioners were well known as men of distinction and ability. The honorable conduct they expected of themselves and their fellow lawyers was only exceeded by what they expected of judges. The Special Commission was an opportunity, if an unwelcome one, to act on their beliefs.

In this instance, their idealism also served as fuel for professional courage, as they took on a task that many lawyers and others saw as very risky. In later years, when Henry Pitts was upbraided by judges and lawyers who disapproved of what he and his fellow commissioners had done, he would simply tell them, "I had to call it as I saw it, as I'm sure you would expect me to do."

The commissioners' report was based, of course, on the evidence that John Paul Stevens had collected and pieced together for them. Although Stevens was known to most of the commissioners at the outset, none of them could have realized then how perfect the fit would be. Never before had Stevens faced a challenge quite like this case, demanding his organizational and leadership skills, strategic judgment, physical stamina, and intellectual powers to resolve questions of great complexity, sensitivity, and public import. Having to do the whole job in six weeks, and with a mostly unproven team of helpers he didn't know, only added to the uncertainty of what he might accomplish.

At the end of the work, there was little doubt about Stevens's extraordinary achievement. It would be an exaggeration to say that no one else could have done the job with the kind of insight, thoroughness, and clear judgment he displayed, but few others would have taken the risk and done it as well. What the commissioners and his team saw in the work of Stevens the lawyer in 1969 would be seen by many others in the work of Stevens the justice. Justice Brennan described his colleague as "remarkably humble and affable," and "a person of extraordinary intelligence." One of Stevens's former law clerks probably said it best: "His charm is not easy to capture. Part of it is a rare combination of exceptional ability and lack of pretense."[10]

As much as any lawyer ever has, Stevens demonstrated how deeply ingrained was his belief that a license to practice law is a privilege held in trust for the public. When he received Henry Pitts's phone call at his home on an evening in June, he made no calculations before accepting the request to serve. He just thought, "It's the kind of thing that I ought to do." What he meant, of course, was that it was the kind of service that any lawyer ought to perform. The unhesitating, automatic readiness of Stevens to honor his ethical responsibilities as a lawyer stands in stark contrast to the unhesitating, automatic readiness of Klingbiel and Solfisburg to disregard theirs as judges.

Just before the twenty-fifth anniversary of his taking the oath of office at the Supreme Court, Stevens issued the dissenting opinion that is likely to be his most famous. In *Bush v. Gore*,[11] he rejected the majority's conclusion that the presidential election recount in Florida in 2000 could not constitutionally proceed as directed by the Florida Supreme Court. Among the points made in his dissent, Stevens charged that underlying the Bush legal team's "assault on the Florida election procedures is an unstated lack of confidence in the impartiality and capacity of the state judges who would make the critical decisions if the vote count were to proceed." Stevens declared, "The endorsement of that position by the majority of this Court can only lend credence to the most cynical appraisal of the work of judges throughout the land."

Stevens plainly felt that his colleagues were inviting unwarranted cynicism about the judiciary in Florida. Many years earlier, of course, Stevens had found good reason for cynicism about Illinois justices he investigated. He believed then that the public is entitled to know when judicial misconduct is proven. The corollary he expressed in *Bush v. Gore* is that the public should not be led to suspect judicial bias or misconduct when there is no proof.

Speaking of the Illinois Supreme Court, the Special Commission had proclaimed in 1969 that "the confidence of the public and the Bar in the Court is a most essential foundation of our society." Stevens had become a judge partly as a result of his battle to restore public confidence in the judiciary in his home state. Years later, his battle continued on the national stage, as he still labored to maintain a solid foundation for what he called "the loser" of the 2000 election—"the Nation's confidence in the judge as an impartial guardian of the rule of law."[12]

A Final Letter

In the summer of 1969, as this unusually vivid clash between honor and dishonor, integrity and corruption, was coming to an end, Frank Greenberg wrote his final letter as chairman of the Special Commission. It was a letter of appreciation to Stevens and his staff. Greenberg considered paying them a compliment that he and the other commissioners were hearing frequently at the time, but he decided against it:

> The phrase "service over and beyond the call of duty" has occurred to me, but I really think that it is inappropriate in this case. This kind of sacrifice that we have all made is not beyond the call of duty. I think that it is our duty, and that our willingness to perform it is the saving grace amidst the charges which have been made against the bar and the judiciary.[13]

The commissioners fulfilled their duty that summer. So did their counsel, and his service over those six weeks led him to immeasurably greater service to the law and the nation than he, or anyone else at the time, could have imagined.

Notes

Preface

1. George Fiedler, *The Illinois Law Courts in Three Centuries* (Berwyn, Ill.: Physicians' Record Co., 1973), p. 314.

2. Hearings before the U.S. Senate Committee on the Judiciary, December 8–10, 1975, p. 65; letter from John Paul Stevens to author, February 4, 1976; speech by Justice John Paul Stevens to American Bar Association Annual Meeting, Pro Bono Publico Awards Luncheon, San Francisco, August 10, 1992.

3. Letter from Frank Greenberg to John Paul Stevens et al., August 1, 1969.

Chapter 1

1. Basil Talbott Jr., "2 Illinois Justices Indicate They'll Show Financial Data," *Chicago Sun-Times,* June 21, 1969, p. 6.

2. Deposition of Sherman H. Skolnick, July 10, 1969, p. 97.

3. *Skolnick v. Mayor and City Council of Chicago,* 415 F.2d 1291 (7th Cir. August 18, 1969) (affirming 1968 district court decision).

4. Paul Galloway, "Reissued: Sherman Skolnick Is Back Raising, Well, Some Unusual Topics," *Chicago Tribune,* January 15, 1988, sec. 5, pp. 1, 2. In what Skolnick called a "major physical improvement in my life," in 1970 he had his self-described "cowcatcher teeth" fixed.

5. See, e.g., *Skolnick v. Martin,* 317 F.2d 855 (7th Cir. 1963); *Skolnick v. Spolar,* 317 F.2d 857 (7th Cir. 1963); *Skolnick v. Martin,* 32 Ill. 2d 55, 203 N.E.2d 428 (1964); *Skolnick v. Nudelman,* 71 Ill. App. 2d 424, 218 N.E.2d 775 (1966); *Skolnick v. Nudelman,* 95 Ill. App. 2d 293, 237 N.E.2d 804 (1968); and *Skolnick v. Martin,* 98 Ill. App. 2d 166, 240 N.E.2d 296 (1968).

6. *Skolnick v. Martin,* 32 Ill. 2d 55, 203 N.E.2d 428 (1964).

7. Galloway, "Reissued: Sherman Skolnick Is Back Raising, Well, Some Unusual Topics," pp. 1, 2.

8. "Skolnick's Guerrilla War," *Time,* August 29, 1969, p. 45.

9. "An Ethical Blind Spot," *Chicago Daily News,* June 23, 1969.

10. F. Richard Ciccone, *Chicago and the American Century* (Chicago: Contemporary Books, 1999), p. 254; Dan Rottenberg, "Messing with the News: How Chicago's Biggest Law Firm Uses—and Misuses—Its Dual Role as Press Adviser and Establishment Spokesman," *Chicago Journalism Review,* December 1970, pp. 3, 5; telephone interview with Charles Nicodemus, December 4, 1997; Christopher Chandler, "The Exposé That Staggered into Print," *Chicago Journalism Review,* June 1969, p. 3.

11. 376 U.S. 254 (1964).

12. Robert P. Howard, *Illinois: A History of the Prairie State* (Grand Rapids, Mich.: W. B. Eerdmans Publishing, 1972), p. 557; Robert P. Howard, *Mostly Good and Competent Men* (Springfield: Sangamon University and Illinois State Historical Society, 1988), p. 341.

13. Carol Oppenheim, "Ted Isaacs—The Man Who Was Everywhere," *Chicago Today,* November 24, 1971, p. 19. A more extensive description of Isaacs's background is presented in Bill Barnhart and Eugene Schlickman, *Kerner: The Conflict of Intangible Rights* (Urbana: University of Illinois Press, 1999), pp. 106–11.

14. Howard, *Illinois: A History of the Prairie State,* p. 558; Barnhart and Schlickman, *Kerner: The Conflict of Intangible Rights,* p. 108.

15. Hank Messick, *The Politics of Prosecution: Jim Thompson, Richard Nixon, Marje Everett and the Trial of Otto Kerner* (Ottawa, Ill.: Caroline House Books, 1978), p. 221; Joseph C. Goulden, *The Benchwarmers: The Private World of Powerful Federal Judges* (New York: Weybright & Talley, 1974), p. 172.

16. Barnhart and Schlickman, *Kerner: The Conflict of Intangible Rights,* p. 98.

17. Ibid., pp. 6, 224.

Chapter 2

1. "The Day the Judges Fell," *Alton Evening Telegraph,* September 25, 1969, p. A-17.

2. The Illinois Commerce Commission is the state's public utilities commission, with authority over various financial and service aspects of utilities in areas such as electricity, natural gas, telephone, and water. It also has responsibilities related to transportation services such as trucking. Commissioners were appointed by the governor.

3. Statement of Roy M. Fisher to Special Commission (undated), p. 1.

4. Deposition of Walter V. Schaefer, June 25, 1969, p. 97.

5. Deposition of Robert C. Underwood, June 27, 1969, p. 67.

6. Deposition of Ray I. Klingbiel, June 30, 1969, p. 99.

7. Lois Wille, "The Seventies," in *One More Time: The Best of Mike Royko* (Chicago: University of Chicago Press, 1999), p. 51.

8. By the end of June, it was publicly reported that Howard had resigned as a CCB director. Christopher Chandler, "The Exposé that Staggered into Print," *Chicago Journalism Review,* June 1969, p. 14. Strangely, confidential bank records revealed that Howard had submitted his resignation on June 4, apparently even before Skolnick brought his suspicions to the attention of Pound and Nicodemus. Memorandum from the author to the Special Commission, July 10, 1969, p. 6.

Although there is no way to be sure, it seems unlikely that the timing was just coincidental. Howard probably was tipped off about the allegations Skolnick was brewing, and the most probable source of a tip was James Linen IV, the principal owner of the *Daily Calumet.* Linen was well connected in journalism circles, especially since his father was the president of Time, Inc. Linen was friendly with Howard and may have thought he would be interested in the information the *Daily Calumet* had intended to publish a few weeks earlier. Perhaps such advance information also explains why Howard, when visited by Fisher and his delegation, never even looked at the story and quickly made it clear that he would not veto it.

9. Ed Pound and Ande Yakstis, "High Court Judge Linked to Bank Deal," *Alton Evening Telegraph,* June 11, 1969.

10. Deposition of Walter V. Schaefer, June 25, 1969, p. 100.

11. Statement of Ed Pound, April 25, 1970, p. 6.

12. "Gift to Klingbiel Bared," *Chicago Daily News,* June 11, 1969, p. 1.

Chapter 3

1. See Paul Simon, "The Illinois Legislature: A Study in Corruption," *Harper's Magazine,* September 1964, p. 74.

2. Under the proposed legislation, salaries for circuit court judges in Cook County would increase from $32,500 to $35,000, while circuit court judges' salaries elsewhere in the state would go from $23,500 to $27,500. In comparison, new associate lawyers in the highest-paying Chicago law firms at that time were receiving annual salaries of about $15,000.

3. Jerome Watson, "House Sets Up Unit to Probe Gift to Klingbiel," *Chicago Sun-Times,* June 13, 1969, p. 3. The other lawyers were Republican Representative Leslie Jones and Democrats Paul Elward, Horace Calvo, and Scariano. The accountant was Republican David J. Regner.

4. The text of the resolution as amended is set forth in *Cusack v. Howlett,* 44 Ill. 2d 233, 234–35, 254 N.E.2d 506, 507 (1969). A Democratic legislator from Aurora also tried to have the committee's scope expanded to include examination of ethical issues related to the Illinois Commerce Commission, but his proposal was ruled out of order. The legislator emphasized the close ties between Chief Justice Solfisburg and various ICC members, including Perbohner.

5. Telephone interview with George W. Lindberg, April 8, 1998.

6. The *Los Angeles Times'* Chicago bureau was adjacent to the *Chicago Daily News'* newsroom, and reporters from the two papers frequently exchanged information. Telephone interview with D. J. R. Bruckner, April 14, 1998.

7. D. J. R. Bruckner, "Legislature to Probe Illinois Supreme Court," *Los Angeles Times,* June 13, 1969, p. 6. Another of the Civic Center Bank's organizers was C. E. McKittrick, a senior executive of the *Chicago Tribune.* Of the four major Chicago newspapers at the time, the *Tribune* took the least active role in the unfolding scandal, but the connection between McKittrick and the bank was probably not the reason. More likely factors were recognition that the *Daily News* was far ahead in developing the story, the *Tribune's* long-standing Republican affinities, and its disdain for information emanating from Skolnick. Although the *Tribune* also owned the *Chicago Today* newspaper, that paper operated quite independently, and it pursued the scandal more actively than the *Tribune* did.

Chapter 4

1. William T. Braithwaite, *Who Judges the Judges? A Study of Procedures for Removal and Retirement* (Chicago: American Bar Foundation, 1971), pp. 97–98.

2. Illinois Constitution of 1870, as amended effective January 1, 1964, Article VI, section 18.

3. George Fiedler, *The Illinois Law Courts in Three Centuries* (Berwyn, Ill.: Physicians' Record Co., 1973), p. 418; Braithwaite, *Who Judges the Judges? A Study of Procedures for Removal and Retirement,* p. 100.

4. Braithwaite, *Who Judges the Judges? A Study of Procedures for Removal and Retirement,* pp. 99–105. See also Administrative Office of the Illinois Courts, *1968 Annual Report to the Supreme Court of Illinois,* p. 8, as quoted in Fiedler, *The Illinois Law Courts in Three Centuries,* p. 424.

5. Letter from Henry L. Pitts to author, July 30, 1997; telephone interview with George W. Lindberg, April 8, 1998.

6. Deposition of Byron O. House, July 3, 1969, p. 75.

7. Telephone interviews with Don H. Reuben, March 17, 1998, and September 10, 1999.

8. *Universal Oil Products Co. v. Root Refining Co.,* 328 U.S. 575 (1946). The Court there said, "The inherent power of a federal court to investigate whether a judgment was obtained by fraud is beyond question." Id. at 580. Skolnick also aptly cited a later federal appellate decision in the same case. *Root Refining Co. v. Universal Oil Products Co.,* 169 F.2d 514 (3d Cir. 1948).

A thorough legal research memorandum prepared for the Special Commission a few weeks later confirmed that these decisions cited by Skolnick were proper bases for the court's action. Memorandum by James T. Harrington, July 1, 1969. Although other Illinois judicial decisions also supported the action, there does not appear to have been any Illinois case in which the specific phrase "integrity of the judgment" was used in a context such as this.

9. Letter from Henry L. Pitts to author, July 30, 1997.

10. Letter from Henry L. Pitts to author, August 13, 1999.

11. See Illinois Governmental Ethics Act, S. B. 506, Illinois Laws 1967, pp. 3401ff., enacted August 21, 1967, effective January 1, 1968.

12. See chapter 7.

Chapter 5

1. 37 Ill. 2d 205, 226 N.E.2d 38 (March 29, 1967) (rehearing denied, May 16, 1967).

2. Jack Mabley, "Kerner Aide Admits Link to Major State Supplier," *Chicago's American,* September 30, 1964, pp. 1, 3.

3. "Kerner Statement Defends Isaacs," *Chicago's American,* September 30, 1964, p. 3.

4. Robert P. Howard, *Illinois: A History of the Prairie State* (Grand Rapids, Mich.: W. B. Eerdmans Publishing, 1972), p. 558. See also Hank Messick, *The Politics of Prosecution: Jim Thompson, Richard Nixon, Marje Everett and the Trial of Otto Kerner* (Ottawa, Ill.: Caroline House Books, 1978), p. 73. Messick writes that Isaacs left the campaign "so the affair wouldn't damage Kerner's image as Mr. Clean."

5. Carol Oppenheim, "Ted Isaacs—The Man Who Was Everywhere," *Chicago Today,* November 24, 1971, p. 19.

6. Bill Barnhart and Eugene Schlickman, *Kerner: The Conflict of Intangible Rights* (Urbana: University of Illinois Press, 1999), p. 110.

7. Telephone interview with Laurin A. Wollan Jr., November 13, 1997. See also, Jack Mabley, "Here's What Led to Probe of 2 Judges," *Chicago Today,* July 15, 1969, p. 4, where it is stated that Isaacs's partner in the printing company "didn't tell Lang of Isaacs's interest in Cook Envelope until 1963," and that Lang resigned shortly after that.

8. Letter opinion from Judge Paul C. Verticchio to Lipnick, Barsy, and Joseph et al., April 25, 1967.

9. Mabley, "Here's What Led to Probe of 2 Judges," p. 4.

10. George Fiedler, *The Illinois Law Courts in Three Centuries* (Berwyn, Ill.: Physicians' Record Co., 1973), p. 315.

Chapter 6

1. Letter from Henry L. Pitts to author, July 30, 1997. Before selecting Stevens, the Special Commission briefly considered another Chicago lawyer as counsel. Milton I. Shadur was proposed by Greenberg and Pitts, but Edwin Austin forcefully indicated that if Shadur was chosen, Austin would not serve on the commission. Austin had long represented the Wrigley family, principal owners of the Chicago Cubs baseball team. Shadur represented minority stockholders that had sued to force the Cubs to install lights at Wrigley Field to allow night games to be played. Although the suit already had been thrown out (*Schlensky v. Wrigley,* 95 Ill. App. 2d 173, 237 N.E.2d 766 [April 25, 1968]), Austin was firmly opposed to the selection of Shadur. Years later Shadur would become a federal district court judge in Chicago.

2. Mike Royko, *Boss: Richard J. Daley of Chicago* (New York: Dutton, 1971), p. 19; Adam Cohen and Elizabeth Taylor, *American Pharaoh: Mayor Richard J. Daley: His Battle for Chicago and the Nation* (Boston: Little, Brown, 2000), p. 212.

3. Letter from Jerome H. Torshen to author, September 2, 1997.

4. Ibid.

5. Letter from Nathaniel Sack to author, October 16, 1997.

6. Letter from John Paul Stevens to author, August 14, 1969.

7. Letter from Henry L. Pitts to author, August 28, 1998.

8. Thomas M. Gray, "High Court Asked to Void Solfisburg-Klingbiel Panel," *Chicago Sun-Times,* June 20, 1969, p. 32; Charles Nicodemus, "House Panel Rejects Quick Look at Records," *Chicago Daily News,* June 19, 1969, p. 1; Raymond Coffey, "Who Will Judge the Judges?" *Chicago Daily News,* June 26, 1969, p. 3.

9. Press release, June 18, 1969, p. 3.

Chapter 7

1. Charles Nicodemus, "Klingbiel Case: Vexing Issues," *Chicago Daily News,* June 21, 1969, p. 6.

2. See chapter 2.

3. Deposition of Robert C. Underwood, June 27, 1969, p. 69.

4. Deposition of Walter V. Schaefer, June 25, 1969, p. 97.

5. Deposition of Robert C. Underwood, June 27, 1969, p. 65.

6. Ibid., p. 69.

7. Deposition of Byron O. House, July 3, 1969, pp. 7, 72.

8. See chapter 2.

9. "The Day the Judges Fell," *Alton Evening Telegraph,* September 25, 1969, p. A-17.

10. Donald L. Barlett, "Illinois Jurists' Bank Ties Probed," *Plain Dealer,* June 19, 1969, p. 1; Donald L. Barlett, "Conflicts Clutter High Court Path," *Plain Dealer,* June 20, 1969, p. 1.

11. Telephone interview with Donald L. Barlett, October 7, 1999; telephone interview with Bernard Judge, October 6, 1999.

12. See Christopher Chandler, "The Exposé That Staggered into Print," *Chicago Journalism Review,* June 1969, p. 3; Dan Rottenberg, "Messing with the News," *Chicago Journalism Review,* December 1970, p. 3.

13. Two years earlier the Illinois Attorney General had issued a formal legal opinion that the state's rental of Solfisburg's office space from Dolph's trust did not create a conflict of interest for Dolph as a state employee. Attorney General's Opinion No. F-1766, March 20, 1967.

14. "An Ethical Blind Spot," *Chicago Daily News,* June 23, 1969.

Chapter 8

1. See chapter 4.

2. Letter of Roy J. Solfisburg Jr. to George W. Lindberg, June 20, 1969, p. 2.

3. Testimony of Roy M. Fisher, Hearings of the Special Commission, July 23, 1969, p. 1624; deposition of Roy J. Solfisburg Jr., July 1, 1969, p. 51.

4. John Camper, "Story Behind Court Probe," *Chicago Daily News,* August 4, 1969, p. 3; statement of Roy M. Fisher to the Special Commission (undated).

5. Roy M. Fisher, "Letter from the Editor," *Chicago Daily News,* August 2, 1969, p. 2.

6. Letter from Henry L. Pitts to author, July 31, 1997.

7. "Nixon Pledges Conservative Court Choices," *Chicago Tribune,* May 17, 1969, p. 3. In retrospect, other tangential aspects of the *Tribune*'s article are amusing. The article opined that it was "almost a certainty" on Capitol Hill that Justice Potter Stewart would become chief justice. It also declared that Judge Warren Burger was one of the "leading Jewish candidates" for the seat left open by Fortas's departure. Burger, of course, was nominated four days later not for Fortas's position, but as chief justice. He was a Presbyterian, of Swiss-German Protestant background. See *Current Biography* (Bronx: H. W. Wilson, 1969), p. 62; Bob Woodward and Scott Armstrong, *The Brethren* (New York: Simon & Schuster, 1979), p. 22.

8. Donald L. Barlett, "Conflicts Clutter High Court Path," *Plain Dealer,* June 20, 1969, p. 1; Donald L. Barlett, "Illinois Jurists' Bank Ties Probed," *Plain Dealer,* June 19, 1969, p. 1.

9. Bruce A. Murphy, *Fortas: The Rise and Ruin of a Supreme Court Justice* (New York: W. Morrow, 1988), p. 556.

10. Letter from Everett M. Dirksen to Roy J. Solfisburg Jr., May 13, 1969.

11. "Court Group Asks Curb on Protests," *New York Times,* April 27, 1969, p. 45.

12. Telephone interview with Judge Michael Barron, February 17, 1999. Judge Barron of Wisconsin has served since 1994 as the conference's secretary and financial officer. Telephone interview with Judge Thomas J. Stovall Jr., February 17, 1999. Judge Stovall of Houston, Texas, was one of the initial organizers of the conference and was active in it for many years. See also National Conference of Metropolitan Courts, "Working to Improve the Administration of Justice" (1994).

13. Barlett, "Conflicts Clutter High Court Path," p. 1.

14. See John L. Steele, "Haynsworth v. the U.S. Senate," *Fortune,* March 1970, pp. 90–91; John P. Frank, *Clement Haynsworth, the Senate, and the Supreme Court*

(Charlottesville: University Press of Virginia, 1991), p. 24; Rowland Evans Jr. and Robert Novak, *Nixon in the White House* (London: Davis-Poynter, 1971), p. 159.

Chapter 9

1. *Illinois v. Harper & Row Publishers,* 301 F. Supp. 484 (N.D. Ill. 1969).
2. Letter from Henry L. Pitts to author, September 22, 1997.
3. Rules of Procedure, sec. I (July 2, 1969).
4. *Jenkins v. McKeithen,* 395 U.S. 411 (June 9, 1969). See memorandum from Clifton A. Lake to Henry L. Pitts, June 28, 1969, pp. 6–7, which concluded:

> In order to avoid the due process requirements of [*Jenkins v. McKeithen*], the Commission must make clear that its function is solely to investigate facts which might affect the integrity of the judgment entered by the Court, i.e., to determine whether cause exists to indicate that such impropriety occurred to justify a full investigation by the Court itself. To accomplish this the Commission should exercise caution and carefully avoid making any recommendations for action by the Court based upon its findings. Should such a recommendation in fact be submitted, the Commission would be open to the charge that it acted in an adjudicatory fashion, and therefore was required to extend all the traditional rights of due process to those who would be affected by the findings (specifically the parties to the judgment, Isaacs and Lang).

5. Rules of Procedure, secs. III(7)–(8), IV.
6. *Skolnick v. Special Commission,* U.S. District Court for the Northern District of Illinois (No. 69C 1342), Complaint, filed June 26, 1969.
7. Minute Order of June 26, 1969.
8. Campbell had been a federal judge since 1940 and had long been a politically prominent Chicago Democrat. Even many years later, the judge was described as having been "one of the most powerful men in a city where Democrats ruled." See Jim Puzzanghera, "Campbell in the Soup," *San Jose Mercury News, West Magazine,* April 18, 1999, p. 14.

Chapter 10

1. "Judiciary Should Not Be Independent," *Waukegan News-Sun,* December 26, 1969, p. 10A.
2. The most analogous incident is probably the impeachment proceedings against the chief justice of the New Hampshire Supreme Court in the summer and fall of 2000.

Chapter 11

1. *In the Matter of the Special Commission in Relation to No. 39797,* Order re Petition for the Entry of an Order Relative to Procedure, July 7, 1969.
2. See chapter 7.
3. Deposition of Robert M. Perbohner, July 11, 1969, pp. 2–3.
4. Deposition of Joseph D. Farrington, July 11, 1969, p. 44.
5. Deposition of Henry Ashe, July 11, 1969, p. 49.
6. Deposition of Doris Steigberg, July 11, 1969, p. 65.
7. There even was speculation that the court had selected August 1 as the completion date for the Special Commission's work "so that if Klingbiel and Solfis-

burg are cleared, the full 7-member court can rule on the constitutionality of the new state income tax." "Judges Probe Opens Tomorrow," *Chicago Today,* July 13, 1969, p. 4.

8. At about this time, Justice Schaefer telephoned Roy Fisher again to ask whether there was anything the *Daily News* could do to make the investigation move more quickly to a resolution. Fisher consulted with the paper's lawyer, Daniel Feldman, but they could find nothing the newspaper could do to ease Schaefer's distress. Telephone interview with Daniel Feldman, August 23, 1999.

Chapter 12

1. Both statements affirmed the trial court's quashing of twenty-three of the thirty-three counts at issue in the appeal. In fact, most of Klingbiel's decision was borrowed verbatim from the Underwood draft. The Underwood opinion would have reversed the lower court on ten counts and required both Isaacs and Lang to stand trial on those. In contrast, Klingbiel's version affirmed the dismissal of two of those counts, and only required Lang—but not Isaacs—to stand trial on the remaining eight counts.

2. Deposition of Walter V. Schaefer, June 25, 1969, pp. 52–53. Schaefer was referring to the lectures given by Harvard Law School Professor Paul A. Freund at Northwestern University School of Law in 1949. Speaking of Justice Brandeis, Freund had said, "Not infrequently the preparation of a dissenting opinion was foregone because the demands of other items of work prevented an adequate treatment, but with the promise to himself that another occasion would be taken when circumstances were more propitious." Paul A. Freund, *On Understanding the Supreme Court* (Boston: Little, Brown, 1949), p. 71.

Chapter 14

1. Telephone interview with William C. Murphy, February 23, 1998.

2. Albert E. Jenner Jr., "Tribute to Walter V. Schaefer," *Northwestern University Law Review,* vol. 74 (1979), pp. 693, 694–98.

3. James Warren, "Albert E. Jenner, Jr.: A Legend in Legal Circles," *Chicago Tribune,* September 19, 1988, p. C7.

4. See Norman Mailer, *Oswald's Tale* (New York: Random House, 1995), pp. 397, 531.

5. Two months before the commission's hearings, in the same *Chicago Tribune* article in which Solfisburg's prospects for appointment to the U.S. Supreme Court were raised, Jenner's name also appeared. The article quoted Senator Hugh Scott of Pennsylvania, a Republican leader, as mentioning Jenner as a possible choice by President Nixon for the high court. "Nixon Pledges Conservative Court Choices," *Chicago Tribune,* May 17, 1969, p. 1. See chapter 8.

6. Telephone interview with Thomas P. Sullivan, October 7, 1999.

7. Deposition of Jayne W. Kegley, July 5, 1969, p. 37.

8. Memorandum from author to Special Commission, July 10, 1969, p. 8. Referring to correspondence identifying three purchasers and the individual who brought them in, the memorandum stated, "Mrs. Kegley was very likely unaware of this letter, and the accuracy of her memory in this particular cannot be questioned."

9. See Joseph Maguire, *Evidence: Common Sense and Common Law* (Chicago: Foundation Press, 1947), p. 43. Maguire also stated, "According to the best professional thought, sweeping prohibition of impeachment by a party of his own witnesses is nonsense—most regrettably not simple nonsense, but very complex nonsense."

10. See John Wigmore, *A Students' Textbook of the Law of Evidence* (Brooklyn: Foundation Press, 1935), p. 188. Wigmore noted that "virtually all courts" allow a witness to be impeached by his own self-contradiction if counsel claims he is "surprised" by the witness's assertion on the stand.

Chapter 15

1. Deposition of Lawrence J. Flynn, July 3, 1969, pp. 17, 21–22.
2. Depositions of Roy J. Solfisburg Jr., July 1, 1969, p. 46; Ray I. Klingbiel, June 30, 1969, p. 46; and Thomas E. Kluczynski, July 3, 1969, p. 5.
3. Deposition of Roy J. Solfisburg Jr., July 1, 1969, pp. 660–61.
4. Letter from Henry L. Pitts to author, July 31, 1997.
5. Deposition of Roy J. Solfisburg Jr., July 1, 1969, p. 90.
6. Ibid., p. 80.

Chapter 16

1. Gary Cummings, "Judge Got 'Campaign Gift' After Election," *Chicago Today,* July 16, 1969, p. 5.
2. Deposition of Ray I. Klingbiel, June 30, 1969, p. 37.
3. Deposition of George R. Bieber, July 2, 1969, p. 7.
4. Deposition of Ray I. Klingbiel, June 30, 1969, p. 75.
5. Charles Nicodemus, "Greenberg Lays Down Law to Illinois Justices," *Chicago Daily News,* July 19, 1969.
6. See chapter 11.
7. See chapter 4.
8. Deposition of Thomas E. Kluczynski, July 3, 1969, p. 27.
9. See chapter 11.

Chapter 17

1. See chapter 11.
2. Letter from Jerome H. Torshen to author, July 23, 1998.
3. Statement of Rubin G. Cohn at Memorial Service for Frank Greenberg, March 21, 1984, reprinted in *Chicago Lawyer,* April 1984, p. 18.
4. "Frank Greenberg, A Noble Soul," *Chicago Lawyer,* April 1984, p. 11.
5. Frank Greenberg, "President's Page," *Chicago Bar Record,* October 1969, p. 2.

Chapter 18

1. See chapter 15.
2. Memorandum from author to Special Commision, July 10, 1969, p. 5.

3. See chapter 13.

4. These conversations are noted in chapter 2 and more fully described in chapter 7.

Chapter 19

1. Deposition of Doris Steigberg, July 11, 1969, p. 57.

2. Deposition of Doris Steigberg, July 21, 1969, p. 7.

3. See chapter 1.

4. Telephone interview with Sherman Skolnick, September 17, 1999.

5. See chapter 7.

6. Deposition of Howard M. Hansen, July 9, 1969, p. 10.

7. Deposition of Theodore J. Isaacs, July 3, 1969, pp. 20–21.

8. Deposition of James J. Pelts, July 9, 1969, pp. 7–10.

9. Deposition of Theodore J. Isaacs, July 3, 1969, pp. 118–24.

10. Deposition of Doris Steigberg, July 21, 1969, pp. 49–56.

Chapter 20

1. See chapter 8.

2. See chapter 8.

3. See chapter 8.

Chapter 21

1. *Majewski v. Gallina,* 17 Ill. 2d 92 (1959).

2. Letter from Nathaniel Sack to author, October 16, 1997; interview with John Paul Stevens, November 7, 1997. The aphorism has been variously attributed to Machiavelli, Emerson, and others, and phrased in numerous ways. See, for example, *General Mill Supply Co. v. SCA Services,* 697 F.2d 704, 712 (6th Cir. 1982): "There is a wise maxim whose original author the writer does not know: 'When you shoot at a king you must kill him.'"; Charles W. Rhodes, "Demystifying the Extraordinary Writ," *St. Mary's Law Journal,* vol. 29 (1998), pp. 525, 593: "An old adage is that you should aim well if you shoot at the King."; Patricia Wald, "Guilty Beyond a Reasonable Doubt," *University of Chicago Legal Forum,* vol. 101 (1993), p. 119: "The old saying [is] that if 'you shoot for the king, you had better not miss.'"

3. Letter from John Paul Stevens to author, August 14, 1969.

Chapter 22

1. Deposition of David X. Meyers, July 25, 1969, p. 17.

2. Deposition of Howard M. Hansen, July 31, 1969, pp. 46–47.

3. On Friday, the day after the hearings ended, the supreme court announced its ruling upholding the constitutionality of the new state income tax law. This historic decision had nothing directly to do with the investigation, of course, but the timing of the court's announcement may have been influenced by it. The court had heard oral argument only eight days earlier, and it ruled quickly for the obvious reason that the tax law was scheduled to take effect on August 1. Addi-

tionally, some of the justices may have feared that if a decision were delayed, the cloud over Klingbiel and Solfisburg might make it difficult or impossible for them to participate. The four votes needed for a decision might then be in jeopardy.

4. See chapter 11.

5. One glaring example was the reference to "Mr. Isaacs's sworn testimony, as corroborated by witness Mertz, that he was called by the bank and advised that by some inadvertence at the bank the $1 discrepancy had occurred." Mertz had given no such corroboration. Even Jenner, while Mertz was on the stand, observed that the witness "has no recollection affirmatively, negatively, or otherwise." Later in the statement, this first reference to Mertz was contradicted by an acknowledgment that he "had no recollection" that Isaacs made up the $300 difference.

6. Telephone interview with Don H. Reuben, March 17, 1998. See also chapter 14.

Chapter 23

1. See chapter 4.

2. "Perjury Charged in Justices Case," *Chicago Today,* August 2, 1969, p. 5; Phillip J. O'Connor, "Court-Quiz Perjury Probe!" *Chicago Daily News,* August 2, 1969, p. 1.

3. Letter from Henry L. Pitts to author, August 2, 1997; telephone interview with Henry L. Pitts, December 28, 1999.

4. See chapter 4.

5. Telephone interview with Alfred Y. Kirkland, November 12, 1997; letter from Henry L. Pitts to author, July 30, 1997.

Chapter 24

1. Letter from Jerome H. Torshen to author, July 23, 1998. *Time* magazine reported that Skolnick, "with rare humility," told the judge, "If I offended you, I apologize." "Skolnick's Guerilla War," *Time,* August 29, 1969, p. 43.

2. "Skolnick's Guerilla War," p. 43.

3. Letter from George W. Lindberg to John Paul Stevens, August 6, 1969.

4. *Cusack v. Howlett,* 44 Ill. 2d 233, 254 N.E.2d 506 (1969). This decision was analyzed at *Harvard Law Review,* vol. 84 (1971), p. 1002.

5. Telephone interview with William G. Hundley, March 3, 1999; telephone interview with Henry J. Hyde, August 31, 1998.

6. William T. Braithwaite, *Who Judges the Judges? A Study of Procedures for Removal and Retirement* (Chicago: American Bar Foundation, 1971), p. 112.

7. George Fiedler, *The Illinois Law Courts in Three Centuries* (Berwyn, Ill.: Physicians' Record Co., 1973), pp. 334–35.

8. See chapter 12.

9. See, for example, *Maki v. Frelk,* 40 Ill. 2d 193, 239 N.E.2d 445 (1968). In that tort case, Justices Ward and Schaefer dissented from the majority decision written by Klingbiel. The dissenters emphasized the ambiguity of legislative inaction. See also *Zuber v. Allen,* 396 U.S. 168, 185 (1969): "Legislative silence is a poor beacon to follow in discerning the proper statutory route"; and *Cleveland v. United States,* 329 U.S. 14, 22 (1946): "Notwithstanding recent tendency, the idea cannot always

be accepted that Congress, by remaining silent and taking no affirmative action in repudiation, gives approval to judicial misconstruction of its enactments."

Chapter 25

1. John Camper, "Story Behind Court Probe," *Chicago Daily News,* August 4, 1969, p. 3; "The Day the Judges Fell," *Alton Evening Telegraph,* September 25, 1969, p. A-17.

2. Letter from John Focht, *Chicago Journalism Review,* vol. 3, no. 3, March 1970.

3. "Enterprise in Alton," *Columbia Journalism Review,* summer 1970, p. 4.

4. Letter from Sherman Skolnick to John Hohenberg, April 11, 1970.

5. Letter from Ed Pound to author, September 27, 1999.

6. Telephone interview with Jameson Campaigne, March 9, 1998; letter from Robert Seltzner to author, August 5, 1999.

7. Ken Watson, "Court Reform Before Con Con," *Aurora Beacon-News,* August 11, 1969, p. 20. See also Wayland Cedarquist, "The Proposed Judicial Article," *Chicago Bar Record,* vol. 51, no. 6, March 1970, pp. 290, 293; Rubin G. Cohn, *To Judge with Justice: History and Politics of Illinois Judicial Reform* (Urbana: University of Illinois Press, 1973), p. 30.

8. Frank Greenberg, "The Task of Judging the Judges," *Judicature,* vol. 59, no. 10, May 1976, pp. 459, 461–62.

9. Joint Committee on Judicial Article, "Summary of Judicial Article Revisions," January 24, 1970.

10. Rubin G. Cohn, "The Illinois Judicial Department: Changes Effected by the Constitution of 1970," *1971 University of Illinois Law Forum,* p. 355; Robert P. Howard, *Illinois: A History of the Prairie State* (Grand Rapids, Mich.: W. B. Eerdmans Publishing, 1972), pp. 563–67; Cohn, *To Judge with Justice: History and Politics of Illinois Judicial Reform*; Elmer Gertz, *Charter for a New Age: An Inside View of the Sixth Illinois Constitutional Convention* (Urbana: University of Illinois Press, 1980).

11. Memorandum from Wayland Cedarquist, chairman, to members, Joint Committee on Judicial Article, September 17, 1970.

12. "Voters Want Court Cleanup, Daley Told," *Chicago Daily News,* December 16, 1970.

13. Greenberg, "The Task of Judging the Judges," pp. 459, 461–62.

14. The Judicial Inquiry Board's official report for fiscal years 1996 through 1998 noted that the board's staff investigated over twelve hundred complaints during that period. From its inception through fiscal 1998, the board filed sixty-three formal complaints with the Courts Commission and in some of these the commission imposed sanctions as severe as removal from office.

15. Max Boot, *Out of Order: Arrogance, Corruption, and Incompetence on the Bench* (New York: Basic Books, 1998), p. 21 (criticizing Courts Commission for only disciplining thirty-three judges in thirty-three years, including the removal of only five); Jeffrey Shaman, Steven Lubet, and James Alfini, *Judicial Conduct and Ethics,* 2nd ed. (Charlottesville, Va.: Michie, 1995), p. 434; James Tuohy and Rob Warden, *Greylord: Justice, Chicago Style* (New York: Putnam, 1989), pp. 51–52.

16. Bill Peterson, "Operation Greylord's Scorecard Nearly Complete," *Washington Post,* August 25, 1989, p. A5. See also Tuohy and Warden, *Greylord: Jus-*

tice, Chicago Style; Matt O'Connor and Bob Sector, "Convicted Judge Defiantly Claims He's Innocent," *Chicago Tribune,* June 17, 1999 (describing the testimony of convicted Judge Thomas J. Maloney in a case seeking to overturn murder convictions allegedly tainted by his corruption); Ian Ayres, "The Twin Faces of Judicial Corruption: Extortion and Bribery," *Denver University Law Review,* vol. 74 (1997), p. 1231 (analyzing implications of Judge Maloney's pattern of corruption).

17. See Jerome Meites, Steven Pflaum, and Carolyn Krause, "Justice James D. Heiple: Impeachment and the Assault on Judicial Independence," *Loyola University of Chicago Law Journal,* vol. 29 (1998), p. 741; Boot, *Out of Order: Arrogance, Corruption, and Incompetence on the Bench,* pp. 19–21; Abdon Pallasch, "Heiple Laughs, Cries, and Dodges Impeachment," *Chicago Lawyer,* June 1997, p. 1.

18. See Bill Barnhart and Eugene Schlickman, *Kerner: The Conflict of Intangible Rights* (Urbana: University of Illinois Press, 1999); John T. Noonan Jr., *Bribes* (New York: Macmillan, 1984), pp. 587–91; Robert Hartley, *Big Jim Thompson of Illinois* (Chicago: Rand McNally, 1979), pp. 31–56; Hank Messick, *The Politics of Prosecution: Jim Thompson, Richard Nixon, Marje Everett and the Trial of Otto Kerner* (Ottawa, Ill.: Caroline House Books, 1978).

19. See Robert P. Howard, *Mostly Good and Competent Men: Illinois Governors 1818–1988* (Springfield: Sangamon State University & Illinois State Historical Society, 1988), p. 299: "Mrs. Marjorie Lindheimer Everett, the dominant figure in Illinois racing, had secretly dispensed her race track stock in the same manner as Isaacs did the bank stock."

20. *United States v. Isaacs,* 493 F.2d 1124, 1144 (7th Cir. 1974).

21. See chapter 18.

22. James Kloss, "Blast Isaacs in Summation," *Chicago Daily News,* February 17, 1973, p. 3; Paul Galloway, "Kerner and Isaacs Guilty," *Chicago Sun-Times,* February 20, 1973, p. 3.

23. Howard, *Mostly Good and Competent Men: Illinois Governors 1818–1988,* p. 299.

24. *United States v. Isaacs,* 493 F.2d at 1139, 1152.

25. Messick, *The Politics of Prosecution: Jim Thompson, Richard Nixon, Marje Everett and the Trial of Otto Kerner,* p. 73.

26. Letter from Edwin C. Austin to author, January 15, 1973. See also Howard, *Mostly Good and Competent Men: Illinois Governors 1818–1988,* p. 293.

27. Mike Royko, "Otto's Fault: He Was Dumb," *Chicago Daily News,* February 20, 1973, p. 1.

28. Barnhart and Schlickman, *Kerner: The Conflict of Intangible Rights,* p. 309.

Chapter 26

1. Henry Pitts, *My Life* (Roswell, N.Mex.: Roswell Printing Co., 1999), p. 48.

2. See Rowland Evans Jr. and Robert Novak, *Nixon in the White House: The Frustration of Power* (London: Davis-Poynter, 1971), p. 108.

3. Joseph C. Goulden, *The Benchwarmers: The Private World of Powerful Federal Judges* (New York: Weybright & Talley, 1974), p. 178.

4. In October 1969 the nomination of a prominent Chicago lawyer to fill the Schnackenberg vacancy ran into trouble when allegations of the nominee's anti-Semitism surfaced in the Senate Judiciary Committee, forcing withdrawal of the

nomination. Sheldon Goldman, *Picking Federal Judges* (New Haven: Yale University Press, 1997), p. 207.

5. Telephone interview with John Paul Stevens, August 27, 1999; telephone interviews with Charles H. Percy, April 6, 1998, and July 20, 1999. A slightly different description of this conversation as related by Senator Percy appears in Robert J. Sickels, *John Paul Stevens and the Constitution: The Search for Balance* (University Park: Pennsylvania State University Press, 1988), p. 35.

6. Letter from James A. Velde to members of the Constitutional Convention, July 1, 1970.

7. Letter from John Paul Stevens to author, November 9, 1992.

8. Speech by John Paul Stevens to American Bar Association Annual Meeting, Pro Bono Publico Awards Luncheon, San Francisco, August 10, 1992. See also Richard Reuben, "Justice Stevens: I Benefited from Pro Bono Work," *San Francisco Daily Journal,* August 11, 1992, p. 11. The principal focus of Stevens's speech was his pro bono work as a young lawyer in the case of *People v. La Frana,* 4 Ill. 2d 261, 122 N.E.2d 583 (1954).

9. Letter from John Paul Stevens to Otto Kerner, December 15, 1971.

10. See, for example, *Skolnick v. Campbell,* 454 F.2d 531 (7th Cir. 1971); and *Cousins v. City Council,* 466 F.2d 830 (7th Cir. 1972) and 503 F.2d 912 (7th Cir. 1974).

11. Letter from John Paul Stevens to Otto Kerner, December 10, 1975.

12. About two weeks before the nomination, I happened to tell a few of my law students about Stevens, and I too asserted that he was someone who should be on the Supreme Court. My students were not particularly aroused by my assertion at the time, but their reactions soon changed.

13. See, for example, Henry J. Abraham, *Justices and Presidents: A Political History of Appointments to the Supreme Court,* 3rd ed. (New York: Oxford University Press, 1992), pp. 326–34; David O'Brien, "The Politics of Professionalism: President Gerald R. Ford's Appointment of Justice John Paul Stevens," in *Gerald R. Ford and the Politics of Post-Watergate America,* edited by Bernard Firestone and Alexej Ugrinsky (Westport, Conn.: Greenwood Press, 1993), pp. 111–36; Victor Kramer, "The Case of Justice Stevens: How to Select, Nominate, and Confirm a Justice of the United States Supreme Court," *Constitutional Commentary,* vol. 7 (1990), p. 333; Gerald Ford, *A Time to Heal: The Autobiography of Gerald R. Ford* (London: W. H. Allen, 1979), pp. 334–35; Leonard Orland, "John Paul Stevens," in *The Justices of the United States Supreme Court,* edited by Leon Friedman, vol. 5 (New York: Chelsea House, 1978), pp. 149–51; Francis Beytagh Jr., "Mr. Justice Stevens and the Burger Court's Uncertain Trumpet," *Notre Dame Lawyer,* vol. 51 (1976), p. 946.

14. *The Supreme Court Justices: Illustrated Biographies* (Washington, D.C.: Congressional Quarterly, 1993), p. 503. See also Goldman, *Picking Federal Judges,* p. 208.

15. O'Brien, "The Politics of Professionalism: President Gerald R. Ford's Appointment of Justice John Paul Stevens," p. 112.

16. Hearings before the U.S. Senate Committee on the Judiciary, December 8–10, 1975, p. 19.

17. See, for example, *In re McDonald,* 489 U.S. 180 (1989); *In re Sindram,* 498 U.S. 177 (1991); *In re Amendment to Rule 39,* 500 U.S. 13 (1991); *In re Demos,* 500 U.S. 116 (1991); *Martin v. District of Columbia Court of Appeals,* 506 U.S. 1

(1992); *In re Anderson,* 511 U.S. 364 (1994); *In re Whitaker,* 513 U.S. 1 (1994); *Whitaker v. Superior Court,* 514 U.S. 208 (1995); *Judd v. U.S. District Court,* 120 S. Ct. 1 (October 12, 1999); and *In re Bauer,* 120 S. Ct. 6 (October 18, 1999).

18. See, for example, Abraham, *Justices and Presidents: A Political History of Appointments to the Supreme Court,* pp. 332–33; Bradley Canon, "Justice John Paul Stevens: The Lone Ranger in a Black Robe," in *The Burger Court,* edited by Charles Lamb and Stephen Halpern (Urbana: University of Illinois Press, 1991), p. 343; William Popkin, "A Common Law Lawyer on the Supreme Court: The Opinions of Justice Stevens," *1989 Duke Law Journal,* p. 1087; Orland, "John Paul Stevens," p. 149.

19. William J. Brennan Jr., "Tribute to Justice Stevens," *1992/1993 Annual Survey of American Law,* p. xxi. The ongoing debate on the nature of this duty is addressed in Ruth Bader Ginsburg, "Remarks on Writing Separately," *Washington Law Review,* vol. 65 (1990), p. 1.

20. See chapter 12.

Chapter 27

1. Early in 1970 disciplinary proceedings against Solfisburg as a lawyer were initiated by the Illinois State Bar Association. After a long and contentious process, in which he was represented by Albert Jenner, Solfisburg was censured by the Illinois Supreme Court in 1975 for the appearance of impropriety created by his conduct in the *People v. Isaacs* affair. See *In re Roy John Solfisburg, Jr., an Attorney,* Case No. M.R. 1723, Order of September 29, 1975, Supreme Court of the State of Illinois.

2. *Midwest Freight Forwarding Co. v. Lewis,* 49 Ill. 2d 441, 275 N.E.2d 388 (May 27, 1971); *County of Kendall v. Avery Gravel Co.,* 101 Ill. 2d 428, 463 N.E.2d 723 (April 19, 1984).

3. Remarks of Milton A. Shadur, memorial service for Frank Greenberg, Bond Chapel, University of Chicago, March 21, 1984; "Frank Greenberg," *Chicago Tribune,* March 14, 1984, p. 6; "The Greenberg Legacy," *Chicago Lawyer,* July 1984.

4. William Hundley, the Washington lawyer for the Lindberg Committee, also figured in Watergate. He represented Attorney General John Mitchell in the Watergate trial. Later, in the proceedings leading to the impeachment of President Clinton, Hundley represented the president's friend Vernon Jordan. George Lindberg went on to become a federal district court judge in Chicago, and Henry Hyde attained national prominence in Congress.

5. F. Richard Ciccone, *Chicago and the American Century* (Chicago: Contemporary Books, 1999), p. 33; Mike Royko, *One More Time: The Best of Mike Royko* (Chicago: University of Chicago Press, 1999), p. 19; Nelson Algren, *Chicago: City on the Make* (Oakland: Angel Island Publishing, 1961), p. 93; John Miller, ed., *Chicago Stories* (San Francisco: Chronicle Books, 1993), pp. xii, 200.

6. Larry Sabato and Glenn Simpson, *Dirty Little Secrets: The Persistence of Corruption in American Politics* (New York: Basic Books, 1996), p. 24.

7. Telephone interview with Daniel Feldman, August 23, 1999.

8. See, for example, *Merriam Webster's Collegiate Dictionary Tenth Edition,* distinguishing "integrity" as structural soundness or completeness from "integrity" as moral incorruptibility. See also Stephen L. Carter, *Integrity* (New York: Basic Books, 1996), noting that the word "comes from the same Latin root as 'in-

teger' and historically has been understood to carry much the same sense, the sense of wholeness: a person of integrity, like a whole number, is a whole person" (p. 7).

9. Letter from John Paul Stevens to author, September 28, 1992.

10. Christopher Eisgruber, "John Paul Stevens and the Manners of Judging," *1992/1993 Annual Survey of American Law,* p. xxix.

11. 121 S. Ct. 525 (December 12, 2000).

12. Id. at 542. Steven's dissent was widely interpreted as viewing the majority decision not only as impugning state judges but also as damaging public confidence in the impartiality of the Supreme Court itself. See, for example, Evan Thomas and Michael Isikoff, "The Truth Behind the Pillars," *Newsweek,* December 25, 2000, p. 48.

13. Letter from Frank Greenberg to John Paul Stevens et al., August 1, 1969.

Sources

Documents

The complete July 31, 1969, report of the Special Commission and the full text of other selected documents underlying this story are available at http://press .uchicago.edu/sites/manaster/.

Hearings

Explanation of the testimony and other developments in the public hearings of the Special Commission is based principally on the official transcript of the proceedings. The 1,800-page transcript covers the period from July 14 to July 24, 1969.

   Sam Abezetian of Leon M. Golding Associates in Chicago gave generous and critical assistance to the author's effort to acquire a complete set of transcripts of the hearings and depositions.

Interviews

During the gathering of information for this book, the people listed below were interviewed on the dates indicated. Interviews conducted in person are identified by the location of the meeting. All others were conducted by telephone.

Allen, Lyle W., 8/4/00
Barlett, Donald L., 3/8/99, 3/24/99, 7/30/99, 10/7/99
Barron, Michael, 2/17/99
Bruckner, D. J. R., 3/20/98, 4/4/98
Bull, Nick, 10/1/99, 11/23/99
Campaigne, Caroline Young, 3/9/98
Campaigne, Jameson, 3/9/98, 9/10/99
Delaney, Catherine, 9/15/98
Feldman, Daniel, 8/23/99, 8/25/99, 9/30/99 (Santa Clara, California)
Fisher, Patty, 3/26/98, 7/16/98, 8/12/98, 10/20/99
Flaum, Joel M., 11/30/98
Hollis, Richard A., 2/20/98
Hundley, William G., 3/3/99
Hyde, Henry J., 8/31/98
Isaacs, Leonard, 4/10/00
Johnson, Elmer W., 10/20/99
Judge, Bernard, 10/6/99, 5/30/00
Kifner, John, 6/18/98

Kirkland, Alfred Y., 11/12/97
Klingbiel, Tom J., 8/16/99
Lindberg, George W., 4/8/98
McGarr, Frank J., 9/1/99
McNally, William J., 10/30/97
Marshall, Prentice H., 3/30/98
Miner, Judson H., 12/3/97
Murphy, William C., 2/23/98
Nicodemus, Charles, 12/4/97, 3/16/98, 3/19/98, 6/19/98, 2/18/99, 3/3/99, 3/9/99, 10/13/99, 5/30/00
Nussbaum, James G., 7/21/99
Perbohner, Arthur, 8/16/99
Percy, Charles H., 4/6/98, 7/20/99, 7/21/99
Pitts, Henry L., 7/15/97, 7/31/97, 9/2/98, 8/25/99, 12/28/99
Plotkin, Robert, 3/27/98
Pound, Ed, 10/30/97, 3/22/98, 8/2/99, 9/20/99, 9/27/99
Reuben, Don H., 3/17/98, 9/10/99, 9/13/99, 5/30/00
Rothschild, Edward I., 11/19/98
Sanders, David, 9/30/99
Seltzner, Robert J., 3/23/98, 7/30/99, 8/5/99
Shadur, Milton I., 8/4/00
Skolnick, Sherman H., 9/17/99
Solovy, Jerold S., 10/1/99
Stevens, John Paul, 9/8/97, 9/15/97, 10/29/97, 11/7/97 (Washington, DC), 6/24/98, 11/13/98, 4/21/99, 4/23/99, 8/27/99, 10/5/99, 12/10/99, 1/18/00, 2/18/00
Stovall, Thomas J., Jr., 2/17/99
Sullivan, Thomas P., 10/7/99
Terrell, Raymond L., 11/24/97
Torshen, Jerome H., 9/15/97, 12/8/97, 3/26/99, 7/30/99, 9/14/99, 10/5/99
Tuite, Patrick A., 12/15/99
Weisman, Joel D., 9/28/99
Wollan, Laurin A., Jr., 11/13/97
Yakstis, Ande, 8/6/99, 10/22/99

Newspapers

In addition to newspaper articles specifically cited, numerous other articles from the following newspapers provided information incorporated into the text. The majority of those articles were published during the period from May through September 1969.

Alton Evening Telegraph
Aurora Beacon-News
Chicago Daily News
Chicago Sun-Times
Chicago Today
Chicago Tribune
New York Times
Rockford Register-Republic

Acknowledgments

Many people helped, in many different ways, in the preparation of this book. I am grateful to them all. The text and notes name some of those who provided essential information. The most crucial of these contributors were Charles Nicodemus, Henry Pitts, Ed Pound, Jerry Torshen, and, most centrally and generously, John Stevens. Without their insights and enthusiasm, this book could not have been written.

The list of individuals interviewed for this project identifies many more who were invaluable in developing the story, even though they may not otherwise be named in the book. Additionally, others around the country who assisted in various ways include David Alfini, Jim Alfini, Bob Bennett, Herb Davis, David English, Jim Friedlander, Rachel George, Randy Gingiss, Paul Goda, Paul Goldstein, Craig LeMay, Eric Lund, Newton Minow, Marty Oberman, Heidi Robertson, David Souter, Jerry Uelmen, and Pam Zekman.

I greatly appreciate the support provided by Dean Mack Player of Santa Clara University School of Law, as well as the encouragement offered by him and other colleagues. A series of Santa Clara law students—beginning with the extraordinary work of Ted Stevens—helped mightily with my research. This talented group includes Jennifer Davis, Melissa Lipon, Karen McLeod, Carl Switzer, and Andrew Temkin. Alyssa deMars, of the faculty support staff, was an indispensable and remarkably efficient aide. Law Library personnel at Santa Clara, especially Barbara Friedrich and Dolores de la Fuente, were creative and persistent in helping me track down obscure materials.

At the University of Chicago Press, John Tryneski and Anne Ford gave me the full benefit of their masterful editorial skill and oversight. They did their best, along with Abner Mikva, to prevent me from turning this unusual tale into a ponderous treatise. Erin DeWitt's meticulous copyediting was indispensable.

I also thank the following for their help: Chicago Historical Society, Illinois State Historical Library, Dirksen Congressional Research Center, Office of the Clerk of the Supreme Court of Illinois, Nixon Presidential Materials Staff, *Chicago Sun-Times* Photo Research Department (especially James Strong), and *Chicago Tribune* Photosales Department (especially Sandra Spikes).

Throughout this project, I was blessed with the steady support of friends who not only listened to my repeated recitations of the story as it was shaping up, but also helped in other ways, some editorial and some emotional. Included in this cherished group are Richard Berg, Don Conant, Brian Dunn, Tom Ferrito, Gary Neustadter, Peter Schuck, and Ed Steinman.

The concern and interest of my daughter, Jenny, and the joyful energy of my son, Cole, helped me through this long task. The thoughtful encouragement of my sister-in-law Linda Brandewie also helped a lot. My brother, Guy Manaster, not only read the manuscript and offered perceptive suggestions, but also fully understood how much this story means to me.

The memory of my parents, Bernice and Saul Manaster, was of special significance. Their interest in my work in the summer of 1969 and always, their fascination as native Chicagoans with all things political, and the pleasure I know they would have derived from this publication were very much with me during this process. I was spurred, too, by the enthusiasm of my uncle George Perlman as we discussed this project and he read some chapters shortly before his recent death at age 103.

Finally, my deepest gratitude is to my beloved wife, Ann Brandewie, for her unfailing support and so much more for which I am thankful beyond words.

Index

acts of impropriety, 225–27

Adam, Sam, 76–79, 177

affirmative acts of concealment, 208, 227. *See also* acts of impropriety; appearance of impropriety

Algren, Nelson, 278

Alton Evening Telegraph: award for, 251; competition of, 251–53; investigation by, 10, 13–14, 16, 49–51; after Special Commission, 277. *See also* Pound, Ed

American Bar Association, 140, 265, 267, 269

antitrust law, 38–39, 63

appearance of impropriety: absent in other justices, 201; commission report on, 221–29; of Fortas compared to Solfisburg and Klingbiel, 235–36; Klingbiel's testimony on, 147; Murphy's summation on, 211; Solfisburg censured for, 301n. 1; Solfisburg's testimony on, 134, 140–41; Stevens's summation on, 209

Archer National Bank, 75, 149

Armstrong, David H., 53

Ashe, Henry, 78, 152

Associated Press, 14, 251–52

Athletics (team), 39

Aurora: justice's office space in, 53; search for typewriter in, 153. *See also* Old Second National Bank (Aurora)

Aurora Beacon-News, 159

Austin, Edwin C.: appointment to Special Commission, 26, 291n. 1; House questioned by, 94–95; Isaacs questioned by, 190; on Kerner-Isaacs trial, 262; Klingbiel questioned by, 147–48

banks. *See* Archer National Bank; Civic Center Bank & Trust Company (CCB, Chicago); First National Bank (Chicago); Old Second National Bank (Chicago); Old Second National Bank

(Aurora); St. Charles National Bank

Barlett, Donald L.: career after Special Commission, 277; investigation of Solfisburg, 52–53, 58, 196, 252; on Solfisburg's recommendation by conference, 61

Barron, Michael, 292n. 12

Barry, Norman J., 39

Better Government Association (BGA), 29, 52, 196

Bieber, George, 144–45

bipartisanship, 282

Bockelman, J. Richard, 125, 131–32, 151

Bolton, John F., Jr., 40

Boyle, John S., 74

Brandeis, Louis D., 99, 268, 294n. 2

Brennan, William J., Jr., 273, 284

bribery, 17–18, 257–62, 299n. 19

Bull, Mason: appointment to Special Commission, 26; dissent on commission report, 221; on Klingiel's career after Special Commission, 275; as member of Joint Committee on the Judicial Article, 255–56; Stout questioned by, 166, 169

Burdick, Quentin, 271

Burger, Warren E., 292n. 7

Busch, Harry: at hearings' beginning, 87; as Isaacs's lawyer, 117, 177, 180–82, 187; money order and, 216

Bush v. Gore, 284–85

Byrd, Robert, 272

Calvo, Horace, 289n. 3

Campaigne, Jameson, 5–6, 253

Campbell, William J., 67–68, 293n. 8

campus disorders, statement on, 60–61

Canons of Ethics, 224–25, 227, 248

Carey, Homer, 63

CCB. *See* Civic Center Bank & Trust Company (CCB, Chicago)

Cermak, Anton J., 7, 262

CPSIA information can be obtained
at www.ICGtesting.com
Printed in the USA
LVHW022108170719
624400LV00007B/975/P

9 780226 350103